The Language of Cinema

DATE DUE

-3. DEC. 1999		
-2 FEB. 2000		
-8. SEP. 2000		
-9. SEP. 2003		
14. SEP. 2004		
-6 JAN 2011		
GAYLORD		PRINTED IN U S A

91197

Also from Carcanet

Fly-fishing: a book of words
C. B. McCully

Horse Racing: a book of words
Gerald Hammond

Theatre: a book of words
Martin Harrison

Whisky: a book of words
Gavin D. Smith

The Language of Cricket
John Eddowes

The Language of the Field
Michael Brander

The Language of Jazz
Neil Powell

Kevin Jackson

The Language of Cinema

CARCANET

First published in Great Britain in 1998 by
Carcanet Press Limited
4th Floor, Conavon Court
12–16 Blackfriars Street
Manchester M3 5BQ

A CIP catalogue record for this book
is available from the British Library.

ISBN 1 85754 232 0

The publisher acknowledges financial assistance
from the Arts Council of England.

Set in 10pt Plantin by Ensystems, Saffron Walden
Printed and bound in England by SRP Ltd, Exeter.

Acknowledgements

Though I have sometimes taken issue with its definitions – see, for example, the entries on *cinéaste* and *cinéma-verité* – or sniffed at its omissions, the indispensable resource for this book has been the *Oxford English Dictionary*, a work on which I now look with a renewed sense of awe. I have also profited from the labours of previous workers in the field of cinema lexicography. Of the cinema reference books cited in the bibliography, the most important for my purposes have been Liz-Anne Bawden's *Oxford Companion to the Film*, Ephraim Katz's *The Macmillan International Film Encyclopaedia* and Ira Konigsberg's *The Complete Film Dictionary*: my occasional acts of dissent from or quiet emendations to the wisdom and erudition of these authors and/or their contributors should emphatically not be taken as marks of disrespect. I have also been informed, inspired and, at times, seduced away from my labours by David Thomson's *Biographical Dictionary of Film*, which I have come to view as the only cinema reference book that is also a work of literature.

Among the friends and colleagues who commented on the manuscript and offered suggestions, amendments and wit, I'd particularly like to thank: John Baxter, not least for his erudite knowledge of pornographic films; Alex Marengo, who pointed me in the direction of a number of recent industry terms, including this book's final entry, 'Zydeco'; Liz Rigbey, who drew my attention to the British slang term 'Dougal'; Chris Peachment, who first explained what a 'Martini' was; and the documentary film-maker David Thompson, who strongly advised me not to undertake such a maddening task in the first place. Other friends and colleagues who aided and abetted this work in a variety of ways (sometimes unwittingly) include: John Archer, Anne Billson, Glyn Johnson, Robert Keirans, Roger Parsons, Simon Pettifar, Linda Reisman, Paul Schrader, Martin Wallen and the audiences for my lectures at Waterman's Arts Centre. Gerald Hammond was a patient and gently encouraging series editor; Robyn Marsack helped trim the book down to reasonable dimensions and eliminate some of its horrrors of style. Brief quotations from reviews and articles by myself and other writers on *The Independent* are reproduced by kind permission of Newspaper Publishing PLC.

This book's dedicatee, Charles Cuddon, was – among his many accomplishments – a great lexicographer; his magnificent *Dictionary of Literary Terms and Literary Theory* was an example to me throughout. My greatest personal debt is to the scholar who has taken on the task of revising new editions of Cuddon's masterwork, Dr C. E. Preston.

As usual in such undertakings, all the failings of the finished product are mine: 'the lexicographer can only hope to escape reproach, and even this negative recompense has been yet granted to very few'. I would welcome suggestions for improving subsequent editions of this work, particularly those from correspondents who have pondered the wisdom of Samuel Johnson's *Preface* to his Dictionary.

Abbreviations

Fr: French
Gk: Greek
It: Italian
L: Latin
ME: Middle English
OE: Old English
OF: Old French

OED: Oxford English Dictionary

Words set in *medium **bold** **italic*** indicate cross-references.

Introduction

On the evening of 9 December 1824, Peter Mark Roget M.D. – the Roget now remembered throughout the English-speaking world for his *Thesaurus* – stood up to read the members of the Royal Society a paper entitled 'Explanation of an Optical Deception in the Appearance of the Spokes of a Wheel Seen Through Vertical Apertures'. Inspired by a curious illusion he had noticed while watching the traffic from the basement kitchen of his house, the paper was the earliest scientific account of an oddity that mankind must first have encountered when some inglorious neolithic artist picked up a burning twig and drew patterns with it in the night air: 'namely', Roget summed up, 'that an impression made by a pencil of rays on the retina, if sufficiently vivid, will remain for a certain time after the cause has ceased.'[1] The good doctor had enunciated the principle of *persistence of vision*; and, as one film historian wrote of Roget's apparently trifling discovery, 'On this peculiarity rests the fortune of the entire motion-picture industry'.[2] It is a conjunction that anyone with an interest in both words and moving images ought to relish: the father of the *Thesaurus* was also the grandfather of cinema.

Roget's paper prompted scientists across Europe – Faraday in London, Plateau in Ghent, Stampfer in Vienna – to start devising toys and gadgets to test out his principle. Before long these inventors were astonishing audiences with their wonderful new gadgets the *phenakistoscope*, the *stroboscope* and the *zoetrope*, all of which offered the unprecedented spectacle of pictures that could move like living things, and it was with their devices – rather, say, than with the *camera lucida* sometimes attributed to Alberti, or the magic lantern described by Athanasius Kircher – that the true pre-history of cinema began. About two years before Roget's paper, a Frenchman called Joseph Nicéphore Niepce, whose difficult name has been obscured by the more euphonious one of his subsequent partner, Louis Daguerre, managed to create a crude but lasting photographic image. It took seven decades for the offspring of Dr Roget and M. Niepce to meet and marry (film historians and patriots continue to argue about whether the nuptials took place in France or England or the United States), but when they did, in 1895 or thereabouts, there was finally something new under the sun.

1. Cited in D. L. Emblen, *Peter Mark Roget, The Word and the Man* (London: Longman, 1970), p. 186. For a bizarre fictional version of what really inspired Roget, see Theodore Roszak, *Flicker* (New York: Bantam, 1992), pp. 447–8.
2. Arthur Knight, *The Liveliest Art* (New York: Macmillan, 1957), p. 5.

1

Not many people immediately recognised it as a new form of art, and there are some pure souls who would continue to deny that the cinema has any right to such an honourable name. Nor did many recognise it as a new industry – the Lumières themselves notoriously said of their *cinématographe* that it was a machine without very much commercial potential.[3] But it did gradually dawn on some interested observers that the cinema might be regarded as a new form of language, and even, perhaps, as the unexpected realisation of an ancient dream Roget himself once described as 'that splendid aspiration of philanthropists – the establishment of a universal language'.[4] Plainly, the (silent) cinema had the potential to communicate across the linguistic boundaries of nations, and across the gulf between the literate minority and the illiterate masses. Intellectuals began to speculate on the possible affinities between film images and Egyptian hieroglyphics or the Chinese ideogram,[5] and as the Brighton school in England and Edison in America began rapidly to invent and deploy such narrative conventions as the *close-up*, *parallel editing* and the like, it also became apparent that the new medium must have a fairly elaborate syntax as well as the simple 'nouns' (people, objects) and 'verbs' (actions) which were its most obvious units of sense. Hence the title of some of the classic text books on film-making in general and editing in particular, such as Raymond Spottiswoode's *A Grammar of the Film* (1935).

Yet at the same time the poets and philosophers were hailing the advent of a language that might be comprehensible to every human with eyes to see, the practitioners of cinema from California to Brighton were rapidly starting to improvise and scratch together an altogether different kind of language, at first largely unintelligible save to their fellow labourers – a technical jargon of film-making, loaded with such terms as *shot, cut, pan, dolly, dissolve, iris-in, track* and hundreds of others; an argot which, like other professional lingos, enabled them to get the job done more rapidly and efficiently. (Film-makers in other countries were busy evolving their own counterparts of such terms, though nation was soon pilfering freely from nation: consider the widespread currency in Anglophone countries of such terms as *montage, mise-en-scène, cinéaste, film noir* . . .) It is this latter language of cinema which is the subject of the following book.

Just as early Hollywood was a Babel as well as a Babylon, and appeared quite happy to employ newcomers from many nations and all walks of life provided they were sufficiently pretty or profitable, so the technical jargon

---

3. For a first-person account of the Brothers' development of the *cinematographe*, see *Auguste and Louis Lumière: Letters*, ed. Jacques Rittaud-Hutinet (London: Faber & Faber, 1995).
4. From Roget's introduction to the first edition of the *Thesaurus* (London: Longman, Brown, Green, and Longmans, 1852); quoted in Emblen, op.cit. p. 262.
5. See, for example, the first chapters of *A Million and One Nights: A History of the Motion Picture* by Terry Ramsaye (New York: Simon and Schuster, 1926). Incidentally, the Chinese term for 'cinema' is rather beautiful: *dian ying*: 'electric shadows'.

of cinema is a mongrel creature, spawned from the promiscuous inter-
course of words from the theatre and the laboratory, the building site and
the painter's *atelier*, the study and the gutter. Technicians concerned with
the quality of moving images borrowed freely from the vocabulary of still
photography (*focus, print, negative* and *positive, lenses* and *cameras,*
and *photography* itself), and from the science of optics. Those more
interested in the stories films could tell borrowed from the stage (*actor,
actress, star, set, cyclorama*; one widely-used early term for a moving
picture was a *photoplay*) and from the novel. Where there was no obvious
term to borrow, film-makers could either adapt some fairly ordinary
existing word to meet their needs – *take, edit, cover, wrap, fade, screen,
director, producer* – or devise an entirely new one: *cinematographe* or
kinematograph.

Before too many years had passed, though, the specialist language of
film-making came to be rather different from the various esoteric sociolects
of other trades and pursuits. From its earliest days, the cinema was an
object of fascination for countless millions of people who had no connection with it save as *fans*; and despite the subsequent invasion of its
territories by its upstart younger sibling, television (a medium with a rich
jargon of its own, left largely unexamined here save where it overlaps with
that of the cinema), it still possesses an unrivalled glamour for many
viewers. As a result of the extravagant amount of attention paid to film
stars and the industry in general by the mass media, thousands of people
can now talk about movies with remarkably fluency and inwardness.
Where other lexicons (notably that of the law) often look suspiciously like
linguistic palisades to keep out the great unwashed and maintain caste
privilege, the cinema's argot has proved refreshingly democratic.

This unusually widespread awareness of the language of cinema has
exerted subtle but distinct pressures on the ways in which English is used.
In the late 1930s, Cyril Connolly observed that the first few years of
talkies had flavoured both contemporary literature and speech: among
other things, they 'popularized the vocabulary with which Hemingway
wrote and enabled him to use slang words in the knowledge that they were
getting every day less obscure'.[6] Hollywood, it has often been observed,
taught generations of young men and women in Britain how to kiss,
smoke, dress and stand, and – as Connolly remarks – how to talk a diluted,
stylised version of the American tongue; habits generally deplored by their
elders. It has less often been observed that Hollywood popularised not
only a mode of snappy talk but an industrial jargon. Today, one would
have to be either very sheltered or very deprived not to recognise at least
three-quarters of the technical words I have so far cited, and even someone
who is hazy about the precise distinction between a director and a
producer, or a dolly and a pan, would have some approximate notion of
the sort of thing they signify – a person involved at a senior level in making

6. Cyril Connolly, *Enemies of Promise* (1938); Penguin edition p. 75.

films, a type of camera movement. Our slang, too, picks up these terms quite frequently, so that one can hear of politicians examining an issue in close-up, generals discussing possible *scenarios*, waffling speakers being told to *cut to the chase*, a project being wrapped, research ending up on the cutting-room floor, and so on.

Words which are well known are not, however, always known well. In the last two weeks alone, I have come across garbled, misleading or simply ignorant uses of the terms '*cine-verité*', '*mise-en-scène*' (the broadsheet journalist in question seemed to think it meant 'plot') and 'producer' (the author of an otherwise extremely erudite study of Cambridge between the wars referred to the great documentary director Humphrey Jennings as a 'film producer'). I have therefore tried to cast some light on the subject – a subdued metaphor from filming, nowadays? – by giving brief, unambiguous definitions for each term and by illustrating, where possible and useful, something of the ways in which the word may be used. Though there are several existing dictionaries of film, three or four of them first-rate (see the Acknowledgements), I believe that this is the first book of its kind to give due weight to language as well as to cinema, by supplying relevant etymological information for each word and by sketching something of its history before and since the Lumière Brothers' *annus mirabilis*, 1895. In addition to the hard core of vocabulary used in the business of film-making, I have also looked into words from related fields, including the financing, distribution, exhibition and preservation of films, as well as from film criticism, film (or, perhaps more appropriately demotic, *movie*) journalism and film history. There are many strange bedfellows here, from *splatter movie* to *Symbolism*, *fish out of water* to *FEKS*. And since a fair amount of general discussion of the cinema requires some awareness of its institutions – a *Cahiers* critic, a *Monogram* film, an *MGM musical* – some of the entries are devoted to thumbnail sketches of the more significant production companies, archives, festivals, institutes, studios and journals.

Though I have tried to make the technical part of each entry as accurate as possible, I have also followed the example of previous books in the series (and relieved the Johnsonian drudgery of the task) by making a virtue of the idiosyncrasy inevitable in any one-man enterprise of this nature, and have included a number of anecdotes, speculations, asides, conjectures and jokes. My prejudices will be apparent on many pages. Some of the entries include suggestions for further reading, and there is a selected bibliography of books which I have found useful, enlightening or simply entertaining.

With several significant exceptions (one of them being the word *cinema* itself) and a number of insignificant ones, both of which I have tried to emphasise at the appropriate points, the words defined in this lexicon would be as readily understood and used by film-makers in Hollywood as those in Pinewood. Though the American film industry is no longer the largest in the world, it remains the most influential, and the *lingua franca* of international film-making is English, generally with an American accent. There may be slightly more attention to British film history here than an American reader would usually expect, but in all other matters of definition and example I have tried to be as impartial as possible. With luck, the results will be of equal interest to readers from either side of the Atlantic.

As the cinema enters its second century, gloomy commentators are already beginning to announce its demise as an art form. With the rise of increasingly spectacular, ever more mindless *blockbusters*, the cinema has, they contend, renounced its always tentative claims to being an art form and reverted to the status of a toy, albeit a colossally expensive, technically magnificent toy; while the explosively rapid development of new forms of electronic communication has made the hundred-year-old ritual of going to darkened rooms to gaze at giant sheets of light seem almost quaint. There may be some truth in this, though I have my doubts. Even if the cinema does go the way of blank-verse tragedy or the Petrarchan triumph, however, it has long since established itself as the most powerful cultural form of our century ('For us', said Lenin, meaning the triumphant Bolsheviks, 'cinema is the most important of the arts.') if not, as one sage put it, 'another dimension for human existence'.[7]

Films have helped shape the world in trivial and in momentous ways, and any history of the cinema must also be, at some level, an oblique history of the twentieth century, with its new horrors and new delights. Any collection of cinema words, however humble, is shot through with the same history (see the entries on *socialist realism*, *UFA*, *film noir* . . .), and I hope that this one may be of interest even to those who have no great fondness for movie-going, or who positively dislike motion pictures. Dr Roget, alas, would almost certainly have been among the latter number, for he was a correct, pious man, and the vulgarity and excesses of the medium he unwittingly invented would surely have appalled (repelled, revolted, sickened, disgusted, nauseated . . .) the *Thesaurus* man. Had he foreseen the consequences of his innocent talk to the Royal Society, he would probably have held his peace. Millions of us should be glad he did not.

Kevin Jackson
13 July 1997

7. The sentiments of Marshall McLuhan, as paraphrased by Emblen, op. cit., p. 186.

A, AA, (A certificate, AA certificate) two categories that were formerly used by the British Board of Film Censors (*BBFC*) to classify feature films and trailers for public exhibition. The first, indicating that the film was for viewing by Adults only, grew increasingly permissive over the years in response to changes in social attitudes, and also because of the introduction of a separate 'X' certificate in 1951. In 1970, the certificate was split into two parts, the A and the AA. From that year onwards, the AA restricted admission to public screenings to viewers over the age of 14, while the A certificate (like today's *PG* rating) simply warned concerned parents that a film contained scenes that might be thought unsuitable for children. Both categories are now defunct. See *censorship, rating*.

A and B printing, A and B roll printing, A and B editing a technique which makes it relatively cheap and easy to achieve *superimpositions, dissolves, fades*, and so on. Short strips of black or blank *leader* are spliced between the necessary shots on two reels of negatives, so producing the *A and B rolls*, equal in length: the shots on the A roll correspond to the leader on the B roll and vice versa. A master print is produced by combining the two rolls in a variety of ways: to produce a dissolve, for example, the A roll would contain all the required shots up to the point of the dissolve and then be replaced by leader; the B roll would have leader followed by the incoming shots.

A-list the róll-call of the most commercially desirable stars or directors at a given moment. 'She met, and was pursued by the Franco-Swiss director Barbet Schroeder, now a successful A-list director in the United States': obituary of Kathleen Tynan, *Independent*, 11 January 1995. William Goldman discusses the term in some depth in his entertaining book of memoirs, *Adventures in the Screen Trade*.

A-picture (a) a major, high-budget production; a term derived from the fact that (b) in the days when double features were the rule rather than an oddity, the A-picture was the main attraction and the *B-picture* its support.

A wind an indication of how a film stock is perforated: if the sprocket holes are on the right as the film is unwound (assuming that you are holding the film before you and unrolling it from the top), it is A wind; if on the left, *B wind*.

Aardman the highly successful Bristol-based animation company, specialising in the use of plasticene models rather than drawings, best known as the producers of Nick Park's wonderfully funny Oscar-winning shorts *Creature Comforts* and *The Wrong Trousers*.

Aaton the trade name for a range of cameras; despite all his leftist scruples and the scathing critiques of the culture of advertising to be found in his films, Jean-Luc Godard was once used in an *Aaton* commercial, promoting an exceptionally steady hand-held camera he had asked the company to develop, the Aaton 8–35.

aberration   the general term for any lens defect that will result in a distorted image.

above-the-line   Literally, the cost of a film before shooting starts, made up of the contracted fees for writer(s), director, leading performers and producers. (*below-the-line* costs, which tend to be cheaper, include the salaries of crew members, facility fees and so on.) However, the term is also widely used in Hollywood to distinguish the 'creative' members of a production from those regarded, fairly or otherwise, as being in more menial positions, such as editors and cameramen.

abrasions   the common term for small scratches on the surface of film, usually accidental, sometimes deliberately inflicted to give the film a dated or bizarre appearance, as in the extraordinary credit sequence for *Seven* (1995).

absolute film   though there is some confusion about the term, which is sometimes used interchangeably with *abstract film*, and has even been applied (misleadingly) to the early films of Buñuel and Cocteau, as well as to Walter Ruttmann's semi-abstract, semi-documentary work of the late 1920s, the term is usually understood to refer to a particular group of silent abstract films made in Germany by Viking Eggeling, Hans Richter and others in the early part of the twentieth century: Eggeling used a technique of drawings on scrolls to produce *Symphonie Diagonale* (1920–2); Richter animated cut-out shapes for *Rhythmus 21, 23, 25* (1921–5), and continued in this vein with the likes of *Filmstudie* (1926), *Inflation* (1927–8) and *Vormittagsspuk*, in which everyday objects stage a revolution to the music of Hindemith. But the clarity of the term is somewhat muddied by the fact that it was Oskar Fischinger, working in sound, who seems to have coined the phrase *absolute film study* to designate the practice of making filmic patterns dance to music – a practice adopted, or (some would say) prettified in the Bach section of Disney's *Fantasia*. And the waters are muddied yet further by the fact that at least one theorist has appropriated the term for his own ends: in his *Theory of Film: Character and Growth of a New Art* (1948; English translation 1952), for example, the Hungarian writer Bela Balázs uses 'absolute film' as a category for any *avant-garde* film which expresses its maker's private view of the world.

abstract film   any film of a non-figurative nature: the term originally dates from the *avant-garde* film-making of the 1920s, and is derived from an obvious analogy with abstract art. *Abstract film* may be either wholly non-representational – and made (a) by direct treatment of film stock, as in certain works by Len Lye and Stan Brakhage (b) from drawings or (c) from computer graphics – or, (d) like Fernand Léger and Dudley Murphy's *Ballet méchanique* (1924), probably the first fully photographed abstract film and still probably the best-known example of the form, it may arrange recognisable images of objects, faces and so on into complex, non-narrative spatial and temporal patterns. The form has a thriving history: notable practioners include Marcel Duchamp, in his anagrammatic *Cinema Anemic*; Len Lye, in *Colour Box* (1935), for which he painted directly onto the film stock, and *Free Radicals* (1958); Germaine Dulac, in *Disc 927, Arabesque* and *Thèmes et variations* (all 1928–9); Henri Chomette, who photographed reflections inside moving crystals for his *Jeux de reflets et de la vitesse* (1925); Man Ray, in *Emak Bakia* (1926); Norman McLaren, in some of his work for the National Film Board of Canada (one of them recently revived in *Thirty-Two Short Films About Glenn Gould*); and Moholy-Nagy in his *Lichtspiele* series. Some narrative films also contain abstract sequences: the 'Star Gate' episode from *2001*, for example. See *cinema-pur*.

Academy any phrase in the cinema world prefixed by 'Academy' pays its tribute to the authority of the American Academy of Motion Picture Arts and Sciences (AMPAS, founded 1927 and based in Beverly Hills) and the technical standards – known as *Academy standards* – it has established for film-makers and exhibitors over the past half-century or so. Among the more important of these conventions are the *Academy aperture* – the ratio of width to height in the aperture of a camera or projector which produces the 1.33: 1 *Academy ratio* (see *aspect ratio*); *Academy leader*, the standardised *leader* used on the heads and tails of *release prints*; *Academy roll-off* or *Academy curve*, the standard which limits high frequencies in cinema sound-systems. The AMPAS is most widely known for its yearly *Academy Awards* for artistic and technical achievements: those outside the industry know these awards by their more familiar name, the *Oscars*.

accelerated motion the effect of rapid movement created by filming action at rates slower than 24 frames per second and then projecting them at normal speed; thus, the opposite of *slow motion*. *Accelerated montage*: increasingly fast cutting, generally for the purpose of creating excitment or suspense; see *montage*.

acceptance angle (or **angle of acceptance**) the area covered by a given camera or light meter; see *angle of view*.

ace a spotlight with a 1,000-watt bulb.

ACE the abbreviation for *American Cinema Editors*, the professional society for editors in the United States, founded in 1950, with a membership of about 350; the initials A.C.E after an editor's credit thus indicate that he or she has been invited to join the society.

acetate base (or *triacetate base* or *safety film*), the relatively non-inflammable base for film which gradually took over from the cheaper but far more combustible nitrate bases between 1937 and 1951, and has been standard ever since (though polyester bases have also come into use more recently). Film stock is made up of this base plus a covering of light-sensitive emulsion. The term 'acetate', meaning a salt formed by the combination of acetic acid with an alkaline or metallic base, has been used in English since the early 19th C; hence Faraday, 1827: 'Nitrate of mercury, acetate of lead.'

Acey-Deucey   the former name for a *peanut light*, a small *Fresnel lamp* with a 200-watt bulb, made by the Acey-Deucey company.

achromatic lens   from the Gk *achromat-os*, 'colourless'; a lens which has been corrected so that it focuses all colours at the same point. The adjective has been used in the field of optics since the mid-17th C: 'I likewise made use of a very good achromatic telescope': Maty, 1766.

actinicity   the technical term for the proportion of light which is registered on film when it is exposed. The term is derived from 'actinism' (from the Gk *aktin*, 'ray'), coined in the the mid-19th C, meaning the property or force of the sun's rays by which chemical changes are produced, especially in photography.

action   from the F *action* and the L *action-em*, a doing or performance, itself from *agere*, to do; English takes up the word, in a variety of spellings, towards the end of the 14th C. (a) As an imperative, the director's command to his performers to begin a scene: 'Action!' OED's first citation is from 1914, from a book entitled *Motion Picture Making* ('the camera man starts cranking the machine and the actors stand ready ... An instant after follows the order "Start your action".'), but its second example, from F.A. Talbot's *Moving Pictures* of 1923 ('Ready! Action! Camera!!! Go!!!!') is rather closer to that immortal triple order known to every English speaker: 'Lights! Camera! Action!' *Action* may also mean variously: (b) what the performers do on being given the command – 'action' was used in the theatrical sense from the early 17th C onwards, as in Steele's account of a performance for a Mrs Bignall: 'Throughout the whole Action, she made a very pretty Figure' (1710); or (c) the longer sequence in which this scene will play its part; or (d) filmed physical activities as opposed to dialogue scenes; or (e) the film's images as distinct from its sound (see *APO*); or (f) the story of the film, etc.

Terms associated with 'action' include: *action axis*, for which see *imaginary line*; *action cutting* (or *cutting on action*): editing a sequence in such a way that its action seems smooth and natural – so natural indeed, that the ideal spectator will accept the action as continuous and scarely notice that it has been edited at all; *action film*: a film boasting fights, chases, explosions, stunts, mayhem, and – if it is extremely expensive – Arnold Schwarzenegger; *action still*, a still made directly from the negative of a film, as opposed to the standard type of publicity shot made by a stills cameraman.

Actors Studio   the New York group which practices the *Method* or method acting, a naturalistic technique originally inspired by Konstantin Sergeyevich Stanislavsky (1863–1938) and made internationally famous or notorious by the charismatic, neurosis-ridden film performances of James Dean and Marlon Brando; also by those of Montgomery Clift, Rod Steiger, Anthony Quinn and others. The *Actors Studio* was founded in 1947 by Elia Kazan and Cheryl Crawford; its Californian cousin, *Actors Studio West*, was founded in 1966.

ACTT   the Association of Cinematograph, Television and Allied Technicians, the British trade union for film workers, founded in 1931.

actual sound   (a) sound which can be seen to originate from some on-screen source, or from some off-screen source the nature of which is reasonably evident, as opposed to other types of film sound such as soundtrack music, narration and so on; hence, more narrowly (b) sound recorded at the time of filming rather than dubbed on at some later point.

actualités   the Lumière brothers' name for their shorts devoted to real-life activities: thus, both the earliest form of cinema, and the earliest form of *documentary*. The term was taken over fairly directly into English within a few years: 'The films began with "actualities", the record of more or less formal current events': H.G. Wells, 1929.

acutance   from the L *acut-us*, the past participle of *acuere*, to sharpen: the scientific measurement of the degree of sharpness in a photographed image; see *densitometry*.

adaptation   a film inspired by, based on or otherwise in debt to a novel, play, article or some other non-filmic source, rather than one conceived for the cinema from the outset.

additive process   a largely outmoded form of *colour* cinematography in which red, green and blue lights were added to black and white films; it has been replaced by the more satisfactory *subtractive process*.

advance   (also known as **sound advance**)   the distance, measured in frames, by which the picture precedes the sound-track when images and sounds are properly in *sync*, This varies from format to format – on 35mm film, for example, optical sound is 20 or 21 frames in advance; on 16mm, 26 frames in advance. See *projection sync*.

aerial-image photography   an optical process which involves bouncing a projected picture off a mirror, refocusing it under the surface of an animation table and then photographing it again in combination with titles, animations and the like. **Aerial shot**, a shot taken from a plane or helicopter. In recent years, the development of more elaborate camera mounts – **aerial mounts** – has allowed *aerial shots* of unprecedented smoothness: see, for example, the opening credit sequence of Bernard Rose's horror film *Candyman* (1992).

AFI   the American Film Institute, a body which serves much the same function in the United States as the *BFI* does in the UK. Founded in 1967, and funded principally by the NEA (National Endowment for the Arts), it maintains a film archive, restores prints, carries out scholarly research, supports young film-makers and the like. The Institute, based in Washington D.C. (though its Center for Advanced Film Studies is in Beverly Hills) also publishes a widely read non-specialist journal, *American Film*.

agent   from the L *agens, agentem*, acting; in the simplest sense, the business person who represents the commercial interests of a 'creative' client – actor, director, writer – in return for a percentage of fees. (This modern, commercial sense of *agent* developed from earlier senses in which an agent was an emissary, steward, factor or deputy; such senses begin to appear in English around the late 16th C.) But this bland description does not remotely do justice to the degree of power which certain agents and agencies – notably *CAA* and *ICM* – have come to exercise in the American film industry since the decline of the *studio system*. When *Premiere* and other industry magazines run their annual lists of the 50, 100 and 200 most powerful people in the business, the names of certain key agents (Michael Ovitz, Jeff Berg) are regularly near the top.

Agfacolor   an early, soft-hued colour system devised in Germany as early as 1908, but only made commercially available by Agfa Filmfabrik in 1936. It underwent development during the Second World War, when it was used to shoot the likes of *Kolberg* (1945) and *Munchhausen* (1943). After the war, the Soviets took over Agfacolor as the basis for *Sovcolor* (and, in East Germany, *Orwocolor*); in America, the system was developed into *Ansco Color*.

AIP   the acronym for American International Pictures, the company founded by Samuel Z. Arkoff in 1954 to specialise in the distribution of low-budget *exploitation* movies – horror movies, biker pictures and the like. AIP is now best known for the work of the prolific producer-director Roger Corman, and particularly for his cycle of films based more or less fancifully on the writings of Edgar Allan Poe and starring Vincent Price. It merged with Filmways in 1979, and later became part of *Orion*.

aleatory   techniques based on chance (from *alea*, a die) or coincidence rather than authorial design. Not as commonly used in film as in other, less audience-dependent twentieth-century arts, though many directors welcome serendipities encountered in shooting or editing, and some *avant-garde* cinema – the films of Andy Warhol, say – at least verges on the aleatory. But the role of chance in film-making should not be underrated; indeed, according to Peter Bogdanovich, Orson Welles once defined a director as someone whose job is to preside over a series of accidents.

aliasing   see *computer graphics*.

Allefex   a versatile sound-producing gadget used to add excitement to screenings in the silent era.

Allied Artists Productions; Allied Artists Pictures Corporation   the American production company, set up in 1946 as a subsidiary of *Monogram* to handle the slightly more up-market, indeed *A-picture* productions of that *B-movie* factory.

Alligator clamps   see *gator*.

allusion   see *hommage*.

ambient light   from the L *ambientem*, the present participle of *ambire*, to go about: a term which usually refers to the diffuse, general light within a scene; hence also *ambient noise, ambient sound*, the various background noises which give acoustic life to a scene.

American loop   see *Latham loop*.

American montage a kind of shorthand technique based on superimpositions, jump cuts and dissolves. Mainly found in Hollywood films of the 1930s and 1940s (but still in use), American montage squeezes time, space and action into a short, rapid sequence. Typical examples: a showbusiness career hits the high spots; a gangster's reign of terror spreads across the city; our hero has a nightmare vision of his possible future.

American shot see *two-shot*.

anaglyph process, anaglyphic process an antiquated 3-D technique, used in the 1920s and 1930s, but abandoned because the coloured spectacles (**anaglyphoscopes**) required to enjoy the illusion caused eyestrain, and because it could not produce images in full colour. The cinematic word was derived from the fairly recondite 'anaglyph', which comes into English in the mid-17th C to designate embossed ornaments in low relief; 'anaglyph' is from the Gk *anaglyphe*, 'work in low relief', from *anaglyph-ein*, 'to hollow out or carve', which also gives us the more familiar word for embossed wallpaper, anaglypta. Paramount produced a series of short anaglyph films in the 1920s called Plastigrams; MGM's slightly later version of the same attractions were known as Audioscopiks.

analogue image synthesis (or **video synthesis**) a computer graphic process which can produce moving shapes, abstract or representational; **analogue recording**, sound recording using non-digital methods; magnetic or optical sound recording.

analytic projector a 16mm projector which can freeze frames for the purpose of closer study.

anamorphic lens the essential tool of many wide-screen techniques, including *Cinemascope*, Superscope and others. An *anamorphic camera lens* will squeeze the width of an image to half its size so that it will fit into the frame; projection through another anamorphic lens will create a wide-screen picture with an aspect ratio of 2.55:1 – or, more usually, 2.35:1, to accomodate an optical soundtrack. 'Anamorphic' is from the Gk *ana*, up and *morphe*, form: 'anamorphism', meaning a distorted projection or perspective, appears to be an early 19th C form, and 'anamorphosis' can be found at least a century earlier: 'To draw the *Anamorphosis*, or deformation of an image, upon the convex surface of a cone': Chambers' *Cyclopaedia*, 1727–51.

angel hair the filaments of celluloid that are accidentally cut away from film when it scrapes against the mechanism of a camera or projector.

angle a word which comes into ME from the F *angle*, derived from the L diminutive *angulum*, a corner: the commonly-used abbreviation for *camera angle* – the attitude, that is to say, from which the camera films its subject: *high angle, low angle, Dutch angle* and so on. Introductory textbooks on film-making tend to imply that certain types of shot necessarily convey certain meanings – that a low-angle shot will make the audience feel dominated by the subject, for example – but such ready wisdom should be treated cautiously. *Angle of view*: the horizontal (or, more rarely, the vertical) slice of the field of vision which a camera or its lens can accomodate. For a 50mm lens and 35mm film, this is about 25 degrees; lenses with short focal lengths give a wider angle of view; long-focus lenses give a narrower angle. *Angle on*: a written direction in a shooting script to change the camera angle of a shot. *Angle-reverse-angle*: the standard method of filming a conversation between two characters. The actors face each other; each new shot is taken from the reverse angle of its predecessor. *Angle shot*: a shot which takes a new angle on a continuing action.

animal handler   see *wrangler*.

Animascope   a cheap animation technique which uses live actors, filmed in stop-motion, rather than complex cel drawings to achieve movement.

Animatics   rough versions of a scene produced using animation methods, and often used in preparing films with elaborate and costly special effects.

animated, animation   today, the term is almost universally understood as referring (a) to the use of stop-frame photography to create illusions of movement in or with drawings, models, cut-outs or objects; or (b) to that illusion of movement itself; or (c) to the drawings used in animated *cartoons*; or (d) to the effects created with *CGI*, or Computer Generated Imagery. 'Animation' is derived from the L *animatus*, filled with life, and *anima*, air, breath, soul, mind: its earlier senses – giving life, vitality, inspiration and so on – can be found in English from the mid-16th C. OED first records our modern cinematic sense of the word 'animated' in *Harper's Weekly*, 11 December 1915: 'Even cartoons began to come in – "animated" cartoons, as they are called'. Before 1919, however, the term *animation* was quite commonly used to apply to all kinds of motion picture, not just cartoons; hence F.A. Talbot in 1912, writing that 'What we describe as animated photography is not animated at all. All that happens is that a long string of snap-shot photographs . . . are passed at rapid speed before the eye.' In its more familiar modern sense, the word also occurs in such terms as *animation camera* (or *rostrum* camera), a stop-frame camera; *animation layout*, the plan for a scene to be animated; *animation stand*, a device which holds and moves drawings and positions the camera in relation to them; *animation zoom*, the illusion of a *zoom* created by photographing increasingly large drawings; *animator*, the artist and/or overall designer of an animated film; and so on. *Animatronics* are essentially elaborate puppets, usually of weird creatures or monsters, widely used in live-action *science-fiction* and *horror* movies (*Star Wars*, *Jurassic Park* etc.) or to stand in for animals in gentler entertainments. The history of animation, which encompasses both the most mindless and the most strange, beautiful and delicate works of the cinema, is so complex that it would require several book-length studies to do it justice; here, let a few animators' names stand for the legions of dead and living: J. Stuart Blackton, by most reckonings the first true animator with his Vitagrapgh production *Humorous Phases of Funny Faces*

(1906), Winsor McCay (*Gertie the Dinosaur*, 1909, and the – highly disturbing – first animated feature, *The Sinking of the Lusitania*, 1918), Max Fleischer (Betty Boop, Popeye), George Herriman (the immortal Krazy Kat), Pat Sullivan (Felix the Cat), Walt Disney and Ub Iwerks, Chuck Jones and Tex Avery (the incomparable Warner Brothers stable), William Hanna and Joseph Barbera (Tom and Jerry), Walter Lantz (Woody Woodpecker); Paul Grimault, Halas and Bachelor, Richard Williams, Bob Godfrey, Walerian Borowczyk, Karel Zeman, Jiri Trnka, Ralph Bakshi, Don Bluth, Matt Groening, the Quay Brothers, Lys Flowerday . . .

Anscolo Color   an integral tripack colour process used from 1941 onwards by Ansco, a American film-manufacturing company originally founded in 1890; this was superseded by *Anscochrome*, a reversal-film process. See *Agfacolor*.

answer print (or **trial composite, trial print, approval print**)   the first print from an edited negative, shown to the producers for approval before release, almost always with corrected light and colour and synchronised sound; it is common for several answer prints to be made before the producers are fully satisfied. OED records the first use in 1940.

anticipatory camera, anticipatory setup   a shot which begins just before the main action takes place.

anti-halation backing   the light-absorbing layer put on the back of film to prevent reflection back onto its light-sensitive surface. See *halation*.

aperture   the opening through which light passes before enterting a lens, a camera, a projector or a printer. From the L *apertura*, itself from *aperire*, to open. The optical sense of the word is quite early: 'I saw . . . with one Aperture of my glass more than 40 or 50' (1664). Hence a photographic report of 1879: 'That roundness and relief that is admired so much in photographs taken with large aperture lenses.'

APO   *Action Print Only* – that is, a print without a sound track.

apochromatic lens   a sophisticated form of *achromatic lens*.

apple box   slang for a box which puts an actor or object into frame at the right height: for example, to make a short male actor seem taller than his leading lady. The original apple boxes were the real thing; their modern counterparts are specially made, and usually about 24″ by 14″ by 8″; see *half apple, pancake*.

approach   a camera movement towards an actor or object.

archival film   a film made entirely from *archival* or *archive footage* – old newsreels and the like. Film *archives* (from Fr *archif, archive*, the late L *archium, archivum* and Gk *archeion*), a public office or magisterial residence), such as Britain's National Film Archive (founded 1935) will usually house not only films but stills, scripts and many other forms of documentation. Other famous archives include those of the *Cinémathèque Française*, the Museum of Modern Art in New York, the Pacific Film Archive in Berkeley, and the film library of Moscow's *V.G.I.K.*

arc lamp   an extremely bright incandescent lamp used to light sets or project pictures. So called because of the luminous shape (L *arcum* means a bow, arch or curve) created between two electrical poles; Sir Humphrey Davy wrote of 'poles . . . connected by charcoal so as to make an arc, or column of electrical light' (1821). *Arc out!* Either: a director's order to an actor to move past the camera in a curve, or an order to the dolly crew to pass the action in a curve; *arc shot*, a shot which curves or circles around its subject. See also *character arc*.

AromaRama   one of the many gimmicks used to add an olfactory dimension to the audio-visual experience of cinema. Devised by an inventor called Charles Weiss, it was first used to lend atmosphere to the documentary *Behind the Great Wall* (1959); the public was not charmed. Aromarama worked by piping scents to the audience via air conditioning ducts. See *Odorama, Smell-O-Vision, Todd-AO*.

Arriflex, Arri   the mirror reflex cameras made by the German company Arnold and Richter, particularly their Arriflex 35 IIC, first put on the market at Leipzig in 1937. Small, battery-powered and readily portable, this camera and its successors – notably the Arriflex 16BL and its 35 mm counterpart, which are sound insulated (see *blimp*) and thus suitable for synchronous sound recording – have proved immensely successful and influential, both for documentary work and in features.

art department   the team responsible for designing and building sets, props, wardrobes and so on – all the things which, apart from the lighting and camerawork, help give a film its distinctive visual character, or 'look'; *art director*, either (a) the person in charge of the art department or (b) where there is a separate *production designer* at work, the person responsible only for the sets.

art house   a cinema which specialises in showing films of acknowledged, reputed or alleged artistic merit, whether these be *art films* or the type of commercial films which might also be enjoyed by typical art-house customers. The English term, equivalent to the French *cinéma d'art et d'essai*, originates in the United States as early as 1920, when Michael Mindlin presented the first American commercial screening of *Das Cabinett des Dr Caligari* (1919), but came into more general use in the early 1950s, when Amos Vogel began to import into America and exhibit those foreign or avant-garde films which would not otherwise have been distributed. The phrase is often used adjectivally: 'an art house movie'.

ASA (or **ASA Speed Rating**)   the most commonly used of the various scales for measuring the sensitivity of a given film emulsion to light; the higher the ASA, the greater a film's capacity to respond to light. The term ASA is an abbreviation for the American Standards Association, a body founded in 1930 to establish technical standards for films, still photography and, later, television (its name was changed to the USA Standards Institute in 1966) ASA measurements are used and understood by professionals throughout the world; other such scales include *DIN* and *ISO*.

ASC   the American Society for Cinematographers. The appearance of these initials in credits indicates that the Director of Photography is a member of the Society (compare *BSC*); membership is by invitation only.

ashcan   a type of floodlight.

aspect ratio   the ratio of width to height in a film or television image. The most familiar of these is the *Academy ratio* of 1.33:1 or 4:3, established by AMPAS in 1932, itself inspired by the pleasing aspect ratio of silent films that was originally established by Edison. The wide-screen ratios which were developed in the 1950s (see *anamorphic lens*) began at 2.55:1 but were adapted to 2.35:1 to accommodate an optical sound track; various other wide-screen ratios have followed. Nowadays, 70mm films are projected at 2.2:1, and non-anamorphic 35mm prints at 1.85:1. See also *Cinemascope, dynamic frame, wide screen.*

assemble, assembly   the earliest stage of editing is to select the best or more useful takes and cut them together in a loose approximation of the form the film-makers have in mind. (The next stage is the **rough cut**.) OED's first citation is from 1949.

assistant cameraman   the crew member who loads and unloads the film, changes lenses, carries out minor repairs and makes sure that focus is kept steady during camera movements; see *focus puller*. The *assistant director (AD)*, is the person who calls for silence on the set and tells the cameraman and sound recordist to start turning over. An AD is also responsible for co-ordinating crowds, and doing many other jobs for the director – liaising with the crew, actors or visitors to the set, keeping order, checking budgets and so on. An *assistant editor* is usually responsible for keeping track of all the pieces of unedited film, maintaining editing equipment in good repair, splicing and more menial tasks.

associational editing   editing together shots of different objects or scenes so as to establish some form of relationship between them, from symbolic equivalence to sharp contrast. See *relation editing*.

astigmatism   a lens flaw that prevents light rays from coming to focus at the same point; the resulting distortion is particularly glaring around the edges of the image. From the Gk *a*, the privative prefix, and *stigma*, point; it became an English medical term, denoting the common eye disorder, in the mid-19th C.

asynchronous sound   any sound which, whether by accident or design, does not match the action or scene, but particularly the intentional overlapping of sound from one scene to the next, or the bringing forward of sound from the following shot. The technique was used brilliantly and innovatively in Humphrey Jennings's *Listen to Britain* (1942), though its use has now become so routine that audiences seldom notice the device any more.

atmosphere   either (a) the background sound of a scene (sometimes abbreviated to *atmos*: see **room tone, wild track**), or (b) a collective term for *extras*, or (c) the mood of a given scene or film.

attenuated filters   filters which reduce the presence of primary colours.
Auricon   the trade name for a range of cameras made by Bach Auricon
Inc. of California.

auteur, **auteur, auteur theory,** *politique des auteurs*   the precise
value and use of the term *auteur* has often been disputed – not to say
derided – by those, especially screenwriters (Gore Vidal and William
Goldman lead the pack), who regard the whole notion as residing
somewhere between idiocy, bunkum and confidence trick. Briefly, however, it can be said that (a) the auteur theory recognises the director of a
film – rather than, say, its producer, writer, stars, or designer – as the
person who gives it an artistic identity; in other words, it maintains that
despite the essentially collaborative nature of the medium, the director
should be regarded as the true 'author' of the film; and/or (b) that the
auteur theory is also a way of establishing a canon of artistic merit among
directors – that is to say, every auteur is a director, but only a few
approved directors are auteurs. Following this, it should therefore be
possible to observe the stylistic development, thematic consistency and
so on of a canonical director across a body of films, despite the
circumstances in which they were made, and this is precisely what auteur
criticism sets out to do. Though the general line of thought in auteur
criticism is often said to have been inspired by the critico-theoretical
writings of André Bazin (1919–58), the term itself appears to date from
an essay published in 1948 in the pages of *Ecran Français* by the critic
Alexandre Astruc, 'Le Caméra-stylo'. (A translation of this essay can be
found in *The New Wave*, ed. Peter Graham, 1968.) The phrase *politique
des auteurs*, usually if not quite accurately translated, following the
example of the American critic Andrew Sarris, as the *auteur* theory
(rather than 'policy' or 'strategy'), was coined shortly afterwards by the
young François Truffaut for an article in Bazin's journal *Cahiers du
Cinéma* in January 1954, 'Une Certaine Tendance du cinéma français'
(translation available in *Cahiers du Cinéma in English*, No.1, 1966 and
elsewhere). Here, Truffaut opposed the creative, indeed visionary *auteur*
director to the mere *metteur en scène*, a characterless hack who simply
helps bring other people's ideas and creations to the screen. He and his
friends on and around *Cahiers*, including Jean-Luc Godard, Jacques
Rivette, and Eric Rohmer, then went on to establish a pantheon of
auteurs, lavishing elaborate and often immoderate praise on such Hollywood directors as Alfred Hitchcock, Howard Hawks and Nicholas Ray,
and also on a handful of older European directors: Jean Renoir, Roberto
Rossellini, Robert Bresson. The *politique des auteurs* was exported to
Britain via the pages of *Movie* magazine, and to the USA by Andrew
Sarris in the journal *Film Culture*: the *locus classicus* is his article 'Notes
on the *Auteur* Theory in 1962' (reprinted in *Film Culture*, ed. P. Adams
Sitney, 1971). Excessive and even ludicrous as its lines of argument
could be, the auteur theory had several healthy consequences (for one
thing, it helped Truffaut and Co. to become *auteurs* themselves: see

nouvelle vague), and despite the displacement of the *politique des auteurs* by newer, more fashionable and significantly anti-humanist French theories towards the end of the 1960s and afterwards, some diluted version of auteurism still informs much middle- to highbrow discussion of cinema. Moreover, though the French are credited with dreaming the whole business up around the end of the 1950s, it had long been thought quite sensible to regard at least some directors (Griffith, say) as the creators of their films, and at least one central tenet of the *auteur* theory appears to have been anticipated as early as 1915: 'Languages as they evolve produce stylists, and we will some day distinguish the different photoplay masters as we now delight in the separate tang of O. Henry and Mark Twain and Howells' – Vachel Lindsay, *The Art of the Moving Picture.* The screenwriter Jean-Claude Carrière has recently noted that, in France at least, the notion of an 'author's film' soon became corrupt: from meaning 'a film which bears the unmistakable stamp of its director', it came to imply 'a film in which the director only talks about himself' (*The Secret Language of Film*, p. 42). See a *film by A.*

automatic (or **automated**) **dialogue replacement (ADR)**   see *looping*.

available light   the natural light of a location or set, not augmented by artifical sources of illumination.

avant-garde, **avant-garde**   though the term can be applied to the cinema precisely as it is to the other arts, and applies to all innovative or experimental (and generally non-narrative) work made outside the commercial mainstream, in film history it often refers particularly to work done in France and Germany between 1918 and 1930, or to the films of the early Soviet directors: Eisenstein, Vertov, Kuleshov and others. But there have been many *avant-garde* schools and outbursts, from the *cinéma-pur* of Henri Chomette and others, influenced by the *absolute* or *abstract* films of Eggeling, Ruttman and co, via the *surrealists* and the *New American Cinema* or *Underground* movements up to the formal innovations characteristic of today's *Queer Cinema* and the many strange and sometimes rich audio-visual works being created on film and video by incalculably large numbers of visual artists, from Nam June Paik and Bruce Nauman to the recent, much-vaunted school of Young British Artists including Damien Hirst, Angus Fairhurst, Georgina Starr, the Wilson Sisters and so on. At the time of writing, Hirst, at least, looks well placed to move into the mainstream of film-making – a logical progression, since the commercial cinema has often plundered the avant-garde. The visual grammar of many rock videos, for example, would once have seemed weirdly incoherent; conversely, a *colourised* extract from the Bunuel/Dali *Un Chien Andalou*, originally bourgeois-baiting, riot-provoking stuff, has been screened on the rock music channel MTV as light filler material, wholly suitable for its juvenile audience.

B **-movie** (also **B-picture, B-feature**) in the days of double-features – mostly the 1930s and 1940s – the more modest of the two attractions on show, generally running about 55 to 75 minutes and starring less well-known actors than *A-pictures*. The usual practice was for cinema managers to book them for a flat fee, rather than a percentage of the gross receipts. Cheap and cheerless as they may have been, they did serve the useful function of providing employment in a notoriously unstable industry, and critical history has been surprisingly kind to some of these productions. For example, Val Lewton's horror films, inexpensively made for RKO, are now widely regarded as minor classics of their kind, and many film buffs continue to nurse passions for directors who worked wholly or mostly in B-movies. Jean-Luc Godard dedicated his own first feature, *A Bout de souffle*, to **Monogram** Pictures, a company which, like *Republic*, made nothing but B-movies. OED's earliest citation for 'B feature' is from 1949.

B wind see *A and B wind*.

baby (or **baby spot**) a small spotlight fitted with a 1000-watt bulb, used mainly for close-ups; the *barn door* on a baby is known as a *baby door*; *baby plate*, a mount used to hold a small spotlight; *baby tripod*, a small tripod used for low-angle shots; also known as *baby legs*.

back-and-forth printing printing an action twice (or more than twice) to create the effect, usually though by no means always comic, of forward and backward motion. Jean Cocteau used reverse motion lyrically in *Orphée* and *La Belle et la Bête*, as, earlier, did Jean Vigo in his short, impressionistic study of the championship swimmer *Taris* (1931). See *reverse motion*.

backdrop as in the theatre, the scenery painted on a cloth or flats at the back of a set; or a large photograph serving the same purpose. Also known as a *drop*.

back end the percentage of a film's receipts which go to a writer, performer or director, either as *gross points* or as *net points*. For an amusing digression on the term, see Buzzell, 317.

back focus (or **back focal distance**) the distance between a plane of focus and the lens's rear glass surface.

background (BG) the area of an image or scene at the greatest distance from the camera; that is, everything set behind the *foreground* area in which the main action takes place, including the scenery, buildings or decor and the *background action* – incidental activities carried out by *extras* and minor actors to add to the general atmosphere of the scene rather than to advance the narrative; such activity is lit by *background lighting*.

background music the music which helps provide the scene with its mood, but which, unlike *source music* (also known as *direct music*) does not originate from something which is happening on screen – a soldier blowing a harmonica before battle, a car radio playing or the like.

background plate a painted glass plate used in *rear projection*.

back projection, background projection   see *rear projection*.
backing   (1) the source or sources of finance for a production; (2) a backdrop; (3) the coating on the reverse side of film stock.
back light   a (usually brilliant) light set behind an actor or object so as to sharpen the outline and make him, her or it stand out clearly from the background: generally a rather stylised effect.
back lot   traditionally, the outdoor area of a *studio* where technical equipment is stored, where trailers for cast, crew and back-up services are parked and, above all, where exterior sets – particularly those for street scenes – are specially constructed or kept ready for repeated use. With the decline of the *studio system* and the rise of *location filming*, however, back lots are becoming a thing of the past.
back story   in screenwriting jargon: (1) any of the significant events which have taken place before the script's main action begins, and which have set its plots in motion, but particularly (2) the personal histories of the leading characters. Sometimes the back story can go back an extremely long way. In his introduction to his scripts for the BBC thriller serial *Edge of Darkness*, for example, Troy Kennedy Martin reveals that the most remote level of back story for two of his leading characters, Jedburgh and Grogan, is that in former lives they were, respectively, a Teutonic knight and a Templar.
baffle   (1) The adjustable shutter which fits over a lamp to control its brilliance and direct its beam; (2) a screen used to cut down echo and reverberation during sound recording; or (3) the part of a microphone or loudspeaker which reduces vibrations.
BAFTA   (1) the British Academy of Film and Television Arts, founded in 1959 by the union of the British Film Academy (created in 1947) and the Guild of Television Producers and Directors (created in 1954), and initially known the Society of Film and Television Arts; it has its HQ in Piccadilly, and the expressions 'a BAFTA screening' or 'a screening at BAFTA' refer to a press or private show at one of small cinemas there. (2) An award given by the academy at its annual ceremony, the BAFTAs; thus, the British counterpart to the *Academy Awards* or *Oscars*.
balance   (1) the arrangement of shapes, colours and light within an image or (2) its acoustic equivalent: the respective levels of voice, music, incidental noises and the like on a sound track; (3) an abbreviation of *colour balance*: the preparation of a film stock for a particular light source – daylight, studio light etc. The choice of an inappropriately balanced stock will result in an unwanted tint to the developed images.
balance stripe   a band of magnetic coating on film designed to make it lie flat as it passes over the magnetic heads.
bank   a row of lights; or, as a verb, to arrange lights in a row.
barn doors, barn door   the four (or sometimes two or one) hinged shutters set on front of a lamp to adjust the direction and brilliance of its illumination.
Barney, barney   the covering which can be slipped over a camera,

either to reduce its noise or to keep it warm and dry in bad weather. The name is said to derive from the American cartoon character Barney Google; perhaps in an allusion to Barney's racehorse, which wore an old blanket, or perhaps to his weird, 'googly-eyed' facial expression.

barrel, barrel mount   a detachable mount that holds a camera's lenses; see *lens barrel*.

bar sheet   a chart used in animation work, which shows the number of frames that must be placed together to match characters' lip movements to recorded dialogue. See *lead sheet*.

base, film base   the layer of film stock on which the light-sensitive emulsion is coated, previously made of nitrate (which unfortunately proved to be highly inflammable), now made of cellulose acetate. *Base down/base up* (or *base in/base out*): the directions in which the film is threaded for editing.

base light (also **foundation light, set light**)   the basic lighting for a set before any individual lighting has been added.

basher   a small spotlight.

bass boost   to augment low frequency sounds during recording; the opposite of *bass roll-off*, to reduce low frequency sounds.

batch   one particular mixture of emulsion for film stock: since the sensitivity of stock will tend to vary slightly from batch to batch, manufacturers supply batch numbers with each roll so that film-makers can be sure that they are using stock from the same batch.

bath   the chemical solutions in which film is processed; or the container for those solutions.

batten   as in the theatre: a supporting pole made of metal or wood, used to prop scenery or mount overhead lights.

battery belt   the portable power source that can be strapped around the cameraman's waist and plugged directly into the camera, and may be used for filming *hand-held* shots.

bayonet mount   a type of lens mount, such as the one used on *Arriflex* cameras. On a bayonet mount, the lens is snapped quickly into place rather than screwed on slowly.

bazooka   support for an overhead light.

BBFC   the British Board of Film Censors, established in 1912 at the initiative of the film industry itself, led by the Cinematograph Exhibitors Association. Under the terms of the Cinematograph Act of 1909, local authorities had been given the right to ban films at their own discretion; the results proved so chaotic that the industry saw the benefit of a body which could certify films for the whole country. By the 1920s, most local authorities were co-operating with the BBFC, though they retain their right to over-rule censorship decisions to the present day; witness, in 1996–7, Westminster Council's refusal to permit screenings of David Cronenberg's *Crash*. See *censorship*.

BCU   the abbreviation for big close-up (see *extreme close-up*).

beaded screen   a viewing room or cinema screen covered with small reflective beads, usually of glass.

beam   a ray or shaft of light; from OF *beam*, 'tree' or 'plank'; the figurative, optical sense is very old in English and can be found as early as the 9th C ('sunne beam'); according to OED, the idea was borrowed directly from the L concept of a *columna lucis*, a pillar or column of light. Bede uses this term to describe the streams of brilliance issuing from the dead body of a saint. *Beam angle*: a measurement, usually supplied by the manufacturers, of the angle of usable light a given lamp will produce. The lowest acceptable level of lighting is taken to fall where the beam is half as intense as at its peak. *Beam coverage* denotes the area that a lamp can light down to half of its peak intensity. *Beam lumens*, the amount of light within a beam; see *lumen*. *Beam projector*: a spotlight that throws a narrow beam, *Beam splitter*: a prism, mirror or other optical device that splits the beam from the lens into two separate images, thus allowing the use of viewfinders, the production of special effects and so-on.

bear trap   also known as a *gator grip* or *gaffer grip*: a strong clamp.

beat, story beat   in screenwriting jargon, the major plot points in a story. The term has been in fairly common use within the industry since the 1980s, and is presumably derived from an analogy between narrative rhythms and musical rhythms.

Beaulieu   a lightweight professional 16mm camera, made by the French company, used in filming documentaries or by television news crews.

beep, beep tone   a noise put on soundtracks by an electronic *clapstick* or *beeper* to help synchronise sound and image.

behind-the-lens filter   a *filter* inserted into a camera between its lens and the film; such filters are generally considered superior to those set in front of the lens, since they are less liable to break and are not susceptible to *flare*.

behind-the-scenes film   a documentary (or, often, *plugumentary*) about the shooting of a large-scale production. This may vary in scale and value from a brief *EPK*, issued to television companies as a promotional exercise, via more serious arts documentaries to full-length films that may be distributed to cinemas as attractions in their own right: for example, *Hearts of Darkness*, an engrossing and intermittently hilarious account of Francis Ford Coppola's laborious attempt to complete *Apocalypse Now*.

Bell and Howell   the pioneering, Chicago-based manufacturer of cameras and projectors, *fons et origo* of a number of standard industry terms including the *Bell and Howell mechanism*, a device for steadying the movement of film through that company's cameras; and the *Bell and Howell perforation (BH)* (also *negative perforation*): a common form of perforation for 35mm negatives, using rectangular holes. Positive prints tend to use the *Kodak standard perforation (KS)*, which is shorter, has curved corners and is less likely to tear.

bellows attachment   a collapsible device, the folding sides of which somewhat resemble an accordion, that extends the lens away from the camera for extreme close-ups.

belly board   a camera mount for low-angle shots.

below-the-line   the basic technical cost of a film – hiring, transporting, housing and feeding the crew, paying location fees and so on – as distinct from the cost of hiring its stars, writers, director, composer and other, notionally more 'creative' personnel. See *above the line*.

bench editing   manual (rather than mechanical) winding of film through a viewer for the purpose of editing.

best boy   the assistant to the chief electrician, or *gaffer*; in other words, the second-in-command on the electrical team. The origins of the phrase are hazy, but since 'gaffer' is a corruption of 'grandfather', some sort of metaphorical family relationship may be at the root of the matter.

BFI   the British Film Institute, founded in 1933 'To encourage the art of the film' (this phrase was taken by Ivan Butler for the title of his history of the Institute, published in 1971) and funded by a combination of government subsidy and membership fees. Often the object of bitter criticism and the site of still more bitter internal wrangling, the BFI none the less carries out a number of valuable activities, including the preservation and restoration of significant films in the National Film Archive (est. 1935 as the National Film Library); the running of the National Film Theatre (formerly the Telekinema, built for the Festival of Britain in 1951) and MOMI, the Museum of the Moving Image, on London's South Bank – as the last acronym suggests, the BFI has increasingly been concerned with television as well as the cinema; the publication of many books on cinema history and theory, as well as the monthly magazine *Sight and Sound*, devoted to criticism, debate and – since the incorporation of the old *Monthly Film Bulletin*, its previous journal of record – providing a detailed and constantly accumulating catalogue of credits and synopses for every film given major release in the UK; the production and distribution of documentaries, shorts and feature films, both for theatrical release and for television; a wide variety of educational activities and resources, including the BFI library and so on.

BG   the abbreviation for *background*.

Bianco e Nero   ('Black and White' or, to be pedantic, 'White and Black'), the influential Italian monthly journal of film criticism and film aesthetics, first published in January 1937 by the Centro Sperimentale di Cinematografia; the journal also specialised in printing screenplays.

bias   the damping or complete removal of hiss and distortion on a sound tape.

bicycling   a rather amateurish practice, common in the early part of the century, which involved a cyclist picking up the hastily rewound first reel of a film from cinema A, pedalling frantically across to Cinema B (where the show began a crucial quarter of an hour or so later), handing it over and then racing back to cinema A for the second reel. Though the

practice became increasingly rare as more and more prints were struck
for each film, the term 'bicycle print', meaning any spare print, survived
for decades after the end of the silent period.

bidirectional microphone   a *microphone* that is sensitive to sound
from behind and in front, but relatively *dead* at the sides.

big eye   a large, powerful floodlight of 100,000 watts.

Billancourt   the Parisian studios built in 1920 on the banks of the Seine
by Henri Diamant-Berger for his film *Vingt ans après*. A number of the
greatest French films were shot there, including Abel Gance's *Napoléon*
(1927), Jean Renoir's *La Grande illusion* (1937) and Marcel Carné's *Le
Jour se lève* (1939). In the 1920s, when it was known as the Abel Gance
studios, it was staffed almost entirely by White Russians.

billing   the degree of prominence given to the actors, directors and
other key members of a production on posters, in screen credits and so
on. The term is taken over from the theatre, where variants of the terms
'bill', 'billing' and so on have been in use since the late 17th C: 'A
Composition that he Bill'd about, under the name of a Sovereign
Antidote' – L'Estrange, *Fables*, 1694.

bin (or **trim bin**)   a mobile container for film which is being edited. It
is generally made of a metal frame, about waist-high, with a large cloth
bag inside it, and a short rack (sometimes known as a *pin rack*) on top;
lengths of exposed film are hung from small hooks set into this rack.

binder   the substance which binds the light-sensitive emulsion of film
to its base.

Biograph   an important early American film company, founded in 1896
by W.K.L. Dickson, H.N. Marvin and H. Casler, which developed its
own series of high-quality cameras and projectors and also produced
many one- and two-reel films. D. W. Griffith was the most illustrious of
Biograph's employees; he made some 400 pictures under its banner from
1908 to 1913, and the company also helped to launch the careers of
Lillian and Dorothy Gish, Mary Pickford and Mack Sennett, among
others. 'I am the one poet who has a right to claim for his muses Blanche
Sweet, Mary Pickford, and Mae Marsh. I am the one poet who wrote
them songs when they were Biograph heroines, before their names were
put on the screen, or the name of their director' (Vachel Lindsay, *The
Art of the Moving Picture*). More properly known as the American
Mutoscope and Biograph Company, its earliest business plan was simply
to market those two devices – the *Mutoscope*, a sort of peep-show
gadget akin to Edison's *Kinetoscope*, and the *Biograph*, a combined
camera-projector. In 1897 the company built its first studio on an office
roof in Manhattan, and a decade later, in 1906, opened a studio at no.
eleven, 14th Street. In 1910, Biograph followed the general industry
trend westward and opened a second studio in Los Angeles, thereafter
dividing its activities between the two cities. The company's downfall
was largely due to a dispute with Griffith and some of his leading players
– to keep costs down, Biograph refused either to give name billing to

their stars or to back Griffith's more ambitious projects. In 1913, Griffith went off to join *Mutual*, taking his cameraman Billy Bitzer with him; Biograph declined rapidly, and went into liquidation in 1915. (Described by OED as 'rare', 'biograph' had previously, in the mid-19th C, meant a biographical sketch or notice.)

biopic   a dramatic treatment of the life story – or, more commonly, episodes from the life story – of famous artists, scientists, soldiers, politicians, criminals and other well-known or notorious people, as opposed to documentary features (though the categories may sometimes blur slightly in the case of fully or semi-dramatised documentaries which use some of the techniques of fiction: *Thirty-Two Short Films about Glenn Gould*, for example). The form has sometimes been thought to be rather corny or middlebrow, which may be one – if no more than one – of the reasons why Sir Richard Attenborough's biopics *Ghandi*, *Cry Freedom* (about the death of Steve Biko), *Chaplin* and *Shadowlands* met with middling to hostile reviews from *bien-pensant* critics. Yet considered broadly, many extraordinary or at any rate notable films, of great variety and scope, have been biopics of some order, from 'epics' such as David Lean's *Lawrence of Arabia* and Abel Gance's *Napoléon* to John Ford's *Young Mr Lincoln*, Paul Schrader's *Mishima: A Life in Four Chapters* and *Patty Hearst*, Derek Jarman's *Caravaggio* and *Wittgenstein*, Hans-Jürgen Syberberg's *Hitler, a Film From Germany*, Spike Lee's *Malcolm X*, Neil Jordan's *Michael Collins*, Julian Schnabel's *Basquiat*. The term 'biopic', which seems to have come into circulation in America some time in the 1930s, when Warner Brothers were starting to produce fairly ambitious movies based on the lives of Zola and Pasteur, is a compound of 'biography' (possibly from Fr *biographie*, but more certainly from the early medieval Gk *biographia*, 'writing of lives', which is first recorded *c.* 500 AD) and 'picture'. 'Biographist' was used by Fuller in 1662, and 'Biography' by Dryden in 1683: 'In all parts of Biography . . . Plutarch equally excell'd'.

biophantoscope   an early British form of the *cinematograph*, the invention of a Mr Rudge of Bath, who is commemorated by a splendid plaque in that city. Coined, presumably by Rudge himself, from the Gk *bio-*, *bios*, 'Life, course or way of living' and *phantasia*, 'a making visible'.

bioscope, *bioskop*   an early German camera and projector system, invented by Emil and Max Skladanowsky and first displayed to the Berlin public in 1895 – the same year as the more celebrated show mounted by the Lumière brothers. The term, however, soon seems to have passed into English to mean not only this apparatus and others of its kind, chiefly the *cinematograph*, but the places where they were used; which is to say, that it was another early synonym for the cinema. James Joyce, in a letter of 28 December 1904, writes that 'the other evening we went to a bioscope. There were a series of pictures about betrayed Gretchen.' OED notes that in South Africa, it remained the common term for a cinema or moving picture long after the use was abandoned elsewhere.

The Bioscope was the title of a superior British weekly trade journal, published in London, specialising in technical developments and advice to would-be cinema managers as well as full synopses of new releases and information on films in production. It was also the first trade journal to review films. The journal ran from 1908 to 1932; the rights to the title were bought by Odham's Press, but it has never been revived.

bipack   the simultaneous use of two pieces of film in projection, photography and, especially, in *bipack contact matte printing*, which combines two separate images into one – live action with animation or other kinds of artwork. *Bipack double-print titles* are produced by printing titles and images from two separate reels; a *bipack magazine* has four chambers, which feed and pick up two reels of film into and from the projector or camera. The word *bipack* has been current within the industry since the 1920s.

birdseye   see *PAR light*; *bird's-eye view*, a shot taken from high above the subject, see *overhead shot*.

Bison   the trade-mark for a number of silent westerns, produced by the New York Picture Company and issued by a variety of different companies, including *Imp* (later known as *Universal*). The most successful of these films were supervised by Thomas Ince (1882–1924), himself a notable director, and starred W.S. Hart (1870–1946), who was often for all practical purposes their director, too. The series came to an end with the demise of the last of its distributors in 1923.

bit part   a small and usually insignificant speaking role, but of slightly higher rank than an *extra*, who has no lines at all; it is taken by a *bit player*.

black-and-white   though there were many experiments with *colour* stocks, the various forms of black-and-white film remained in standard use around the world until the late 1950s and early 1960s, and have sometimes been revived by film-makers interested in the textures and atmospheres such stock can create: Martin Scorsese's *Raging Bull*, Steven Spielberg's *Schindler's List* and Woody Allen's *Manhattan* and *Shadows and Fog* are among the best-known of these, though many other less celebrated directors have also chosen to work wholly or mostly in black-and-white, including Lars von Trier (*Europa*), Chris Newby (*Anchoress*), the Quay Brothers (*Institute Benjamenta*) and Abel Ferrara (*The Addiction*).

black leader   see *leader*.

black level   the darkest part of a film image.

black limbo   see *limbo*.

blacklist   any list of proscribed actors, writers, directors and others, but particularly that which was drawn up in Hollywood after the HUAC (House Un-American Activities Committe) investigations of alleged Communist infiltration of the entertainment industry in the late 1940s and early 1950s, and which drove many people out of work, out of America or into the use of aliases. This period has inspired a number of

feature films, mostly sympathetic to the blacklisted, including *The Front,
Guilty by Suspicion* and *Fellow Traveller.* See *Hollywood Ten.*

Black Maria   by some accounts – that of Hans-Jürgen Syberberg in
Hitler, A Film From Germany, for example – the world's first movie
studio, designed, built (in New Jersey, in 1893) and used by the Edison
company to produce filmstrips for their *Kinetoscopes.* It was not much
more than large shed, covered with black tar paper, and lit solely by the
rays of the sun (the roof, and indeed the whole structure, could be moved
to follow the sun). Actors performed against a black backround and were
shot by the *Kinetograph* camera.

black net   a screen used to damp down the radiance of a lamp.

blacks   large sheets hung over windows, doors and so on used to
exclude unwanted light from a set

blaxploitation (also, much more rarely, **blacksploitation**)   a compound of *exploitation (film)* and 'black': broadly speaking, any sensationalist, low-budget American movie targeted at the black cinema-
going audience of the US, but especially the popular thrillers of the early
1970s, of which the best-known were *Shaft* (directed by the photographer
Gordon Parks in 1971) and its less well-known sequels (*Shaft's Big
Score!, Shaft in Africa*), *Superfly* (also directed by Gordon Parks, in
1972), the vampire film *Blacula* (William Crain, 1972) and so on. (To
the satisfaction of their producers, many of these films also proved
successful with white audiences.) The genre fell into understandable
disrepute with the arrival of a younger and sometimes more politicised
generation of black directors, some of whom have spoofed it mercilessly,
but in the mid-1990s has been reappraised in more affectionate and even
admiring spirit. At the time of writing, the highly regarded young African-
American director John Singleton is reported to be at work on a remake
of *Shaft.*

bleach   the chemical bath used in processing reversal film.

bleached out   the pale, insipid or poorly detailed look of film that has
been over-exposed.

bleeding   the spilled light or colour at visible at the edges of matte shots
or titles when the image has been badly shot or processed. The term was
taken over from the printing industry, where it applies to pictures that
run off the edge of the page.

blend   an order – as in 'blend in with the crowd' – for an actor to move
closer to other performers.

blimp   the casing which blocks off sound made by the camera's motor,
so that the microphones will not pick it up. The blimp was developed as
a replacement for the *ice box,* which allowed very little camera movement. Since, however, it still made the camera equipment too heavy to
be manoeuvred except by large *cranes* or *dollies,* the industry went on
to develop lightweight *self-blimped* cameras, such as the Arriflex BL,
which can be used for hand-held shots and sequences. The term *blimp*
came into use because such camera casings were thought to resemble the

non-rigid airships of that name, themselves apparently so-called because their floppy structure made them seem (b)limp: the man who coined the name seems to have been the aviator Horace Shortt, some time before 1916.

blistering   the symptom of heat damage on a film stock's surface; blistered film is almost always unusable.

block   see *blocking*.

block booking   a film distribution practice, made illegal in the United States in 1948, which involved forcing distributors to rent productions which were unlikely to do well at the box office as part of the package deal including some sure-fire hits. The practice was begun by Paramount in 1915–16.

blockbuster   a term which came into use in the 1960s to denote either (1) an inordinately expensive, intensely *hyped* film (Hollywood was fighting another of its battles against television by trying to produce *hard ticket* films, such as *Lawrence of Arabia* and *Cleopatra*, calculated to draw audiences in search of sounds and visions more overpowering and lavishly realised than the small screen could provide), or (2) an extremely profitable film. At the time of writing, *Independence Day* (1996) answers admirably to both definitions, though the assumption that films in the first category will be bound to fall into the second category has received any number of harsh refutations over the years. For instructive reading on this point, see Steven Bach's *Final Cut* (subtitled 'Dreams and Disasters in the Making of *Heaven's Gate*') and Julie Salamon's *The Devil's Candy* (subtitled '*The Bonfire of the Vanities* goes to Hollywood'). The original 'blockbusters' were powerful aerial bombs, capable of devastating an entire city block.

blocking   as in the theatre: (1) mapping out the ways in which actors will sit, stand, lie, hang or move about in a scene; deciding the disposition of props and scenery; and working out camera movements; (2) demonstrating those actions or inactions to the performers and crew.

blood bag, blood capsule   the small containers of artificial blood that can be hidden on performers and burst open (often by miniature explosive caps) for gory sequences in thrillers, horror movies and the like.

bloom   to dull down bright surfaces that might cause unwanted glare (or *blooming*) in a shot, generally by using a spray.

bloop   a sound fault – the noise heard when a break or splice in an optical soundtrack goes over a scanner; or the part of the optical-sound track that renders such noises inaudible. See *deblooping*.

blooper   (1) in American English, an actor's verbal gaffe or howler, or (2) the device used in deblooping, a process which involves the use of *blooping ink* and *blooping tape*.

blow-up   either (1) to make print of larger gauge from one of smaller gauge (8mm to 16mm, 16mm to 35mm), or (2) to use an optical printer to enlarge part of an image.

blue cometing   a colour flaw – blue streaks in the image caused by metal particles.

blue movie   a cheap or home-made sex film. The term can also be used to disparage more mainstream ventures into 'erotica', such as *9-½ Weeks* (Adrian Lyne, 1985). An odd, and occasionally quite witty view of the world of blue movie making can be found in the British period film *Inserts* (John Byrum, 1975), which stars Richard Dreyfuss as a director fallen on hard times, and obliged to make pornographic silents. The adjective 'blue' comes to mean 'obscene' in colloquial English around the early to mid-19th C; Carlyle uses the term 'blueness' in 1840: 'The occasional blueness . . . shall not altogether affright us.'

blue-screen process   a widely used technique for producing multiple images, particularly for special effects sequences, as in the *Star Wars* films. Briefly: actors are filmed in a studio against a featureless blue background, and the resulting film, after several stages of development, is combined with images of a different background in an optical printer. See *travelling matte*.

blur pan   see *zip pan*.

BO, b.o   abbreviations for *box office*.

board   in a recording studio, the control panel; in lighting, the master control.

body brace   (also **body frame, body pod**) the metallic support worn by the cameraman when shooting hand-held sequences; see *Steadicam*.

boffo   *Variety*-speak: extremely successful.

Bolex   a Swiss make of 16mm camera, lightweight and easily portable.

Bollywood   familiar term for the Indian film industry, the largest in the world, coined simply by marrying the names 'Bombay' (home to the sub-continent's busiest and most important studios) and 'Hollywood'.

bomb   American slang (as in the punning title of Joseph Heller's air-force play *We Bombed in New Haven*): a critical and commercial disaster. At one time, a source of confusion for uninformed Britons, for whom the expression 'going like a bomb' meant huge success.

book   (1) the unsung, narrative part of a *musical*; (2) a type of double *flat*, hinged for folding open and shut like the covers of a book; (3) to hire a performer, or rent a film from a distributor; hence *booking, booking agent, booking contract*.

boom   a word brought into English in the mid-17th C from from the Dutch *boom* (cognate with OE *beam*), 'tree, pole, beam', and originally used almost exclusively in nautical senses, to mean any long spar which holds out the base of a sail; OED's earliest citation is from 1662, 'The violence of it snappt off their boom by the board.' Hence various related cinematic senses: (1) the long arm, fitted with a microphone at one end, which the *boom operator* or *boom man* (who on modest productions may also be the sound recordist) holds over the heads of the performers and (usually) out of shot; (2) the *camera boom*, a large camera mount which can move the camera up, down and sideways for a *boom shot* (see *crane*);

(3) the *light boom*, a pole from which lights can be suspended. Hence *boom up*, *boom down* – upwards and downwards movements of a boom, or the order to move them thus.

boomerang   the semi-circular mount which holds a filter in front of a lamp; the word, adapted from a name in a language spoken by the original inhabitants of New South Wales, first found its way into print in 1798, in a short vocabulary book put togther by the Judge Advocate of the colony.

boomy   an acoustic which exaggerates low frequencies and muffles high frequencies. 'Boom' – or its earlier variant forms such as 'bombe' and 'bomb' – has been used in English to mean a loud, deep sound since *c.* 1500.

booster light   any illumination used to augment natural daylight, or simply to brighten a set.

boot   (1) a flexible protective cover for the head of a tripod, usually made of plastic or fabric; some tripods are also fitted with boots for their legs; (2) in processing, the part through which film is fed from the magazine into the storage area.

border light   a strip of several lights.

bounce board, bounce card   a white card or sheet used to reflect light on to a subject (see *reflector*); *bounce light*, lights shone off the surrounding walls of a set or location to create general lighting.

box   a four-walled set.

Box Office, box office   (1) commonly, either (a) the amount of money made by a film during its period of theatrical distribution, or (b) the marketplace, either national or global, for a film in the course of its theatrical release: 'How did it do at the American box office?' and so on. This meaning of the term is, of course, a derivation for the more literal sense (2): the small kiosk or booth at the front of a cinema where tickets are bought and sold.

B picture   see *B Movie*.

brace   a scenery support.

bracketing   a kind of safety-net process used in exposing film: the practice of reshooting a scene that has already been filmed at the exposure indicated by the meter at slightly lower and higher exposures, so as to make sure of a completely satisfactory take.

breakaway   a prop, such as a chair or bottle, made from some flimsy substance so that it will break easily without wounding performers.

breakdown   (1) a chart, table or diagram of all the different costs involved in producing a film. (2) A reading of a script which works out which scenes can or must be shot at the same location or set, so as to keep costs at a minimum. (3) An editor's list of the different shots in a roll of exposed film; or the act of drawing up such a list.

breathing   the accidental, intermittent movement of an image in and out of focus during projection, often caused by a loose *gate*.

Breen Code   see *Motion Picture Production Code*.

bridge music   the music which links two or more scenes. *Bridging shot,* a shot which provides some logic for the transition from one scene to another.

brightness   subjectively measured by the human eye, is accurately measured in *lumens.* A light meter will measure the *brightness range* of a given scene.

Brighton School   a pioneering group of British film-makers, based (as the name suggests) on the south coast of England and working around the turn of the century. This informal group did not refer to themselves by the name, but were so christened by the film historian Georges Sadoul in his *British Creators of Film Technique* (1948). Though now little-known outside scholarly circles, one of the group's leaders, G.A. Smith (1864–1959), deserves greater public acknowledgement, since he not only appears to have been an innovator in many of the basic camera movements and the *close-up* (for example, in *Grandma's Reading Glass* and *The Big Swallow,* both *c.*1900) but in 1906 was the co-inventor of the first commercial cinematographic colour process, **Kinemacolor.** The Brighton School began to use close-ups and parallel editing earlier than the Scottish-born American director Edwin S. Porter, who is sometimes credited with inventing these conventions in his work for the Edison company, notably *The Life of an American Fireman* and *The Great Train Robbery,* both made in 1903. In fact, it appears to have been another Scot, James Williamson, who came up with the earliest film to employ a recognisably fully-grown film grammar in his *Attack on a Chinese Mission* (1900); Williamson also made some elementary experiments with colour, staining scenes from his short drama *Fire!* (1902) with a red dye, to what he described in a catalogue as 'sensational' effect. The most famous Brighton School production was Cecil Hepworth's *Rescued by Rover* (1905).

broad, broadside   a floodlight, built in the rough shape of a square, used for soft general illumination.

B roll   see *A and B roll printing.*

brute   originally a trade name, now the general term for the largest studio lamp, a 225 amp arc light.

buckle switch, buckle trip   a device which shuts down a camera or projector if the film becomes loose.

buckling   distortion of film under pressure or heat – for example, when a projector becomes overheated. This sense of the word *buckle* has been known since the 16th C: 'And as the wretch whose fever-weaken'd joints,/ Like strengthless hinges, buckle under life . . .' – Shakespeare, *2 Henry IV* (1597).

buddy movie   from the colloquial US word for 'friend', generally assumed to be a corruption of 'brother', and widely used in North America since the mid-19th C. An enduringly popular genre in which the key elements tend to be friendship (usually male), adventure (usually quite violent) and comedy (usually quite broad). The protagonists may be friends of long standing, but more often they start out as strangers from dramatically contrasting social, national, racial or cultural backgrounds and only achieve mutual respect and buddyhood after a trying period of antipathy: Nick Nolte (loutish white cop) and Eddie Murphy (suave black criminal) in Walter Hill's successful *48 HRS* and its less happy sequel *Another 48 HRS*; James Belushi (Chicago policeman) and Arnold Schwarzenegger (Soviet policeman) in the same director's *Red Heat*; Danny Glover (conventional black cop) and Mel Gibson (supposedly unhinged white cop) in the *Lethal Weapon* series; Wesley Snipes (black basketball hustler) and Woody Harrelson (white basketball hustler) in *White Men Can't Jump*. Among the many variants: Clint Eastwood and Clyde, an orang-utan, in *Every Which Way But Loose*; Tom Hanks and a large, slobbery dog in *Turner and Hooch*; space traveller Dennis Quaid and bisexual alien Louis Gossett Jr in *Enemy Mine*. *Thelma and Louise*, starring Susan Sarandon and Geena Davis, is one of the few examples of a successful female buddy movie.

buff   a knowledgeable, and often pedantic, and – so the prejudice runs – often socially inept movie fan. The word, American in origin but widely used in the UK, has a curious history: Webster, in 1934, defines a buff as 'an enthusiast for going to fires'; such types were so-called because the volunteer fireman in New York used to wear buff-coloured uniforms. It had come to mean an enthusiast of any kind by the 1950s.

bug eye   see *fisheye lens*.

building the tracks   see *track-laying*.

bulk eraser   see *degausser*.

bump   a sound error: the mismatch of background noise when two takes are edited together.

bumper (or **bumper period**)   the time allowed for a production team to clear its equipment from a studio before the next team can move in.

bumper footage   in animation: the additional frames before and after each scene which allow for different editing options.

burn-in matte   see *matte*.

burn out   see *matte*.

business   as in the theatrical term, recorded by OED as early as 1671: either (1) the action generally, as distinguished from dialogue ('The carpenters say, that unless there is some business put in here . . . they shan't have time to clear away the fort' – Sheridan, *The Critic*, 1779) or (2) a small piece of action, often humorous.

busy   adjective applied to a scene so crammed with characters, action and decor that it is hard to absorb all its details.

butterfly   a large *scrim* used to diffuse and soften light.

butt splice   film strips joined end to end with tape, rather than overlapped; *butt-weld splice*, film strips joined end to end by heat.

buzz   slang term for the rumours, gossip and so on about a production before its general release; see *word of mouth*. This sense of the word, derived from the onomatopoeic term for the noise made by bees, flies

and other small creatures, common in English since the early 16th C, is
first used in something like this sense as early as 1627: 'The frothy buzze
of the world.' (Feltham, *Resolves*).

buzz track   (1) a low-level background sound track, used to stop silence
from seeming too artificial or eerie, (2) a strip of test film used in
adjusting a projector.

C **-mount** a device for attaching lenses to 16mm and some video cameras.

CAA the abbreviated name of the American *Creative Artists Agency*, which represents the interests of actors, directors, writers and other industry types. It is now said to be one of the two most powerful companies of its kind in Hollywood, the other being *ICM*.

cadmium cell either (a) the electric batteries used in portable equipment, or (b) a standard voltage unit, based on the battery, of 1.0186 volts at 20 degrees centigrade.

Cahiers du Cinéma There have been many distinguished and provocative film journals, but surely none quite so influential as *Cahiers du Cinéma*, which not only helped change the way films were understood and discussed but, by launching a major cinematic movement, radically altered the way in which they were made. *Cahiers* rose from the ruins of an earlier journal, *La Revue du cinéma*, which had folded in 1949; it was first published in 1951 and edited by three men: Lo Duca, Jacques Doniol-Valcroze and – far and away the most important of the trio – André Bazin (1919–58). A disciple of the Catholic philosopher Emmanuel Mounier and a protégé of the journalist and critic Roger Leenhardt, Bazin made the early *Cahiers* an arena in which he could work out his personal, systematic theory of the cinema – a theory which, to simplify somewhat brutally, took issue with Eisenstein's notions of *montage* as manipulative, and held that the nature of the medium was most truly realised in extended shots and *deep focus* cinematography. (For a more adequate statement of this position, see the essays by Bazin collected and translated into English in the two volumes of *What is Cinema?*) He championed the work of Renoir – on whom he wrote an excellent book, published posthumously – and of Rossellini, as well as many Hollywood directors from Von Stroheim to Welles. Some of these views were taken up and given more pungent and pugnacious, if sometimes cryptic, formulation in the writings of a group of younger men who began to publish in *Cahiers* from about 1955 onwards: Jean-Luc Godard, Jacques Rivette, François Truffaut and company. Between them, this posse of brilliant scholar-hoodlums thrashed out the elements of what became known as the *politique des auteurs*, loosely rendered into English as the *auteur* theory, and then made a triumphant crossover from theory to practice by directing their own iconoclastic films in the late 1950s. It would not be too wide of the mark, then, to say that *Cahiers du Cinéma* was the seed-bed of the *Nouvelle Vague*. Partly thanks to the success of that movement, *Cahiers* became internationally famous: its fads and theories, some of them sublimely cranky, some of them now orthodoxies in their own right, were imported and adapted by other magazines, including *Film Culture* in the United States and *Movie* in Britain. After the death of Bazin, however, the magazine which had poured scorn on the *cinéma de papa* ('daddy's cinema' – the conventional dross turned out by much of the French film industry at that time) turned viciously on its own fathers. By the late 1960s, old and new *Cahiers* writers alike were denouncing what they had come to regard as the humanist, idealist and crypto-mystical ideology of its early contributions, embracing a stern, 'scientific' brand of Marxism and promulgating the structuralist theories of Christian Metz and others. This movement also passed; *Cahiers* continues to publish, but is now a much blander creature than it was in its glory days. The British Film Institute has published several volumes of writings from the various *Cahiers* periods, which make instructive and sometimes exhilarating reading.

calculator, cine calculator   a plastic or cardboard gadget used by camera crews to work out light settings and so on; it is marked with information on the relationships between f-stop and t-stop numbers, depth of field, filter factors, colour temperature, shutter angles and the like.

calibrations   the markings on the barrels and rings of a lens, indicating the diaphragm aperture and focus.

caligarisme   the international success of Robert Weine's occult classic *The Cabinet of Dr Caligari* (1919) prompted some French writers to use the term *caligarisme* to evoke either (1) the anxious spirit of Europe in the period after the Great War or, more narrowly, (2) the *expressionist* style and technique in cinema which Weine's film helped make popular.

call (also **call sheet, shooting call**)   the daily schedule given out to all members of a production, indicating the scenes to be shot that day or night, times when performers are needed on set, special requirements (extras, props), likely weather conditions, hours of daylight and so on.

Callier effect   a term from physics, denoting the breaking-up of light beams as they pass through optical instruments.

cameo lighting   a form of lighting which makes the subject stand out sharply against a dull background; a *cameo role* is a swift but telling appearance, usually by a well-known performer; *cameo staging* makes action stand out against a dull background. From It *cameo* and related forms and medieval L *cammeus*; the derivation is uncertain. Between the mid-16th C – its first recorded use – and the mid-19th C, the word appears almost exclusively in its literal, lapidary's sense, to mean a carved ornament of two colours, figure against ground. The figurative sense enters the English language in 1850 or thereabouts, first for literature (a short sketch or portrait) and then for the stage (a small character part that stands out from other parts).

camera   the machine which makes cinema possible, by exposing strips of film to focused light at short, regular intervals – usually 24 frames per second. The word *camera* was taken over by English from L *camera*, meaning a vault or arched chamber, a word which in turn derives from Gk *kamara*, denoting anything with an arched cover. The OED maintains that the word was only used as 'a Latin or alien word' until modified and popularised by the invention of still photography in the nineteenth century. The modern sense is recorded as early as 1844: 'Producing

pictures with the aid of the Camera, by the process of M. Daguerre'.
The word is, as most bright schoolchildren know, an abbreviation of
camera obscura ('dark room'), though that fascinating instrument, had
itself long since been referred to simply as a 'camera', as in *Tristram
Shandy* (1793): 'Others . . . will make a drawing of you in the Camera'.
The earliest cameras designed for taking moving pictures – the Lumière
brothers's *Cinématographe*, Edison's *Kinetograph* – combined the functions of camera and projector in one apparatus, but almost all subsequent
models, whatever other adaptations have been made to their structure,
have been used solely for filming. Among the dozens of terms associated
with the history, technology, maintenance and aesthetics of the camera
are: *camera angle* (or simply *angle*), the perspective from which the
camera films its subject, or – more commonly in writing about film – the
image which results from that filming. The most basic camera position is
head-on to the subject, parallel to the horizon and at a height of about
five to six feet – an approximation, in other words, of what would be
seen by a standing adult of average stature. (In working terms, it can also
be defined as the image that results from a 35mm camera with a two-
inch lenses operated at shoulder height.) Any position lower than this
will produce a *low* or *extreme low angle*; higher than this a *high* or
extreme high angle and so on. Some introductions to film technique
will suggest that certain camera angles have an intrinsic meaning or
emotional tone; for example, that a high-angle shot will tend to dominate
or even tyrannise its subject, a low angle shot will seem cower beneath it,
a *dutch angle* (tilted sharply upwards or sideways) will create a sense of
insecurity or dramatic instability and so on. There is something in this,
though the meaning of any shot obviously depends on far more than its
physical attitude. The selection of camera angles has long been held to
be one of the key mysteries of the director's art; see J.B. Priestley, *Angel
Pavement* (1930): 'He knew nothing about camera angles and "cutting"
and all the intricacies of crowd work.' *Camera body*, the central apparatus
of the camera, not including the magazine, lens or other attachments;
camera boom, a mobile camera mount which allows the camera to film
from a great variety of angles (see *boom* and *crane*); *camera car*, a
vehicle – despite the name, usually a lorry rather than a car – adapted to
carry cameras and operators, and used for *travelling shots*; *camera crew*,
the small team of technicians, generally known as *cameramen*, who work
with the *cinematographer*; in most full-scale film productions, this
team will be made up of (1) the *camera operator* (*operating cameraman*,
operator), who on some productions may be may be one and the same
person as the cinematographer (in America, *director of photography*),
and whose task is the direct management and manipulation of the
camera; (2) the *focus puller* (in America, *first assistant cameraman*),
who keeps the image sharp – or *pulls focus* – as the camera is moved,
and changes magazines; (3) the *clapper loader* (in America, the *second
assistant cameraman* or *slateman*), who claps the board at the start

of each take, loads magazines and keeps notes of what has been shot; and (4) at least one *grip*, a burly fellow who moves the *dolly* and performs other strenuous tasks; the term 'grip' is said to have originated in the early days of cinema, when the job involved holding on to the cameraman when he was filming in precarious circumstances. Large-scale productions will usually employ a *stills cameraman*, too, whose job is to take publicity photographs of the film in production.

camera leading   a type of moving shot which retreats as the actor advances, so that the distance between them remains roughly constant; *camera left/ camera right*, the left (right) side of the camera when pointed towards its subject, and thus the left (right) side of the image when it appears on screen; *camera lucida*, a prototype of the photographic camera used by artists during the Renaissance, an invention is sometimes attributed to Leone Battista Alberti (1404–72), the great Florentine architect, painter and humanist; *camera mount*, the various appliances which make it possible to pan, tilt or otherwise move a camera – *tripods, hi-hats, booms* and so on, as well as *copter mounts, Steadicams* and the like; *camera movements*, the movement of a camera relative to its subject. The principal ways in which a camera may be moved are (1) to be turned horizontally, see *pan*; (2) to be rotated vertically, see *tilt*; (3) to be raised and lowered, either straight up and down or in combination with a smooth lateral repositioning, see *crane*; (4) to be pushed smoothly towards, away from, around or in parallel with its subject, see *dolly*; (5) to be mounted on a platform and run along a set of rails, see *tracking*; (6) to be mounted on a moving vehicle, see *travelling* and *trucking*; (7) to be carried by the operator, see *hand-held* and (8) to be mounted on a body brace, see *Steadicam*. *Camera obscura*, see *camera*; *camera original*, the film exposed inside a camera; *camera rehearsal*, a full dress rehearsal held before a proper take; *camera report* (or *sheet* or *log*), the document sent to the lab with exposed film, explaining what has been shot and how it should be processed; *camera riser*, a platform that lifts the camera above its usual level; *camera shake*, unintentional wobbling, particularly on hand-held cameras; **camera speed**, the number of frames which pass through the camera every second during shooting; 24 frames per second (24 fps) has been the standard speed for sound film (the silent cinema used 16), though faster and (occasionally) slower speeds are used for particular effects; *camera stylo*, a critical term coined by Alexandre Astruc; see *auteur*; *camera test*, either (a) the filmed audition of a performer, also called a *screen test*, or (b) a try-out of a camera's working parts – its lens, feed and so on; *camera trap*, the hiding place for a camera which will be filming different angles of an action but must not be visible from the main camera or cameras; *camera tracks*, see *tracks*; *camera wedge*, also known as a *tilt plate*, a gadget which attaches to the tripod and allows the camera to be tilted more sharply than usual.

can   the flat circular container used for storing film. The slang term *in* *the can* means that a film (or, less often, an individual scene) has been completed.

candela the standard unit of light intensity (symbol: *cd*), agreed in 1950 and defined by *Nature* in 1968 as 'the unit of luminous intensity, in the perpendicular direction, of a surface of 1/600 000 square metre of a black body at the temperature of freezing platinum under a pressure of 101 325 newtons per square metre.'

Cannes, Cannes Film Festival the annual jamboree of the international film industry on the French south coast, where directors, producers, financiers and publicists gather to premiere new films, hustle for projects, give and receive prizes, seek publicity and (in the case of would-be *starlets*) be photographed without bikini tops. It celebrated its official 50th anniversary in 1997, after some tactful fudging of chronology. See *festival*.

cant, canting to tilt the camera forwards, backwards or to the side so as to create a sharply angled image; in other words, to set the camera at a *dutch angle*. This sense of the word has been common since the early 18th C ('The sea broke in upon us, and the canoe being filled half full, canted her broadside to it' – *Mariner's Chronicle*, 1711); it comes from an earlier noun, rare before 1600, meaning border, side, brink, edge, corner.

cap the metal or plastic covering that protects the lens when not in use; *capping shutter*, a shutter found in animation cameras that is set between the lens and the ordinary shutter and is used to block off frames that must not be exposed.

capstan the small metal cylinder in a tape recorder which helps steady the tape as it passes over the heads. Probably from the Fr *cabestan*, and known in English in its nautical sense from early 14th C onwards.

caption written information superimposed onto an image, either as indications of place, time and suchlike – for example, the quasi-official print-outs in *The Silence of the Lambs* or *The Hunt for Red October*, which can convey the flattering impression that we are being made privy to the top secret events on screen – or in the form of sub-titles to a film made in a foreign language. OED cites the *Yorkshire Post* for 17 December 1923: 'A continuous alternation of pictures and those pieces of text that are, one believes, known as captions.' The original meaning of the word is 'taking, catching, seizing, capture', from the L *caption-em*; it comes to mean a heading in a book or newspaper by the mid-19th C, particularly in America.

carbon arcs, carbons the extremely bright, direct current lamps used to light sets.

card a type of screen *credit* which does not move but rather fades in and out.

cardioid microphone a directional microphone that is highly responsive to noises in front but relatively insensitive to noise from behind, and is therefore useful for recording dialogue. So called because a diagram of the areas to which it is most sensitive roughly resembles the classic representation of a human heart.

car rigs   pieces of scaffolding and the like that fasten cameras and lights to a vehicle for moving shots.

Carry Ons   the series of vulgar British comedies – our national cinema's equivalent of the Donald McGill seaside postcard – produced by Peter Rogers and directed by Gerald Thomas. It began in 1958 with the comparatively tasteful *Carry On, Sergeant*, a comedy about National Servicemen based on a play, *The Bull Boys*, by R.F. Delderfield; which is as much as to say that the collective title has its origins in a term of command from H.M. Forces, punningly flavoured with the slang term 'a carry on' – a fuss, a ruckus, an outlandish performance. *Carry On, Sergeant* proved successful enough to set in train many 'sequels' which had nothing in common save the 'Carry On' prefix, ever more awful double (or single) entendres about body parts and excretory functions and a familiar repertory company of actor/comedians: Sid James, Kenneth Williams, Hattie Jacques, Barbara Windsor, Charles Hawtrey, Kenneth Connor, Joan Sims, Jim Dale and others. Despite the best efforts of high-minded critics, no fewer than 28 Carry Ons were made between *Carry On Nurse* (1959) and *Carry On Emmanuelle* (1978) – the title of this last hinting at one of the main reasons why they ceased to become a staple of production: after the mainstream cinema had become free to show scenes that were previously the exclusive preserve of pornographers, the series' largely innocent titterings about breasts and bottoms looked sillier than ever. *Carry On Columbus*, a belated attempt to revive the format with the help of a younger generation of comedians (Alexei Sayle, Rik Mayall) was not conspicuously successful, but, thanks to an alliance of nostalgia and departments of Contemporary Cultural Studies, the series is now being written about both more affectionately and more ponderously (Bakhtin has been evoked . . .) than ever before. It's appropriate that the most intelligent essay about the Carry Ons should also be the funniest: Gilbert Adair's spoof-Barthesian analysis 'The *Nautilus* and the Nursery' in his *Myths and Memories* (1986).

cartoon   any film made up of animated drawings, paintings or computer-generated images, but particularly the short, humorous kind inhabited by feisty and talkative animals – Disney's Donald Duck, Warners' Daffy Duck. The application of the word 'cartoon' to the cinema is recorded at least as early as December 1915, in *Harper's Weekly*: 'Even cartoons began to come in – 'animated' cartoons, as they are called.' The sense of 'humorous or satirical drawing' dates from the mid-19th C; when first carried over into English from Fr *carton* and It *cartone* (from *carta*, paper), it meant a large-scale drawing used as the design for a painting, tapestry or mosaic. 'I perceived him carving that large cartoon, or crucifix, of Tintoretto' – John Evelyn, *Diaries*, 18 January 1672.

cascading   a deliberate strobing effect, created by printing several frames in a single frame.

cast   much as in the theatre, variously: (1) the performers in a film; or
(2) the full roll-call of parts and performers that appears on the screen at
the end (or, less frequently, the beginning) of a film; or (3) as a verb, to
choose actors for roles. The director and producer will usually cast the
main roles well before pre-production begins; other parts will be filled by
the *casting director* or *casting department*, who will send out scripts to
actors and agents, set up *readings*, consult with the director and issue
contracts; *casting couch*, in movie folklore, the place where an attractive
young actress tries to begin her career by servicing the sexual appetites
of a producer or casting director; Mencken, in 1948, attributed the origin
of the expression vaguely to 'Hollywood wits'. The theatrical senses of
the word 'cast', which has had a long and active life in English, first
appearing in the early 13th C meaning 'to throw' (the ME form is
derived from the ON *kasta*), start to come into play in the early 17th C
('Whimzies: or a new Cast of Characters', 1631). Interestingly, OED's
first citation for 'casting' is from *Mansfield Park* (1814): 'From the first
casting of the actors, to the epilogue, it was all bewitching'.

catalyst cinema   see cinema vérité

catchlight   a small light use to isolate a performer's eyes; in Martin
Scorsese's *The Age of Innocence*, for example, a catchlight illuminates the
stricken upper face of Newland Archer (Daniel Day-Lewis) as he reads
a fateful letter. See *kick*.

cattle call   the cruel slang term for a mass audition for minor roles.

catwalk   in a studio, the narrow walkway built above a stage from which
lights and microphones may be suspended.

cd   the abbreviation for *candela*.

cel, cel animation   before computer animation became relatively commonplace, the standard method of animation used several layers of
transparent cels – rectangular sheets of plastic in standard screen ratios.
The term is an abbreviation of 'celluloid' or 'cellulose nitrate', the original
substance of which these sheets were made, though it serves equally well
as a shortened form of 'cellulose acetate', its modern replacement. In cel
animation, the sheets are arranged in planes, with some (the lowest)
depicting the immobile sections of the image – scenery, motionless body
parts – and others (the highest) being minutely altered frame by frame
so as to create the illusion of movement when the film is run.

celluloid   the base on which light-sensitive emulsion is coated, so
producing *film*. As with *cels*, this was once made from cellulose nitrate,
but, since nitrate stocks were highly inflammable, it is now made of
cellulose acetate. Hence, colloquially, the adjective used to evoke an
aspect of the cinema (OED cites this use from 1922: 'The celluloid hero
flashed his impartial smile across the screen') or a metonymy for cinema
itself: 'The British Board of Film Censors . . . who draw the line between
the decorous and libellous in the world of celluloid' (A.G. MacDonnell,
How Like an Angel, 1934). Such figurative use is often pejorative,

implying something ersatz, lifeless or deformed by Hollywood fantasy, as in D.H. Lawrence's sneer at 'celluloid women' in *Lady Chatterley's Lover*.

cement splice   the fixing together of two strips of film with a form of glue known as liquid cement.

censorship   in the UK, film censorship began with an eye to the safety rather than the morals of the viewing public: the Cinematograph Act of 1909, which is the foundation of today's system, was primarily concerned with establishing that cinemas were unlikely to collapse or burn down. With this law in place, local councils began to bring actions against certain films on grounds of indecency; recognising that this could prove a serious nuisance, the industry itself lobbied for a centralised system of regulation. Their efforts led to the establishment of the British Board of Film Censors (*BBFC*) in 1912, and local councils gradually recognised that they had no power to prosecute a film that had been certificated by the BBFC. As the tussles over David Cronenberg's *Crash* in 1996–7 made all too plain, however, local councils retained the right to ban films. For a brief account of the early American experience of censorship, see *Hays Code*; see also *certificate, rating*.

Centro Sperimentale di Cinematografia   the influential Italian film school, originally founded as part of the Rome Academy of Music in 1932, at the behest of the Fascist government. Visting lecturers at the school have included Robert Bresson and Jean Renoir; its graduates include Michelangelo Antonioni.

century stand or **C-stand**   a stand, supporting various flags or screens, which is placed in front of lamps to soften or direct their rays, or to cast particular shadows.

certificate   the censor's *rating* given to a theatrical feature or commercially distributed video cassette, stating the age groups that is allowed to watch the film in question; in this country, certificates are issued by the *BBFC* and in the United States by the Motion Picture Association of America (*MPAA*). There are at present five categories of British film certificates:

U (Universal) Passed for general exhibition. Open to all.

PG (Parental Guidance) Passed for general exhibition. Open to all. Unaccompanied children admitted, but parents/guardians are advised that the film contains material they might prefer children under 12 not to see.

12 Passed as suitable only for exhibition to persons of 12 years or over. When a programme includes a '12' film, no person under 12 can be admitted.

15 Passed as suitable only for exhibition to persons of 15 years or over. When a programme includes a '15' film, no person under 15 can be admitted.

18 Passed as suitable only for exhibition to adults. When a programme includes an '18' film, no person under 18 can be admitted. See also *censorship*.

CGI   the standard abbreviation for *Computer Generated Imagery*.

change-over, changeover, reel change   in projection: the (ideally) smooth and seamless transition from one projector to another as the first reel ends and the second begins. The projectionist is alerted to the imminent change by cues at the top right hand corner of the frame.

change pages   once a production has begun shooting, any changes to the script are printed up on coloured paper (a different colour for each stage of the rewriting) and handed over to the cast and crew.

changing bag   a portable substitute for a darkroom: a sturdy bag made of light-proof material, inside which magazines can be loaded and unloaded

chapter play   one of the silent cinema's alternative terms for a *serial*, now rather quaint-sounding.

character   as in the novel and theatre: a person (or sometimes ghost, demon, animal, electronic consciousness or extra-terrestrial life form) in the fictional world of a film; a role for an actor. (Fielding, *Tom Jones*, 1749: 'Whatever characters any . . . have for the jest-sake personated . . . are now thrown off.')

character actor   a non-starring performer, regularly cast in the same type of role (or *character part*) in film after film, usually because of some readily identifiable physical attribute, such as obesity or a strong regional accent, or some plausible temperamental quirk, such as irascibility. The term 'character acting' was originally pejorative – 'What is known as character acting has definitely established its supremacy in England upon the ruins of tragic art' (J. Knight, *Athenaeum*, 1878), but 'character actor' is relatively neutral.

character arc   in screenwriting jargon, the development of the leading character (and often some subsidiary characters, too) in the course of the film's action: thus, crudely: the coward rebels, the repressed spinster learns unbridled passion, Scrooge comes to dote on Tiny Tim.

chase film, chase movie, chaser etc   most simply, a film in which the main action consists of one character or set of characters chasing another, such as *The Fugitive* or Arthur Penn's *The Chase*; or a film in which there are plenty of chase scenes. 'I would add to the list of Action Films . . . the recent popular example, Douglas Fairbanks in The Three Musketeers. That is perhaps the most literal 'Chase-Picture' that was ever really successful in the commercial world' (Vachel Lindsay, *The Art of the Moving Picture*).

cheat   'In film and television the term "cheat" refers to a technical fudge – an edit that makes two objects appear closer than they actually were or a camera angle that obscures some unwanted detail. In other words, deceit and moving pictures have been close associates from the earliest days' – Thomas Sutcliffe, 'Glossary', *Independent* 28 July 1994. In more general terms, a cheat or *cheat shot* is any kind of spatial fakery, often involving either (a) a performer apparently turning to look at something but in fact simply striking a more photogenic pose, or (b) moving a supposedly immobile performer or thing between takes so as to contrive a more interesting shot. The first English use occurs in Pudovkin's *On Film Technique*, translated by Ivor Montague, 1929.

checkerboard cutting   see *A and B printing*.

check print   a print that may be made to see if any chemical or mechanical errors have occured in processing, usually just before making an *answer print*. See also *sample print*.

cherry picker   as in other technical fields (OED mentions particularly aeronautics and space travel), the widely used nickname for a *crane*.

chicken coop   a wire-covered *luminaire*.

china girl   the picture of a woman seen in the leader frames of colour film, used as a standard during processing. David Bowie used the term in one of his hit songs of the early 1980s.

Chinese, Make it   on-set slang command to the lighting crew, indicating that the *barn doors* in front of a light should be closed to a vertical to horizontal; the racist origins of the term will be all too plain; *chinese dolly*, a movement of the camera backwards while the shot is panned.

chippie   slang term (in the UK only) for the production carpenter, just as it is for carpenters who work in the building and other trades.

chopsocky   the jokey *Variety* slang for kung-fu and other martial arts movies: a compound of 'chop suey' and 'to sock', or strike violently.

Christmas tree   logically enough, a stand set up with a number of lights, similar in apperance to the festive ornament; also a vehicle used for carrying lights.

chroma   a measurement of the intensity of a colour: from the Gk *chroma*, colour: OED records a technical use of the term as early as 1889; a good modern definition dates from 1905: '*Chroma*, the degree of departure of a color sensation from that of white or grey; the intensity of distinctive hue; color intensity' (A.H. Munsell, *Color Notation*).

chromatic aberration   a lens defect, which causes colours to be dispersed instead of focused.

chrominance   the measured variation between two or more colours of equal luminance.

chronophotographs   a crude, early form of cinema, developed in the 1880s by Etienne-Jules Marey, and created with a camera which exposed a revolving plate twelve times a second. (The *Pall Mall Gazette*, 13 November 1895, refers to 'the various kinds of apparatus required for the difficult operations of "chronophotography"'.)

cinch, cinching   (as in horsemanship, etc.) to tighten a roll of film. Hence *cinch marks*, scratches on film caused by abrupt or excessive tightening, or dirt trapped between its layers.

cinéaste   generally anglicised to *cineaste* or, less frequently, *cineast*. There appears to be some confusion about the correct meaning of this term, which is often used to mean a film *fan*: OED, offering a derivation from Fr *ciné* plus -*aste*, as in *enthousiaste*, defines it simply as 'an enthusiast for, or devotee of, the cinema' – and particularly, as some of its quotations make clear, the serious or pretentious kind of enthusiast. In so doing, it tacitly endorses an earlier definition from *Chambers Technical Dictionary*, 1940: 'One who takes an advanced view of the artistic possibilities of motion pictures.' And yet some of OED's own sources point to a quite different sense: see, for example, its citation of an article published in 1930: 'The amateur *cineaste* . . . has . . . the opportunity to experiment for the exact, the perfect cinematic effect'. This, and several other OED entries ('Foreign writers, poets, cineasts, scientists . . .'; *Twentieth Century*, April 1960) demonstrate beyond reasonable dispute that the term is frequently used to mean not film *fan* but film-*maker*. There are good reasons for preferring this latter definition: it will, for example, explain to the puzzled British tourist why the well-known French television series *Cinéastes de notre temps* was dedicated to directors rather than *buffs*. On the few occasions when a grander word than 'film fan' or 'movie buff' seems called for, why not plump for the unambiguous *cinephile?*

Cinecittà   the large and celebrated studios on the outskirts of Rome, built on the site of the earlier Cines studio after that facility burned down in 1935. (Cines was a major Italian production company, founded in 1906 and dissolved in 1921, though the name was revived for other companies in 1929 and 1949; it is best remembered for the eight-reel epic *Quo Vadis*, released in 1913, the most spectacular production of its day.) The Italian government took over Cinecittà on the death of its original owner, the industrialist Carlo Roncoroni; it was heavily bombed by the Allies during the war, but was fully restored as the home of the national film industry by 1950. Cinecittà has served as the production base for blockbusters such as the 1959 *Ben-Hur*, as well as more critically reputable productions by Antonioni, Visconti and Fellini, who shot *Roma* there.

cinema   broadly, either (a) the art and/or industry of producing moving images, or (b) the buildings where films are commercially exhibited. This second use is comparitively rare in the United States, where the term 'theatre' or, in local spelling 'theater' (or 'movie theater') is considered less affected, paradoxical as it may sound to British ears. Indeed, on both sides of the Atlantic, *cinema* both as a general noun and as an adjective ('belonging to or associated with the industry or art of moving pictures'; see also *cinematic*) has become quite high-toned over the past few decades; the appropriately demotic terms for a democratic art would usually be *movie* or *the movies* in the United States, and in the UK *film* or *films*. ('Movie' still sounds horribly mid-Atlantic in most British mouths; 'the *pictures*' or 'the *flicks*' either old-fashioned or aggressively low.) The upward mobility of the term 'cinema' has been roughly contemporary with the growth of an uneasy awareness, in all but the most hidebound or benighted quarters, that moving pictures can occasionally be more than a mindless pastime. Thus, universities may nowadays have departments with the appropriately solemn title of

Cinema (or Film, or Moving Image) Studies, but would be unlikely to offer courses in Movie Studies; the same principle applies, of course, to the title of this lexicon. The word 'cinema' is an abbreviation of *cinematograph*, taken over into English from the Lumière brothers' patented coinage *cinematographe*, and ultimately from Gk *kinema*, *kinemat-*, 'movement', plus *-graph*. Cinematographs were the machines with which early films were both shot and projected: *Times*, 22 February 1896: 'The Cinematograph ... is a contrivance belonging to the same family as Edison's kinetoscope ... but in a rather higher stage of development.' The abbreviation of 'cinematograph' to *cinema*, initially meaning only a place where the products of the cinematograph were shown, dates from as early as 1899, though this use was still novel enough in 1910 to provoke raised eyebrows in the columns of the *Daily Chronicle*: '"Cinematograph" – which has just been cut down in a glaring advertisment to "cinema".' Despite journalistic disapproval, the abbreviation became fully established in the course of the next decade or so: D.H. Lawrence uses it without any perceptible emphasis on its novelty in 1922. The use of *cinema* to mean films in general, and/or the art of film, is recorded by Webster in 1918: '*Cinema* ... moving pictures collectively.' and used by the *Spectator* in 1921: 'The cinema is a democratic entertainment ... which abounds in purely visual effects.' It is curious to note that in France, that most film-crazy of nations, the word can have associations of mendacity: *c'est du cinéma* is an expression meaning, roughly, 'that's a load of rubbish, that's nonsense', while *Il fait son cinéma* means 'He's conning you, he's full of blarney.' For a discussion of this oddity, see Jean-Claude Carrière, *The Secret Language of Film*.

Cinema Nôvo   the left-wing nationalist Brazilian 'New Cinema' collective of the late 1950s and 1960s, whose principal activists included the producer, director and essayist Glauber Rocha (*Barravento*, 1962) – the leader of the school, and its best-known member, who left Brazil after 1969 – Nelson Pereira dos Santos (*Vidas secas*, 1962) and Ruy Guerra (*Os Fuzis*, 1963). Though the movement aimed at establishing a Brazilian cinema that would be both economically and ideologically opposed to Hollywood, it was criticised by leftists for its aestheticism; the movement collapsed under governmental and military pressure by the early 1970s.

cinéma-pur or **pure cinema**   a term coined by the director Henri Chomette to designate a type of film (such as his own *Jeux des Reflets et de la Vitesse* of 1923 and *Cinq Minutes de Cinéma Pur* of 1925) which renounced most of the representational ambitions of the conventional cinema and concentrated instead on formal properties such as ryhthms of editing. This movement was influenced by *absolute cinema* and was short-lived, though many subsequent avant-garde film-makers have worked in similar fashion without necessarily being aware of M. Chomette's practice or polemics.

CinemaScope or **Cinemascope**   a wide-screen system, now largely defunct, which used anamorphic lenses to film and project images at a ratio of 2.55:1, or, later, 2.35:1. It was introduced by Fox in 1953 for *The Robe*, and soon inspired other studios to introduce their own '-scope'; thus, the term *scope* is now colloquially used to denote most types of wide-screen system.

Cinémathèque Française   one of the few institutions of its kind that may actually merit the weary adjective 'legendary', this extraordinary and sometimes beleaguered cultural resource was the creation of Henri Langlois, who had begun his career as a collector of film prints while still a schoolboy. In 1935, at the age of 21, he and his friend the director Georges Franju (with whom he had made a short film, *Le Métro*, the previous year) founded the *Cercle du cinéma* to hold screenings from the Langlois hoard, and in 1936 the two young men joined forces with the historian, theorist and experimental film-maker Jean Mitry to develop this body into the more formal *Cinémathèque Française*. The original purpose of the Cinémathèque was simply to preserve silent films that were threatened by the advent of the talkies, but this soon developed into a more risky enterprise: during the Occupation, Langlois and his assistants (including Lotte Eisner, later to become an important film historian in her own right) saved hundreds of films by hiding them from the Nazi forces. He was subsequently honoured by the French government for these activities, and began to receive government subsidies for his work. The Cinémathèque thrived in the years after the war, and helped both to make the reputations of new, obscure directors such as Bergman and Kurosawa and, through retrospectives of the Hollywood films that French audiences had not been able to see before the Liberation, to remake the reputations of more established American directors. Langlois' tastes were of great importance to the **Cahiers du Cinéma** critics who later became the **Nouvelle Vague** of film-makers, and they remained loyal to him in his years of dispute with the **FIAF** (with which he broke off diplomatic relations in 1960) and with the French government. According to some versions of history, it was the sacking of Langlois and his staff in February 1968, and the subsequent demonstrations outside the Cinémathèque, which lit the fuse for the *événements* of May '68; for a fictional version of these and related matters, see Gilbert Adair's novel *The Holy Innocents*.

Langlois was reinstated, though the government withdrew its funding, and established its own archive at Bois d''Arcy in 1969. Unbowed, Langlois and his staff went on to found the Musée du Cinéma in 1972; it continues to screen the holdings from its vast collection to the present day.

cinematic   an adjective, usually found either in technical, critical or would-be solemn writing, meaning either 'belonging to the cinema, proper to the cinema' (*Daily Express*, 10 October 1927: 'A masterpiece of cinematic treatment') or 'resembling the cinema'; theatre reviewers, for example, will sometimes praise or blame a stage production for its cinematic effects – rapid 'cutting' from scene to scene and the like.

Cinematograph or **Cinematographe**   The name of the machine for producing moving pictures which was patented by the Lumière Brothers in 1895; see *cinema*.

cinematographer   in America, usually called the *director of photography* or *DP*; also known more simply as the *cameraman*, or as *first cameraman* or *lighting cameraman*. In its original use, the term *cinematographer* simply meant anyone who practised **cinematography**: that is to say, who shot moving pictures rather than still photographs. The OED Supplement preserves that simple definition, citing examples from 1897 ('A hand-camera man chooses a time when such figures are not in the way; the cinematographer can do the same, but a hundred people may surge in front of his instrument before the exposure is finished' – C.M. Hepworth, *Animated Photography*) and 1909 ('If our cinematographers had the instruments which could look into the dark backward and abysm of time' – J.H. Skrine, *Pastor Ovium*). But this is highly misleading, since the term *cinematographer* is now almost always applied to practitioners of a specific craft or art within the general activities of film production: the cinematographer is the person in charge (generally after consultation with the director) of lighting the set and actors; setting up and moving the camera; selecting appropriate lenses, stock, filters; establishing the composition of images and so on; in general, then, the person who helps create what can loosely be called the 'look' of a film, its visual identity. Similarly, *cinematography* now tends to be applied in most instances solely to the art or craft of the cinematographer, though the older and far more general sense of 'motion picture photography' survives, particularly in non-specialist writing. Despite the exceptional importance of the job, relatively few cinematographers – the short roll of honour includes the late Nestor Almendros, Vittorio Storaro, Vilmos Sigismond, Raoul Coutard, Sven Nykvist – have enjoyed reputations in any way comparable to that of the directors whose films they have worked on, though television screenings of a recent American documentary about the art, *Visions of Light*, have offered some small recompense to the fraternity.

cinéma-verité (sometimes *ciné-verité*)   is a vexed label, since it is often used and defined misleadingly – the OED Supplement is, alas, a prime offender here – as if it meant simply any style of documentary, such as *fly on the wall*, that manages to give the rough and gritty appearance of unmediated, unmanipulated reality. Worse, it is generally confused with the American documentary school more correctly known as *direct cinema*, whose products are not merely distinct from *cinéma verité* but stand in principled opposition to it. The term was coined (or more precisely borrowed and translated from a Russian slogan originally brandished by the revolutionary director Dziga Vertov: see *Kino Pravda*) by the anthropologist and director Jean Rouch to categorise the work he was doing in his documentary *Chronique d'un été* (*Chronicle of a Summer*, shot in 1960, released in 1961). Inspired by the results he had achieved from interviewing local Africans for his films *Jaguar* and *Moi, un Noir* (*I, a Black*, 1958), Rouch decided to apply this anthropological style of questioning to the 'strange tribe' of Parisians. Rouch would stop passers-by in the street and simply ask them 'Are you happy?' – a question which, thanks to the Algerian war, was rather less bland than it might now appear, and which provoked some extraordinary reactions. Rouch and his collaborator Edgar Morin both appeared on camera, and then invited those who had taken part in the film to come and watch the footage and discuss their reactions; these discussions were themselves filmed, and then edited into the final cut. In short, *cinéma verité* is not a technique or philosophy of passive observation, but demands the personal intervention of the director in the events filmed. The film historian Eric Barnouw, who sometimes calls *cinéma verité* 'catalyst cinema', crisply underlines the distinctions between that school and the work of direct cinema film-makers:

> The direct cinema documentarist took his camera to a situation of tension and waited hopefully for a crisis; the Rouch version of *cinéma verité* tried to precipitate one. The direct cinema artist aspired to invisibility; the Rouch *cinéma verité* artist was often an avowed participant. The direct cinema artist played the role of uninvolved bystander; the *cinéma verité* artist espoused that of provocateur.
>
> Direct cinema found its truth in events available to the camera. *Cinéma Verité* was committed to a paradox: that artificial circumstances could bring hidden truth to the surface. (Barnouw, 254–5)

A short list of other notable documentaries within the true *cinéma verité* tradition soon spans the globe, and includes *Le Joli Mai* (1963) by Chris Marker (though Marker's subsequent essays in the field, such as *Sans Soleil* and *The Last Bolshevik*, both transform and transcend his *verité* inheritance; his work defies ready classification); *Memory* (*Pamat*, 1969) by the Soviet director Grigori Chukrai; *Minamata*, an angry attack on the callousness of the Japanese industrialists whose mercury effluents made women give birth to misshapen babies, by Noriaki Tsuchimoto; and, perhaps most famously, *Le Chagrin et la Pitié* (*The Sorrow and the Pity*, 1970), a study of the Nazi occupation of France, by Marcel Ophuls. Many of these works are grim in tone, though a black comedy such as Michael Moore's 1989 film *Roger and Me* (in which the corpulent, rather clownish director frantically pursues the president of General Motors to quiz him about lay-offs in the Michigan motor industry) can readily be seen as following the *verité* tradition, as can the documentaries of Nick Broomfield, in which the director's participation is so obstrusive as to have provoked accusations of narcissism. On a more frivolous note, the school's name also inspired the British television and film producer Verity Lambert to christen her company Cinema Verity.

Cinéorama   an allegedly spectacular but doomed experiment in 360-

degree film projection, patented by Raoul Grimoin-Sanson in 1897 and first shown to the public at the Paris Exhibition of 1900. Designed to give audiences the illusion of flying in a hot air balloon, it was abandoned after just three shows because of fire hazards. Cinéorama relied on ten separate projectors showing ten separate films on the inside walls of a circular building.

cineplex (or *multiplex*, the more common form in Britain)   a cinema split up into a number of auditoria with medium to small screens showing new films; a visit to such centres is becoming the standard form of cinema-going, to the dismay of everyone who thinks that one point of the big screen is that it should be just that.

Cinerama   the trade name of a once-popular wide screen process, with an aspect ratio of about 2.5:1, which used multiple projectors and a large curved screen. The cinerama spectaculars of the 1950s were mostly travelogues; full-length features began to be produced in the 1960s: *How the West was Won* (1962) and so on. By the time of Stanley Kramer's *It's a Mad Mad Mad Mad World* (1963), the original multiple-film process had been abandoned, though the trade name was maintained. Gilbert Adair has pointed out (in his history of the cinema's first century, *Flickers*) that 'cinerama' is an exact anagram of 'American'.

Ciné-Roman   a French term meaning (a) a type of romantic film produced by Pathé in the early years of the century, beginning with *Roman d'amour* (1905); (b) another term for *feuilleton-cinema*, the photographic comic-books issued in tandem with cinema serials; (c) a novel or other narrative written with the screen in mind or (d) the published script of a film, heavily illustrated with stills.

Cinex strip, Cinex   a strip of positive film that shows how the same frame looks at various different exposures, and so helps the director and cinematographer to work out how best to print the entire shot.

Circarama, Circle Vision   the trademark names of two extremely wide wide-screen systems developed by the Disney corporation for their amusement parks: the former offers a 360 degree image projected on to a cylindrical screen, the latter a more modest 200-degree image on a large curved screen which closes around the audience.

city symphony   a documentary sub-genre devoted to the portrayal of urban life and architecture, generally in a self-consciously 'poetic' style tending towards abstraction. The canonical example, which has lent its name to the form, is Walter Ruttman's *Berlin, die Symphonie einer Grosstadt* (1927). American exercises in the genre include Frank Stauffacher's *Sausilito* (1948) and *Notes on the Port of St Francis* (1952), about San Francisco; Philip Leff's *Symphony* (1951); Allen Downs's *Freight Stop* (1954); and Francis Thompson's *N.Y., N.Y.*, which views New York through distorting lenses.

circled takes are the takes marked up on a camera report or production report for printing by the lab.

clapboard (also **clapper** or **clappers, clapper board, clapstick**

board, number board, slate board, production board, take board and so on) the simple but heavily mythologised device – in its basic form, no more than a small sheet of plastic, metal or wood joined by a hinge to a *clapstick* or *clapsticks* – used to help the editor identify rushes and synchronise image with sound. The names of the production's director, producer and sometimes cameraman are written on the front of the board, along with details of the scene and take; the board is held up to the camera for each new take, and the *clapper boy* (or *clapper loader, second assistant cameraman* etc.) snaps the clapstick shut. ('A clapper-boy self-consciously clapped his instrument together in front of the lens' – Edmund Crispin, *Frequent Hearses*, 1950).

classical cutting   see *cut.*

classification   the censor's *rating* for a film; see also *certificate.*

claw   the part of the camera or projector mechanism which draws film into the gate; a small metal device whose jagged projections engage with the sprocket hole(s), advance the film by one frame, then withdraw so as to connect with the next hole(s). The result is the *intermittent movement* that makes both filming and projection possible.

claymation   strictly, a form of stop-frame animation using clay rather than drawings, but the term is also loosely applied to the plasticene products of the *Aardman* studios, of which the most famous are Nick Park's sublime creations Wallace and Gromit, stars of the Oscar-winning *The Wrong Trousers* and *A Close Shave.*

clean entrance, clean exit   the movements of an actor or thing completely in to and out of shot, with no messy overlaps, shadows or the like.

clear   an order to performers to move around anything that may partially block the camera's view of them; or, in the command 'clear the frame!', to move entirely out of the camera's field of view.

clear filter   a colourless filter sometimes used to protect the lens in harsh weather conditions.

click track   a sound track with a regular beat – normally a *loop* of film with holes punched at regular intervals – used by composers and instrumentalists to help synchronise their music to the action.

cliffhanger   generally, any suspense film that relies on a tense climax in which hero or heroine are in peril. The name pays homage to the silent serials or chapter plays which traded in the most literal form of suspense – characters dangling from a cliff as the episode came to an end. (The earliest example offered by OED comes from 1937, though the definition here is at once broader and more narrow: 'type of serial melodrama'.) Not many cliffhangers actually involve cliffs nowadays; the Sylvester Stallone vehicle *Cliffhanger* (1993) is an undistinguished exception.

clip   a brief extract from a film, used in advertising, in documentaries about the cinema and so on. OED records a use in 1958.

closed form   a term from film aesthetics, denoting a highly stylised, artificial narrative technique, in which the director and/or cinematographer dicate(s) every aspect of the on-screen world rather than striving for the illusion of reality: examples might include films by Von Sternberg (*The Saga of Anatahan*), Powell and Pressburger (*A Matter of Life and Death*) or possibly Francis Ford Coppola (*Bram Stoker's Dracula*). See *open form*.

close down   see *stop down*.

closed set   a set that has been declared off-limits to press, visitors and all non-essential crew members, usually because a nude scene is being filmed.

close shot   sometimes used interchangeably with *close-up*, but more exactly a *head and shoulders close-up* – a shot that is slightly larger than a head close-up, and which generally shows not only the traditional features of a bust but also a few background details.

close-up (CU)   a shot taken at short range to emphasise details, particularly of human or animal faces; according to the OED Supplement the term is found in print in America as early as 1913. Most reference books attribute the first uses of the close-up either to Britain's Brighton School, or to the American director Edwin S. Porter, though it was left to D.W. Griffith to grasp and refine the artistic possibilities of the technique, which is why he is often loosely credited with 'discovering' it. As far as filming actors is concerned, there are four main types of close-up: the *medium close-up (MCU)*, which covers the area from waist to head; the *close shot*; and the *extreme close-up (ECU)*, which isolates just one or two features of the face. As so often, Jean-Luc Godard has a pregnant maxim on the device: 'Close-ups make us anxious about things' (*Godard on Godard*).

clothes light   *kicker lights* which emphasise the grain or texture of a performer's clothes.

cloud wheel   a spinning wheel set in front of a lamp to interrupt its beams and give the effect of daylight.

cluster bar, cluster mount, cluster pipe   a mount for several lamps.

coated lens   a lens that has been coated on the exterior side to cut down its reflectiveness and so allow more light to pass into the camera; the coating is made of magnesium flouride.

collage film   a type of *avant-garde* or experimental film, such as those made by the surrealist Joseph Cornell, which brings together disparate celluloid images in much the same way that a painter might incorporate bits of newspaper or can labels into a still collage.

collision   a term coined by Sergei Eisenstein to stress the defining feature of his particular theory of *montage*.

Colorization, Color Systems Technology   trademark names for the computer processes that electronically 'paint' colour on to black and white films for the benefit of audiences (chiefly the network television viewers of America) who are assumed to find monochrome unappealing. Colorization has been the object of a good deal of justifiable anger and ridicule, and has prompted any number of jokes. In Christopher Guest's satirical film *The Big Picture*, for example, the hero (Kevin Bacon) sits in a bar at Christmas watching Frank Capra's *It's a Wonderful Life* on television and wallowing in seasonal self-pity. His nostalgic reverie is shattered when the barman notices that the picture is in black and white and hits the set, which blooms into garish late-century colour.

colour   the adjective applied to any film that is not made in black and white. The opposition of 'colour' to 'black and white' was used in writings on photography from the late 19th C onwards (OED Supplement gives an example from 1893), and in writings on cinema at least as early as 1912. By 1931, one commentator noted that 'Colour has been coming almost imperceptibly, and the public hardly notice whether a film is in colour or black and white', though the observation seems highly unlikely. The earliest kind of colour films were simply black and white films which were then tinted by hand – a tiresome process which has long since been abandoned save by a handful of avant-garde film-makers. (At the time of writing, for example, Stan Brakhage is still busy making short abstract films in which he paints colours directly on to strips of celluloid; he has also produced images in other unconventional ways, such from the body parts of moths. See *direct cinema*.) Often this was simply a matter of washing a particular scene in a single atmospheric colour such as red, but sometimes the process was more complex: in *Gli ultimi gioni di Pompeii* (*The Last Days of Pompeii*, 1913), Vesuvius erupts in dazzling flame against a deep blue sky. When truer forms of colour cinematography began to emerge, they were marketed under a bewildering variety of trade names but were based on just two main methods, the *additive* and the *subtractive*. Additive methods were the more primitive: they included Kinemacolor (1906), Chronochrome (1912), Prizmacolor (1918) and later, in the 1930s, *Dufaycolor*. Modern colour film, however, has been developed from pioneering work with the subtractive process. A prototype of the *Technicolor* process was used in *Ben Hur* (1925) and *The Black Pirate* (1926). More advanced forms of the Technicolor method were so successful that between 1935 (the year of Mamoulian's *Becky Sharp*, sometimes described as the film with which colour cinematography came of age) and the mid-1950s, 'Technicolor' – or, often, 'glorious Technicolor' – became synonymous with all colour films in the public mind (and, to some extent, still lives on, at least among older cinemagoers), much as the word 'Hoover' denotes a vacuum-cleaner and 'Kleenex' a paper handkerchief. The reign of Technicolor was overthrown by the advent of *Eastman Color*, first produced in 1952 as a professional counterpart to the multi-layer home-movie stock Kodakchrome; and of the resurgence of *Agfacolor*, originally developed in Germany before the Second World War. All of the colour film methods now in professional use are the direct offspring of these two stocks.

Among the major terms associated with colour cinematography are: *colour balance*, meaning either (a) the degree to which an image concentrates on a particular colour, or (b) whether a particular film emulsion is suited to artificial light or daylight; *colour-blind film*, which does not register particular ranges of the spectrum (particularly those which do not register yellow, and so allows film to be printed in rooms illuminated by yellow safelights); *colour card*, which shows a graduated scale of hues and is photographed to help with colour correction; *colour cast*, the underlying tone of the film image, either accidental or contrived; *colour-compensating filters*, lens filters which subtly change the colour balance of a shot, especially by way of compensating for imbalances in the stock, and more radical *colour-conversion filters*, which change the *colour temperature* (usually measured on the Kelvin scale) of a shot, so that, for example, stock suitable for outdoor shooting in daylight can be used in a studio; *colour grad filters*, which fit over the camera and tint one part of the resulting image – see *grad filter*; *colour lily*, a chart of colour values shot at the beginning of a scene for lab reference purposes; *colour reversal intermediate* (*CRI*), a colour *dupe* made directly from the original negative, and used to strike release prints; *colour saturation*, see *saturation*; and so on.

Columbia Pictures   the American production and distribution company, founded as CBC Sales Corporation in 1920 by Harry Cohn, Jack Cohn and Joseph Brandt, who had come from Universal. It has been immensely successful at various points of its career, particularly in the 1930s when Frank Capra made a strong run of films that achieved healthy box office returns and critical acclaim: *It Happened One Night* (1934), *Mr Deeds Goes to Town* (1936), *Lost Horizon* (1937), and *Mr Smith Goes to Washington* (1939). But its output went into a serious decline after Capra left in 1939, and only began to recover in the 1950s, when it produced *Born Yesterday* (1951), *On the Waterfront* (1954) and *The Bridge on the River Kwai* (1957). Another landmark in its business history was the youth movie *Easy Rider*, which, whatever its aesthetic shortcomings, produced huge revenues for minimal outlay, and so helped pave the way for the more innovative American cinema of the 1970s. Columbia is now owned by the Coca-Cola Company, and known as Columbia Tri-Star.

coma   a type of flaw in a spherical lens which causes blurred images.

combined move, compound move   a combination of camera movement with performer movement – the camera dollying back while the performer moves forwards, say. A compound move can also mean a combination of physical and/or optical camera techniques, such as dollying back while zooming in.

cometing   small flaws on a film, the result of impurities in the processing bath.

commag print   the in-house BBC term for a print combining picture and magnetic sound.

commentary   the spoken text in a documentary film; see *voice-over*.

coming attractions   the early part of a cinema programme which shows *trailers* for the films that will be shown in the next few weeks. In the (very funny, and lamentably short-lived) satirical television cartoon series of the early 1990s about the misadventures of an unduly scrupulous film reviewer, *The Critic*, the hero's cable TV show is called 'Coming Attractions'.

commissary   in Hollywood: the studio's in-house restaurant or canteen.

compilation film   a type of anthology or collage film, made up entirely of shots and sequences from other, earlier films, edited into new sequences and fresh meanings. Though the practice of looting and re-editing existing film is almost as old as the cinema itself (Francis Doublier raided his library to fake up a news story about the capture of Dreyfus in 1898), the true origins of the compilation film are Soviet: suffering from an almost total lack of raw stock, directors of the revolutionary period such as Dziga Vertov drew on newsreels and other footage for their experiments in *montage*; and in the late 1920s, the editor Esther Shub put together an epic trilogy in support of the new regime, using countless thousands of feet of archive material. For a fuller discussion of the form, see *Films Beget Films* (1964), by the American cinema historian Jay Leyda, who coined the English term in this pioneering study.

complementary angles   shots of different objects or actions within the same scene that are filmed from similar positions so that they will edit together easily and produce a sense of coherent space; *complementary two-shots*, the standard method for filming a conversation between two speakers: a sequence of two-shots in which each speaker is favoured in turn.

completion guarantee   a contract between the backers and the makers of a film which specifies the maximum time and budget allowed; *completion services*, all the activities – *printing*, *editing*, *looping*, *mixing*, *conforming* and the like – which follow the shooting of a film. See *post-production*.

composite   either (a) a *composite print*, a print which has picture and sound properly synchronised, or (b) an image made up of several different elements – minatures, animation, computer graphics, live action and so on. *Composite film*, a full-length feature containing more than one story, such as the classic Ealing ghost-yarn collection *Dead of Night*, directed by Cavalcanti and others, the somewhat less classic *Twilight Zone: The Movie* (Steven Spielberg, Joe Dante and others), Rossellini's *Paisan* (1946), or the various English films based on short stories by Somerset Maugham.

composition   as in painting: the arrangement of shapes, colours and lighting within a frame; and/or the movement within a shot or scene.

compressor   an electronic device used in recording to diminish sound levels

Computer Generated Imagery (CGI), computer graphics (or **computer-generated animation**)   images, usually of the *special effects* kind, produced by computer technology and used either on their own (as in certain scenes of the science fiction thriller *The Lawnmower Man*, loosely adapted from a story by Stephen King, or in the 'virtual reality' sequences of Barry Levinson's *Disclosure*) or, more often, in combination with filmed pictures. The advent of CGI has meant that it is now possible, given a sufficently large budget, to create eerily convincing moving pictures of anything from dinosaurs to alien invasions. In the eyes of some critics and other concerned parties, this is a disastrous development, which may mean the end of the cinema as an art form dedicated to the human face and frame and *la condition humaine*, and may finally reduce it to the state it has been approaching for the last two decades or so: a glorious but sterile light show.

computerized multiplane system (COMPSY)   an animation system invented by Douglas Trumbull and first used in *Star Trek: The Motion Picture* (1979).

concave lens   (also **plano-concave lens**), any lens in which one or both (*bi-concave*) sides curve inwards; see *convex lens*.

condenser lens   the type of lens used in a projector; **condenser microphone**, a microphone based on the principle that sound vibrations, picked up by a diaphragm in relation to a fixed plate, will result in fluctuations of voltage; also known as an *electrostatic microphone*.

cone   (a) a lamp designed to cast a soft light, built in the shape of a cone, or (b) the conical, vibrating unit inside an amplifier.

conforming   the job of the *conformer* (or *negative cutter*, or *negative matcher)*, who matches the original film to the *workprint*, usually by following the edge numbers (or *key numbers*). The practice of editing a work print rather than from footage ensures that the original film remains in pristine condition until the final editing decisions have been made.

construction crew   the team which builds sets.

contact print   a positive made by *contact printing*, a process in which the positive and negative films are run together, emulsion to emulsion, in front of an aperture for light: the images on the latter are thus directly transferred to the former.

content curve   the time supposedly needed for an audience to pick up the principal meaning of a shot – generally no more than a couple of seconds.

continuing zoom   a zoom which does not stop when the subject is closely framed, but continues until the frames have been filled and beyond.

continuity   usually (a) the fictional 'time' of a film – its logical or narrative sequence: the carefully contrived effect of a smooth flow from shot to shot, sequence to sequence, or (b) the shorthand term for a *shooting script* of a production in which details of all dialogue, shots, sound effects and so on are written out in full.

Among the associated terms: *continuity breakdown*, the sheet of technical information for a day's shooting; *continuity cutting*, the unobtrusive, standard cutting style for a feature, which moves smoothly from shot to shot, avoiding sudden leaps in time, place or action unless they are clearly signposted as a change of scene. It should seem so inevitable, so natural to an audience that it is hardly noticed; *continuity girl* (or *continuity clerk, script clerk, script girl, script supervisor*); the person – traditionally a young woman – who keeps detailed notes of the positions of actors, props, recorded dialogue and so on for each take, chiefly so as to avoid continuity errors or to permit the scene to be restaged identically at some later date. These records are known as *continuity notes* (or *continuity sheets, take sheets*); *continuity shooting*, the unusual (because generally costly) practice of shooting the scenes in a film in precisely the order of the screenplay; *continuity sketches*, drawings of sets and/or of action, used by the director and others as a guide to see narrative sequence or overall feel of a production; see *storyboard*.

continuous action   action within a single sequence which, though filmed in segments from a variety of different angles, gives the impression of being unified after editing.

continuous drive   in a camera: the mechanism which feeds film from the magazine into the camera body and back into the magazine.

contract player   an actor who is under long-term contract by a studio or production company, and may be assigned to any of the films the company has in production.

contrapuntal sound, contrapuntal music   a sound-track whose connotations clash with the visual meaning of a scene, usually to ironic effect: in the recent independent film *Johns* (1997), for example, the sordid life of two young male prostitutes is set against jolly Christmas carols and sacred music. The effect can be rather trite if handled indelicately, but at its best can be extremely funny, disconcerting or harrowing: *Mother Night* (1997) makes wonderfully pointed use of a sound-track featuring Bing Crosby, Arvo Part and other musicians.

contrast   the opposition of light and dark tones within a film image, usually determined by the choice of lighting and stock, or by processing. *Contrast filter* in black and white photography, filters used to add contrast to colours which read as similar shades of grey. *Contrast glass*: a filter or other dark glass used by the cinematographer to gauge the *contrast range* of a set or location; the term *contrast range* also applies to the capacities of film stock: high contrast film will reproduce extrely bright and extremely dark tones; low contrast film gives the grey areas between the extremes.

control band   in printing: a strip of perforated paper which controls the amount of light that can reach the film.

convergence   in projecting 3-D films, the point at which the left- and right-eye views converge – which is to say, roughly at the surface of the screen.

convex lens (plano-convex lens)   any lens with one or both (*bi-convex*) surfaces curved outwards.

cookie (or **cuke, cukaloris, cookaloris, kook**)   an irregularly perforated sheet of metal, plastic or wood, placed in front of a lamp to break up its light, so giving a more varied texture to otherwise featureless surfaces. See *ulcer*.

cooking   overdeveloping a film, usually to compensate for inadequate lighting.

co-production, copro   a film made by two or more different countries, or, more generally, by two or more different production bodies. (Joke in Godard's *Vent de l'est*: 'We're the Italian actors in the co-production'.)

copter mount   a camera mount which enables the cameraman to take aerial shots smoothly from a helicopter.

cordless sync   any form of *synchronization* between camera and sound recorder that does not use a sync-pulse cable.

core   the small plastic hub, about 2 or 3 inches in diameter, around which film is wound for storage; cores are made in sizes of 16mm, 35mm and 70mm to hold these three stocks.

costume designer   the person responsible for making all the specialist clothing for a production, from togas to space suits.

costume drama   the type of historical feature in which a major attraction for audiences is the lavish appearance of the period clothes: most of the Merchant/Ivory productions, for example, or Martin Scorsese's *The Age of Innocence* (1993).

costumer   the person who buys, fits and, if necesary, helps the actors into their costumes; an alternative term for *wardrobe master*.

counter   an abbreviation for *footage counter*.

counterkey, counter key   a *luminaire* set opposite the *key* light, used either to balance the lighting so that it appears less artificial, or to bring out the contours and textures of a subject; in the latter case, it is also known as a *modelling light*.

counter matte   see *matte*.

cove   the area at the bottom of a piece of background scenery or *cyclorama* which holds a row of lights, hidden from the camera by a board painted to blend in with that background.

cover, coverage   (a) to cover a scene is to shoot it from a number of different angles, so that its space can be reconstructed dramatically in the edit; the *coverage* is the sum total of shots that have been taken of a particular scene or action. (OED does not mention these senses, but it does note an early 20th C use of the term meaning 'to photograph the whole of an area from the air', and also notes that 'coverage' has been used to mean 'the range of a lens' since the 1930s); (b) *coverage* is also the term applied to the professional summaries of a book or screenplay that are drawn up for the benefit of busy producers, studio executives and so on so that they can make an early decision about its suitability for production; see *reader*.

covering   an actor's error, in which he or she blocks the camera's view of the action or the lighting plot.

covering power   a lens with high covering power can produce images that are sharp even at the edges.

cover set   an substitute indoor set, kept ready in case of bad weather.

cover shot (or **insurance shot, protection shot**)   a shot – often a long shot or *master* – taken to bail the director out if there should prove to be problems of continuity or other editing difficulties, or when there are suspicions that a particular shot may have gone wrong in some way.

cowboy film   a demotic synonym for *western*. As Gilbert Adair has pointed out, the word 'cowboy' has hardly ever appeared in the title of a film with pretensions to seriousness (possible exceptions: Delmer Daves' *Cowboy*, 1957, and Mark Rydell's *The Cowboys*, 1971). However, one could add that, thanks to its camp associations, the word has appeared in the titles of films with a rather more pronounced erotic element: John Schlesinger's *Midnight Cowboy* (1969), the Andy Warhol/ Paul Morrissey *Lonesome Cowboys* (1968), etc.

crab, crab dolly   a four-wheeled *dolly* that, like the crustacean, can move rapidly sideways or in any other direction. Hence *crabbing, crab shot* and so on.

cradle   a mount set on a camera to support the weight of large lenses.

crane (or **cherry picker**)   a device consisting of a large trolley on top of which is mounted an extended arm or boom with a platform for the camera and cameraman. The trolley can be moved back and forth, the arm up and down, so allowing a wide range of possible camera angles, static or mobile – a *crane shot* means a mobile shot taken from a crane; such shots are also known as cranes, and the action as *craning*. Quite a lot of features still adhere to the convention of ending on an upwards crane shot: it tends to have the rhetorical effect of a valediction (the filmic equivalent of the *travelogue* cliché 'and so we bid farewell') or a concluding flourish.

crash zoom   an extremely fast zoom in to a subject, usually for comic or shock effect; generally a rather disreputable gimmick, though it has been used to humorous effect by self-conscious stylists such as the Coen brothers, in *Raising Arizona* and elsewhere.

crawl (or **crawl title, crawling title, creeper title, roller title, roll-up title**)   words (or, occasionally, images) which move slowly up from the bottom of the frame until they disappear at the top; a device most commonly used for:

credits, credit titles   the list which formally acknowledges or advertises all those involved in the making of a film. In most cases, these will appear at the beginning (*front credits, opening credits*, which are usually quite brief, and list only the major participants – director, writer, producer and production company, leading players) and/or at the end (*closing credits, end credits*) of the film.

crew   the team of craftsmen, technicians and labourers employed in the production of a film; or one of the smaller teams (such as the camera crew) within the overall crew. The term, taken over from OF *creue*, 'augmentation, reinforecment', originally (mid-15th C onwards) designated reinforcements for an army, but within a century had also come to mean any gathering of persons into a company: 'a courtly crew of gentlemen soiourning in his palace' – Lyly, *Euphues*, 1579. After another century, it began to take on the sense of a body of workmen engaged on a specific task, and, as the United States was opened up, came to be applied particularly to teams building railways or cutting wood. It seems to be from this last sense, rather than the nautical one (common from the late 17th C) that the film world adapted the word for its own purposes, some time in the early 20th C.

CRI print a release print made from a *Colour Reversal Intermediate.*

cricket dolly an small Italian gadget which combines all the functions of a *crab dolly*, with a central column that can be raised or lowered by several feet.

critics, criticism with a few exceptions, film critics are journalists and professional writers who review or analyse current films, or comment on the aesthetic properties of earlier films, as opposed to the (notionally) more scholarly film historians and (allegedly) more rigorous theorists of the academic world. The practice of discussing films in newsprint was quite rare until the 1920s – one notable exception being the detailed accounts of new releases offered by the British periodical *The Bioscope* – though more theoretical accounts of the new medium had been hammered out in *avant-garde* coteries from Paris to Moscow. Theorists and jobbing critics have seldom been on good terms, and on the whole continue to regard each other with mutual contempt, though there are signs that hostilities are easing on some fronts. A recent (1997) book of writings about Howard Hawks by the leading film theorist Peter Wollen happily includes a number of pieces which are recognisable as mainstream criticism. A striking number of practising critics have also been novelists, playwrights or poets: James Agee, Peter Barnes, Graham Greene, G. Cabrera Infante, Vachel Lindsay, Susan Sontag, David Thomson; the theatre and opera director Jonathan Miller also served a stint as critic for the *New Yorker*, as did his friend Kenneth Tynan. For reasons which might merit investigation, it is a literary form in which many women have thrived or excelled: Anne Billson, Colette, Angie Errigo, Penelope Gilliatt, Molly Haskell, Sheila Johnston, C.A. Lejeune, Dilys Powell, Amy Taubin . . . a short list that would be scandalously incomplete without the name of the most influential critic of the second part of this century: Pauline Kael, whose exhilarating, scathing, cranky, witty and unabashedly confessional reviews for the *New Yorker* have been compared to the musical and dramatic reviews of Shaw, but are in fact without obvious peer. Ms Kael once told me that she was proud to be a critic, and considered it an honourable calling: she is one of the writers who have helped make it so.

critical focus as in still photography: the distance between the lens aperture and the subject in focus.

cropping   as in still photography: to change the composition of an image by masking some part of it, projecting through a small aperture and so on. The most common type of cropping occurs in television, in which film images are sliced down to fit into the narrower aspect ratio of a domestic set; see *panning and scanning*.

cross-cutting   cutting between two or more sets of action, often to create suspense or some other kind of exciting effect, or more generally to establish some narrative or metaphorical connection between them; a technique discovered in the early years of the century, before cinema had even reached its teens: in *The Great Train Robbery* of 1903, for example. A symbolic, perhaps excessively symbolic, use of cross-cutting occurs at the climax of *Apocalypse Now*, in which the assassination by Willard (Martin Sheen) of Colonel Kurtz (Marlon Brando) is cross-cut with a Cambodian tribe's ritual slaughter of cattle; an earlier shot of Kurtz's library had shown him to be a student of *The Golden Bough*.

cross dissolve   see *dissolve*; *cross fade*, strictly speaking, a relatively uncommon type of transition from one scene to the next, made by fading the scenes into and out from some colour other than black; but, since the term is derived from audio recording (where it means progressively fading out one tape or track while bringing up the volume on the next) it can also simply mean a *fade*.

cross in, cross out   the movements of performers respectively into and out of frame.

crossing the line (breaking the 180 degree rule, crossing the imaginary line, crossing the proscenium)   a violation of one of the most basic laws of film grammar, which states that the camera should never be allowed to move behind a hypothetical line drawn between the principal actors or speakers, unless there is some strong dramatic justification for the movement (Example: a bomb goes off behind them and we cut to see their shocked faces.) If the line is crossed, the actors appear to swap positions and the audience may become disoriented. In practice, the rule is broken more often than some text books suggest: Orson Welles, trying to teach himself how to direct a film before embarking on *Citizen Kane*, sat through repeated screenings of *Stagecoach*, noted that John Ford crossed the line time after time in the chase sequences, and concluded that the rule did not matter.

cross light (side light)   lighting a subject from the sides.

cross modulation   a type of distortion that can occur in optical sound recording.

crowd scene   any scene displaying large masses of people, whether fighting (*The Birth of a Nation*), revelling (the end of *Les Enfants du Paradis*), revolting (Eisenstein's *October*) or just roaming around. Some notable examples from the last few years include the fantasy dance held inside Grand Central Station in Terry Gilliam's *The Fisher King* and the packed, rain-soaked streets of *Blade Runner*.

Crown Film Unit   the British government-sponsored film unit that operated between 1940 and 1951 (when it was closed down by the new Conservative government), specialising in the production of documentary shorts. It was the successor to the earlier Empire Marketing Board (founded 1928) and GPO Film Units, which absorbed the EMB's production wing in 1933; films by all three bodies are sometimes loosely, and confusingly referred to as 'Crown' films. Crown produced work of exceptional quality, and has been discussed in detail in many histories of the cinema. Among the names you will find in such histories: John Grierson, producer of the Unit from 1929 until his resignation in 1937, and his protégés of the 'Grierson School' Arthur Elton, Stuart Legg and Basil Wright; the Brazilian *avant-garde* film-maker Alberto Cavalcanti; Benjamin Britten and W.H. Auden, who composed and wrote verse for GPO films, most famously in *Night Mail*; and several other directors, including Paul Rotha, Edgar Anstey, Harry Watt and Pat Jackson. Perhaps the most extraordinary talent to emerge from Crown's studios was Humphrey Jennings (1907–50), who was described by Lindsay Anderson as the British cinema's one true poet.

CU   see *close-up*.

cucaloris   see *cookie*.

cue   any verbal, visual or other signal for an actor to begin an action or speech; *cue cards* (*idiot cards*), large cards with dialogue written across them held up for the benfit of actors with poor memories, bad nerves, minimal intelligence or some other professional liability; *cue light*, often green in colour, used to cue actors or (more commonly) narrators or (in television) presenters; *cue marks* either (a) a change-over cue, or (b) any synchronisation mark on film or sound tape; *cue sheet* (or *cue breakdown*), in dubbing: a chart of columns that show the various sound-tracks to be mixed together.

cult film, cult movie   any film which survives an initially poor reception in the general marketplace thanks to being taken up by a particular faction of movie *buffs*, drug connoisseurs, college students, ironists, insomniacs or faddists. Many of them will be cheaply made genre films – Westerns, thrillers, science fiction or horror, and almost any road movie – with some odd quirk to their plot, direction, acting or general sensibility. Many cult films are of negligible artistic merit, and valued for just that reason: the classic case is Ed Wood's *Plan 9 from Outer Space*, whose maker has recently become immortalised in Tim Burton's *Ed Wood* (1995). Others are of clear, or at least arguable distinction: *Witchfinder General*, *The Wicker Man*, *Performance*. Sometimes attendance at the cult demands audience participation, as with *The Rocky Horror Picture Show* (for which, two decades after its first release, audiences will still dress up in fishnet stockings, throw rice at the screen, howl 'Slut!' and so on) or the Joan Crawford biopic *Mommie Dearest* (a more short-lived cult of the 1980s, for which audiences would come equipped with wire coathangers).

custard pie   according to Mack Sennett's autobiography, the first custard pie was thrown by Mabel Normand at Ben Turpin, as a spontaneous on-camera gag, some time in 1913. As the reference books point out, this cannot be strictly accurate, since Turpin did not join *Keystone* until 1917; Sennett was probably confusing Turpin with Fatty Arbuckle, who took the cinema's first recorded pie in the face from Miss Normand in *A Noise from the Deep* (July 1913). The custard pie became one of Keystone's staples – they used the real thing, not some foam imitation – and was soon borrowed by other comedians; hence the term *custard-pie humour* and similar expressions.

cut   in its common sense: (a) the most basic unit of film grammar, and, it can been argued, one of the foundations of film as a distinct art form rather than an epigone or mongrel offspring of the theatre, painting or the novel. It means the immediate transition from one shot to another, created by splicing two strips of film together. Whole books have been written on the matter of cutting, but, in brief, it can be said that most of the principles which have dominated the cinema of this century were invented by D. W. Griffith (but see the entry for the *Brighton School*) and elaborated by the Soviet theorists and film-makers, *Kuleshov*, Pudovkin and Eisenstein (see *montage*). In a sense, what Griffith was offering his audiences were several new perspectives on time and space: (1) by breaking up an individual action into a number of different pieces in filming, then re-building these pieces into a new unity for the projected film; (2) by varying the frequency with which these pieces were displayed, as well as their duration; and (3) by bringing actions that were physically separate within the same time frame – that is, by *cross-cutting*. To be sure, there are some precedents and loose analogies for all these techniques in more ancient narrative arts, which is one reason why Christopher Logue, in his much-applauded free translations from *The Iliad*, so frequently resorts to film terms such as 'reverse angle'. But cinema was the first medium that could perform these fragmentations and reconstructions in wholly visual terms, for the gazing eye rather than the mind's eye.

Other senses of the word *cut* include: (b) the act of making such cuts; (c) the splice itself (d); a particular stage or version of the edit of the entire film, as in the *rough cut* (a loose assembly, put together to give the makers or the backers some idea of what the finished version will look like) or the *director's cut* – the version of the feature handed over to the studio by the director and sometimes – as, in recent years, with *Heaven's Gate, Blade Runner, Lawrence of Arabia, The Abyss, Dances With Wolves* and so on – subsequently released in theatres after the studio cut has had its chance in the marketplace (e) on set, 'Cut!' is still the order usually shouted by the director to stop the camera and sound from turning over. OED, which offers slightly ambiguous examples to illustrate the various meanings of the word, suggests that it had come to mean 'to edit' or 'to make a quick transition from one shot to the next' as early as 1913, though its example from 1916 is more certain: 'You can cut to some single person who overlooks the crime and later tells the story' – E.W. Sargent, *Technique of the Photoplay*.

Related words include *cutaway* (or *cutaway shot*) a cut from the main action towards some subsidiary action, person or thing, often (a) to show someone's reaction, (b) to change the rhythm of the scene, (c) to cover a jump cut or (d) to supply additional information – the time on a clock, the burning of a fuse; *cutter*, another, less commonly used word for an editor (alternatively, an editor's assistant), though it can also be the generic word for any device that cuts down illumination – a *cookie*, a *flag* and so on. The written direction *cut to* is often found in screenplays and treatments, emphasising the movement from scene to scene. A *direct cut* goes from one scene to the next without any transitional device.

cutting   some of the more important compound terms include: *cutting continuity*, a detailed written (and sometimes published) account of a film in its finished version, including not only the dialogue but descriptions of action, camera movements, music and so on; *cutting copy*, the print of a film as it passes through the editor's hands; *cutting in the camera*: filming in such a way that little or no editing of the completed footage will be required; *cutting on action* (see *invisible cutting*); *cutting room*, the editor's workplace, containing one or more **Steenbecks**, trim bins and so on; *cutting sync*, editing with separate sound and vision tracks.

cyc, cyclorama   as on the stage: a curved backdrop to a set, or artificial horizon. The term, which was coined from the Gk *kuklos*, 'circle' and -*orama*, 'spectacle', originally denoted a novel type of popular diversion of the 1840s: the viewer would stand inside a large cylindrical space, the surface of which was painted with a landscape or some other scene. OED records the first theatrical use in 1915 ('This is the "Horizont", which we may name for the purpose a cyclorama' – H.K. Moderwell, *Theatre To-Day*).

D **ada** see *surrealism*.
   Daieiscope the trade name of a Japanese wide-screen process,
   which was actually the *Vista Vision* process as licensed from
Paramount by the Daiei company.

dailies also known as *rushes*: positive prints of each day's shooting in
the course of a production, usually processed overnight and viewed first
thing the following morning by director, cinematographer and others; in
normal circumstances, dailies will have synchronised sound-tracks. 'Every
time a scene is successfully "shot" it is called "a take"; the whole of the
day's "takes" are then assembled and shown to the producer in a private
projection room, but are then known as "the rushes" or "the dailies"' –
Tit-Bits, 31 March 1934. Dailies are used to assess the calibre of
performances, the quality of lighting and sound and the general effect of
the film-in-progress.

daily production report (DPR) the production manager's breakdown of a given day's work, drawn up to give the producer or studio an
idea of how the film is proceeding and how much it is likely to cost; each
of the individual production departments (camera, sound and so on) will
usually draw up a DPR of their own activities.

dampen to cut down unwanted echoes and vibrations on a set, usually
by surrounding the area where the microphones are placed with sound-
absorbing walls. The verb 'to damp', from the G *dampfen*, is frequent in
English from the mid-16th C; the musical and acoustic senses are known
from the early 19th C.

dark end the section of a processing machine into which film is fed to
be developed, and which must be kept in complete darkness to prevent
accidental exposure.

Dawn processes two early forms of multiple-image technique. The
first, devised by Norman Dawn and used for cinematography from 1907
into the 1930s, combined live action with scenery painted onto a glass
sheet; the second, also invented by Dawn, was a type of in-camera *matte*
shot.

DAY in a screenplay, the heading – as, for example, in 'ONE.
INTERIOR. DAY.' – which indicates that the following scene takes
place in the daytime, though not necessarily in daylight.

day-for-night, day for night (DN) the practice or technique of
giving a daytime shot or sequence the appearance of night. The effect is
achieved with dark filters, or by underexposing or under-printing the
film. One of the best known of all technical terms, thanks to the
international success of François Truffaut's entertaining light comedy
about film-making, *Day for Night* (*La Nuit Américaine*, 1973; *la nuit
Américaine* being, of course, the French name for the process).

day player a performer contracted on a day-by-day basis.

daylight conversion filter a lens filter that alters the colour-tempera-
ture of the light passing through the camera, so that film which has been

65

balanced for shooting by artificial light can be used outdoors, in natural light.

daylight loading spool   a metal spool that allows short lengths of film to be loaded into the camera in ordinary light conditions.

daylight projection   a process involving either back-projection onto a translucent screen, or front projection onto a reflective screen, and carried out in a lit set or location.

dead   an acoustic with little or no reverberation, such as a room hung with heavy curtains. The word 'dead' has meant 'profoundly quiet, still' at least since 1548, and 'without resonance' since 1530, if the OED reading is correct: 'The lady called them again, but . . . very softly, for it was with a dead voice'. Hence *dead end*, the most sound-absorbent part of a recording studio, *dead side*, the least sensitive side of a microphone, and *dead spot*, the point at which reverberations from the same sound source become mutually cancelling. *Dead sync*, see *editor's sync*.

deal   the deceptive term has many uses in Hollywood, but is often used to refer to a type of contract which guarantees a certain number of productions to a director or star: 'Stallone has just signed a five-picture deal with Columbia' and so forth.

deblooping   the process of removing, by physical or electronic means, the unwanted noise – that is the 'bloop' (presumably an onomatopoeia) – caused (a) by a break in the film sound-track when it passes over a scanner, or (b) from damage created by editing tools.

decamired   a measurement of colour temperature; see *mired*.

decibel (DB)   the standard unit of sound intensity; the -bel syllable is a tribute to Alexander Graham Bell and the deci- prefix indicates that the unit increases exponentially by a factor of ten.

Decla Bioscop   the short-lived German production company responsible for the sinister likes of *Das Cabinett des Dr Caligari* (1919) and Fritz Lang's own 'Doctor' film, *Dr Mabuse der Spieler* (1922). Founded as Decla in 1916 by Erich Pommer as a German counterpart to the French Eclair, it merged with Bioscop in 1919 and was taken over by *UFA* in 1923.

decor   loosely speaking, the 'look' of a particular scene or film as created by its costumes, furniture, props, and colour scheme.

découpage   a term from French film criticism sometimes (though less commonly in recent years) borrowed by Anglophone writers: the literal meaning is 'cutting up', but the term is taken figuratively, and means 'editing style'. *Découpage classique* is the French term for *invisible cutting*.

deep field, deep focus   a style of shooting which thrived in the early silent cinema (when fast *orthochromatic* stock was standard), went into abeyance for a couple of decades (with the introduction of *panchromatic* stock), and then resurfaced with Gregg Toland's wonderfully atmospheric camerawork for *Citizen Kane* (1941); it was the critical success of Welles' film which brought the term into common use. Deep focus permits several planes of action to be held sharply in view simultaneously, thus opening up the possibility for richer and more complex images; in shallow focus, most of the picture except the single plane of action is left blurry or vague. The ethical and metaphysical virtues of deep focus were lauded in some influential essays from a four-volume study *Qu'est-ce que le cinéma?* (published in French between 1958 and 1962; selections from this work were translated into English as *What is Cinema?*, by the French critic and theorist André Bazin (1919–58).

definition   the precision or sharpness of an image; or of a film stock or lens.

defocus   either (a) to pull an image slowly out of focus as a transitional effect (this is known as a *defocus transition*, and is now relatively uncommon), or to switch focus more suddenly from one plane to another – that is, to *pull* or *rack focus*.

degauss (or **demagnetise**)   to use a magnetic tool (a *degausser*) to wipe the recording on a tape, etc. The term is derived from the work of Karl Friedrich Gauss, the mathematician and natural philosopher (1777–1855); in physics, a Gauss is the unit of intensity of a magnetic field.

degradation   the coarsening of a film or video image which results from its being transferred through several printings or generations in editing.

Denham   the famous British film studios, at one time the centre of the national industry, which operated between 1936 and 1953, and served as the production base for many distinguished films, including *Things to Come* (1936), *The Life and Death of Colonel Blimp* (1943) and the Olivier Shakespeare films *Henry V* (1944) and *Hamlet* (1948). It was sold in 1953 by the *Rank* Organisation, which wanted to concentrate its activities in *Pinewood*.

denouement   from the Fr *denouer*, 'to untie': as in the theatre or prose fiction: the outcome of a film, the 'unravelling' of its main plot and sub-plots.

densitometer   a photo-electric instrument used in processing for measuring the *density* of an image – that is to say, of its degree of opacity.

depth   the illusion of three-dimensional space created by and within a two-dimensional image. **Depth of field**, the extent to which objects that are in front of or behind the principal plane of action may be held in focus. A cinematographer who wishes to achieve a considerable depth of field – *deep focus* – will have resort to a wide-angle lens, greater exposure times and so on.

desaturation   the intentional or accidental dilution of a colour by white light, resulting in a pallid hue. See *saturation*.

detail shot   an extreme close-up on some small object, usually of significance to the narrative – the caption to a newspaper photograph, a bottle of sleeping pills, a spent cartridge.

detective film   a hardy perennial within the thriller genre, with many and varied blooms. For most viewers, the classic examples date from the

1940s, notably John Huston's *The Maltese Falcon* (from the novel by Dashiell Hammett, with Bogart as Sam Spade), Howard Hawks' *The Big Sleep* (from the novel by Raymond Chandler, with Bogart as Philip Marlowe) – the type of hard-bitten, wise-cracking movie mercilessly spoofed in Carl Reiner's *Dead Men Don't Wear Plaid*, starring Steve Martin, and pastiched with dazzling ingenuity in Martin Rowson's cartoon version of Eliot's *The Waste Land* (1990). The 1970s saw some inspired returns to this arena, in Roman Polanki's lush, fatalistic *Chinatown* (screenplay by Robert Towne, starring Jack Nicholson) and in Robert Altman's *The Long Goodbye* (starring Eliott Gould in the Marlowe role). For good and ill, the torrent of 'tecs shows no sign of abating: see *film noir*.

deuce   a floodlight of 2,000 watts, also known as a *junior*.

develop   (a) to treat exposed film with chemical solutions – *developers* – and so bring out the images that are latent there; from Fr *developper* and related terms in It, meaning 'to unfold, unroll' etc. The photographic sense of the word, which appears to be a specific application of a more general earlier sense 'to bring out that which is potentially contained within', is found in English from c. 1840.

   (b) To work on an idea, synopsis, treatment, draft screenplay or some other property with a view to eventual production; a process sometimes made smoother by *development funding*, or guaranteed by a *development deal*.

DGA   the Director's Guild of America: the union for film and television directors in the United States.

dialing   controlling the levels from different microphones or sources during sound recording.

dialogue   as in the theatre: (a) the words written on the page for the actors to speak (b) those same words as spoken by the actors; or words improvised before the camera. The word comes from 13th C Fr *dialogue*, which itself has roots in the L *dialogus* and Gk *dialogos*. OED records the specialist sense of 'a literary work in the form of a conversation' as early as 1225; the present theatrical sense of the word appears to be established by the early 18th C ('A tragedy is a thing of five acts, written dialoguewise' – Fielding, 1732). Dialogue in the cinema can often be a good deal looser than most theatrical dialogue: consider, for example, the films of Robert Altman, where dialogue is allowed to overlap, drift in and out of earshot or remain only partially, tantalisingly audible. This relative freedom is partly due to the fact that the eloquence or permissible stylization of much dramatic language can sound odd in the context of Hollywood realism (even when the stylization is that of a David Mamet), and partly to the recognition that – or so it can be argued – 'screenwriting isn't really writing: it's really part of the oral tradition and it has a lot more to do with the day your uncle went hunting and the dog went crazy and the bird got away than it does with literature.' (Paul Schrader, in *Schrader on Schrader*, 1990). Certainly, one of the lessons drummed into novice screenwriters is that dialogue is one of the less important aspects of a *screenplay*: screenplays, as William Goldman insists in *Adventures in the Screen Trade*, are *structure*, and the writer's natural wish to dazzle with words must generally be kept subordinate to the building of that structure. Some purists would go further, and maintain that the cinema reached its artistic zenith in the silent period, and that the advent of sound, and particularly of recorded dialogue has merely diluted or cheapened the art.

A *dialogue coach* is a person employed to help the actors learn or comprehend their lines; *dialogue replacement* is the process of re-recording dialogue in studio and synchronising it with the lip movements of the original recording (see *looping*); *dialogue track* is the sound track which holds the recorded dialogue.

diaphragm   the adjustable metal device inside a camera that regulates the amount of light that can pass through the lens; see *iris*.

diapositive   a simple device for producing composite images: a glass plate through which action is shot, partly clear, partly occupied with a photograph (generally of scenery).

diegesis   a term made fashionable in theoretically inclined circles during the 1970s by the writings of the French semiotician Christian Metz, and also found in criticism influenced by such theory: roughly speaking, the fictional world of the narrative, particularly as opposed to the elements of the film which contribute in some other way to its meanings. (Soundtrack music, for example, is not an element of the diegesis.) Taken into English directly from Gk *diegesis*, meaning either 'narrative' or, in a speech, the statement of a case; OED gives the first English use of the word in the early 19th C.

diffuser   in the early cinema, a gauze or cotton sheet put over a lamp, window or other source of illumination to soften the light it cast. Today, either (a) any of the materials used to soften light – netting, wire, frosted glass or a plastic *diffusion curtain*; or (b) a *diffusion filter*, which is placed in front of the lens to achieve the effect of *diffusion*, the softening of detail and creation of glowing highlights. At one time, diffusion was standard method for filming actresses in close-up or romantic clinches; used too obviously, it now appears hackneyed.

dimmer   the gadget which increases and decreases the brilliance of a light source by boosting or cutting back its power supply. Dimmers were commonly used in black-and-white film-making, but are employed more sparingly in polychrome productions since they create an obvious change in colour temperature.

DIN   the abbreviation for Deutsche Industrie Norm, one of the standard measurements, like *ASA* and *ISO*, of the speed or sensitivity of a film.

dinky   a small lamp with a 100-watt bulb.

diopter   (or **diopter lens, plus lens** or **close-up diopter**)   an additional lens set in front of the main lens for filming extreme close-ups. From the 16th C Fr *dioptre*, L *dioptra* and the two Greek words *dioptra*, an optical instrument for measuring heights, and *dioptron*, a spy-glass. The word has been widely used in English since the 17th C, meaning at different times and variously a theodolite, a surgical speculum, an instrument for obtaining drawings of the skull by projections and a unit of measurement for lenses.

direct, direction, director   adopted by English from the L stem *direct-*, itself from *dirigere*, to straighten, set straight, direct, guide. The cinematic sense of the verb grows out of the more general meanings (a) 'to give intructions, to order or ordain' ('I'le first direct my men what they shall doe with the basket': *Merry Wives of Windsor* (1598), IV, ii) and (b) 'to guide, conduct, lead', common since the mid-16th C. OED gave neither the theatrical nor the cinematic definitions of 'direct' and 'director' until its Supplement, which states that both of these artistic senses come into use in America some time in the early years of the century, and implies that they soon caught on in Britain, too. Hence *Moving Picture World*, 22 July 1911: 'The director explains to the players the action of a scene'; and a reference in R. Grau's *Theatre of Science* (1914) to 'The world-famous director, D.W. Griffith'. The dictionary suggests, in other words, that the British stage gradually – in the 1930s and 1940s – took over the American theatrical and cinematic term 'director' for the role which had previously been designated as 'producer', citing W. Somerset Maugham and other authorities to this effect.

   In the cinema, the director continues to be what he or she has been since the silent era: the person who gives orders and/or advice to the actors and/or camera crew, and so helps turn the words on the screenplay's pages to sounds and images on screen – a very general job of work, which in its practical elements consists largely of talking, shouting and gesticulating. (This is why, as the critic James Monaco once amusingly suggested, it might appear to the uninformed outsider that a director is someone who gets paid large sums of money to point at things; interestingly, one old sense of the verb 'direct' is 'to point': 'Little white brisles [*sic*] whose points all directed backwards' – Robert Hooke, *Micrographia*, 1665.) But rather more lofty interpretations of the terms 'direct' and 'director' will be familiar to anyone who has skimmed or studied film criticism of even the lightest kind. At a less prosaic level, the director is generally understood to be the person (or, infrequently, persons: directorial teams include siblings such as the Taviani brothers, the Hughes brothers, the Maysles brothers and the Quay brothers; and heterosexual couples such as Annabel Jankel and Rocky Morton) who, by supervising and steering the efforts of all the artistic and technical staff of a production, gives the finished film its shape, tone and distinctive visual signature. Moreover, for loyalists of the *auteur* theory, the director is or should be the true artistic genius of the film, regardless of who wrote, produced or starred in it. It is fairly easy to pick large holes in this last view, not least because the recognition that a director might in some way be stamping his (rarely, until recent decades, her) mark on the written source material dawned fitfully and slowly, at least in the American film industry. With one or two exceptions, such as the above-cited D.W. Griffith, the names of non-acting directors were little known or publicised until the 1950s and 1960s; Hitchcock and John Ford were among the first directors who were able to sell films to the public on the strength of their names rather than those of their stars. But from the late 1950s onwards, and thanks in large measure to the efforts of auteurists and the auteurists-turned-directors of the *Nouvelle Vague*, this relative anonymity gave way to the cult of – as a collection of interviews with practioners published in the early 1970s was memorably entitled – The Film Director as Superstar. Despite the critical disrepute into which auteurist views have fallen, and the obvious consideration that many directors are hacks and dolts, the view that the most distinguished, creative and (the job of movie star excepted) glamorous role in the film industry is that of director has become a potent myth of the late twentieth Century. In the 1980s, there were rumours that sardonic, or painfully frank souls in Los Angeles had taken to wearing t-shirts printed with the slogan 'What I Really Want to Do is Direct', or words to the same effect. But this interesting topic is matter for an essay or book, not a lexicon. Some of the major terms asociated with 'director' include:

director's cut, either (a) a *rough cut* of a film, produced by its director and editor without (in theory) any interference from the producer or studio; in Hollywood, the right to such a director's cut is usually guaranteed by the DGA's guide to basic terms of employment, or (b) in recent years, the term applied to what is, at least in theory, a complete version of a large-scale film by a prominent director that was trimmed back by the studio for its first release but has been restored and re-released in response to pressures from critics, fans or (a more cynical reading) accountants who see the director's cut as a strategic way of compounding the profits from a hit or recouping some of the expenses of a flop; see *cut*; *director's viewfinder, director's finder*, a calibrated optical instrument used by both directors and cinematographers to work out how a shot will appear in different sizes and through different lenses. It is usually worn on a cord around the neck, and may thus also serve as an unofficial decoration or a badge of rank comparable to the doctor's stethoscope. *Direction* may mean either (a) the act or art of directing, or (b) the instructions written into a screenplay, dictating either action (*general direction*) or the motions and motives of a single character (*personal direction*).

director of photography (DP)   see *cinematographer*.

direct cinema   a term coined by the American director Albert Maysles for the style of documentary he and his contemporaries – graduates of a company, Drew Associates, formed by Robert Drew and Richard Leacock in 1959 – were starting to make in the early 1960s. Among the luminaries of the direct cinema movement were Donn A. Pennebaker, best known for his rockumentaries *Don't Look Back* (1968: a splendidly mordant study of Bob Dylan on tour in Britain, and, indirectly, of the sorry-looking country itself) and *Monterey Pop* (1968); Frederick Wiseman, who has specialised in studies of American institutions, from an asylum for the criminally insane (*Titicut Follies*, 1967) and the US Army (*Basic Training*, 1971) to the self-explaining *Central Park* (1989) by way of *Hospital* (1970), *Meat* (1976), *The Store* (1983) and *Missile* (1988); and the Maysles Brothers, Albert and David, who made direct cinema films about both the famous – *The Beatles in the U.S.A.* (1964), *Meet Marlon Brando* (1965), *Gimme Shelter* (1970, about the ghastly Rolling Stones concert at Altamont) – and the obscure: *Salesman* (1969), a chronicle of four door-to-door Bible merchants. Direct cinema was made possible by a number of technical innovations, such as mobile synchronised-sound shooting, fast film stock and lightweight, hand-held cameras. Its products were chararacterised by their appearance of utter spontenaiety, by the blank; non-committal gaze of the camera and lack of any authorial comment, and by occasional technical roughness. Watching them, it is easy to believe that the people on screen have forgotten or never noticed the presence of the film crew, and that the events shown are taking place precisely as they would have if there were no one around to observe. Sometimes, particularly in Wiseman's films, the effect is curiously similar to the offence the Army used to term 'dumb insolence': when people behave terribly on screen, their behaviour seems all the worse for being regarded so affectlessly, for provoking no reaction on the part of the director. Most of the original direct cinema film-makers are still at work – for example, Pennebaker's *The War Room*, released in 1993, was an entertaining account of the workings of the campaign team that helped put Bill Clinton in the White House. The movement has also influenced many other documentary film-makers over the last few decades: Jan Troell in Sweden; Bert Haanstra in Holland; Kon Ichikawa in Japan; and, most famously, Louis Malle in France. For a more detailed discussion of the subject, see Erik Barnouw's *Documentary: A History of the Non-Fiction Film*; and see also *cinéma verité*.

direct cut   a sudden *cut* from one shot to another, without any softening transitional device such as a *fade*.

direct film   a type of abstract film made without the use of a camera by painting, drawing or otherwise making non-photographic marks on film stock – in the case of Stan Brakhage's *Mothlight*, for example, by gluing the body parts of dead moths to the celluloid. The pioneer of this form of cinema is generally held to be the New Zealand painter and director Len Lye (1901–80), whose direct film projects, commissioned by the GPO Film Unit, include *Colour Box* (1935), *Rainbow Dance* (1936) and *Trade Tattoo* (1937). Some reference books maintain that Lye's work was a major influence on the well-known animator Norman McLaren, but Dai Vaughan's biography *Portrait of an Invisible Man: The Working Life of Stewart McAllister, Film Editor* (1983) establishes that McLaren had already worked on an untitled three-minute abstract film of the 'direct' kind with McAllister in 1933, applying shoe polish, India ink and oils to strips of 35mm stock. Both McLaren and McAllister were excited by the experimental films of Eggeling, Ruttmann, Fischinger and others. Incidentally, Stan Brakhage, in his book *Film at Wit's End* (1989), credits the American avant-garde film-maker Jerome Hill (1905–72) with being the first to use 'in any intelligent way' the technique of hand painting or drawing directly on to a negative for his autobiographical *Film Portrait* (1971). See also *absolute film*.

direct sound   film sound that comes directly from the action happening in the scene, rather than that which is added later.

disaster film, disaster movie   apt terms for the commercially success-ful but, on the whole, aesthetically wretched films which depict some large-scale natural or man-made catastrophe; or, more typically, which depict the struggles and sufferings of a studiedly diverse group of people (played by actors whose reputations have either seen better days or which subsequently perish as swiftly as they bloomed) in the grip of such disasters. The presiding genius – if that is the appropriate term – of the genre is the producer/director Irwin Allen (b. 1916), whose productions include *The Poseidon Adventure* (1972, maritime disaster), *The Towering Inferno* (1974, high-rise disaster) and *The Swarm* (1978, killer-bee disaster). Long considered dormant, the genre has recently risen again, with unfortunate results: witness *Daylight*, *Dante's Peak* and so on. For a discussion of the deeper appeal of this form, see Susan Sontag's essay on science fiction movies, 'The Imagination of Disaster' (1965) in *Against Interpretation*.

disclaimer   the nervous words that creep on to the screen at the end of the feature, reassuring litigious members of the audience that the events they have just witnessed are pure fictions and are in no way intended as portraits of any real person, living or dead.

discontinuity   the deliberately (or, less often, the accidentally) jarring effect created by unexpected jumps from one action, object or scene to the next, or by some other interruption to the steady narrative flow of the film; see *dislocation*.

discovery shot   a moving shot, such as a track, pan or dolly, that eventually 'finds' an object or action that was out of sight when it began. The effect can be humorous, dramatic, horrific, erotic: though overused at times, it can be one of the cinema's simplest and most satisfactory devices. Also known as a *reveal*.

dishing   an accident that can happen when handling rolls of film by the sides rather than keeping one hand underneath: the central part of the reel starts to droop, and, unless caught, may fall out completely.

dislocation   an effect of emotional distance between the audience and the on-screen action brought about by technical means: unexpected angles or cuts, distorted sound, incongruous sound-track music and so on; a kind of *Verfremdungseffekt*, though not necessarily influenced by Brecht.

Disney   see *Walt Disney Company*.

dissolve (also **lap dissolve, cross dissolve, mix**)   a slower and generally more atmospheric means of transition from scene to scene than the *direct cut*, often implying the passage of a dramatically significant period of time. The end of one scene fades out while the beginning of the next scene fades up, so that the two are on the screen simultaneously for a few seconds. In older films, there was a particular type of dissolve which signified a flashback, a reverie or a dream: called a *ripple dissolve*, it wavered and wobbled as it faded. Today, the device seems corny and is generally only found in broad comedies, such as *Wayne's World* (directed by Penelope Spheeris). The word appears to have been in use as long as the device itself; OED's earliest citation is from 1912.

distortion   bending, stretching or otherwise deforming the image, principally with the use of special lenses or *distortion filters*, and often to convey drugged or other extreme mental states.

distribution, distributor   the business of releasing films to cinemas, regulating their long-term availability and determining the time they spend in the marketplace; the companies which specialise in this trade. The leading distributors in the UK at the moment include Warner, Columbia Tri-Star, Fox and Rank at the more commercial end of the market, and Artifical Eye, Electric amd Mainline for independent and art-house releases.

ditty bag   a bag slung beneath the camera tripod, used for keeping tape, camera tools and the like ready to hand.

divergent turret   a camera turret that sets its three or more lenses sufficiently far apart that shots taken with the wide-angle lens do not accidentally include any of the other lenses.

documentary   from the OF *document*, 'lesson, written evidence', and L *documentum*, 'lesson, proof, instance, specimen' etc. The word 'documentary', in the sense 'of the nature of or consisting in documents', is found in English in the early 19th C, and other senses are introduced later in the century. But the cinematic sense of the word, meaning a particular kind of non-fiction film, appears to have been brought to English – appropriately, since he had such a profound influence on the development of the form in Britain and, later, Canada – by John Grierson in his review for the *New York Sun* of Robert Flaherty's *Moana* (1926); Grierson was borrowing from the French *documentaire*, 'travelogue'. (The earliest instance given by OED is four years later, and comes from Paul Rotha's *The Film Till Now*: 'The Documentary or Interest Film, including the Scientific, Cultural and Sociological Film.') Though sometimes treated as a kind of poor relation of the fiction film, the documentary can, in some hands, be one of the richest jewels in cinema's crown. For a more adequate discussion of the form, see Erik Barnouw's *Documentary: A History of the Non-Fiction Film* (1974, 1993), and for a stimulating compendium of writings by and about some of the leading practitioners, see *Imagining Reality: The Faber Book of Documentary*

(1996), ed. Kevin Macdonald and Mark Cousins. See also *cinéma verité* and *direct cinema*.

docudrama   a dramatised re-enactment of some real-life event; a staged documentary, using either actors or non-professional performers, sometimes including the actual participants. The form is more common on television than in the cinema.

Dolby   the trade name of a high-fidelity sound recording system, developed in the 1970s for use in tape recording but soon applied to the optical sound tracks of 35mm film; its principal function was to reduce unwanted noise and hiss by means of an electronic circuit, and it brought about a major improvement in the quality of film sound-tracks. It is now in extremely common use, though the name still seems to trip some tongues: the girlfriend of one of the oafish rock musicians in Rob Reiner's hilarious mockumentary *This is Spinal Tap* refers to the process as 'Dobbly'.

dolly   (a) a mobile camera platform, mounted on wheels, and generally pushed about by a crew member (a *dolly grip*) rather than propelled by motor; it may either move freely, or run along tracks. (b) The shortened term for a *dolly shot*, a moving shot taken from a dolly; hence *dolly in* or *dolly up* – camera movement towards the subject – and *dolly out* or *dolly back* – movement away from the subject. Dolly shots are sometimes known as **tracking shots** (also *trucking shots* or *travelling shots*), though note (1) that strictly speaking, a tracking shot is one which follows a person or other moving subject, and (2) that any moving shot can be called a dolly, whether or not a camera platform is used. A *doorway dolly* is very narrow, so as to pass through doors; see also *crab*. OED is silent on the question of etymology, but notes the general use of 'dolly' as any kind of small platform on wheels or rollers from 1901 onwards, and the specific cinematic sense in 1929.

dope sheet   a list of information – 'dope' – about footage shot, film stocks used, and so on. Hence the title of the journal *Film Dope*, a British serial dictionary of the cinema.

dot   a small circular *gobo*.

double   the performer who stands in for a leading player, usually to perform some act of skill or daring – falling from a plane, riding a camel; or, as a verb, either (a) to act as a double, or (b) much less frequently, 'to play more than one part in a production' – the older, theatrical sense of the verb, used from the early 19th C onwards. OED Supplement records early cinematic uses in 1918 ('A young man, doubling for a leading lady in a bit of hazardous fire jumping') and 1928: 'Picturegoers should look out for the portions of the film in which Miss Thorndike was "doubled" by other actresses.' One or more *body doubles* may be used for nude scenes, particularly of the erotic kind, to spare the players' modesty and/or foster the illusion of their physical perfection; for these, the body doubles' faces are kept carefully out of shot. Hence the title of Brian de Palma's sordid thriller *Body Double*.

A *double bill* (in America, *double feature*), was, and at a handful of repertory cinemas continues to be, a theatrical presentation of two films for the price of one. In America, the practice became popular in the Depression, and by the 1940s had become standard practice, but declined in the 1950s. Other 'double' usages include: *double eight*, another, much less common term for *8mm* film; *double exposure*, a method, now largely outmoded, of creating two simultaneous images by exposing the same film twice, at levels low enough to prevent overexposure; *double frame*, a film frame of twice the normal size used in certain wide-screen systems; *double framing*, the practice of printing each frame twice: the result is an unusual kind of slow motion effect, less fluent than the familiar slow motion produced by overcranking; *double key lighting*, lighting two parts of a scene with a *key*; *double pass system*, a kind of *matte* process; *double perf stock*, film with perforations along both edges, used in cameras with a double-sprocket drive; *double take*: either (a) in comedies, the old bit of business involving a calm look towards something, an unperturbed turning away, then a sudden spin around in astonishment or dismay; or (b) an editing flaw in which an action or part of an action appears to be performed twice; the result of an unintentional overlap between two shots.

Dougal   a name sometimes given by British film and television crews to the *wind sleeve* used to cover microphones in outdoor shooting; so called because its fuzzy surface and cylindrical shape are somewhat reminiscent of the shaggy, philosophical dog of that name in the children's puppet programme *The Magic Roundabout*.

down shot   a shot filmed looking down on an object or action.

down time   a hiatus in production caused by equipment failure or some other unavoidable delay.

dowser   a device that cuts off the beam of light from a spotlight or from a projector as the reels change.

dream balloon   in the silent cinema, a small circle or oval floating near the character's head and containing dreams or fantasies.

dress   to prepare a set with furniture and the like; *dresser*, as in the theatre: the wardrobe assistant who helps performers into and out of costume; *dress extra*, an extra who wears his or her own clothes or uniform, and is therefore given a bonus; *dress rehearsal*, a full-costume rehearsal of a scene (rather than, as in the theatre, of the whole text) staged immediately before shooting.

drive   the mechanism, powered by the motor, that feeds film through a camera.

drive-by shot   a shot of a (usually more or less static) object, person or scene taken from a moving vehicle as it passes by.

drive-in   a kind of outdoor cinema, rare to the point of invisibility in the UK (poor climate, poor economy, fewer cars) but highly popular in the United States between 1945 and the mid-1960s: viewers could simply drive their cars into a parking lot, rent individual speakers for the sound-track, and watch the film on a giant screen. The most famous image of a drive-in is, however, televisual, parodic and animated: it appears in the credit sequence for cartoon series *The Flintstones*, and shows the blue-collar caveman Fred Flintstone taking his family to a neolithic drive-in for a screening of a movie called *The Monster*. This is a fair indication of how common drive-ins had become by the early 1960s. Both the term and the institution of the drive-in cinema followed the example of America's earlier drive-in restaurants. In recent years, most of America's remaining drive-ins have been given over to *exploitation movies*, particularly *slashers*: for a critical survey of such fare, see Joe-Bob Briggs, *Joe-Bob Goes to the Drive-In*.

drop   much as in the theatre, an abbreviation of *back-drop*, a large curtain, painted with scenery and hung from a fly at the back of the set. The *Oxford Companion to the Theatre* states that drops came into theatrical use some time around 1690.

drop shadow   as in printing and graphics work: the method of making letters (usually in credit sequences or captions) stand out more clearly by giving them a slight shadow, so creating the effect of three-dimensionality.

dry box   a warm container in which processed film is gently dried after its chemical bath; it can be found at the *dry end* of the machinery for processing.

dry run   a technical rehearsal, either with or without actors, of camera movements.

dual role   the appearance by one actor in two roles within the same film, particularly in dramas or comedies about identical twins: Bette Midler and Lily Tomlin as two sets of town and country mice in Jim Abrams' *Big Business*; Matthew Modine as good and evil brothers in Alan Rudolph's *Equinox*.

dub (dubbing, postdubbing)   to dub a film is either (a) generally to add new components – dialogue, atmospheres, effects – to its sound-track after the shooting has been completed, or (b) more specifically, to add recorded dialogue, particularly when substituting dialogue in English for original dialogue in a foreign language. OED Supplement suggests that the verb is a shortened form of *to double*, and this seems highly likely. The *New York Times* in 1929 used *dub* to mean 're-recording from film to film'; and a cinema text-book from 1930 defines *dubbing* as 'a method of doubling the voice on the screen after the photographing of the picture'. A *dubbed version* is a foreign film for which an English translation has been supplied by dubbing rather than sub-titling (OED Supplement records an instance of the phrase from 1938); even when sensitively done, the effect is often faintly ludicrous.

Hence *dubber*, the playback machine used for *dubbing*; also *dubbing room* (also *dubbing stage, dubbing studio, dubbing theatre*); and a *dubbing session*, in which actors record dialogue for pre-shot scenes (see *looping*).

Dufaycolor   an additive colour process of the 1930s, said to have been abandoned because the images it produced tended to be too dark. It was, however, used to pleasing effect by Humphrey Jennings in two short films, *English Harvest* (1939) and *Design for Spring* (1938, a.k.a. *Making Fashion*), a display of new designs by Norman Hartnell. Both films have recently been re-released in new prints by the BFI.

dump tanks   these hold large quantities of water which, when released, can be filmed at close range and in slow motion so as to create the effect of floods, torrents, tormented seas and the like. Also known as *spill tanks*.

Dunning process   a relatively primitive method for filming actors against a moving background that had been shot somewhere else; in other words, a prototype *matte* process, devised in the 1920s by C. Dodge Dunning. It relied on separating foreground from background with coloured lights, and was therefore unsuitable for colour films.

dupe (also **dupe negative, duplicate negative**)   a copy – 'duplicate' – of the complete original or master negative of a film, made either as a precaution against possible damage or to allow simultaneous printing on one machine or more in the making of release prints. (Also known as an *interdupe*.) The term can also refer to a copy of an individual shot or shots, made to allow for various effects, superimposed credits and so on.

dutch angle   an image tilted noticeably either to the left or the right, and created by shifting the camera from its usual vertical and horizontal axes. Origin uncertain, but presumably related to the various insulting uses of the term which began during the period of commercial and military hostilities between Britain and the Netherlands in the 17th C, and particularly to the slur that the Dutch were heavy drinkers, as in 'Dutch courage'. (America seems to have borrowed the prejudice whole: there have been any number of opprobrious terms formed from 'Dutch', including 'in Dutch', meaning 'in disgrace' and 'to do a Dutch', meaning 'to desert, commit suicide'.) A Dutch angle would thus be the point of view characteristic of a drunk who is having difficulty in maintaining a vertical posture. The process of tilting the camera in this way is also known as *canting*.

Dykstraflex   the trade name for a motion control system – that is, a system capable of exactly repeating a sequence of movements and shots, most often used with *miniatures* – invented by John Dykstra and his team at the special effects company Industrial Light and Magic. It was first employed in George Lucas's *Star Wars* (1977).

Dynalens   the trade name for a device that may be mounted in front of a lens to prevent wobbling for zoom shots and the like.

Dynamation   the name – a portmanteau of 'dynamic' and 'animation' – coined by the stop-motion animator Ray Harryhausen (b. 1920) for his method of combining miniature models with live action, first deployed in *The Seventh Voyage of Sinbad* (1958).

dynamic cutting   a jagged, abrupt, highly obstrusive cutting style – the opposite of *continuity cutting* – in which images from various different sources are yoked violently together to create striking dramatic or visual effects effects rather than serve the purposes of linear narrative.

dynamic frame   the term was coined by Sergei Eisenstein in his lecture 'The Dynamic Square', delivered in Hollwyood on 17 September 1930 to a meeting of the Technicians Branch of the Academy of Motion Pictures Arts and Science; it was published in *Close-up*, vol. 8, no. 1 (March 1931) and no. 2 (June 1931), and has been republished in a slightly revised version in *Eisenstein: Writings 1922–1934*, edited by Richard Taylor (BFI, 1988). What Eisenstein proposed here was that the 'compositional possibilities' of the cinema had been crippled for three decades by a slavish and unthinking adherence to a horizontal rectangular frame; that, for various reasons, the ideal shape for the film image was actually the square; and that the square in question should be 'dynamic' – 'that is to say,' Eisenstein continues, 'providing in its dimensions the opportunity of impressing, in projection, with absolute grandeur every geometrically conceivable form of the picture limit.' (*Dynamic* enters the English language in the early 19th C as a term in mechanics, meaning 'of or pertaining to force producing motion' – and thus also, by the later 19th C, as an antonym for *static*. It came from Fr *dynamique* and Gk *dynamikos*, 'powerful'.) Eisenstein's implication – though his phrasing is slightly cryptic at times – seems to be that film-makers should be able to alter the size and shape of their images to match their subject-matter. Needless to say, the Academy did not rush to embrace the Soviet director's proposals, and there have been very few experiments with the dynamic frame since 1930. Probably the most notable of this handful is *The Door in the Wall*, made under the patronage of the BFI's Experimental Film Fund by Glen Alvey Jr in 1955. Alvey was able to change the size and shape of his images by devising up a masking film which, when printed over the original, would screen off the unwanted parts of the frame.

dynamic range   in sound recording, the difference between the softest and the loudest points of an audio system.

Eady levy   the now defunct money-raising scheme for British cinema, also known as the British Film Production Fund. It was named for Sir Wilfred Eady, a treasury official, and introduced as a voluntary measure in 1950, becoming compulsory in 1957 under the terms of the Cinematograph Films Act. The scheme was simple enough: a small percentage of takings at the UK box-office were collected by HM Customs and Excise and passed on to the British Film Fund Agency, which would in turn distribute it to the nation's film-makers in proportion to their domestic earnings.

Ealing   as most British and many overseas viewers still know, the phrase 'Ealing film' refers to one of the much-loved productions made at Ealing Studios in West London between 1931 and 1952 (and for a few years after that at Pinewood), and particularly one of their small but distinguished clutch of eccentric comedies about bizarre events taking place in banal circumstances, such as *The Lavender Hill Mob* (Charles Crichton, 1951), *Passport to Pimlico* (Henry Cornelius, 1951), *The Ladykillers* (Alexander Mackendrick, 1955) and so on. The studios were built by a company called Associated Talking Pictures, and originally specialised in inexpensive productions aimed at the home market – musicals starring George Formby, Gracie Fields and other popular entertainers. During the war, Ealing turned to producing action features and military information films such as Thorold Dickinson's *The Next of Kin* (1941); they kept up the action tradition after the war with the likes of *Scott of the Antarctic* (1948) and *The Cruel Sea* (1952), but it was the Ealing comedies, most of them made between 1949 and 1955, that have earned the company its immortality. The brilliance and unmistakable house style of these films has generally been attributed to Ealing's careful maintenance of a regular production team of writers (notably T.E.B. Clarke) – most Ealing films were based on original screenplays, loosely inspired by real-life incidents – and of directors (notably Crichton, Mackendrick and Robert Hamer). Ealing was also responsible for *Dead of Night* (1945), a portmanteau ghost-story film which, for all its patchiness, contains some of the most chilling and poetic scenes the British cinema has produced: the episodes by Hamer and Alberto Cavalcanti are particularly fine. Financial difficulties drove the company out of business in 1955; the studio buildings survive, however, and since 1952 have been owned and operated by the BBC, though it now seems that they will be taken over by the National Film and Television School.

Eastman Color   a tripack *colour* film, first introduced by the Eastman Kodak company in 1952, which, since it was both cheaper and far more flexible than its precursors, quickly replaced *Technicolor* as the principal colour process used in moving pictures. The stock has been improved at various stages over the last four decades, and is now widely used throughout the United States and Europe.

Eclair   the proprietory name for the cameras made by Eclair International Diffusion, a French manufacturer; notably for their lightweight, portable 35mm camera, the Eclair Camiflex 35. Virtually soundless and fitted with a magazine that could be changed in a matter of seconds, it rapidly became an invaluable tool for documentaries with synchronised sound, though European film-makers also used it for shooting feature films.

ECU   see *extreme close-up.*

edge fog (or **edge flare**)   accidental over-exposure sometimes found at the edges of a reel of film, resulting from light leakage in the magazine, from the film having been too loosely rolled, or from its being clumsily handled during loading; *edge numbers*, see *key numbers*; *edge track*, the sound track on magnetic film.

edgewax   a lubricant of trichlorethane and paraffin wax used to protect the edges of film in editing or projection.

edit, editing   from L *edit-us*, past participle form of *edere*, to put forth; the literary sense of the word – 'to prepare or publish a work by an earlier author' – comes into English in the late 18th C. To edit a film is to create a set of visual narratives, arguments or metaphors by the simple process of joining together various strips of exposed film (or, in the case of video editing, by entering frame numbers into a computer); and, usually, to complete the process by mixing and adding sound tracks to the resulting images. OED suggests that the first cinematic use of the verb *edit* comes in 1917, from *Scientific American*: 'Editing a film is perhaps the most interesting phase of laboratory work'; and though the Dictionary's suggestion that the principal labour involved in editing is 'eliminating unwanted material, etc.' is more than a little misleading, this definition does accurately catch one specific use which still persists: to edit (or *edit out*) can simply mean 'to remove one or more pieces of film' or 'to shorten'. But the business or art of editing amounts to far more than simple elimination: it is in many respects a process analogous to writing, and is a matter of creating not just stories but, so to speak, counterpoints, harmonies and dissonances with individual units of film. The task of editing is carried out by an *editor* (or, less often, *cutter*); the same *Scientific American* article from 1917 suggests that the editor is 'usually the director himself in dramatic productions', though this doubling of roles is now extremely rare in the commercial cinema, and a more reliable definition comes from Brunel's *Filmcraft*, 1935: 'one who cuts, assembles, edits and titles a film'. Today, the editor usually works in close association with the director (and sometimes the producer), and one or more *assistant editors*. The basic tools found in a traditional *editing room* (*cutting room, edit suite*) include various **bins** and an *editing table*, such as a **Steenbeck**, on which film can be viewed, cut and spliced. Editing usually begins while the film is still being shot, with the assembling of **dailies** or **rushes** into short, provisional sequences. From this, the editing will gradually proceed to a **rough assembly** (or *rough cut, rough edit*) of the whole film, often a good deal longer than the completed version; a more polished *fine cut* and eventually the *final cut*, approved by the studio, to which the negative may then be conformed. Such a straightforward list of tools and tasks cannot, however, begin to hint at the complexity of the subject of editing and editing styles, about which many books have been written. Despite the importance of their contribution to the cinema – in certain instances, it can be argued, every bit as great as that of directors – few editors have yet to achieve very much attention outside the industry itself; rare exceptions to this rule include Martin Scorsese's usual editor Thelma Schoonmaker. For an eloquent investigation of this neglect, see *Portrait of an Invisible Man : The Working Life of Stewart McAllister, Film Editor* (BFI, 1983) by Dai Vaughan, himself an editor.

Editor's sync, also known as *dead sync* or *editorial sync*, is the stage of post-production in which images and sound are matched against each other frame for frame; it is the stage immediately prior to the final mix.

Editola, is the trade name of a brand of editing machine widely used in the 1930s and afterwards, but now uncommon if not unknown.

effects (FX) (or, in the case of **special effects, SFX**)   the most illusory elements of an art founded on illusion; either (a) the various transitional devices, such as *dissolves* or *fades* or *wipes* that are introduced into the film during *post-production*; or (b) the more or less spectacular sights and sounds which are added to footage after it has been shot, for example by *matte* processes; or (c) the mechanical devices (prosthetics, exploding blood sacs, robotic dinosaur feet and so on) used on set to create magical or horrible sights. The word 'effects' is from the L *effectus*, the noun of action from *efficere*, 'to work out, accomplish', and comes into English via OF *effect* in the late 14th C. OED notes a theatrical use of the term in 1881, and a cinematic sense as early as 1911.

An *effects film* is a feature which leans heavily on its special effects for box office appeal; an *effects filter* is any optical filter used to create an artificial appearance in the resulting image, such as *day for night*; an *effects projector* is a front- or rear-projector used in in a special effects sequence; and an **effects track** is the channel which contains the sound effects to be added during the *dub*.

EHS   the abbreviation for Extreme High Shot – a shot taken from a position far above the subject.

EI   an abbreviation for *emulsion in*, the opposite of *EO, emulsion out*: both terms refer to the direction in which film is wound around a core or spool.

eight-ball, eight-ball microphone   a microphone used for sound effects or for recording single voices, so called because of its resemblance to the black ball used in playing pool.

eight-millimetre, 8mm   before the advent of relatively inexpensive forms of video technology, 8mm film, the narrowest, was the standard gauge of the home-movie enthusiast, particularly (after 1965) in the widely available form of *Super-8*, which, since its perforations are smaller than standard 8mm stock, has a wider and higher frame. Though standard 8mm film is now obsolete, Super-8 has in recent years been used by a number of professional film-makers – not merely for creating the effect of home-movie sequences within feature films, but for its distinctive colours and grain, which can be very appealing when blown up to 16mm or 35mm. (Its cheapness is also appealing, of course.) The late Derek Jarman made use of 8mm in some of his films, notably *The Angelic Conversation*, as has the Australian director Paul Cox.

EK   originally an abbreviation for Eastman Kodak, the term now applies to any release print made directly from the original negative, and thus of extremely high quality.

Ektachrome   a low contrast 16mm colour stock introduced to the market by Eastman Kodak in 1958 as a replacement for Kodachrome. It is most commonly used for making prints.

electric department   the crew which carries out all electrical work on a shoot, particularly its lighting. Members of the team are known, straightforwardly, as electricians. The chief electrician is the *gaffer*, his assistant the *best boy*.

electronic press kit (EPK)   a short video documentary about a production, usually including clips of the finished film, issued to press and television by way of promotion; see *press kit*.

electroprinting   the process of transferring sound directly from the master magnetic track to the release print, rather than from an optical sound-track printing master.

Elemack dolly   see *spider dolly*.

elevator   a support which moves the camera vertically up or down, so producing an *elevator shot*.

ellipsoidal spot   a spotlight that uses ellipsoidal lenses to produce an extremely sharp beam.

elliptical cutting   a rapid and sometimes disconcerting editing style which omits many or all of the usual transitional devices that make for an apparently seamless flow of images.

ELR   the abbreviation for *Electronic Line Replacement*; see *loop*.

ELS   see *extreme long shot*.

EMI   the British company which became involved in film production after 1969 (when it bought Associated British, the owner of Elstree Studios). In 1979, it was merged into Thorn-EMI; in 1986, it sold its film business to the Cannon group.

Empire   a popular British film magazine, founded in the 1980s and appealing to a young general audience of fans rather than the more specialist and generally older readers who would buy, say, *Sight and Sound*; the apparently jingoistic title alludes to the fact that many British cinemas used to be named 'Empire'. (Some still are – the Empire, Leicester Square, for example.) *Empire Marketing Board Film Unit*, see *Crown Film Unit*.

emulsion   the dull, light-sensitive chemical layer coated on to the celluloid base of film stock. The word is used from the very beginnings of photography: thus J.F.W. Herschel in 1840: 'My first attention was directed to the discovery of a liquid, or emulsion, which by a single application, whether by dipping or brushing over, should communicate the desired quality [of sensitiveness]'; *emulsion batch*, the quantity of emulsion produced at a given time; because each batch will have slightly different properties, some companies print an *emulsion number* – a code which indicates the specific chemical batch – on each roll of film; *emulsion position*, in projection, the position of the emulsion relative to the projection lamp; in *A Wind* it faces towards the lamp, in *B wind* towards the screen; *emulsion speed*, the degree to which an emulsion is responsive to light. High emulsion speeds are necessary in dim environments, or the film will be underexposed; low emulsion speeds are used in bright environments. The choice of emulsion also helps determine the quality of the final image: its grain, its degree of *saturation* and so on.

end credits   see *credits*.

end slate   the clapperboard as used to signal the end of a given scene.

enlargement printing   the process of enlarging (see *blow-up*) a frame size in an optical printer – from 16mm to 35mm, say.

environmental sound   the actual background noises of a location; its atmosphere.

epic   a term handled somewhat more loosely or brusquely by the film world than by literary scholars, and generally used to mean either (a) a costly, or costly-looking production set in some version or other of the ancient world, such as *Ben Hur, Cleopatra, Spartacus* or, more recently, *Rob Roy*; or (b) any film with a broad canvas, from Abel Gance's *Napoléon* to David Lean's *Lawrence of Arabia*, from Kubrick's *2001, A Space Odyssey* to Coppola's *Apocalypse Now* – all of which may be considered among the more intellectually respectable epics, since the form has tended to be more appealing to with mass audience than to the cognoscenti. Aldous Huxley actually speaks of *Birth of a Nation* as an 'epic in pictures' in a letter dated 19 March 1916, and the habit of use seems to have been established by about 1940. A more flippant, and much-repeated definition states that an Epic is 'any film starring Charlton Heston'.

episode film   a portmanteau film; a dramatic feature made up of several self-contained or interlocking short stories, either by one director, such as D.W. Griffith's *Intolerance* (1916), Roberto Rosselini's *Paisa* (1946) and Jean Renoir's *Le Petit Théâtre de Jean Renoir* (1969), or by several, as in *RoGoPaG* (1962), by Rossellini, Godard, Pasolini and Gregoretti. They can tend to the uneven, as in Ealing Studios production *Dead of Night* (Alberto Cavalcanti and others, 1945; see *Ealing*), or – to stay within the Gothic field – *Dr Terror's House of Horrors* (Freddie Francis, 1964), *Creepshow* (George A Romero, 1982), *Twilight Zone – the Movie* (Steven Spielberg, Joe Dante and others, 1983) and *Necronomicon* (1994).

EPK   see *Electronic press kit, press kit*.

equalizer   an electronic device used to modify the frequency response of a circuit, particularly in sound equipment; hence

equalization (EQ)   the process of *equalizing* sound tracks, either in recording or (more often) in re-recording or mixing; that is to say, for changing the relationship of bass to treble sounds and generally to improve the sound quality.

Equity   the actors' union in both the United Kingdom (founded 1929) and the United States of America.

erect image   an image that is right-side up.

errors and omissions (E and O)   a category of insurance, drawn up to protect production companies and studios either from charges of plagiarism (as in the celebrated case brought by the humorous writer Art Buchwald against Paramount, Eddie Murphy and Arsenio Hall over *Coming to America*, which he claimed had been lifted without acknowledgement from his own treatment), or charges of defamation of character and the like.

escape film   any film about a break-out from a prison, POW camp and the like; most examples of the genre have been routine thrillers (*The Great Escape*, directed by John Sturges and starring Steve McQueen, is the most popular example), but at least two – Renoir's *La Grande Illusion* and Bresson's *Un Condamné à mort s'est échappé* – are acknowledged masterpieces.

Essanay   An early production company in the United States, now remembered mainly for the comedies it made with Charlie Chaplin from 1915–16, the period of his career between leaving Keystone and joining Mutual. The company's name was taken from the initials of its co-founders, George K. Spoor and G.M. Anderson; it remained in business from 1907 until 1917, when it was bought out by Vitagraph.

establish   to introduce and make plain to the audience the identity and nature of a character, a location and so on; hence the more common term *establishing shot*, the image – usually a *long shot* or *extreme long shot* of a cityscape, building, prairie or what have you – which, in conventional editing, begins each new sequence, showing the audience the location in which the subsequent action will be taking place until the scene changes. OED records the first occurence of 'establishing shot' in Lindgren's *Art of Film*, 1948, but it is safe to say that it must have been in use for some time before this date.

Estar   the trade name for a widely-used polyester base developed by Eastman Kodak, favoured for being stronger than acetate bases.

Everyman   the well-known repertory cinema in Hampstead that has been in business since 1933, played host to the British premières of, *inter alia*, Renoir's *La Regle du jeu* (1933) and Vigo's *Zéro de conduite* (1933). It has somehow, heroically, managed to survive a commercial climate that has wiped out almost all of the capital's other repertory cinemas.

exciter lamp   a small, extremely bright lamp which shines through the optical sound track of a film (a) when sound is being recorded or (b) when sound is being played back in projection; the resulting light pattern is converted into sound waves by an optical sound reader.

executive producer   the title given to the person or persons who (a) keeps an eye on the projects of the producers employed by a particular studio or company, or who (b), on a single production, is in charge of financing the film directly or raising the finance, and then of allocating funds.

exhibition   the screening, generally for profit, of a film to an audience. (From L *exhibit-*, from *exhibere*, to hold out. Forms of the verb have been in use in English since the late 15th C.)

exhibitor   the person or persons who arrange the screening; or sometimes, the cinema where films are shown.

expanded cinema   a term coined in the early 1970s and applied to films that use new forms of image-making technology, such as holograms or computer graphics.

experimental film   see *avant-garde*.

explainer, *explicador*   In the early days of cinema in Spain, when audiences were unfamiliar with the basic grammar of film which today seems perfectly natural to us, a man – the *explicador*, or explainer – would be stationed by the side of the screen to explain what was happening. The *explicador* would use a long pointer to indicate characters on the screen, and would give a running commentary on the action as it unfolded so that no one would be baffled. By about 1920, most audiences had got the hang of the new medium and the *explicadors* had to find new jobs. (Gert Hoffmann's novel *The Film Explainer*, recently published in an English translation by his son Michael, is about a German practitioner of the art.) Elsewhere in the world, however – in African countries, for example – 'explainers' were employed as recently as the 1950s. (See Carriere, 7–8.)

exploitation film   usually: a cheaply made film which relies on explicit displays of sex (hence the portmanteau term 'sexploitation'), graphic passages of violence or sordid and sensationalist subject matter to reach an audience. Occasionally: an expensive film made in much the same spirit, such as Paul Verhoeven's *Showgirls*.

exposure   (a) the general term for the act of bathing film stock in light so as to produce the latent images which are then brought out in processing, or (b) the amount of light needed to create such images, or (c) the length of time needed to create such images, or (d) the area exposed. (From L *exponere*, to put out, by way of the 14th CFr *exposer*; the English term is as old as photography: 'in one specimen which had been exposed only thirty seconds, the plate was still intensely black, excepting in the sky': 1839). As these various uses may suggest, the degree of exposure is determined by the amount of light on a given scene; the length of time for which the film is exposed; and the extent to which the lens is opened. An over-exposed image will be too bright and pallid; an under-exposed image too murky.

Exposure index (EI) (or *exposure rating*), the manufacturer's indication of the sensitivity to light of a given stock, expressed in ASA, ISO or DIN numbers; *exposure latitude,* the range within which a film can be satisfactorily exposed; *exposure meter* (or **light meter**), the instrument used by the cinematographer or cameraman to measure the intensity of light in a scene. There are two main types: the incident light meter, which measures direct light, and the reflected light meter.

Expressionism   the cinematic counterpart to the Expressionist movement in painting (and, later, the other arts), which can be seen to originate in the works of Van Gogh, Gaugin, Munch, Ensor, the Fauves (especially Matisse) and others, though nowadays the term is mainly applied to a group of German artists working in the period following the First World War, particularly those influenced by the surviving members of the *Blaue Reiter* group. The term, which appears to have been coined by German art critics, was taken up in Britain as early as 1908: 'The appearance of these later and more extreme forms of expressionism . . .' (*Edinburgh Review*).

Though Expressionist works in other media may be said to date from around 1903, or even earlier, the principal Expressionist films were made between 1919 (the year of Robert Weine's *The Cabinet of Dr Caligari*) and 1933 (the year of the great book-burning ordered by Dr Goebbels). The defining features of these films were a fascination with the monstrous, the morbid and the macabre, conveyed in a visual style dominated by shadows, angular or otherwise distorted compositions, and manifestly artificial interiors – factors which, despite some evocative accounts of the movement's debt to the dark vein in German Romanticism, can quite often be directly attributed to the frequent power shortages and slender budgets of the day. *Caligari* apart, probably the most influential of all Expressionist films was Murnau's *Nosferatu, eine Symphonie des Grauens* (1922), an early film treatment of the Dracula myth (loosely remade by Werner Herzog as *Nosferatu: Phantom der Nacht* in 1979); other important Expresionist films by Murnau include *Der Letzte Mann* (1924) and *Faust* (1926), though many other directors contributed to the cycle of films, including Fritz Lang, Ewald Dupont and the American-born Arthur Robison. Expressionist visual compositions were widely imitated in other countries – James Whale's *Frankenstein,* for example, is strongly expressionist, as at certain points is *Citizen Kane* – and its characteristic angular compositions and highly contrasted lighting schemes are often said to have been taken over almost wholesale in *film noir;* a great deal of the critical commentary on this point has been somewhat overstated, however, and the widespread assumption that the characteristic murk and contrast of *film noir* is directly attributable to German emigré cinematographers and directors who had been schooled in Expressionist cinema does not seem to stand up to prolonged investigation. Expressionism's most immediately recognisable marks have often, in recent years, been pastiched by the directors of rock videos and movies with a self-consciously Gothic feel, such as Tim Burton's hugely successful films about the comic-book hero *Batman* and *Batman Returns*, which latter boasts a villain (played by Christopher Walken) called Max Schreck, by way of *hommage* to the extraordinary, cadaverous star of the original *Nosferatu*.

EXT   the standard screenplay abbreviation for *exterior*: any scene shot out of doors

extended scene   in editing: part of a workprint with a piece of leader (see *slug*) cut in to indicate that a scene needs to be made longer or completed.

extension tube   a type of lens attachment used in filming *close-ups*; it takes the lens away from the camera so as to bring the subject into sharp focus.

external rhythm   see *rhythm*.

extra   a non-speaking and usually uncredited member of the cast used in street scenes, crowds, bars and the like; extras tend to be semi-profesionals or amateurs, employed on a casual basis. The term has been used in the theatre since the late 18th C, and was in common use by film-makers by 1916. The poet Fiona Pitt-Kethley, who has supplemented her literary income by working as an extra, has written a number of poems about the experience, including 'Old Extras', 'Merging' and 'Bond Girl'.

extreme close-up (ECU, XCU)   a close-up so tight that it shows only a small detail: an eye, a mouth, a bullet, a key; *extreme high-angle shot, extreme high shot (EHS, XHS)*, a shot taken from a very long way above the subject, for example from a high building or helicopter; also known as a *bird's-eye shot; extreme long shot (ELS)*, a shot taken at a considerable distance from its subject, and often serving as an *establishing shot; extreme low-angle shot*, a shot taken from roughly floor level (or below, if the floor is transparent), or otherwise looking up at the subject; *extreme wide-angle lens*, a *fish-eye lens*, which can give a field of vision as wide as 180 degrees, causing a great deal of circular distortion.

eye   *eye contact* the moment when a performer in a feature looks directly into the camera – a technique quite popular in the 1960s, for example in *Tom Jones* and *Alfie; eye-level shot*, a shot taken from about five to six feet above the ground, thus approximating the point of view of the average person when standing; *eye light* (or *catch light*), a small light mounted near the camera that can put a shine in a performer's eyes without affecting the overall exposure of the scene; see also *kicker; eye line*, (a) the direction in which a particular actor can see; visitors to a set and other non-essential personnel may be told to clear the actor's eye-line so as not to be a distraction; (b) a type of cut, in which a shot of a performer looking at someone or something is immediately followed by a shot of what is seen; *eye piece*, the part of the camera through which the cameraman can see what is being filmed.

F see *f-stop*
f number see *f-stop*.
    f-stop   as in still photography: the number on the lens which indicates how far the aperture is open, and thus how much light can pass through the lens onto the unexposed film. Also known as the *f number*.

factual film   see *documentary*

fade   derived from the verb meaning to grow dim, faint or pale, used in English since the early 14th C, and derived from the OF *fader*, itself from the adjective *fade*: 'vapid, insipid, dull'. OED records the first occurence of the cinematic sense in 1918 as a verb, meaning to make an image pass gradually in or out of view on the screen. Today, 'fade' tends to be used mainly as a noun, meaning a type of optical effect in which the image on screen gradually ebbs away, often though not always to black; the verb form also persists.

A fade generally indicates a major change of time and space within the narrative, though some less conventional film-makers have used it for other purposes. In Kieslowski's *Trois couleurs: bleu* (1993), for example, fades to black are repeatedly introduced to otherwise continuous action, apparently so as to represent the heroine's disordered frame of mind, while in Scorsese's *The Age of Innocence*, a sudden fade to red from a close-up on the face of the Countess Olenska (Michelle Pfeiffer) hints that social ostracism in old New York might be regarded as a metaphorical form of bloody murder. In his essay 'Don't Make Waves' (1967), the screenwriter George Garrett gives an admirably concise definition of the effect in its most common form:

In the Fade the image disappears and the screen goes black. It is a real interruption in the sequence. Quite as formidable as the curtain coming down in the theater. For that reason it was and still is often used in much the same way as a curtain ending an act. There is always a risk that it may break the spell; for in fact everything does stop.

Strictly speaking, however, Garrett is here describing a *fade-out* (or *fade down*); the practice of opening a major scene with *fade-in* (or *fade up*) is also common. Moreover, until the 1960s, fades were not always reserved for major end-of-act transitions, but might also be used to begin and end less significant scenes. Fades can be executed in the camera by opening or closing the aperture, but are more often achieved with an optical printer. In the early years of the cinema, the term *fadeaway* was also used: 'Note the "fadeaway" at the beginning and the end of the reel, whereby all things emerge from the twilight and sink back into the twilight at last' (Vachel Lindsay, *The Art of the Moving Picture*). Sound tracks – particularly music tracks – can also be faded in and out; a *fader* is the device which adjusts the stength of a signal in an optical or audio system. See *dissolve*.

failsafe   a device used in projection, which automatically stops the projector if the film breaks, buckles or is otherwise damaged.

fall-in   the point at which a sychronous motor hits the correct speed for synchronisation.

fall-off   the term most commonly refers to the way in which illumination becomes more feeble as the distance from a light source increases; it must be taken into account when a scene is being lit. In projection, it refers to the decreasing brightness from the centre to the sides of the screen.

false reverse   a reverse shot that disturbs the audience's sense of the space within a scene, because it breaks the 180 degree rule; see *imaginary line*.

fan   abbreviated from 'fanatic': the term originates in America *c.* 1889, and was originally applied to followers of team sports, particularly baseball. A member of the viewing public with an ardent (possibly excessively ardent) admiration for a particular actor, actress, genre (as in 'horror fan'), director or what have you. Someone who is a fan of the cinema as a whole is more typically referred to as a *buff*.

fantasy   though all products of the cinema, including documentaries, in some measure consist of or make an appeal to fantasies, a fantasy film is generally understood to be the type of production which relies heavily on exploiting the medium's infinite capacity for creating marvels and curiosities: science fiction films, horror movies, fairy tales and the like. If the Lumière Brothers were the fathers of cinema in its realist and/or documentary modes, then Méliès was the father of the fantastic strain: his descendants include the likes of James Whale (*Frankenstein* and *The Bride of Frankenstein*), Tod Browning (*Dracula*), Jean Cocteau (*Orphée, La Belle et la Bête*), Jacques Tourneur (*Night of the Demon*), Powell and Pressburger (*A Matter of Life and Death, The Red Shoes, Tales of Hoffman*), Neil Jordan (*The Company of Wolves*), Jan Svankmajer (*Faust*), David Cronenberg (*The Fly*) and Steven Spielberg (*Close Encounters of the Third Kind, Jurassic Park*). In another sense, the cinema itself is nothing other than a fantasy: the ultimate Greek root of the word is *phantasia*, 'a making visible', from *phantasein*, 'to make visible'. The word comes into English via OF *fantasie* in the 14th century, in a range of meanings including a spectral apparition or phantom; an illusory appearance; a hallucination or delusion ('This fool of fantasie': Chaucer, *Troilus and Criseyde*), and so on.

farce   as on the stage: a broad, fast-moving comedy, involving a good deal of physical humour and, often, a tightly restricted plot and/or location. Not all cinematic farce is aesthetically negligible: that most delightful of all genres, the *screwball comedy*, is heavily dependent on farcical action.

far shot   outmoded name for a *long shot*.

fast   *fast cutting* see *accelerated montage*; *fast film* (or *fast stock*): stocks that are highly sensitive to light, and therefore well suited to filming in dark sets or in natural light; any film with an ASA higher than

100; similarly, a *fast lens* has a fairly large aperture, and is used in combination with fast film; *fast motion*, see *accelerated motion*.

favour   to bring the camera or microphone closer to one particular performer, so emphasising his or her presence in the scene; or to create a similar emphasis by selective lighting.

Feathercam   the proprietory name of an unusually light (about 9lb) and easily portable 35mm camera, the full name of which is the Feathercam CM35.

feature (feature film)   a full-length dramatic film, as opposed to a short, a documentary etc. The term was originally used to suggest the type of film that had some attractive element, such as a well-known actor or sensational subject matter, which could be 'featured' in publicity. Then, as audiences gradually learned to consider extended running time an attraction in its own right, a 'feature film' came to mean any film over two reels in length. Until the 1960s, it was common practice for cinemas to run a *double feature* policy, with a *main, first* or *A feature* as the main attraction and a shorter *supporting* or *B feature*, as well as cartoons, newsreels and the like. To qualify as a full-length feature, rather than a short, a dramatic film must nowadays have a running time of at least 85 minutes; the most common running times are between 90 to 120 minutes; features much longer than 180 minutes are rare, partly because they are strongly disliked by cinema owners, who like to squeeze in several shows a day. A *feature documentary*, according to the rules of the American Academy, must be at least 30 minutes long. As a verb, to *feature* nowadays generally means 'to present in a non-starring role'; a *featured player* is an actor somewhere down the totem pole from the leads, though above all the *day players*, who take minor speaking parts in the production.

feed   (a) as a verb: to run film into a camera or projector; (b) as a noun, the mechanism or mechanisms which perform this function. Hence *feed chamber*, the chamber full of unexposed film which feeds film through the camera and then back up into the take-up chamber of a magazine; *feed plate*, the disc opposite the take-up plate on a *Steenbeck* or other editing machine; *feed reel*, the front reel on a projector, etc. In shooting, *feed lines* are the lines of dialogue spoken off-camera as a cue for the on-camera actors.

feet per minute (FPM)   see *footage*.

FEKS   abbrevation for *Fabrika eksentricheskovo aktyora*, or 'Factory of the Eccentric Actor', a group founded in Leningrad in 1921, originally with the intention of reforming Soviet theatre, though its members (notably Grigori Kosintsev and Ilya Trauberg) soon found themselves involved in film-making. The group's first proper film was a weird and fanciful comedy about a bank robbery, *Pokhozhdeniya Oktyabrini* (*The Adventures of Oktyabrinia*, 1924), and they went on to make several more in equally fantastic vein, some of which show the influence of *Futurism*. Before long, however, Kosintsev and Trauberg became dissatisfied with the crankiness and aestheticism of the FEKS approach, and the group was disbanded in 1929. Kosintsev carried on directing until the 1970s, and is best known in the West for his Shakespearean productions *Hamlet* (1964) and *King Lear* (1972).

'fell off the back of a movie'   jocular British phrase sometimes applied to props, costumes and so on stolen from a production, usually by way of souvenir; compare the well-known expresion for stolen goods 'fell off the back of a lorry'.

FEMIS   see *IDHEC*.

festival   an event at which film-makers, publicists, press and public congregate to see, sell or celebrate new (and occasionally old) films, give and receive prizes and advance careers, or pursue the chance for amorous and other kinds of diversion. The most famous international festival is the annual gathering at *Cannes*, which has been held regularly since 1946 with the exception of 1948, 1950 and 1968; the first two were cancelled as a result of in-fighting within the French film industry and a shortage of funds, while the third was abandoned after a series of political demonstrations, supported by Godard, Truffaut and others. Venice, Berlin, London and Edinburgh also play host to annual festivals, as do many major American cities; in recent years, the Telluride festival in Colorado has become an important launch-pad for independent films and film-makers. There are also a number of smaller, specialist festivals, devoted to animation, horror films, thrillers and the like.

FG   abbreviation for *foreground*.

FIAF (Federation Internationale des Archives de Film)   a union of national film archives, first established in 1938 by agreement between the four major institutions of the day: the Cinémathèque Française, the British National Film Archive, the Berlin Reichsfilmarchiv and the Film Department of the Museum of Modern Art, New York. Though its activities were cut short by the war, it reconvened in Paris in 1946 and rapidly began to attract new members.

field (also **field of action, action field, field of view**)   the space or angle covered by the lens, and therefore the area eventually visible on screen. It varies according both to the focal length of the lens and the distance between the camera and the subject being filmed. *Field camera*, a light-weight camera used for documentaries and the like; or the camera used by the *second unit*. The optical sense of the word 'field' enters the language in the mid-18th C: 'It filled the field of the telescope' – Maty, 1765; in its obvious geographical and related senses, the word has been common in English for almost a thousand years, and is derived from OE *feld*.

fill   (a) a blank or junk piece of film put into a *work print* during the early stages of editing to keep it in sync; or (b) an abbreviation for *fill light*, a smaller, secondary lamp placed near the camera and used to tone down the shadows cast by the *key light* and soften the look of the image.

film   from OE *filmen*, a membrane, caul or prepuce; by the 17th C, 'film' can mean an extremely thin pellicle or lamina of any material ('The painted film but of a stronger bubble' – Francis Quarles, *Emblemes*, 1635). The photographic sense appears to be about as old as the practice of photography: OED's earliest citation is from 1845. The first cinematographic citation is from 1897, where it means a celluloid roll used for a cinema picture: various modern senses of the word follow thick and fast in the first decade or so of the twentieth century. These senses include (a) a motion picture, movie or feature; (b) a frequently used abbreviation for *film stock* – the long strips of material used in shooting moving pictures, made of an acetate base, coated with a light-sensitive emulsion, and perforated at the edge; or the exposed, processed and distributed prints used in projection; (c) the art of the cinema in general (OED's first citation: 1911); (d) a common verb for either (i) the whole process of making a motion picture (OED: 1915) or (ii) the specific act of shooting a particular scene or action or object, etc; hence *filming*.

An exhaustive list of the compound terms for which 'film' is the qualifier would fill a short book of its own. To list a few of the more significant ones: a *film archive* is a store or library where films are kept, generally for scholarly or other cultural purposes, as at the National Film Archive; *film base* is the foundation of *film stock*, on which light-sensitive emulsion is coated; *film buff*, an knowledgeable enthusiast for the cinema; see *buff*; *film capacity*, the amount of film a given unit can hold; *film chamber*, the lightproof container on a camera for both exposed and unexposed film; *film clips*, see *clips*; *film criticism*, see *criticism*; *film festival*, see *festival*; *film grammar*, see *grammar*; *film loader*, the crew member on a large production in charge of loading and unloading rolls of film into and from the camera, a job otherwise performed by the *first assistant cameraman*; *film loop*, see *loop*; *film magazine*, see *magazine*; *film review*, a more or less critical evaluation of a film by a print or broadcast journalist; *film running speed*, the speed, measured in frames per second, at which film passes through a camera or projector; *film speed*, the exposure index of a given stock; *film splicer*, see *splicer*.

Film by, A   flashed up on screen at the start or (less often) the end of a movie, these three apparently innocent words are often the blazon of an overweening directorial ego – 'A Film by Sid Truck' – and are the long-term, largely unexpected fallout of the French *auteur theory* or *politique des auteurs*; indeed, they are the anglicised form of the rather more neutral French expression *un film de*. They imply, or more accurately shriek to the world, that it is the director, rather than the producer or writer or star or cinematographer who is the true genius behind and sole possessor of the work in question. Gore Vidal has made rather too much mileage of the first time he was horrified and amused at encountering the phrase, applied to the best-forgotten work of a jobbing director; but his spleen has a point. *Caveat emptor.*

filmic   a slightly uncommon synonym for *cinematic*, which crops up in such expressions as *filmic space* – the illusion of real, three-dimensional space created by and within two-dimensional moving images – and *filmic* *time*, the corresponding illusion of temporal sequence created within the 90 minutes or so of real time during which the film is projected.

film-maker, filmmaker   often used simply a synonym for *director*, though it can also refer to anyone who has a relatively important part in a production (the producers, writers, crew etc.), especially when used in the plural.

film noir or **film noir**, sometimes abbreviated to **noir**   literally 'black film': at the simplest level, a term coined by French critics (though long since given full citizenship of both the UK and the USA) to designate the cynical, fatalistic thrillers made in the United States during the 1940s and 1950s. The term continues to be widely used in journalism, criticism and general cultivated chit-chat, for all the world as though it were perfectly clear what it meant; and yet there is such vagueness about it what exactly it designates that it tends to fall apart under close scrutiny. Does *film noir* designate a genre (one writer called it 'the genre that never was'), a visual or ethical style, a cycle of films, a social or intellectual tendency? Are there, in fact, really such things as *films noirs* at all? Some of the confusion here is due to the fact that the phrase doesn't originate among film-makers: a director of the 1940s would never have consciously set out to make a *film noir* as he might have set out to make a Western or a war picture.

The first recorded use of '*film noir*' appears to be in an article run on 28 August 1946 by one Nino Frank in the pages of *Ecran français*, No. 61. The films to which he applied this new label were *Double Indemnity* (Billy Wilder, 1944), *Farewell My Lovely* (Edward Dymytryk, 1944), *Laura* (Otto Preminger, 1944) and *The Woman in the Window* (Fritz Lang, 1944). Frank's coinage was enthusiastically taken up by other critics, noticeably Jeanne-Pierre Chartier in 'Les Américains aussi font des films noirs' (*La Revue de Cinéma*, No. 2, November 1946) and Raymond Borde & Etienne Chaumeton in their full-length and for many years definitive study, *Panorama du film noir americain* (1955). What had driven these Frenchmen to their typewriters was not only their enjoyment of these bracingly bitter films on their own terms, but a delighted shock of recognition. During the Nazi occupation and its immediate aftermath, the French had been unable to keep up with the cultural products of the West Coast, but once the barriers were lifted, they were astonished to discover that the countrymen of all those rich, healthy, generous and victorious GIs had been busy producing films of what seemed unprecedented gloom, cynicism and even despair. Unprecedented in terms of their patchy experience of Hollywood, that is to say; the French had produced a *noir* cinema of their own in the pre-war and war years, in such seductively murky dramas as Marcel Carné's *Quai des brumes* (1938) and *Le Jour se lève* (1939), both starring the most charismatic French actor of the 1930s, Jean Gabin – who also played the lead in one of Renoir's darkest films, *La Bête humaine* (1938). Hence the otherwise perplexing title of M. Chartier's piece: 'les Americains *aussi* font des films noirs . . .'; *'film noir'* was itself a play on the literary term *roman noir*, the equivalent of the Anglo-Saxon term 'Gothic Novel'. By and large, the criticism written in the following ten years or so, on both sides of the Atlantic, was a consolidation of the positions sketched in those first few articles, and was often preoccupied with squeezing a widely disparate group of films under the single heading of *noir* despite the occasional awkwardness of the fit.

The definitions of *noir* which we live with and, if so inclined, wrangle over today were all fairly well established in the decade immediately following the end of the war, although the canon of films drawn up then has since been subjected to kinds of scrutiny – by feminists, psychoanalytic theorists, historical materialists and others – which might have alarmed those French *cinéphiles*. While the term has been the subject of intense and occasionally vitriolic debate, a modest fleshing-out of our initial definition of *film noir* might run along these lines: it designates a set of movies made in Hollywood between about 1941 (the year of John Huston's *The Maltese Falcon*, conventionally if somewhat arbitrarily regarded as the first dawning – or dusking? – of the form, and also of Welles's *Citizen Kane*, sometimes annexed as a more idiosyncratic founding father) and 1958, the year of Welles's *Touch of Evil*, traditionally seen as the last true *noir*, after which everything else that bears the stigmata should be seen as pastiche, *hommage*, parody or *neo-noir*. Almost all *noirs* are urban tales, usually concerning murder or some other vicious crime, set largely at night, and shot in a harsh, mysterious – and, as cameramen and directors of the day point out, extremely cheap – lighting style often refered to as 'expressionist', though purist art historians might squirm at the borrowing. (And rightly: the veteran cinematographer John Alton, who lit and shot, among other outstanding films, *The Big Combo*, *He Walked by Night*, *The People Against O'Hara* and *The Crooked Way*, told the makers of a recent documentary on *noir* that his chief visual inspiration was Rembrandt.) These films took their cues from the hard-boiled detective fiction of such writers as Dashiell Hammett, James M. Cain, Cornell Wollrich and Raymond Chandler, and their plots can be convoluted to the point of delirium: Howard Hawks's *The Big Sleep* (1946) – a film which reminds us that *noir* can also be deeply romantic and outrageously funny – is the most notorious instance. As the French noted with a *frisson* of pleasure, the prevailing tone of *film noir* is corrosively world-weary and misanthropic, sometimes to the point of nihilism, and to some eyes this has made the form seem like the vehicle for potent, if covert social criticism. It's certainly striking that many of the best *noirs* were directed by European emigrés – Fritz Lang, Billy Wilder and so on – and it's possible to spot some distinctly un-American qualities in what might seem the most American, not to say Californian of movie forms. (There is a growing body of literature linking *noir* to the growth of Los Angeles; see, for example, Mike Davies's extremely interesting, if occasionally misleading *City of Quartz*, 1990.)

The heroes and heroines of *film noir* tend to live outside the safety and comforts of American middle-class life: they're either poor and rootless, or trapped in fragmenting, sick families that will be squalid (if at the wage-slave end of the class ladder), perverted (if rich), or both. Quite often, they will be the stories of solitary men, ordered around the hero's point of view and sometimes told by him in voice-over, even if, as in *Sunset Boulevard*, he is inconvenienced by being dead; and at some point – the point at which feminist critics sit up, notebooks at the ready – he will encounter a *femme fatale*: a seductress, a deadly dame who will fascinate the hero, drag him into deep waters and then, as if by some eternal law, perish herself. (See *The Postman Always Rings Twice* (Tay Garnett, 1946), *Double Indemnity* . . .) Readers will probably not be startled to learn that writers of a Freudian bent have sniffed out the old Oedipal tangle in such films, and that there is a substantial literature about sexuality in *film noir*; but that way lies a whole treatise. (For an unusual, highly intelligent and pugnacious essay on the subject, see Paul Schrader's 'Notes on *Film Noir*', in *Film Comment*, Vol. 8, No. 1, Spring 1972; reprinted in *Schrader on Schrader*, 1990.)

However hazy and disputed the boundaries of the form, it refuses to vanish. More than any other genre, it enchants and haunts every true buff: and every decade seems able to reinvent the *film noir* in unexpected ways – consider, say, Polanski's *Chinatown*, Altman's *The Long Goodbye*, Scorsese's *Taxi Driver* in the 1970s – or to cross-breed it with more clearly defined genres: the science-fiction film, as in *Blade Runner*; the occult horror film, as in *Angel Heart*; the satirical comedy, as in *Barton Fink*. In recent years, the leading exponent of *noir*, or *neo-noir*, in its purest form has been John Dahl in *Red Rock West* (1993) and the immensely enjoyable *The Last Seduction* (1994).

filmography   a coinage derived from 'bibliography': a chronological list of the films made by a particular director, actor, cinematographer, etc, usually including main production details; or, at the end of a critical essay, a similarly detailed list of all the films cited.

filmology   a term borrowed from the writings of the once-influential French theorist Christian Metz, designating a particular – roughly, sociological-cum-semiological – method of studying the seventh art. Not much used nowadays.

filter   from ME *filtre*, OF *filtre* and medieval L *filtrum*, 'felt'; it develops some of its modern sense by the 16th C, when felt and other fabrics are used to strain and purify liquids in which solids are suspended. In the modern optical, photographic and cinematographic senses, it refers to a type of lens attachment, made of glass or gelatin, that colours, diffuses or polarises the resulting image, or protects the lens from damage in harsh conditions. When shooting through a filter, cameramen must be aware of the *filter factor* – the degree to which the exposure will have to be increased to compensate for the light it absorbs.

final cut   the version of the film that exists at the end of editing, to which the negative is then conformed so that release prints may be struck; the term *fine cut* is sometimes used synonymously, but this more generally refers to an edit which is almost ready for final approval – that is, the version immediately preceding the final cut. *Final trial composite*, see *sample print*.

financing   the money available for making a particular film; *financing entity*, the backer who provides that money.

finder   see *viewfinder*.

fine cut   see *final cut*.

fine-grain duplicate negative, fine-grain master print (also **fine-grain master posititive**, or simply **master positive**)   very sharply defined negatives and prints, so called because the size of the grains in the original light-sensitive emulsion is much smaller than in older types of stock.

finger   a thin *gobo* or *flag*.

first assistant (or **first assistant director**)   see *assistant director*; *first assistant cameraman*, the crew member reponsible for loading magazines, changing lenses, filing reports, measuring the distance between camera and subject and so on (see *cinematographer*); *first draft*, the earliest complete version of a screenplay (which will seldom also be the last, particularly in Hollywood where, as the independent director John Sayles pungently observes, there is a tendency to treat screenwriters like toilet paper); *first grip*, the head of a production's team of *grips*, also known as the *key grip*; *first run*, the initial release of a film in a particular market; *first unit*, the main film crew on a production.

fish-out-of-water   a much-repeated plot premise (or *formula*) which simply involves taking characters from their usual habitat and transplanting them into a strikingly different environment. Hence *Crocodile Dundee* (amiable roughneck from the Australian outback lands in New York), *Beverly Hills Cop* (amiable if sardonic detective from Detroit is assigned to the richest and most pretentious district in Los Angeles) or *The Beverly Hillbillies* (amiable Arkansas rustics come into a fortune and are similarly relocated).

fisheye, fisheye lens   an extreme wide-angle lens which greatly enlarges the centre of the image, shrinking and distorting the remainder into a receding curve; it can be used to create hallucinatory effects, make faces seem grotesque and so on.

fishpole   see *boom*.

fix   to set a developed image by processing it in a chemical bath – a *fixer*. From the OF *fix*, and the L *fixus*, the past participle of *fingere*, to fasten; the verb occurs in various senses in English from the 15th C onwards.

fixed camera   a camera locked into a set position for the duration of a scene; a camera that does not *pan*, *dolly*, *crane* or move in any other way. In Hollywood and other commercial productions, such shots tend to be used quite sparingly, since audiences are now accustomed to a highly mobile camera style and tend to find fixed shots dull if used repeatedly; yet there have been a number of great directors – Yazujiro Ozu, for example – whose films have been largely if not wholly made up of such shots.

fixed-focus lens   see *lens*; *fixed-focus viewfinder*, see *viewfinder*.

fixed matte   see *matte*.

flag   a small rectangular *gobo*; in other words, a piece of dark material used to soften the beams from a lamp; it will either be attached to the lamp or put on a separate stand.

flame drum   a mechanically rotated cylinder which, when set in front of a lamp, casts flickering, flame-like shadows across the set.

flange   in the cutting room, a metal or plastic disc against which the film, mounted on a *rewinder*, is spooled onto a core.

flare   a burst of light, diffused glow or bright fog on exposed film, usually unwanted, and often caused by a reflection (for example, of bright sunlight from a window) that was not noticed during shooting. It can be reduced, in shooting, by the use of lens coatings or hoods.

flash   (a) as a noun: an extremely rapid, sometimes almost subliminal shot, generally used to startle the audience; or another word for *flare* (b) as a verb, to expose stock to light for a brief moment so as to increase the overall exposure of the footage which is subsequently shot. The word 'flash' seems to have been onomatopoeic in origin, and in ME generally expresses the movement of liquid, rather like 'splash'; it begins to be applied to the movement of fire or light in the second half of the 16th C. 'Flakes of fire . . . Out of her steely armes were flashing seene' – Spenser, *Faerie Queene*, 1596.

flashback, flash forward   swift narrative jumps to the past and future within a film; that is to say, breaks in the temporal sequence of the story, made for dramatic effect and/or to provide some essential plot detail, offer insight into a psychological quirk (as in the scene towards the end of Hitchcock's *Marnie* which explains the heroine's compulsions and disorders by showing that her mother was brutally assaulted when Marnie was a child) or to lend some other kind of depth. Many films consist almost entirely of an extended flashback, beginning in a present tense, going back to the past which explains its significance, and returning to that present only in conclusion: Penny Marshall's comedy about the women's baseball teams of the 1940s, *A League of Their Own*, is a recent example. The screenwriter Jean-Claude Carrière has waxed lyrical on the 'wonderful' narrative technique of the flashback, the delights of which are, he speculates, a clue to the cinema's secret ambition to overthrow the tyranny of time: 'An hour and a half later we find ourselves at our point of departure, which has now become our destination. A loop of time closes, time which has been virtually preserved, as if immune from ordinary ageing.' Among the films that have made memorable use of flashback: *Le Jour se lève*, *Citizen Kane*, *Rashomon*, many films by Resnais . . .

flash cutting   extremely fast cutting; *flash frames*, either (a) frames which have been accidentally or deliberately overexposed, or (b) shots that last just a few frames; *flash pan*, see *zip pan*.

flat (or **scenic flat**)   as in the theatre, a moveable part of the set – generally a light framework covered with cloth on which scenery is painted.

flatbed   an editing machine with a horizontal work area, equipped with pairs of circular plates on which film can be spooled to and fro; see *Steenbeck*.

flex arm   see *gobo*.

flick, flicks, flix   a rather dated slang for a film or, in the plural, the cinema in general. The word appears to have been suggested by the phenomenon of *flicker*, a mild strobing effect which results from film being projected at rates slower than 24 frames per second, and which was therefore characteristic of the silent cinema, which used only 16 frames per second (though the flickering effect was somewhat moderated by the use of a rotating shutter; see *persistence of vision*.) 'Flicker' comes from the OE *flicorian*, an onomatopoeic word expressive of quick movement, such as the action of a bird's wings in flight. Hence Chaucer, in the *Knight's Tale*, c.1386: 'Above hir heed hir dowves flickeringe.' It starts to be applied to the variations in light mainly in the 19th C. *Flicker film*, a type of *avant-garde* film which fires colours, shapes or images at the viewer with bewildering rapidity. Theodore Roszak's extraordinary and highly recommended novel *Flicker* (1991), an intellectual thriller which suggests among other things that the cinema was the product of a Cathar conspiracy, owes its title to all of these cinematic uses and more.

flies   as in the theatre, the high area above the set from which lights and sceneries are suspended.

flip, flipover   an infrequently used type of transition device, which tends to be at least mildly comic in effect, in which the screen image appears to be flipped over horizontally or vertically like a playing card, so 'revealing' another image on its 'reverse side'. It is achieved in an optical printer with a *flipover lens*.

float   the accidental effect of wobbling and swaying in a projected image, usually the result of film not being tightly wound. *Floating wall*, a scenery wall that may be easily removed to accomodate new shooting angles.

flood, floodlight   the large, powerful lamp that can cast diffuse light over large areas of the set.

floor   the shooting area of a studio; *floor crew*, in a production which is being directed from a separate control room (fairly uncommon in film-making, standard in television), the team of camera operators, grips and so on who work in the studio area, under the immediate control of the *floor manager*.

fluid camera   a shooting style characterised by a highly mobile camera that weaves in and out of, prowls round, swoops over or circles around the action in long, uncut takes; in recent years, these have generally been executed with a **Steadicam**, though the convention significantly antedates the invention of that useful gadget. Stanley Kubrick's *The Shining* contains the most famous and flamboyant examples of the style, used to tellingly eerie effect – partly, perhaps, because of the unnerving implication in some sequences that these fluid movements represent not just the impersonal narrator's point of view of most features, but rather the baleful gaze of the haunted house in which its action is set.

fluff, fluffer   in pornographic film-making, the crew member (usually female, young, and attractive) who makes sure that male performers rise to the occasion.

flutter   accidental wobbling, jumping or slipping of the film in a camera or projector, usually caused by uneven feeding; or the corresponding sound errors in recording or playback.

flux   the light in a particular space, measured in *lumens*.

focal length   the size of a lens, measured in millimetres; that is, the distance between the centre of the lens and the surface – the *focal plane* – of the unexposed film on which it comes to focus. A small focal length gives a wide angle; a long focal length a smaller angle. The usual focal length for lens on a 35mm camera is 50mm.

focus   (a) as a noun: the point within the camera at which parallel light rays converge after refraction through its lens; or, much more loosely, the plane of action where the subject must be placed in order to register sharply on film – to be *in focus*.

(b) as a verb: to sharpen the image by adusting the lens. Hence to *pull focus* or *rack focus* – to adjust the focus of a lens in the middle of a shot so as to switch attention from one plane of the image to another; for example, to pull back from a couple embracing to a close-up on the face of a jealous observer. Such movements are the responsibility of the *focus puller*, who is also charged with maintaining the camera, changing lenses and magazines and the like; 'focus puller' may also refer to the lens attachment which is used to pull focus. (In the US, the focus puller is usually called the **assistant cameraman**, or **first assistant cameraman**.) 'Focus' is derived from L *focus*, a hearth; the optical sense of the word comes into English in the late 17th C: 'Sunbeams refracted or reflected by a burning-glass to a focus' – Boyle, 1685.

fog   (a) the image flaw caused by the accidental exposure of film stock to light, or (b) the effect of mild mist, medium smog or dense pea-souper created either by the use of a *fog filter* over the lens or by a *fog machine* or *fogmaker*, which generates clouds of cool, heavy artificial mist that lies close to the ground and is relatively easy to control and disperse.

foil marks   on projected film, metal cue marks that help make for smooth changes between reels.

Foley   any of the sound effects, but particularly the sound of body movements (footsteps, rustling clothes, punches), that are recorded after shooting has been completed – i.e., in **post-production** – and then dubbed on to the soundtrack to match the action. Hence *Foley artist*, the technician who creates such sounds by shuffling his feet, panting and the like, and may sometimes be called a *Foley mixer* or *Foley walker; Foley stage*, a large room equipped with many different floor surfaces and sound effects props – bells, whistles, engines and the immortal coconut shells; *Foley studio*, the place where foleys are created and made to synchronise; *foley tracks*, the recordings of such sound effects, and so on. The device is said to have been named after one Jack Foley, the technician who pioneered the modern process. Though Foley artists are, as one commentator observed, 'little-celebrated', their contribution to the art of the cinema was acknowledged by the young British artist Tacita Dean (b.1965) in 'Foley Artist', her installation for the Tate Gallery in the autumn of 1996.

follow, follow focus   to keep the subject sharply and continuously in focus during a tracking shot or other camera movement, or when the action moves towards or away from the camera: this task is the responsibility of the *focus puller*.

follow shot   a shot which appears to chase after a performer or object in motion; *follow spot*, a spotlight that can be kept trained on a moving performer.

foot   the end, or *tail*, of a roll of film.

footage   (a) the measurement of any length of film in units of feet and frames. One foot of 35mm film contains 16 frames, so that, at a filming rate of 24 frames per second (FPS), a single second of filming exposes 1 foot and 8 frames. Hence the *footage counter*, mounted on the camera to show how many feet and frames have been shot. (b) More loosely, any length of exposed film.

footcandle   a unit of illumination; see *lux*; *footlumen*, see *lumen*.

forced coverage   a means of covering over a shooting mistake by simply filming a brief shot that can be edited in place of the botched action rather than having to retake the whole scene.

forced development   see *development* and *push*.

foreground (FG)   as in paintings, the area of the scene closest to the spectator (because closest to the camera in shooting); *foreground music*, see *source music*.

foreign version   a print of a film adapted for theatrical release in a country other than its nation of origin: it will almost always be *dubbed*, and sometimes trimmed or adapted so as not to offend local sensibilities.

forelengthening, foreshortening   deliberate distortions of scale created with, respectively, a wide-angle lens and a telephoto lens. The former has the effect, *inter alia*, of exaggerating motion, the latter of minimising it.

form   either (a) the shape of a film, considered both pictorially and in terms of its editing rhythms and/or overall narrative proportions, or (b) a synonym for *genre*.

formal editing   a rather dignified or even stately editing style in which each shot is roughly the same length as those which surround it, and the shots as a whole tend to be long.

format   see *aspect ratio*.

form cut, form dissolve   transitions from a person or object in one shot to a thing or person with a similar outline, either so as to create some metaphorical connection between them or simply (and at times self-indulgently) for the *frisson* the effect can cause. Perhaps the best-known of all such transitions in recent years is the little joke at the beginning of *Raiders of the Lost Arc*, where the blue and white Paramount logo of a mountain gives way to an establishing shot of a peak of similar shape rising above a jungle.

formula   the term, usually mildly cynical or disparaging in tone, for a film which capitalises on elements of story and/or chararacter – *fish-out-of-water*, for example – that have proved successful in the past; sometimes a less high-toned synonym for *genre*.

forward-backward   see *rock and roll*.

foundation light   the basic lighting for a given scene, to which other lights may be added as required.

found footage   see *archival film*.

four-walled set   a set – such as a real classroom or court room – which completely encloses the filmed action and film-makers alike; most purpose-built sets have three or fewer walls.

four-walling   US term for a type of distribution: the distributor pays the exhibitor a flat fee, handles all the usual exhibitor's business, such as advertising, and then pockets any profits.

Fox Film Corporation   see *Twentieth Century-Fox*.

FPS   see *footage*.

frame   ultimately from OE verb *framian*, to be of service, make progress: (a) as a noun: the smallest individual unit of a film; a rectangular area on a strip of film which holds a single image; when such images are exposed and then subsequently projected at the rate of 24 images per second, the illusion of movement at normal speed results. Hence *frame counter*, the instrument on a printer or projector or camera (see *footage counter*) that shows how many frames have passed through the mechanism. *Frame lines*, the thin black lines which separate one frame from the next. The cinematographic sense of 'frame' seems to be derived, via the obvious analogy of a picture frame, from a use meaning 'that in which something is set', first recorded in Shakespeare's *Sonnets*: 'My body is the frame wherein 'tis held' (*c*.1600); Samuel Pepys refers to buying a picture frame for £1 5s in 1666.

(b) As a verb, either (1) to adjust the position of the camera so as to compose the desired image, or (2) to adjust the film in a projector or an editing machine so that the resulting image is correctly aligned and completely visible. When the bottom part of the picture is cut off, the projectionist should *frame down* – shift the gate downwards until the image is centred; when the top part is cut off, one must *frame up*.

Free Cinema   a small but vocal and influential movement in the British cinema of the 1950s, concerned with finding and representing 'the significance of the everyday', breaking away from the commercial restraints of the dominant film industry and asserting a social role for the film-maker. The name was originally coined for a series of six programmes screened at the National Film Theatre from 1956 to 1959 – programmes which eventually included films by directors as varied as Norman McClaren, Franju and Polanski – but now applies almost exclusively to the documentary films made by the young men who organised them: Lindsay Anderson (who had helped pave the way for Free Cinema in the pages of the Oxford University Film Society magazine *Sequence* from 1946 to 1952), Karel Reisz and Tony Richardson. Early Free Cinema films include *O Dreamland* (1953), a study of a Margate amusement park, by Anderson and *Momma Don't Allow*, about a jazz club, by Reisz and Richardson; later productions include Anderson's *Every Day Except Christmas* (1957) and Reisz's *We are the Lambeth Boys* (1959). All three of the main Free Cinema directors went on to make notable feature films, some of which maintained the Free Cinema spirit.

freeze, freeze frame   the sudden effect of still photography within a moving picture, created by printing a single frame again and again. The device became somewhat overused in the 1960s, particularly as a way of ending a film, but in the right hands can still be quite striking. It is also known as a *stop frame*.

Fresnel lens   a type of lens which has stepped-down circles of glass on its convex side, and which is put in front of a bulb to concentrate and control its beam. It is often used on searchlights or other large lamps, and was invented by the physicist Augustin Jean Fresnel (1788–1827), who intended it for use in lighthouses.

Frezzolini   trade name for a lightweight camera, most often used in filming documentaries.

friction head   a device which attaches to a tripod and permits smooth *pans* or *tilts*.

from the top   the director's command to the cast and crew to play, or repeat, an action from its beginning.

front credits   see *credits*. *Front end*, a term referring to the costs incurred by a film before its full-scale pre-production begins, such as the price of the screenplay. *Front lighting*, lighting that comes from the general area or the camera; it tends to flatten the subject out. *Front projection*, the system of projecting a film onto the front of a screen, over the heads of the audience; thus, the alternative to **back projection** (or *rear projection*).

frying pan   a type of screen used to diffuse the light from a *luminaire*; so called because of its shape.

full shot (FS), full figure shot   a shot which keeps the main subject completely in view from head at the top of the frame to toe at the bottom.

fungus spots   the fungoid growths that may sometimes appear on old film stocks; some of the chemicals in film emulsions are derived from vegetables.

fusion frequency   a term for the speed at which film must pass through a projector so that the still images will 'fuse' into the illusion of motion, as a result of *persistence of vision*. In modern film-making, this is 24 frames per second.

Futurism   despite the fact that Marinetti and other Italian Futurists were fanatical advocates of all things technological, and that it might therefore have been logical for them to devote their considerable energies to the most technologically advanced of all arts, the Futurist contribution to cinema is slight to the point of near-invisibility. Its output appears to consist chiefly of a manifesto, published in September 1916 and, at least in parts, less demented than most Futurist effusions:

The cinema is an autonomous art. The cinema must therefore never copy the stage. The cinema, being essentially visual, must above all fulfill the evolution of painting, detach itself from reality, from photography, from the graceful and the solemn. It must become antigraceful, deforming, impressionistic, synthetic, dynamic, free-wording.

(See Umbro Apollonio, ed., *Futurist Manifestos*, Thames and Hudson 1973, 207–19.) That, and two films: Ginna's *Vita futurista* and Bragaglia's *Il perfido incanto* (*Wicked Enchantment*), though purists will even dispute the precise Futurist credentials of the latter. The Russian Futurists, led by Mayakovsky, left a more substantial legacy, if only indirectly: their ideas, propagated and thrashed out in early revolutionary journals such as *Lef*, appear to have influenced both Vertov and Eisenstein.

fuzz-off   to blur or tone down harsh outlines in a *matte* process.

FX   the standard abbreviation for *effects*.

G (or **G rating**)   the *MPAA* rating for a film that can be viewed by a general audience; the American counterpart of the British U rating.

gaffer   the chief electrician on any production, in charge of lighting the set under the guidance of the cinematographer or DP. The word is generally assumed to be a corrupted form of 'grandfather', and was originally 'a term applied by country people to an elderly man or one whose position entitled him to respect'; this sense is current from the late 16th C. The cinematic sense appears to be taken over from a mid-19th C–late 20th C use: 'the foreman . . . of a gang of workers'. *Gaffer grip*, a clamp used to fix lights to rigging and so on. *Gaffer's tape*, a useful, multi-purpose adhesive tape of cloth, silver in colour.

gain   sound amplification in an audio recording or playback system; *gain control*, the volume control: the knob, switch or dial that controls the gain of an amplifier.

Gainsborough Pictures   the British production company, founded in 1924 by Michael Balcon, that launched Alfred Hitchcock's career as a director (with *The Mountain Eagle*, 1926, a co-production made in Munich; Hitchcock had already worked as an assistant on Gainsborough's very first film, *The Passionate Adventure*, 1924) and then went on to make some of the most distinguished local productions of the late 1930s and 1940s, before going into artistic and commercial decline and ultimately going out of business in the early 1950s. Among Gainsborough's high points were Hitchcock's last film before he left for Hollywood, *The Lady Vanishes* (1938), and a sequences of romances usually starring one or more of the 'Gainsborough Foursome' of James Mason, Stewart Granger, Margaret Lockwood and Phyllis Calvert: *The Man in Gray* (1943), *Fanny by Gaslight* (1944) and *The Wicked Lady* (1945). The best known production from Gainsborough's period of decline is probably *Miranda* (1948). The Gainsborough logo, which had various avatars, was based upon the portrait of Mrs Simmons by the British painter of the same name. An amusing moment in Budd Schulberg's novel *What Makes Sammy Run?* turns on a confusion of the artist and the company, and on the ambiguity of the word 'picture':

'Father hates being late,' Miss Harrington was saying. 'It's all my fault. I came home frightfully late after looking at pictures all day.'

'Perfectly all right,' Sammy said in his best party voice. 'What pictures did you see?'

'Well, one I've really been chasing all over the world,' she said. '*Blue Boy*.'

'*Blue Boy?*' Sammy said. 'A foreign picture?'

'Not exactly,' Laurette said. 'It was done in England.'

'Oh, Gaumont-British,' Sammy said.

'No, by an Independent,' she said. 'Gainsborough.'

People started to laugh. She began to laugh with them.

gang control   the control of various different but connected electronic or mechanical devices from a single unit.

gangster film   (a) very loosely, any film about violent criminals; (b) in a more restricted sense, those fast-moving, atmospheric films made during the 1930s about the villains who ran America's organised crime syndicates of the previous decade. (*Gangster* appears in American English in the late 19th C; OED's first citation is from 1896.) *Warner Brothers*, whose stars included Humphrey Bogart, James Cagney and Edward G. Robinson, easily led the field in the gangster movie, though all the major studios and some minor ones, such as *Monogram*, tried to muscle in on Warner's territory. At their best, these 1930s films were not only well-crafted, irresistibly entertaining and the source of some potent American mythology, but a vehicle for more or less explicit satire (they would hint, for example, at uncomfortable similarities between gangsterism and more conventional business methods) and more or less subtle commentary on the origins of criminality in unjust social conditions. In this classic form, the gangster film may be said to begin with Mervyn LeRoy's Warner Brothers production *The Lights of New York* in 1928, rapidly develop its basic conventions and, possibly in response to the approach of war, gradually run out of steam around a decade later, after Raoul Walsh's *The Roaring Twenties* (1939) – though Walsh went on to make two more outstanding gangster films, *High Sierra* (1941) and *White Heat* (1949), with Cagney as a psychopathic mummy's boy. Between these dates come the films which define the genre: LeRoy's *Little Caesar* (1930), starring Edward G. Robinson as Rico Bandell, a gang boss obviously based on Al Capone; *Public Enemy* (William Wellman, 1931), the first film to cast James Cagney as a heavy – Tom Powers, no less plainly based on Hymie Weiss – and fondly remembered for the scene in which Cagney shoves a grapefruit into Mae Clarke's face; *Scarface* (Howard Hawks, 1932), produced by Howard Hughes and starring Paul Muni as the Capone figure (the film was freely remade by Brian de Palma in 1983, starring Al Pacino as a latter-day Cuban immigrant version of Capone); *I Am a Fugitive From a Chain Gang* (William Wyler, 1932); *Dead End* (also by Wyler, 1937), which launched the careers of a bunch of cute ruffians who came to be known as the Dead End Kids, and made their reappearance in the sentimental *Angels With Dirty Faces* (Michael Curtiz, 1938), starring Cagney as Rocky Sullivan and Pat O'Brien as the priest who persuades Rocky to play the coward as he is dragged to the electric chair so that the Dead End Kids will lose faith in him and learn not to follow his ways.

All this bullet-riddled celluloid has both antecedents and progeny. The urban crime genre was founded in the early days of cinema (D.W. Griffith's *Musketeers of Pig Alley* dates from 1912, to be followed by the likes of von Sternberg's *Underworld*, 1927), and, after its heyday, proliferates and mutates into a number of forms. Though the gangster movie is no longer the guaranteed crowd-pleaser it once was, its basic components have clearly persisted: self-consciously revived in Brian de Palma's *The Untouchables* (1987), minutely re-thought in Martin Scorsese's *GoodFellas* or wittily re-invented, as in Quentin Tarantino's *Reservoir Dogs* and *Pulp Fiction*. Elsewhere, the old gangster film has reappeared, variously, in the guise of *film noir*; as the object of homage in the work of movie-crazy directors such as Jean-Luc Godard (*A Bout de souffle*) and Jean-Pierre Melville (*Le Samourai*), and then in the films of younger directors influnced by the French gangster school, such as Hong Kong's John Woo (*The Killer*); in the countless cops-and-robbers shows made for television; in witty or arch parodies and pastiches from *Some Like it Hot* (1959) to the Alan Parker kiddy gangster musical *Bugsy Malone*; in more serious period films such as Arthur Penn's *Bonnie and Clyde* and Robert Altman's *Thieves Like Us*; and in lavish American epics such as Coppola's three *Godfather* movies. John Baxter has written an enlightening study of the genre, *The Gangster Film* (1970).

garbage matte   a type of *matte* used simply to hide unwanted objects – 'garbage' – from the camera's view.

gaslighting   current slang term for the process whereby a studio will drive a writer and/or director mad by ordering changes to a script/film and then almost immediately demand to know why said changes have been made. The term derives from Patrick Hamilton's gothic play *Gaslight*, and its two main film versions (Thorold Dickinson, 1939; George Cukor, 1944), about the Victorian criminal who tries to drive his wife insane.

Gasparcolor   an early three-colour process, developed in England in 1934 and named after its inventor, Bela Gaspar.

gate   the aperture inside a camera where the film is held to be exposed in shooting, or the corresponding apertures in the mechanisms of printers and projectors. The logic of the name is that the mechanism can be swung on its hinges to allow for cleaning or for threading film. It has been a standard term since the early 20th C: 'The film gate shall be of massive construction and provided with ample heat radiating surface' – 1909. '*Check the gate*', a director's command after a take to make sure that the shot has not been spoiled by dust or hairs (see *hair in the gate*) trapped inside the camera.

gator clamp, gator grip   a powerful metal clamp, usually with insulated handles, also known as an *alligator* or *gaffer clamp*. Originally developed solely as electrical clamps, gators are now widely used for fixing all kinds of props and equipment together.

gauge   the standard formats for the width of film: 8mm or Super-8mm for home movies, 16mm (also known as *narrow gauge*) for many documentaries and some low-budget features, 35mm (also known as *standard gauge*) for most theatrical movies, 65 or 70mm for prestige productions. Snobberies are involved with each of these gauges, and at a festival of Super-8 film held in Leicester in the mid-1980s I heard people solemnly using the term 'gaugism' to designate the kind of disrespect in which the home movie gauge is held by many professionals. 'Gauge' – 'a fixed or standard measure' – is derived from 13th C Fr *gauge* and *gauger*, itself of unknown origin; it enters English in the mid-15th C.

gauze   a thin material, usually made of fibreglass, stretched over a lens to achieve a softer image or over a lamp to diffuse its beam.

gay films   broadly speaking, either (a) films made by homosexual film-makers, on homosexual themes, for homosexual (or unbigoted general) audiences; or (b) any of the mainstream, ostensibly 'straight' films traditionally admired and enjoyed by gay men or lesbians, such as those starring Judy Garland (one humorous, not unsympathetic euphemism for a gay man – 'a friend of Dorothy' – is derived from the role the young actress played in *The Wizard of Oz*), Bette Davis or Joan Crawford. The term would not, therefore, usually be applied to any of the countless films made by directors, writers and performers who were, are or may have been homosexual (such as Sergei Eisenstein), but which do not address gay themes either tacitly or directly, unless these films make some other distinct appeal to gay sensibilities. Clandestine productions apart, the first gay films proper appear to have been *Salome* (1923), a Hollywood production directed by Natasha Rambova and starring her lover Alla Nazimova; and, in Germany, *Anders als die Anderen* (1919), by Richard Oswald – a production followed by a number of other gay films, of which the best-known is *Maadchen in Uniform* (1932), at one time a staple of university film societies and repertory cinemas. But such high-profile films were anomalous, and with extremely few exceptions, gay cinema became an underground movement for most of the next four decades, from Kenneth Anger's *Fireworks* (1947) – a short which prompted a Supreme Court ruling that the portrayal of homosexual acts was not necessarily obscene – and Jean Genet's *Un Chant d'Amour* (1947) to Andy Warhol's films of the mid-1960s onwards. The main-stream cinema caught up with exceeding slowness and caution, and it was not until the 1970s and 1980s (or not even then, some gay critics would insist) that it became widely acceptable to portray gay characters without some strong note of condemnation, condescension or contempt. The mainstream cinema eventually came up with the likes of *The Boys in the Band* (1970), *Cabaret* (1972) and *La Cage aux Folles* (1978); the international art cinema fared a good deal better, from Pasolini to Fassbinder to Derek Jarman and Terence Davies, and throughout the 1980s and 1990s has developed a distinct and flourishing canon of gay work, commonly referred to as *queer cinema* or New Queer Cinema. The literature of gay cinema is extensive, and growing apace; among the various recent studies of the topic are Richard Dyer's *Now You See It: Studies on Lesbian and Gay Film* (Routledge, 1990).

gear head, geared head   a device similar in function to a *friction head*, which fits onto a camera tripod and can be wound into new positions to achieve fluent *pans* and *tilts*.

gel   a transparent coloured sheet put in front of a light to tint its rays; or a uncoloured sheet that acts as a diffuser. An abbreviation of 'gelatine', from Fr *gelatine* (originally meaning, according to OED 'an excellent white broth made of the fish Maigre'), the Italian *gelatina* and *gelata*, jelly; and a gel will sometimes be referred to as a *jelly.*

Gemini system   the trade name for a method used for simultaneous filming by a 16mm film camera and a television camera; it was used in making films for television in the 1960s but was superseded by more efficient forms of transferring and editing videotape.

general directions   the notations in a screenplay, usually ranged left on the page, that indicate exits, entrances and other kinds of movement.

general release   the commercial distribution of prints to cinemas throughout a national market or the world, as opposed to a selective release or exclusive run.

generations   the sucessive stages of duplicating film (or, in television and video productions, tape) from the original negative (or *rushes*) to a release print. A certain amount of definition is lost with each new duplication, fairly negligible in the second and third generations but thereafter more and more obvious.

genre   as in literary, musical or art studies: a particular narrative form or convention of the cinema, such as the thriller, the Western, the musical, the horror movie. From OFr *genre*, 'kind, type', itself descended from L *gener-*, the stem form of *genus*, 'race', and Gk *genos*, from the root form *gen-*, 'to produce'. As 'gender' (and related spellings), it enters English in the late 14th C; commonly used in the artistic sense from the mid-18th C onwards. Hence Mr Jennet to Mr Garrick, 1770: 'With regard to the *genre*, I am of opinion that an English audience will not relish it so well as a more characteristic kind of comedy.'

ghost image   a transparent wraithlike form, created by the simple method of double exposure or with a two-way mirror. Jacques Derrida once observed that the cinema is 'the science of ghosts'; the point was taken up by the British director Ken McMullen in his film *Ghost Dance* (1983), in which M. Derrida makes a cameo apperance and complains about an incident in which, he explains, the Czech secret police planted cocaine on his person.

gigolo   see *jiggolo.*

gimbal   a rig used for large-scale special effects: it can rotate an entire room, so that the performers inside appear to be walking across the walls and ceilings (the camera, of course, being clamped to the set so that it appears not to move). The word is surprisingly ancient: meaning 'joint, link in machinery' it can be found (in various spellings) from the late 16th C; an approximation to the cinematic sense begins with the development of a technology for keeping compasses and the like horizontal on board ship (late 18th C onwards). It is an altered form of *gimmal*, 'a type of finger-ring that may be divided into two or more parts', from *gemel* 'twin, twins' (etymology: OF *gemel*, L *gemellus*, a diminutive of *geminus*, 'twin').

giraffe   the trade name for a type of *crane*, inspired by that exotic quadruped's long and highly mobile neck.

glass filter   a lens filter made either of tinted glass or of a layer of tinted or neutral gelatin fixed between two pieces of glass. *Glass shot*, a relatively inexpensive way, common in the 1920s and 1930s, of producing composite images by simply painting scenery and the like on to a sheet of glass and shooting action through it.

glossometer   an instrument used to measure the 'gloss' – degree of reflectiveness – of a surface.

Go film (movie, picture etc)   slang term for a production that has been given a *green light* and is actually going to be made.

gobo   usually (a) a large black cloth or wooden screen, set on a movable stand and used either to screen the camera fron unwanted light or to diffuse the rays from *luminaires* (OED records something like this use from 1936: 'a small black screen used to deflect light'); or, less often, (b) a movable wall used to damp down sound inside a studio (as in the first example given by OED Supplement, from 1930). Etymology unknown, though said to be American in origin.

golden frame, golden ratio   the 1.33:1 (or 4:3) standard aspect ratio or Academy aperture (see *aspect ratio*), so called from the supposititition – repeated in some film textbooks to this day – that it is identical with the 'Golden Section', the name applied from the 19th C onwards to that harmonious, indeed mystical proportion, known to mathematicians since Euclid and the foundation of so much art and architecture, which results from the division of a straight line into two parts so that the ratio of the whole to the larger part is the same as that of the larger part to the smaller: $a/b = b/(a+b)$, where a is the length of the shorter side of the rectangle and b that of the longer. (The phrase 'golden section' comes into English from a German phrase published in 1835 in a book by Martin Ohm, who writes of '*den goldenen Schnitt*', but it seems unlikely that Ohm coined it.) In fact, since the Golden Section is an irrational number which can be roughly expressed as 1.618:1, the academy ratio is really quite a long way from the Golden Section. On the other hand, Pythagoreans may be cheered to learn that the 1.618:1 ratio is indeed a reasonable approximation to the standard Euopean wide screen ratio of 1.66:1.

golden time   American screen union term: the most highly paid hours of work, including time worked on Sundays, holidays, and after the standard agreed overtime hours.

goldfishing   a term sometimes applied to documentary films to describe the slightly irritating effect created by running footage of people talking with the sound of their words cut off or at a very low level (so as, for example, to allow a commentary to run over them), so that they appear simply to be opening and closing their mouths like goldfish.

Goldwynism   a quaintly witty or fractured English use ('include me out', 'verbal contracts are not worth the paper they're written on') or downright malapropism ('I would be sticking my head into a moose') of the type attributed, often inaccurately or spitefully, to the producer Samuel Goldwyn (1882–1974). The *Saturday Evening Post* used the word 'Goldwynism' as early as 1937; on the deliberate manufacture of Goldwynisms, see Philip French, *The Movie Moguls* (1969), chapter four.

goon stand   a large *century stand*. Derivation uncertain; perhaps originally inspired by *goon box*, the Allied prisoner's slang term for the tall watch-towers manned by armed guards in German POW camps during the Second World War?

goose   (a) as a noun: colloquial term for the camera and sound trucks. (b) as a verb: to boost or augment some process or action; presumably derived from the slang verb (late 19th C to present), meaning to poke, pinch or tickle in a sensitive area, particularly anal or genital. ('I don't like to see vulgar girls in the town/ Pull their clothes up, and stand to be goosed for a crown' – 1879/80.)

gothic film   a term sometimes used interchangeably with *horror film*, though it usefully distinguishes between the type of 'horror' film which deals in the eerie or supernatural (*The Haunting*, say) and the type, much more common in the last couple of decades, which trades mainly in violence and gore (*The Texas Chainsaw Massacre*), whether brought about by supernatural or human agents. Adapted, obviously, from the familiar literary term 'Gothic novel' as in the full title of Horace Walpole's *The Castle of Otranto, a Gothic Story* (1764). (From the L *gothic-us*.)

GPO Film Unit   the important British documentary body of the 1930s, run by John Grierson, which became the *Crown Film Unit* in 1940.

grad, grad filter, graduated filter   a lens filter which, usually, is clear in one part (say, the bottom) and then gradually becomes more tinted, so that the resulting images will be correspondingly coloured: for example, many of the vivid sunsets seen in shots of the American West owe less to the local climate than to warm-toned grad filters.

grader   the lab technician in charge of *grading* – judging and correcting the density of each frame of a negative as it is being processed; that is to say, making adjustments to its colour and brightness. (In the USA, the process is also called *timing*.)

grains   the microscopic particles of silver halide in film stock that respond to light and so help form images; in some stocks, particularly on smaller gauges, the grains may tend to clump together and become visible, so producing the characteristic mottled effect of *graininess*.   '

grammar   the system of cutting, camera movements and optical effects which make films intelligible and fluent. Some theorists, such as the Yugoslavian editor and painter Slavko Vorkapich, have tried to elaborate the correspondences between filmic grammar and the grammar of spoken and written languages. Though such attempts have not proved universally persuasive, it is clear enough that within a few years of its invention, film-makers developed a working set of rules for the representation of time and space which, albeit in modified form, are still followed and understood today: the cut, the fade, the reverse angle, the close-up, the establishing shot and so on. Such conventions are so familiar throughout the world that neophyte film-makers are often surprised to find that they can be broken, either through clumsiness and ignorance (an obvious case would be crossing the *imaginary line*, and so disrupting the illusion of coherent space) or wilfully, as is the case with the *jump cuts* in Godard's *A Bout de souffle*.

Grandscope   a Japanese anamorphic wide-screen process with the same aspect ratio as Cinemascope (2.35:1), developed by the Shochiku Company.

gravel box   one of the basic tools used in creating sound effects, or *foleying*: a shallow box filled with grit in which the Foley man can walk on the spot to create the effect of footsteps on gravel.

green department   the section of the crew whose job is to dress the set with fresh (or artificial) foliage – *greenery* – or to paint vivid colours onto leaves which are losing their health. Such a worker is usually called a *greensman* or *green-man*.

green light   to approve a script or project for production; more loosely, to say 'yes' to any proposal.

green print   a freshly processed print, on which the emulsion may not have fully hardened.

grid   the metal rigging that is suspended above a sound stage.

grip   broadly: any type of manual labourer on a set; the cinematic equivalent of a stage-hand, paid by the hour and responsible for all the tasks that involve muscle. More narrowly: the workers responsible for laying *tracks* and executing camera movements. Most large productions, however, will have a range of specialist grips – Construction Grips, Dolly Grips, Lighting Grips and so on. From the OE *gripe*, 'clasp, clutch'; the cinematic sense appears to derive from the late 19th C American theatrical sense 'a scene-shifter', though it has been suggested that another possible origin lies in the seat-of-the-pants techniques of the early cinema, in which the 'grip' would be the person who held the cameraman steady during tracking shots and other camera movements. See also *key grip*.

Griswold   the trade name for a type of *machine splicer*.

gross   either (a) the total amount taken by a film at the box office between its release and the time of reporting, or (b) a smaller, adjusted figure which means the amount received by the distributors after the exhibitor has extracted the agreed percentage from box office receipts. *Gross points*, the percentage of a film's gross profits to which a writer, producer, director or actor may be contractually entitled. In Lawrence Kasdan's film *Grand Canyon*, the hideously vulgar producer played by Steve Martin has car licence plates which read GRSS PTS.

ground noise, surface noise   the faint noise audible on sound tracks when all other sound has been eliminated, caused by minor scratches, dust particles and so on.

Group Three   a short-lived (1951–55) British production unit set up by the National Film Finance Corporation with John Grierson as executive producer and Michael Balcon as chairman. Devoted mostly to the production of cheap second-features of negligible international appeal, Group Three is chiefly notable for having launched the screen careers of Peter Finch, Tony Hancock, Kenneth More and Peter Sellers, though its most profitable production was a documentary scripted by Louis MacNeice: *Conquest of Everest* (1953).

guide line   a mark made by an editor across a length of filming to act as a visual cue for an actor in *looping*. *Guide track*, a rough version of the sound track recorded as a guide for editing, dubbing etc, which does not survive into the film's final cut.

guild   an American synonym for 'union', found in the names of the Screen Actor's Guild (SAG), the Writer's Guild of America (WGA) and so on.

guillotine splicer   a tool used in editing, which can join two strips of film end to end without cutting off any frames in the process. Derived, of course, from the notorious execution device of Dr Guillotin.

gyro head   a gyroscopically stablised camera mount, used in taking hand-held shots or shots from a moving vehicle.

H, **H certificate**   at one time, the British censor's classification for horror films: it was introduced in June 1937 ('Lord Tyrell, President of the British Board of Film Censors, introduced a new film classification called 'H' to apply to horror films. Pictures so labelled will not be shown to children under 16, whether accompanied by an adult or not'), and then dropped in 1942, at which date all horror films were banned, presumably because of the threat they posed to wartime morale. Revived after the war, it was finally adandoned for good in 1951, when it was supplanted by the all-purpose adult certificate, 'X'. But the term lingered on in popular metaphorical use well into the 1960s – 'real H-certificate stuff' and so on – and is still quite widely understood even by generations born after its demise.

hair in the gate   at the end of a take, the director will ask for the camera's *gate* to be checked to make sure that there were no hairs, dust particles or any other foreign bodies between the lens and the gate to spoil the shot. 'Hair in the gate' is thus the all-purpose complaint about such contamination.

halation   an accidental effect of flaring or haloing that appears on processed film, generally caused by light being reflected back from the film's base onto its sensitive emulsion. The term appears to have been coined by the photographer G.W. Perry in or before 1859: '[the phenomenon] to which, until a better one is found, I have applied the term halation', and it was applied to any kind of spreading of light beyond its proper boundaries on a photographic negative. The English 'halo' is derived from the L *halos* and the Gk *halos*, 'disc of the sun or moon, shield, threshing floor', and its general optical sense appears in the language as early as the mid-16th C; the first religious application noted by OED comes significantly later, from Sir Thomas Browne in 1646. ('Our saviour, and the Virgin Mary . . . are commonly drawne, with scintillations, or radiant Halo's about their head.') To prevent the flaw in filming, film stock is usually coated with an *anti-halation* backing – a dark coat which absorbs almost all of the refelcted light.

half-apple   an *apple box* of half the ordinary height – that is, about 4 inches high.

half-broad   a 1,000-watt floodlight.

half-scrim   a circular frame, half covered with mesh, used to diffuse light.

halide   the compounds of silver and various halogens – silver bromide, chloride, flouride and so on – found in film emulsion which react to contact with light, so forming the latent images that can be brought out by processing.

halogen lamp, or **tungsten-halogen lamp**   a lamp in which the tungsten that is burned off the bulb's filament reacts with halide gas and is relaced on the filament. Result: a bulb that lasts longer and does not blacken.

Hammer   the British film production company, founded in 1948 (and still, or so their receptionist insists with some heat, a thriving concern, though it has not produced a feature film since *The Lady Vanishes* in 1979) by Will Hammer and John Carreras (knighted in 1969), which became internationally famous for its hugely successful, low-budget horror films, particularly those starring Christopher Lee and Peter Cushing. Though many Hammer productions were greeted with contempt and even disgust on first release, hindsight has made at least some critics a good deal more respectful to the old firm. Among the best of the Hammer productions: the early colour additions to the Frankenstein and Dracula cycles with Lee as the monster in both productions, the various films about Nigel Kneale's creation Professor Quatermass (especially the third, *Quatermass and the Pit*, 1967), and *The Devil Rides Out* (1967), an adaptation of the creaky novel about upper-class Satanism by Dennis Wheatley, which, in the eyes of most connoisseurs, greatly improves on its source. The director of *The Devil Rides Out* was Terence Fisher (1904–80), who towards the end of his life earned a (disputed) reputation as an *auteur*, particularly in France. There have been a number of studies of the Hammer horror films, of which one of the earliest, David Pirie's *A Heritage of Horror*, is also one of the best; and the company's productions are still winning fans around the world as its back catalogue becomes widely available on video. *Hammer Horror*, a glossy magazine dedicated to its gothic canon, was launched early in 1995 and soon had a readership of some 40,000 in the UK, USA and Japan. See also *Kensington Gore*.

hand camera, hand-held camera   lightweight portable cameras that can be carried in the cameraman's hand. They are often used by documentary film-makers, news cameramen and the like; or, in feature films, to simulate the effect of such footage. The term hand-held camera is often used synonymously with *hand-held shot*. Memorable hand-held sequences include the attack on the military base in Stanley Kubrick's *Dr Strangelove* (1963) and the interior fight scenes in the same director's *A Clockwork Orange* (1971).

hand-cranked camera   an early type of motion picture camera in which the film was passed through the mechanism by muscle rather than motor power: the operator turned, or cranked, a handle on the side of the camera as regularly as possible.

handlebar mount   a camera mount supplied with bicycle-style handlebars for greater mobility.

hands-on animation   see *animation*.

hanger   a mount which supports a *luminaire*.

hanging miniature   a model of part of a set hung several feet in front of the camera, so creating the illusion of a much larger structure at a greater distance.

hard   (a) an image with high contrast or (b) lighting that produces sharp edges and high contrast in the resulting images.

hard-front camera   a camera which – unlike most professional models, which are equipped with a turret and three or four lenses – has only a single lens.

hard ticket, hard ticket movie in the late 1950s and early 1960s, the American trade term for an expensive, *blockbuster*-style production, such as *Cleopatra* (1963), admission to which could only be gained by buying a more expensive, pre-bookable ticket to a separate performance; the production of hard-ticket films was one of the industry's more succesful attempts at wooing back its audience from television. Anthony Burgess's autobiography *You've Had Your Time* refers to the practice, fudging the chronology slightly but otherwise summing up the phenom-enon with admirable precision: 'The hard-ticket movie was one of the more pleasing innovations of the late sixties . . . It was solid entertain-ment, and the solidity was fancifully attached to the ticket one bought.' The peerless Burgess had been hired to write a 'hard-tick' musical about the life of Shakespeare, never, alas, produced. More recently, 'hard ticket' has come to mean a ticket sold at full box office price, as distinct from a concession or complimentary pass.

Harry the trade name for a Quantel *paintbox* device, used to manip-ulate images electronically; other models in the same family include *Henry* and *Harriet*.

Hays Code, Hays Office the popular names for, respectively, the Motion Picture Production Code (established 1930, made mandatory in 1934, twice revised but only completely discarded in 1968, when it was replaced by a rating system) and the Motion Picture Producers and Distributors of America (formed 1922, changed its name to the Motion Picture Association of America, *MPAA*, in 1945); in other words, folk names for the system of movie censorship which operated in America after a moral panic about sex scandals in Hollywood, and particularly the notorious Fatty Arbuckle affair. The 'Hays' comes from the surname of Will H. Hays (1879–1954), president of MPPDA from 1921 to 1945 and a former Postmaster-General under the Republican President Warren Harding. The Hays Code set rigorous limits to what was permissible on screen, especially in matters of sex, and encouraged the production of wholesome matter.

haze filter a lens filter that absorbs blue and ultraviolet light, so cutting down atmospheric haze; *haze lens*, a soft-focus lens.

HBO the acronym for Home Box Office, the American cable television network that screens feature films around the clock for its subscribers, and also produces features of its own, some of which are given a theatrical release in the USA and other markets.

head variously: the beginning of a reel of film or tape; or the beginning of a scene or shot; or a type of camera mount; or the recording, play-back and erase surfaces in a tape recorder. *Head-on shot*, a shot of action coming directly at the camera; *head-out* (or *head-up*), a reel of film wound with the first frame on the outside, ready for projection, *head shot*, a tight close-up on a performer's head; *head sheet*, a photograph showing several head shots of an actor; *head slate*, the slate displayed at the start of each scene; see *clapperboard*.

heat filter   the optical filter inside a projector that reflects or absorbs the heat from the lamp and so prevents the film from warping or catching fire.

heavy   a thuggish male villain, particularly in a *gangster* movie; so called because, in the early days of cinema, the bad guy was usually played by a bulky actor. Among the actors who have specialised in playing heavies: Lee Marvin (who later graduated from the heaviness of *The Big Heat* and *The Killers* to stardom, though even some of his starring roles – as the vengeful hero of John Boorman's *Point Plank*, for example – have their heavy side), Richard Widmark, Lee Van Cleef, Jack Palance. In American slang, 'heavy man' had been a common name for a criminal since the early 20th C; theatrical villains had sometimes been known as 'heavies', 'heavy actors' or 'heavy villains' since the mid-19th C ('As the heavy villain at the Surrey Theatre would say' – Helps, 1868), though at this time the word was also applied to any sober, sombre or tragic role.

heel   the bottom rear part of a film magazine.

helmer   in *Variety*-speak, a director: plainly a nautical metaphor, which appears to suggest that a director is less like a ship's captain than its Palinurus or steersman; hence *helmed, helming* etc.

herder   the second assistant director: an agricultural or pastoral metaphor, which plainly suggests that extras are like cows or sheep. (Cf, perhaps, Sir Alfred Hitchcock's notorious opinion that actors are cattle.)

hero shot   slang term for the best take of the day, or the one that finds its way into the final edit.

h.i.   common abbreviation for a high-intensity *arc light*.

high-angle shot (also **high shot, down shot**)   a shot that looks down on the subject or action from above.

high concept   a crowd-pleasing film which can satisfactorily be summed up in a single phrase; for example, dinosaurs run amok (*Jurassic Park*), lunatic runs amok (*Halloween*), extra-terrestrials run amok (*Aliens*), or shark swims amok (*Jaws*). The term seems to have come into currency some time in the late 1970s or early 1980s: it is said, for example, that a successful film of the day by Paul Schrader was pitched on its star's name and title alone: 'John Travolta: *American Gigolo*' (the part eventually went to Richard Gere, but the anecdote still illustrates the concept of 'high concept' accurately enough). Such tales continue to circulate: another legend has it that Ivan Reitman's comedy was launched on similar terms: 'Arnold Schwarzenegger and Danny De Vito: *Twins*' . . .

high contrast   an image which stresses the extremes of darkness and brilliance and thus has few intermediate tones; *high-contrast film*, stock which can achieve such effects; *high-key lighting*, an even lighting scheme used to emphasise bright colours; it gives a cheerful effect, and is often used in musicals and comedies.

highlight   (a) to light a object or actor so that it, he or she stands out vividly in the image, generally by using a spotlight; (b) a measure of how much light a subject can accept without becoming distorted by glare (c), in the plural, *highlights* are the brightest parts of an image.

high-speed camera   a camera, used in *high-speed cinematography*, which can expose films (*high speed films*) at much faster rates than the standard 24 frames per second, either (a) to achieve slow-motion effects or (b), in the case of much faster speeds, up to 600 frames a second, for the purposes of scientific research, judging the results of horse-races and so on. Because film tends to snap when run at high speeds through an intermittent motion mechanism, high-speed cameras have a continuous action and achieve distinct exposures by other means: synchronised flash lamps, mirrors, prisms.

highroller   a tall *century stand*.

hi-hat (or less frequently **high-hat**)   a short tripod, used to mount the camera for low-angle shots.

HMI light   a high-intensity arc lamp often used to simulate the warm look of daylight. The initials stand for Halogen Medium Iodide (or, on other accounts, Hydragyrum – i.e. mercury – Medium Iodide). An HMI will be three or four times brighter than incandescent lamps of the same power.

hold   (a) a take that is not immediately printed up, but kept in reserve in case of second thoughts; that is, a *keep take*, or (b) static frames at the head and tail of a reel that has been through the camera, or (c), in animation, the equivalent of a *freeze-frame*: a drawing which is photographed identically for a number of frames so that it appears as a still on screen. *Hold cel*, in animation: the cel which holds the part of an image which is going to remain static while other parts of the image appear to move. *Holdout matte*, see *matte*.

hole   any part of a soundtrack without sound.

Hollywood   the suburb about eight miles north-west of Los Angeles which was for many years – from, say, 1913 until the decline of the *studio system* in the 1950s – the home of the American film industry; thus, today, a somewhat outdated though universally used and understood synecdoche for the American Film Industry and its products; or for its characteristic tastes and methods; or for the mentality witnessed or believed to prevail in and around the major studios. Evocative of glamour, luxury, stardom and the whole complex mythology of American motion pictures since the mid-1920s (the first OED citation is from 1926: Huxley's *Jesting Pilate*), the name 'Hollywood' is also, indeed quite often, used pejoratively, to express disdain for the various lapses of taste and intelligence apparently endemic in commercial film-making: morbid distrust of irony and complexity, rigid notions about what will or will not 'play', formulaic narrative habits, all-round infantilism. OED notes a number of associated nouns and adjectives: *Hollywoodese* (film industry jargon), *Hollywoodesque, Hollywoodian* (or *Hollywoodean*), *Hollywoodish, Hollywoodism,* and *Hollywoodize.* By and large, these are terms of contempt, usually though not always metaphorical; hence *Scrutiny,* in 1941, sneering at 'Puccini, that voice pervasively symbolic of the Hollywoodizing of human emotions.'

The name 'Hollywood' was originally bestowed on the district by a Mrs Horace W. (or Deida) Wilcox, who retired to a ranch there with her husband in 1886. A small community began to grow up around the ranch after 1891, when the Wilcoxes began to divide up their plot, and Hollywood was incorporated as a village in 1903, becoming annexed to Los Angeles in 1910 so as to make use of the city's water supply. Producers had begun to work in Southern California from as early as 1907, and the first studio in Hollywood itself was established in 1911, at the corner of Gower Street and Sunset Boulevard, by the Nestor Company. Though the Nestor studio was joined by some fifteen other small companies by the end of that year, it was in 1913 that the movies really came to Hollywood in in big way, in the person of Cecil B. DeMille, who was scouting around with his co-director Oscar C. Apfel for a suitable location in which to film their western project *The Squaw Man* (Arizona's mountains had looked too snowy). DeMille and Apfel helped set off a new form of gold rush: attracted by the climate and the chance to escape the tyranny of the **Motion Picture Patents Company**, many other producers flocked to this as yet unspoiled land. The new industry, dominated by the likes of William Fox, Samuel Goldwyn, Thomas Ince, Carl Laemmle, Louis B. Mayer and Adolph Zukor, grew with a rapidity that local citrus farmers could only regard with envy and wonder. By 1920 some 800 films a year were pouring out of its hastily assembled studios, and Hollywood was firmly established as the home of the most powerful film industry in the world. That industry continues to dominate the world screens, but its production base has been dispersing from its old haunts since the 1960s, when location shooting became much more common practice and the Hollywood district began to specialise in television movies rather than theatrical features. None the less, the name 'Hollywood' has remained as mythologically potent as ever (compare the enduring flavours and legends of 'Grub Street' or, more recently, 'Fleet Street'). As well as producing films, Hollywood has been the subject of many outstanding movies, from *Sullivan's Travels* and *Sunset Boulevard* to *The Player;* Hollywood novels are no less numerous: *The Day of the Locust, The Last Tycoon, The Deer Park, Flicker.* . . .

Hollywood Blacklist   the roll-call of internal proscriptions carried out by the American film industry in the late 1940s and early 1950s by way of a show of patriotic zeal; these were prompted by the investigations into the alleged communist infiltration of Hollywood carried out by the House Committee on Un-American Activities (HUAC) in 1947 and

1951. Among those whose careers suffered were the so-called *Hollywood Ten*, who refused to testify before HUAC in 1947: Ring Lardner Jr, Dalton Trumbo, Edward Dmytryk and so on. This period has been the subject of a number of movie treatments, including the Woody Allen vehicle *The Front* (about the trick used by blacklisted writers, who would smuggle their work into production under pseudonyms or by passing it off as the work of a willing front man), *Fellow Traveller* and *Guilty by Suspicion*.

homage, or quite commonly if a good deal more archly, **hommage**   the compliment paid by one director to another in the form of an ostentatious formal or thematic allusion. Brian De Palma, for example, many of whose films play variations on the themes of Alfred Hitchcock, often signals this fact by reproducing a well-known moment from the British master's *oeuvre* – the shower scene from *Psycho* at the beginning of *Dressed to Kill*, for example. (Though it must be conceded that every shower scene for the last three decades has either invoked, parodied or fought valiantly to deny its association with Janet Leigh's lethal ablutions.) De Palma's *The Untouchables* also includes an *hommage* to the Odessa steps sequence from Eisenstein's *Battleship Potemkin*.

honey wagon   the mobile combination dressing-room, rest area and lavatory units used by the cast and crew during a shoot.

hook   an attention-grabbing device, used at the start of a film to make sure the audience is enthralled.

horror film   broadly, any film which sets out to chill, terrify or (especially in latter years) disgust its audience, particularly, though not exclusively, with tales of monsters, ghouls, ghosts and other manifestations of the uncanny. 'Horror' comes from L *horror-em*, itself from *horrere*, 'to bristle, shudder'; as 'a painful emotion compounded of loathing and fear', it is first found in English in the late 14th C, and has persisted with a variety of different spellings to the present. 'Horror film' and its counterpart 'horror comic', however, only seem to become widespread in Britain from the mid-1950s, at a time when our moralists were concerned about the pernicious effects of such products on impressionable minds; as late as 1960, *The Times* is still handling the word with gingerly inverted commas: 'The world-wide success of the so-called 'horror' pictures made by Hammer films . . .'. In America, by contrast, the term appears to have been recognised by the late 1930s: 'Mr Arthur L. Mayer took over the . . . theatre, put in horror pictures (zombies and draculas), and he has made it pay every week' – *New Yorker*, 9 January 1937; in Raymond Chandler's *The Big Sleep* (1939) there is a reference to a boy reading a 'horror magazine'. The genre is still disreputable, often deservedly so, but has produced some of the cinema's most poetic, extraordinary or simply enjoyable images: Murnau's *Nosferatu*, Dreyer's *Vampyr*, James Whale's *Frankenstein* and *The Bride of Frankenstein*, *I Walked with a Zombie*, *Cat People*, *Night of the Demon*, *The Seventh Victim*, *Eyes Without a Face*, *The Haunting*, *Hallow-*

een, The Shining, Poltergeist . . . In recent years, there have been a few attempts to give the doggedly B-movie horror film the kind of high production values and high profile that have, in the era since *Star Wars*, helped transform science fiction into an A-film genre; hence *Bram Stoker's Dracula, Mary Shelley's Frankenstein, Interview with the Vampire* and so on. See also *Gothic films, splatter movies*.

horse   a stand found in editing rooms, used to hold the reels that are being fed through the viewer or synchroniser; *horse opera*, jocular or dismissive term for a *Western*; the obvious source is 'soap opera'.

hot   a set or image that is too brightly lit, *hot box*, a junction box into which lighting cables are plugged; *hot frame*, a deliberately overexposed frame at the beginning or end of a shot, used to facilitate editing; *hot lens*, a luminaire lens that can cast a thin, intense beam; *hot set*, a set that is ready for shooting; *hot splice*, another term for a *cement splice* – a strong, permanent splice between two strips of film (usually an original negative or release print) made by using cement and pressure from a simple gadget known as a *hot splicer*; the other, more temporary method of joining film is the *tape splice*, generally used when assembling a *work print*; *hot spot*, a part of the image that is burned out from having been too brightly lit.

house   a business term for a cinema. The word is taken over from the theatre (as one might expect: in the USA, *theater* is a common and unpretentious synonym for 'cinema'), where it has meant 'the building in which plays are performed' since the 16th C. Hence *house lights*, the overhead and side lights in a cinema auditorium, dimmed during screenings; *house reel*, the large, sturdy metal projection reel used in cinemas.

hype   as in other fields: promotion (or, usually, excessive, overblown or unrealistic promotion) of a film by word of mouth and the like as well as by more routine advertising methods. fairly clearly derived from 'hyperbole', though OED notes that the US slang verb 'hype', meaning to swindle or cheat, especially by false publicity, is of unknown origin; the first record of this use was in 1926.

hyperfocal distance   the point at which a lens must be focused to achieve greatest *depth of field*.

Hypergonar   the trade name for an anamorphic lens system that was the prototype for the *CinemaScope* system. It was originally developed by the inventor Henri Chrétien (1879–1956), who first exhibited it in 1927. The Hypergonar was used by Claude Autant-Lara in his short *Construire un feu* (1928), but was otherwise largely ignored by the world until 1952, when 20th Century Fox bought the rights and adapted it for their new wide-screen attraction.

hyphenate   a creative person who does more than one job on a production – actor-director, writer-producer, writer-director-actor and so on; such versatility has become more common since the collapse of the *studio system*, since it allows greater power and freedom to those who can demand it. The term is derived, of course, from the hyphen that links two otherwise distinct job titles.

hypo   the chemical solution that halts the development of film at the appropriate point by dissolving and washing away undeveloped silver halide particles.

I ce box   in the early days of sound films, the slang term for the sound-proof glass chamber in which the camera was mounted so that microphones would not pick up the noise of its mechanisms. Since the use of ice boxes severely limited the possibilities of camera movement, the industry soon developed a new and more mobile form of sound-proofing, the *blimp*. More recently, the term 'ice box' has been applied to a motion-control system developed by Douglas Trumbull and used in *Close Encounters of the Third Kind* and other science-fiction films.

ICM   the abbreviated name of *International Creative Management,* an extremely influential American talent agency, founded in 1975 from Creative Management Associates and the International Famous Agency. It grew in power and scale throught the 1980s, taking over small agencies en route, and its only real rival as a force in the American film industry is *CAA,* the Creative Artists Agency.

identification   the tendency of audiences to respond to the adventures of on-screen heroes and heroines as strongly, or almost so, as if they were living through such experiences themselves. To be sure, this is also an phenomenon that plays its part in our apprehension of the older arts, but, it has been argued with some plausibility, identification can be more vivid or (for those suspicious of the medium's coercive powers) tyrannical in the cinema than anywhere else; such assumptions can play their part in debates about film and video censorship. The screenwriter Jean-Claude Carrière has called identification 'that jewel of cinema, magical transference, the secret journey from one heart to another', and suggests that it is probably beyond rational explanation. The various psychological senses of 'identification' start to enter the English language in the mid-19th C: 'In Livy it will be the manner of telling a story, in Sallust, personal identification with the character': Willmott, 1857; earlier, from the mid-17th C, it had usually meant making one thing identical with another, or regarding it as so. From the late L *identificare,* itself derived from L *idem,* 'same'.

IDHEC (Institut des Hautes Etudes Cinematographiques)   the French state-subsidised film school, founded in 1943 under the control of the director Marcel L'Herbier, and reconstituted in 1970 after the disruptions of May '68. It is now known as *FEMIS.*

idiot cards (or **idiot boards**)   sardonic term for *cue cards* – the sheets of script sometimes held up in front of actors, particularly those incapable of learning their lines by heart. The insult needs no gloss; the term has been in common use since the 1950s (particularly in television, before the advent of the autocue) and probably earlier.

illuminaire, illumination   any source of light, whether artificial or natural, that can be used in filming: a lamp, a reflector and so on. Both words are derived from L *illuminare,* 'to throw light on', and its stem *illuminat-*; the verb 'illuminate' appears from the early 16th C onwards ('Ane feilde of birnest gold so bricht/ That all the land illuminat with greit licht' – Stewart, 1535), and its adjectival sense from the early 15th C. Hence **illuminant**, the bulb used in a projector.

image   the term can be more slippery than it appears, but in the simplest
senses, usually refers either (a) to the still pictures formed on the frames
of film stock after exposure to light, or (b) to the moving pictures
subsequently projected onto a screen.

In the sense of 'an artificial imitation or representation of any object,
esp. of a person' (OED's first definition), the word *image* is very old: it had
already been circulating around Britain for some 150 years before
Wyclif's Bible, in which the book of Exodus commands that 'Thou schalt
not make to thee a grauun ymage . . .'. The word comes to English, via
the 13th C F *image*, from L *imago*, *imagin-em*: imitation, copy, likeness,
statue, picture, phantom; conception, thought, idea; similitude, sem-
blance, appearance, shadow . . . The earliest optical uses of the word
image, meaning the illusion of an object created by reflection in a mirror,
refraction through a lens and so on are also remarkably old, and appear
from the early 14th C, growing more scientific from the mid-17th C, as
one would expect: 'When we see the Image of a Man cast into the Air by
a Concave Spherical Looking-glass' – Boyle, 1674.

The public-relations use of *image*, roughly denoting the fantasy that
the general public is encouraged to have about a particular famous person
or *star*, dates from the early 20th C: 'Between the King and his public
image there was really no relation' – Chesterton, 1908.

Among the technical terms compounded from 'image' are *image plane*,
the field inside the camera at which the image is focused by the lens;
image replacement, any special effects process that adds to, substitutes for
or otherwise modifies an image, for example by a *matte* technique.
Image Stabilizer, the trade name for an Arriflex camera mounting that
uses a gyroscopically gimballed mirror to prevent undue vibration or
jolting when filming from a moving vehicle.

imaginary line   one of the elementary rules of film grammar holds that
all the actions within a given scene should be filmed from the same side,
so that when individual shots are cut together the space will remain
consistent; in other words, that a character on the left hand side of the
image will not suddenly appear to jump to the right hand side and vice
versa. To ensure this, the director and cameraman must make sure never
to cross an imaginary line (also known as the *action axis*, *centre line*,
director's line, *line of interest* and so on) between the major players – a
principle also known as the *180 degree rule*. In practice, it is almost always
possible to cross the line for particular dramatic effects, but if the move
is not carefully justified by the narrative it will tend to appear amateurish.
See *crossing the line*.

Imax   the trade name for a system, originally developed in Canada, of
filming and projecting extremely large images – generally 75 by 100 feet,
well over twice the size of the standard wide screen of 19 by 45 feet, and
closer to a square than the familiar rectangle. These images are achieved
by passing 65mm film horizontally through a specially designed camera.
Since the nature of this system only permits brief takes, the earliest Imax

productions – it was first displayed to the public at Expo 70 in Osaka – mostly took the form of spectacular nature shorts, though recent years have also seen a concert film, *Rolling Stones at the Max*, which runs for about forty minutes with an interval for changing the massive reels. In 1995, the Imax system took a double step forward: into drama, and into 3-D. *Wings of Courage*, a period adventure film about pilots flying an air mail service across the Andes, was directed by Jean-Jacques Annaud and starred Tom Hulce (as Antoine de Saint-Exupéry) and Val Kilmer. It was premiered at the Sony Theatres, Lincoln Square; viewers were required to wear not only 3-D glasses but infra-red headphones (or, as the management charmingly called the headset, a Personal Sound Environment); reviews were tepid. To date, the only Imax system in the United Kingdom belongs to the Museum of Photography in Bradford; at the time of writing, two more are promised for London.

imbibition   from the L *imbibere*, to imbibe, via 14th C Fr *imbibition*; in its earliest English sense of the mid-15th C, 'to soak or saturate with liquid'. A dye-transfer process, also known as *imbibition printing* or *imbibition transfer printing*, used in making release prints for Technicolor and other colour films until the 1970s. Three positives (the *matrices*) would be individually exposed to a negative through a primary colour filter inside an optical printer; each would then be 'imbibed' with its complementary colour, cyan for red, magenta for green and yellow for blue. Though the system itself is now outmoded, the different layers of emulsion in present-day colour film are still called matrices.

IMP   the abbreviated name of the *Independent Motion* (or *Moving*) *Picture Company*, which was in reasonably successful business from 1909 until 1912, when it was absorbed by *Universal*. Its founder was the eccentric Carl Laemmle (1867–1939), who, in addition to his other accomplishments, can be credited with inventing the *star system* in 1910. After seducing *Biograph*'s most famous player, Florence Lawrence 'The Biograph Girl', over to his own company, he planted a fake story about her death in the press, then followed it up the next day with 'indignant' denials and the declaration that the Biograph Girl was now the Imp girl. We are still living with the repercussions of this stunt.

impressionists   a critical label sometimes applied to an informal group of film-makers active in France during the 1920s: Louis Delluc (the movement's chief theorist), Germaine Dulac, Jean Epstein, Abel Gance and Marcel L'Herbier. The relationship of this group to the painterly impressionists appears to be at best indirect.

improvisation   as in the theatre: acting out a scene without the safety net of a script – a technique more commonly found in low-budget, independent features than in studio films, though some of the most famous moments in cinema have been achieved through improvisation. Travis Bickle's unforgettable psychotic monologue 'You lookin' at me?' in Scorsese's *Taxi Driver*, for example, was a piece of inspired improvisation by Robert De Niro. The word originates in Italy, where *improvisare* meant 'to sing or speak extempore', by way of 17th C Fr *improviser*.

in-camera   an adjective denoting any process which is achieved by the camera itself in the course of shooting rather than at a later stage of production; thus: *in-camera editing*, shooting exactly the sequence that will appear on screen, and making all necessary cuts simply by stopping and re-starting the camera; *in-camera effects*, which include slow, fast and reverse motion, multiple exposures, day-for-night shooting and so on; *in-camera matte shots*, for which a portion of the action is blocked off by sheet of glass painted black (or more accurately *was* blocked off: this technique was most common in the early days of cinema, though it has not been wholly superseded) while the other portion is exposed; the film is re-wound, the exposed area blocked and the blank area exposed in turn; *in-camera pass*, in special effects sequences, an electronically controlled camera movement past a model. Since each programmed move is identical, it is possible to build up an image composed of many takes.

in frame   a projected image that has been correctly aligned so that the frame lines are not visible.

in-house unit   a production team that is part of a studio or company's permanent staff; *in-house film*, generally an instructional or propaganda film made for the edification or indoctrination of a company's work-force.

in shot   a person or thing which unintentionally appears in vision. This is a plague of low-budget productions; a boom mike drops all too obviously into vision several times, for example, in Hal Hartley's other-wise admirable independent feature *Trust*.

in sync   the precise marriage of picture and sound; the converse is *out of sync*. See **sync, synchronisation**.

in the can   an expression used to mean either (a) specifically: stock which has been exposed, put in cans and is ready to be processed or, by analogy (b) that shooting has been completed on a particular scene or a whole production.

in turnaround   see *turnaround*.

incandescent light   the warm light produced by a glowing tungsten-halide lamp (or, formerly, a simple tungsten filament lamp), as opposed to the cooler, harsher light produced by flourescent bulbs; also the lamp itself, sometimes called by the slang abbreviation *inky* or *inkie*. The adjective *incandescent* comes from L *incandesc-ere*, to become warm, glow, inflame.

inching   moving film slowly, a frame or so at a time, through a camera, projector or editing machine, by turning an *inching knob* or *incher*.

incident light   all the light, whether from natural or artificial sources, that falls on a subject, as opposed to the light reflected by that subject. It is measured by an *incident light meter*. *Incident*, from L *incidere* and its present participle form *incident-em*, by way of Fr *incident*, is first applied to light in the mid-17th C: 'Looking-Glasses . . . are conspicuous only by the incident beams of the Sun' – Boyle, 1667.

incidental music   the background music for a film – the soundtrack music that accompanies its actions or 'incidents', accentuating or modifying their dramatic meaning, as opposed to the music made by on-screen performers and the like (see *source music*). Cinema takes the term over from the theatre, where it has been in use at least since the mid-19th C.

incoming scene   the scene that emerges on screen during a dissolve, fade-in or wipe.

independent   the adjective commonly applied to any American film made outside the major studios, though more often to relatively conventional features and documentaries than to experimental or avant-garde work; or to any of the comparatively small production companies that produce or have produced such work – AIP, Castle Hill, the Samuel Goldwyn Company, Miramax, New Line Cinema and so on. Hence *independent feature* (*film*, *production*), or, in a common abbreviation, *indie prod*, and *independent film-maker*. Both the films and film-makers may simply be referred to as 'independents'. Some of the most interesting and gifted American film-makers of the past decade or so began as independents, and in one or two cases have remained stubbornly outside the system: Hal Hartley, Jim Jarmusch, Spike Lee, David Lynch, John Sayles, Kevin Smith, Whit Stillman, Quentin Tarantino. Tom DiCillo's *Living in Oblivion* (1995), itself an independent feature, offers a funny and persuasive account of the tribulations encounted by the independent film-maker; *Eating Crow*, a diary DiCillo wrote in the course of making it, corroborates the film.

indigenous sound   the real sound of the location being filmed; or, more narrowly, sound for which there is an obvious on-screen source, such as a production line or a traffic jam. See *direct sound*.

indirect voice-over   see *voice-over*.

industrial film   an informational documentary film sponsored by a particular industrial company, group of companies or marketing body to promote their activities to shareholders or the public, to educate their work-force, or simply to sell their products.

Industrial Light and Magic (ILM)   the company founded by George Lucas in 1975 to devise special effects for *Star Wars*, and which has gone on to be the American film industry's most successful and innovative effects company. Originally based in a warehouse in Van Nuys (California), and run by John Dykstra, ILM relocated to San Rafael near Lucas's home; it has served many of the best-known special-effects movies of the last couple of decades, including *Jurassic Park*, the *Back to the Future* series, the *Star Trek* movies and so on. ILM has pioneered work in *morphing*, *digital effects* and various other sophisticated forms of visual illusion.

infra-red   the long light waves immediately below visible light; some stocks are sensitive to infra-red and thus enable film-makers to shoot in relative darkness if necessary.

ingénue   an innocent female character in her late teens or early twenties; or an actress suitable for such a role. Taken directly from the feminine form of Fr *ingénue* 'ingenuous', and found in English from the mid-18th C: 'When attacked sometimes, Becky had a knack of adopting a demure *ingénue* air, under which she was most dangerous' – Thackeray, *Vanity Fair*, 1848.

inked   *Variety*-speak: signed to a production.

inky   the slang abbreviation for *incandescent light*, the type generally used in studio filming.

insert   a short close-up that can be cut into a sequence either for narrative purposes or to cover up a jump in continuity. The title of John Byrum's *Inserts* (1975), a period comedy (of sorts) about the blue film business starring Richard Dreyfuss, is a lewd pun on the technical term, which has been used at least since 1916, from which year OED notes a sentence in *Phantom Herd* by the pseudonymous 'R.M. Bower': 'He made all of his "close-ups", his inserts and sub-titles'. Inserts may sometimes be shot separately from the main production on an *insert stage*.

insurance shot, insurance take   another term for a *cover shot* – a shot taken in case previous ones are faulty.

INT   in a script, the standard abbreviation for *interior*.

integral reflex viewfinder   see *reflex viewfinder*; *integral screen*, a screen that can create a three-dimensional image, or at least goes some way in that direction; made up of reflective strips that are designed to split left and right eye images, it is meant to free the audience from wearing 3-D glasses, but in practice has not proved very effective; *integral shot*, an unedited shot which lasts the entire length of a scene; *integral tripack colour system*, a film stock with three different layers of light-sensitive emotion, each responsive to different wavelengths; see *colour*.

intensity   the strength of a lamp or other source of illumination; measured in *candelas* or, sometimes, *footcandles*. *Intensification* is the chemical process used to build up contrast in an image, particularly when it has been shot with insufficient light.

intercut   cutting between two or more sets of action in such a way as to make them form a single dramatic unit. In Budd Schulberg's Hollywood satire *What Makes Sammy Run?*, the ghastly anti-hero Sammy Glick is kicking around ideas with his colleagues for a film to be titled *Monsoon*:

'A monsoon is a sequel to a typhoon,' Kit explained.

'Only bigger,' Sammy interpreted. 'So the monsoon'll have to be coming up all the time they're in the cave. It'll be a natural for inter-cutting. Symbolical.'

But intercutting is not always 'symbolical', or even suspenseful; some-times it is used to speed up action, creating swift filmic time from more sluggish real time actions. See also *cross-cut, parallel action*.

interdupe   see *dupe*.

interior   any scene set indoors. *Interior monologue*, in effect, the cinematic equivalent of the stage soliloquy: a voice-over expressing a character's inner thoughts and reactions to what is happening in the drama; for example, the breathy, portentous voice-over of the assassin Willard (Martin Sheen) as he travels up-river towards Colonel Kurtz in *Apocalypse Now*.

interlock   the mechanical process which enables the editor to run images and sound in sync, hence *interlock motor* (also known as a *Selsyn motor*), a motor that can be run in precise sync with a similar motor, so that, for example, two separate cameras can be started and stopped at exactly the same point; *interlock projector*, a projector that can be run in sync with a separate sound machine; *interlock screening*, a screening, held before editing is complete, using an interlock projector.

intermediate   apart from the original negative, any of the films used to make duplicates, such as the *interpositive* and *internegative*.

intermission   either (a) a break in a cinema's daily screenings, calculated to boost sales of confectionery and the like, or (b) the brief hiatus introduced around the mid-point of very long films – *Lawrence of Arabia*, *La Belle Noiseuse* – as an act of mercy to the audience's spines and bladders.

intermittent movement   the rapidly alternating stop-go camera and projector action which makes the correct exposure of frames possible: that is, a mechanism which feeds film regularly through the camera, printer or projector at 24 frames a second, but pauses for a fraction (usually 1/24th) of a second on each frame so that a sharp image can register or be cast. OED gives no example earlier than 1959, but the term must surely be much older, probably as old as the technique itself.

internal rhythm   the pattern of image and sound durations within a particular scene or sequence; the overall rhythm of a film is known as the *external rhythm*.

internegative (IN)   a negative made from the film's original negative, and used to strike *release prints*; this process is designed to preserve the original negative in mint condition.

interpositive (IP)   a positive print made from the original negative. Interpositives are used to make *dupes* – duplicate negatives – and are not for projection.

into frame   in a script: the instruction that a character, object or action that was previously off-screen should now become visible to the audience.

inverse square law   a principle of physics which states that the strength of lighting (or sound) is inversely proportional to the square of the distance between the subject and the lamp (or microphone). For directors who failed their elementary physics, this means that levels of illumination (or audibility) start to drop off much more rapidly than common sense might seem to dictate: moving an object twice as far away from the camera does not produce half the existing level of illumination but a quarter, and so on.

invisible cutting   the unobtrusive style of editing developed by Hollywood in the days of the studio system and still employed in many, if not most commercial productions. Essentially, it consists of a number of conventions that have become so familiar over the years that they no longer register as conventions, but seem natural and inevitable: for example, the technique of filming a conversation between two characters in a sequence of alternating shots and reaction shots, punctuated with a master two-shot. The foundation stone of invisible cutting is the principle of *cutting on action*: the audience is sufficiently entranced by the continuity of narrative that it is untroubled by the discontinuity of space and/or time. This style of cutting is also known as *academic* or *continuity cutting*.

invisible splices   the type of splices used in *A and B Roll Printing*: when the two rolls are joined togther, no cuts should be visible. Hence Stan Brakhage on Bruce Conner's *The White Rose*, which, unlike this avant-garde director's other films, aimed to conceal the mechanics of its editing: 'In it, he deliberately worked with "A" and "B" roll printing, used to conceal the splices.... He went a long way to have no splices showing; thus if we do see a splice, we know he meant it to be seen.'

IPS or **i.p.s.**   stands for Inches per Second, the rate at which sound tape passes through a recorder: seven and a half IPS is considered the slowest acceptable speed for music recording.

iris (or **diaphragm**)   (a) the adjustable metal or plastic device, made up of small overlapping sheets, used to create the aperture in a camera and so to regulate the amount of light which can pass through its lens. Hence, (b) a punctuating effect, most frequently found in the silent cinema, indicating the beginning and/or end of a scene (see *fade*), and achieved simply by closing the iris, so that blackness would gradually encroach on the image from all sides, creating a circular picture which would grow smaller until it vanished. This effect is also known as an *iris in*; its counterpart, achieved by opening the iris, is an *iris out*; both may also be referred to as *iris shots*. The photographic sense of *iris* (ultimately derived from the Greek goddess whose emblem was the rainbow) is taken over from its anatomical use; 'iris' has designated the structure within the eye that regulates the amount of light that can pass to the retina since the early 16th C. The first cinematic sense recorded by OED comes in 1911: 'alteration of diaphragm is effected by the movement of a ring or pin on the lens mount which causes the "iris" inside to open and close like the iris of a cat's eye, except that the hole in the middle always remains circular in shape.' Some histories credit the invention of the cinematic iris to D.W. Griffith's celebrated cameraman Billy Bitzer, and Griffith himself was certainly an inventive exploiter of the device, often using it as a sort of adjustable frame within the frame, isolating a particular character or action. Other silent film-makers also came up with iris shots in a variety of different shapes, including squares, rectangles and stars. Today, iris shots are hardly ever used except in pastiches of silent films, since advances in optical printing techniques made this and other in-camera effects seem rather crude. Among the few recent exceptions to this rule is the BFI production *Anchorite* (Chris Newby, 1993), a drama about a medieval hermit, where the effect echoes other dark, circular shots – for example, the view through a rudimentary telescope, the opening of a well as seen from inside and so on.

ISO the abbreviation for International Standards Organisation, a body which draws up the exposure index for films: hence **ISO exposure index**, **ISO numbers**.

It Girl a short-lived ideal of feminine sexual magnetism, dreamed up by the novelist and screenwriter Elinor Glyn (1864–1943) and incarnated for the cinema by the actress Clara Bow (1905–65), notably in *It* (1927) and *The Wild Party* (1929). 'It' had been a euphemism for sexual magentism since the turn of the century; Kipling, for example uses it – or It – in *Traffics & Discoveries*, 1904.

Itala Film a short-lived Italian production company, founded in Turin by Giovanni Pastrone in 1908 and absorbed into the Unione Cinematografica in 1919. Though the company was a sucessful producer of short comedies, it is remembered by cinema historians primarily as the production base for Pastrone's epic of a slave girl's adventures during the Second Punic war, *Cabiria* (1914), for which d'Annunzio was alleged to have written the screenplay. (In fact, though d'Annunzio was extremely well paid for putting his name to the production, his principal contribution appears to have been the wording of some intertitles.) *Cabiria* was technically innovative in several respects – its use of dolly and crane shots, its lighting, the tinting of the original release prints – and proved both popular and hugely influential around the world. Griffith, for example, who is said to have studied the film minutely, was able to use its box-office success to encourage backing for his own epic productions.

Italian a lighting clamp.

J **ack** a type of electrical socket, with one or more pairs of terminals, used to connect equipment to an electrical circuit when a *jack plug* is inserted. The electrical sense of this exceptionally rich word has been current, so to speak, since the late 19th C: the *Practical Telephone Handbook* of 1891 observes that 'The effect of inserting a plug in one of the jacks is that the end of the plug lifts the line spring . . .'. The origins of this particular application are uncertain, but *jack* has been a common word for various types of machine or machine parts since the late 16th C, apparently on the principle that the machine undertook labours which would previously have been the lot of a man or boy; and *Jack* has been the generic name for a man of the common people at least since the early 16th C. Hence Shakespeare's 'A mad-cap ruffian and a swearing Iacke', and the expression 'every man jack', still heard in many parts of Britain. *Jack tube*, a support for a *luminaire*; the tube can be telescopically extended, and so wedged between two surfaces, usually walls.

jam the accidental clogging of a camera or projector mechanism by loose film; the earliest OED citation for the mechanical use of the term is from 1890, though the sense of 'tight packing' or 'crushing together' can be found in the early 19th C.

jelly see *gel*

jenny colloquial name for the portable generators used for location shooting. Brief etymology: 'generator' = 'gen' = 'jen' = 'jenny'.

jib, jib arm the part of a *dolly* or *crane* to which the camera is attached: a movable extended arm. The projecting arm of a crane (or boom of a derrick) has been known as a jib (or *gib*) since the mid-C18; though the origin is not clear, it is generally supposed to have been derived from the plain visual similarity between a crane and a gibbet.

jiggolo or sometimes **gigolo**, a gadget developed to overcome a projection difficulty found in the early days of the *Cinerama* process. Designed to blur the points at which the sides of projected images joined or overlapped unevenly, it consisted of a pair of jagged-edged *masks* fitted inside the projector. Etymology uncertain, but possibly derived from *jiggle* 'to move backwards and forwards or up and down with a light unsteady motion' (late 19th C onwards), itself a diminutive of *jig* (late 16th C onwards), uncertainly derived from OF *gigue*, a stringed instrument; but modern Fr *gigue*, a dance, is held to have been borrowed from English, so the mystery remains.

jitter a flickering effect generally caused by incompetent camerawork in animated films, or by fluctuations of the pulse in a cathode-ray tube. 'Jitter', meaning to shake, and 'the jitters', meaning a state of nervous tension, are early 20th C US slang; 'jitter' and 'jittery' became applied to shaky television or film images after about 1940. 'The main danger of rostrum tracks or pans is strobing, or jitter' – Halas & Manwell, *The Technique of Film Animation*, 1959.

jog a term sometimes used in videotape editing: to move the image forwards or backwards frame by frame.

Johnston office   from 1945 to 1961, the colloquial name for the Motion Picture Association of America (*MPAA*), whose president was Eric A. Johnston (1896–1962). The office had previously been held by Will *Hays*; Johnston was a slightly less severe censor than Hays had been, but his office was still extremely powerful.

Joinville   or 'Babel-sur-Seine', the home of the Pathé studios, specially adapted by Paramount in the early days of talking pictures for the production of foreign-language versions of their movies; the first of them was completed in March 1930. Using a production-line system, in which teams of actors would replay scene after scene on the same sets but in different languages, the Joinville studios could rapidly and cheaply turn out as many as a dozen versions of the same original film. As one would expect, the quality of these alternative versions was seldom high, and few of them except those recorded in Spanish (and exported to the South American market) made much of a profit. Paramount abandoned this labour-intensive system after two years, and the practice of *dubbing* became the standard method of penetrating non-Anglophone markets.

Joker   a production company founded by Carl Laemmle in 1913, and specialising, as its name suggests, in undemanding comedies.

joystick   any mechanism for operating a camera by remote control, particularly for special effects sequences. OED first records 'joystick', meaning the control lever of an aeroplane or other vehicle, in 1910.

juicer   colloquial name for an electrician, but especially for a lamp operator – the person who, by switching them on and off, feeds lights with electricity or 'juice'. Electricity has been colloquially known as 'juice' since the early 20th C ('The first he asked . . . whose town had got the juice': 1903).

jump cut   a violation, usually wilful, of the classical conventions of editing, created either (a) by suddenly moving the camera much closer to the subject without softening the effect by significantly altering the camera angle, or (b) by trimming film from the middle of a shot. Jump cuts became much more common in the 1960s after the critical success and scandal of Jean-Luc Godard's début feature, *A Bout de souffle* (*Breathless*) and other products of the *Nouvelle Vague*, and are now relatively commonplace in rock *videos* and the feature films which emulate their style. OED's earliest citation is from Karel Reisz's classic *Technique of Film Editing* (1953), where he defines it as a 'cut which breaks continuity of time by jumping forward from one part of an action to another obviously separated from the first by an interval of time.'

jump out   to trim unwanted frames from a shot.

Junger Deutscher Film   the movement of young German film-makers which can be dated from the *Oberhausen Manifesto* of 1962, and which was an act of rebellion against the dismal aesthetic and technical standards of their national cinema in the 1950s and early 1960s. Leading lights of the movement include Volker Schlöndorff, Alexander Kluge,

Edgar Reitz and Jean-Marie Straub, followed by Rainer Werner Fassbinder, Werner Herzog and Wim Wenders.

junior   a small focusable spotlight, of 1000–2000 watts, used to single out a given performer or space.

justified camera movement   a camera movement that is clearly motivated by dramatic or narrative logic – we follow a character as he walks down a corridor; we dolly to the smoking revolver lying on the table – rather than by the director's desire to change the composition of the shot.

juvenile   as in the theatre: either the character of a young man, or, more often, the actor who plays that character. From L *juvenis*, a young person, and *juvenilis*, young or belonging to youth; the theatrical sense of the English term dates from the late 19th C.

K **abuki** though the influence of Japan's classical theatre on its national cinema has been relatively minimal, since its highly formal and stylised techniques are on the whole ill-suited to the realism of the medium, a number of the country's leading directors have produced adaptations from the Kabuki repertoire from time to time: Mizoguchi, for example, with *Genroku Chusingura* (1942) and Kurosawa with *Tora no O o Fumu Otokotachi* (*The Men Who Walk on the Tiger's Tail*, 1945). The form's real route into world cinema is by way of Eisenstein, who was impressed by a visit of Kabuki players to Moscow in 1928; their methods helped form his thinking about *montage*, and his film *Ivan the Terrible* (1944 and 1958), with its exaggerated characters and heightened emotion, shows some more direct borrowing from Kabuki. 'Kabuki' is a compound of three Japanese characters, *ka* 'song', *bu* 'dance' and *ki* 'art, skill'.

Kalem an early American film company, founded in 1905 and taken over by Vitagraph in 1916; the name was a slurred acronym of its three founders, George Kleine, Samuel Long and Frank Marion. The company made only one feature film, a life of Christ entitled *From the Manger to the Cross*, directed by its most distinguished film-maker Sidney Olcott (1873–1949) in 1912. Olcott's film may be regarded as the *Last Temptation of Christ* of its day, since it provoked angry accusations of blasphemy and, in Britain, demands for film censorship; unlike Scorsese's film, however, it was also a hit with the mass audience. But Kalem also enjoyed a good deal of success with its many one-reelers and series, and Olcott's taste for dramas about topical public issues helped give the company a reputation for social conscience and gritty authenticity. Kalem has its place in legal histories as well as chronicles of the cinema, since the court case which resulted from its unauthorised production of *Ben Hur* (1907, again directed by Olcott) established the principle that films of copyrighted material, like adapations into other media, can only be made with the owners' consent. Moreover, Olcott helped establish the practice of location shooting, travelling to Florida (where he shot *Florida Crackers*, 1908), Europe and, for his sole full-length feature, the Holy Land. He left the company in 1913, and eventually made his way to Britain, where he became a production director for British Lion; Kalem never quite recovered from his loss.

Kammerspeilfilm literally, 'chamber-play film' – the cinematic outgrowth of Max Reinhardt's *Kammerspiel* work: plays for a small, intimate theatre. Strictly speaking, the term applies to a number of silent films made in Germany during the 1920s: *Hintertreppe* (1921), *Scherben* (1921), *Sylvester* (1923) and, most famous of the group, Murnau's *Der Letzte Mann* (*The Last Laugh*, 1924). All of these were scripted by the Austrian screenwriter Carl Mayer (1894–1994), who was also the most important theorist of the genre. The typical *Kammerspielfilm* is a middle-class drama, featuring a small number of characters who have roles or functions rather than names; its settings will be dark, drab and sparsely furnished; and there will be no intertitles, a constraint which may lead to great visual fluency but tends to limit such pieces to rather elementary story-lines and crude psychological portraiture. As this may suggest, the *Kammerspeilfilm* was sharply distinct from the other leading movement in the German cinema of the time, *expressionism*; curiously enough, Mayer also co-wrote the script for *Das Cabinett des Dr Caligari* (1919), though he and his partner disowned the filmed version as a complete reversal of his original intentions. Nowadays, the term can be more loosely applied to certain kinds of deliberately unglamorous domestic dramas – Paul Schrader, for example, has referred to his blue-collar family study *Light of Day* as a *Kammerspeilfilm*; see *Schrader on Schrader* (ed. Jackson, 1990).

Kensington Gore industry (particularly stunt-persons') slang for the fake blood used by the British film and television industries, and seldom more copiously than by *Hammer Films*. This jocular term was derived from a play on the street of the same name in London SW7 (which presumably owes its orgins to the second sense of 'gore' noted by OED, 'a triangular piece of land') and the more horrific sense of 'gore', 'blood in the thickened state that follows effusion' (from OE *gor*, dung or dirt).

keep takes the takes that are preserved for possible inclusion in the completed film.

keg a 750-watt spot, so called because its shape vaguely resembles that of a beer barrel.

Kem the brand name of a American flatbed editing machine, similar to the more familiar *Steenbeck*.

key animation a form of computer animation in which the artist – known as the *key animator* – draws only those frames (the *keys*) which contain the most significant points of motion (or change) and the computer carries out the drudgery of filling in all the intermediate points.

key grip the person, usually male, in charge of the manual labourers on a set – in other words, the *grips*.

key light the main light in a scene, generally set up first and used as the basis for the rest of the lighting scheme. It is usually set in front and to one side of the principal subject or action.

key numbers the serial numbers printed by the manufacturer along the edge of the film, and used by the negative cutter as a guide in the process of conforming the negative; the editor will also make lists of key numbers when he is ordering fades, dissolves and the like from the optical department, to specify precisely how long each transition should last.

Keystone the company whose one- and two-reel films dominated American comedy in the silent era, particularly during the period from 1912 to 1917 when Mack Sennett was its head of production and principal director. The keynote of Keystone was frenetic, acrobatic, madcap humour, laced with plenty of chases, pratfalls, trick photography and custard pies. Sennett, who had learned the art of editing from D.W.

Griffith at *Biograph*, produced some 500 films for the company before he moved to Paramount, most notably 35 films with Charlie Chaplin; one of these, the six-reeler *Tillie's Punctured Romance* (1914), is usually cited as the first full-length comedy feature. Other comedians to work with the company included Fatty Arbuckle, Wallace Beery, Frank Capra (as a gag writer), Buster Keaton, Harold Lloyd (briefly) and Ben Turpin. Sennett also assembled the Mack Sennett Bathing Beauties (of whom the most famous was Marie Prevost, though Gloria Swanson – in fact a leading lady for the company – was often described as having risen from their ranks) and, of course, the sublimely incompetent *Keystone Kops*. The company folded soon after Sennett's defection to become an independent producer, distributing his work through Paramount, in 1917.

keystoning a type of image distortion, caused (a) during a shoot, by the camera not being at a true right angle to the plane it is meant to be filming, or (b) in the cinema, by the projector not being at a true right angle to the screen: instead of a right-angled rectangle of standard ratio, the result is a keystone shape.

kicker light (also **kick light, cross backlight, eye light, slice light**) a small light used to make some object in the foreground stand out sharply against the background, or to make a performer's eyes shine more brightly.

kill on set, an order to turn off a piece of electrical equipment: the apparently Herodian cry of 'Kill the baby!' simply means 'turn off the small light!' Film-makers seem to have taken the command over from the theatre, where it had been current since the early 20th C; the earliest strictly cinematic use cited by OED is from 1940. Compare the use of 'kill' – 'cancel, delete, remove' – in printing and journalism from the mid-19th C onwards; or, in the world of engineering and mechanics, the sense 'to turn off or stop'.

kine-, kinema- early, or, nowadays, deliberately archaic prefixes for a variety of moving picture technologies, particularly the kinematograph (see below), itself ultimately derived from Gk *kinema, kinemato*, 'motion', plus *-graph*, from Fr *-graphe*, L *-graphus* and Gk *-graphos*, 'written' or 'that writes' and *graphein*, 'to write'. (See, of course, *cinema*. Incidentally, before the Lumières, the adjective *kinematic* was a scientific term meaning 'relating to pure motion, i.e. motion considered abstractly'.) Thus, for example, *Kinemacolor* was an early British colour film process using an additive method. Its inventors, G. Albert Smith and Charles Urban, introduced the process in 1906 and soon built up a successful library of short colour films. The hardiest of the various kine-compound words, *kinematograph*, was an early and popular English variant spelling of *cinematograph*, itself taken more or less directly from the Lumière Brothers' name for their invention the *cinématographe*. The *Daily News* for 21 February 1896 reports 'An exhibition of the "Cinématographe" in the Marlborough Hall of the Polytechnic, Regent Street, yesterday afternoon. The "Cinématographe" is an invention of MM. Lumiere, and it is a contrivance by which a real scene of life and movement may be reproduced before an audience in a life-size picture.' But the word soon became a naturalised British citizen, swapping its capital C for a K and shedding its tell-tale acute accent. Hence in 1897: 'It was the lamp of the kinematograph which set the place on fire'; from 1899, 'What is called the "American Biograph" – an improved form of the kinematograph'; and, a metaphorical use from the same year, 'Reducing to order and viewing synoptically the kinematograph of life'. The adjective *kinematographic* or *cinematographic* occurs as early as 1897: for example, in 1900, 'A novel by . . . Galdos . . . with a wonderful kinematographic style.' Though it became more scarce as the insitutions of cinema, and the word 'cinema' itself, grew more common, 'kinematograph' survived well into the latter half of the 20th century in odd corners, notably in the name of the British trade organisation KRS, or *Kinematograph Renters Society*, established in 1915. Note also the largely forgotten *Kinematophone*, which was a gadget for producing sound effects during the screening of silent films.

kinescope   an abbreviation for 'kinescope recording', the American term for a recording of a live television broadcast onto film. (Though the term was also applied to the cathode ray tubes used in television sets; indeed, it was a propriety name for such devices until 1950.) In the days before the advent of videotape, this was the only available means of preserving programmes; see *telecine*. 'On June 2 a United States television network transmitted a kinescope version of the B.B.C.'s television of the Abbey Coronation service' – *Manchester Guardian Weekly*, 2 July 1953. Incidentally, the BBC still abbreviates its telecine facilities to TK rather than TC, to avoid possible confusion with its more common in-house use of TC to designate the Corporation's White City headquarters, Television Centre.

kinestasis   any use of still photographs or other images in moving pictures; the term includes camera moves across a photograph, dissolves from still to still and so on. The process is also known as *photokinesis* and *photokinestasis*.

kinetograph, kinetoscope   the kinetograph has a fair claim to being the first moving picture camera, albeit a rather crude one, since it was developed by Edison and his laboratory staff (particularly his chief engineer W. K. L. Dickson) around 1888–9 and was patented in 1891, four years before the Lumières' celebrated screening. 'The kinetograph is a machine combining electricity with photography' – *The Times*, 29 May 1891. The machine fed 35mm celluloid-base film stock (manufactured by the Eastman company) horizontally behind a lens by means of a sprocket-and-perforation system similar to that still used today; the results could then be seen by the paying public on the kinetoscope, a peep show inside which ran a 50-foot loop of film. Edison also experimented with the *kinetophone*, which combined peep show and phonograph, but this was not a success. (The same term was later applied to another Edison invention – a pioneer form of sound cinema that was tried out on a largely unresponsive public from 1913 to 1916.) Though the kinetoscope itself was soon overtaken by a truer form of cinematic apparatus, the Lumière brothers' *Cinématographe*, the name appears to have survived for a couple of decades after the gadget itself became defunct as a loose synomym for 'movie camera'; thus, in 1915: 'Just as the Action Motion Picture has its photographic basis in the race down the high-road, just as the Intimate Motion Picture has its photographic basis in the close-up interior scene, so the Photoplay of Splendor, in its four forms, is based on the fact that the kinetoscope can take in the most varied of out-of-door landscapes' (Vachel Lindsay, *The Art of the Moving Picture*). And well before Edison set to work, Webster had defined the kinetoscope as 'a sort of movable panorama' (1864). OED also records the term *kinetoskotoscope*, citing the *Westminster Gazette* for 18 March 1896: 'The kinetoskotoscope ... By means of this barbarously termed piece of apparatus it is possible, so we are told, to see the motions of the bones of the finger when bent backwards and forwards.'

Kino-Glaz, Kino-Pravda terms derived from the ideology and practice of the early Soviet director, theorist and poet Dziga Vertov (1896–1954), whose real name was Denis Kaufman. *Kino-glaz* (Russian: 'film eye') was the name of the group he formed with his brother Mikhail Kaufman and his wife Elizaveta Svilova (the alliance was sometimes known as *Kinoki*, 'film eyes'); it was also the title of one of the films they made, in 1924; and, above all, it was the label for the theory that guided their work. *Kino-pravda* ('film truth') was the collective title of a series of 23 newsreels the group produced from 1922 to 1925, working with footage shot by hundreds of different cameramen, that was then – in accordance with Vertov's theories – processed and edited into complex patterns of slow and reverse motion, superimposition and so on. Vertov's dazzling or, to their detractors, flashy ways with montage became well-known outside the USSR after 1931, when he toured Western Europe with a print of *Chelovek s Kinoapparatom* (*Man With a Movie Camera*, 1929), the swift-moving and flamboyant documentary feature by which he is best remembered today. Many European documentary film-makers of the 1930s were greatly inspired by Vertov's work, but the state he had served so diligently and creatively attacked him with charges of 'formalism' on the rise of Stalin, and he only made one more feature film. By the time of his death, his international reputation was at a low ebb, but it began to pick up again in the 1960s, particularly after the newly radicalised Jean-Luc Godard began to issue the films he made with Jean-Pierre Gorin under the signature 'Groupe Dziga Vertov': these included *Un film comme les autres*, *British Sounds* and *Pravda*.

Klangfilm a German production company, founded in 1928 by AEG, Polyphone and Siemens. In 1929 it went into partnership with the Tonbild Syndikat AG; see *Tobis*.

klieg light   an extremely powerful arc floodlight, suitable for open-air use. The name is an abbreviation from that of its manufacturers, the Kliegel Brothers (J.H. and Anton), American designers of German birth.

knee shot   a shot of a person or persons from the knee up; see *medium shot*.

Kodak   the film company has attached its brand name to a number of commonly used words and terms, notably *Kodachrome*, the tripack reversal process for 8mm and 16mm film, of which the entertainer Paul Simon has (literally) sung the praises, and *Kodak standard perforation* (*KS*; also known as *positive standard* or *positive perforation*), the rectangular sprocket hole on positive 35mm, 65mm and 70mm film which superseded the more easily damaged Bell and Howell perforation. The word, patented in 1888, was devised by George Eastman, who wanted a name short, easy and memorable enough to register the product in the minds of recent immigrants to the USA even if they had only a minimal grasp of English. Its most famous compound term is the company's colour film process *Kodachrome* (Kodak plus Gk *chromos*, 'colour') first noted by OED in 1915.

Kuleshov effect   one well-known aspect of the many general theories of *montage* developed in the Soviet Union during the early 1920s. Briefly, the term designates the emotional or intellectual meaning that is created by the juxtaposition of shots in editing rather than by the isolated content of a single image: thus, it was argued, a shot of a man with his mouth wide open might mean any number of different things, depending on the shots that preceded or followed it – a dead child (paternal grief), a circus clown (hilarity), an attractive woman (lust). The effect owes its name to the director and theorist Lev Kuleshov (1899–1970), who taught in the early 1920s at the State Film School in Moscow, the *VGIK* (Vsesoyuznyi Gosudartvenyi Institut Kinematograffi), founded in 1919. Kuleshov's students and associates – known as the *Kuleshov Workshop* – included V.I. Pudovkin (1893–1953) later the director of *Storm Over Asia* (1928) and other internationally admired films and himself an important theorist of *montage*. It is sometimes said that necessity was the mother of the Soviet cinema's invention in its early years: lacking the money and resources actually to shoot and edit films of their own, the Kuleshov group would act out short 'films' in the form of playlets, or re-edit existing films, such as Griffith's *Intolerance*, or random stock footage into new and inventive forms. With the possible exception of *The Extraordinary Adventures of Mr West in the Land of the Bolsheviks* (1924), Kuleshov's own films are hardly shown these days, but his example told deeply in the work of his better-known comrades, including Eisenstein.

L **ab, laboratory** from medieval L *laboratorium*; used in English in more or less its modern sense ('a place for practical experiments, especially in chemistry') from the early 17th C: 'Wee commonly prouide that they bee prepared in our laboratorie' – Timme, 1605. In the world of cinema, the laboratory is the place (or company) where (or by which) film is developed, processed and printed; *lab* or *laboratory effects*, special effects produced in the processing of the film rather than on set or in the camera; *lab reports*, lists of film damage or any other problems sent to the cinematographer with each set of developed rushes.

lace from OF *laz* and the popular L *lacium*, 'noose': to insert film into a projector, or tape into a recorder. The earliest cinematic use given by OED is in 1948, from C.A. Hill's manual *Cine-Film Projection* ('this should never be necessary if you always lace the film correctly'), but since 'lace' had meant 'to insert a cord, etc, through a hole, etc' since the early 17th C, the practical use of the term is likely to be as old as the camera and projector themselves.

lacquer, lacquering the protective coating on the surface of film stock; the word is known, in various diffrent spellings ('lacker', 'leckar', 'lacre' etc.) from the late 16th C: 'Enquire of the price of leckar . . .' – Hakluyt, *Voyages*, 1579.

lambert a unit of brightness (or *luminance*) equal to one *lumen* per square centimetre, or approximately 3180 *candelas* per square metre. The term commemorates the German mathematician Johnan Heinrich Lambert (1728–77); it appears to have been coined some time shortly before 1915 by Dr P.G. Nutting, and OED cites an article by Dr Nutting in *Electrical World* for February of that year as its first appearance in print.

lamp (from Fr *lampe*, L *lampas* and ultimately the Gk *lampas*, from *lampein*, 'to shine'; it can be found in English from about 1200 onwards) any of the electrical sources of light used in a studio or on location; or, in some circumstances, the entire lighting unit. *Lamphouse*, the part of a projector or optical printer that holds its lamp in position; *lamp operator*, the crew member who operates any large lighting unit.

lap dissolve an abbreviation for 'overlap dissolve', which is itself generally abbreviated still further to the simple *dissolve.*

large format camera any camera that can produce a negative image larger than 35mm; uncommon in practice, since the costs involved are very high.

laser an acronym – Light Amplification by the Stimulated Emission of Radiation – for the device that can produce concentrated beams of light, used in holography and other processes. It was first developed, from the earlier maser, in 1960. Hence *laser disc* or *laser videodisc*, the audio-visual equivalent of the compact disc, on which sounds and images are recorded by light rather than magnetically.

latent image the invisible, potential image on film which has been exposed but not yet processed or developed. 'Latent' is from L *latent-em,* the present participle of *latere*, 'to be hidden'; it comes into English in the early 17th C; the photographic sense can be found as early as the mid-1860s: 'The latent image becomes developed' – J. Wylde, c 1865. *Latensification*, is a process for building up the density of an image by very slowly exposing an underdeveloped negative to very low light. The process was new in 1940, when *American Cinematographer* introduced the term to its readers in inverted commas: '"Latensification", the name describing this new process, is an outgrowth of the work being done by Du Pont Film Manufacturing Corporation on high speed 35mm film'.

lateral colour   a lens flaw that creates unwanted fringes of colour in the image; *lateral flicker*, a flaw caused by panning too rapidly.

Laterna Magica or **Magika**   an ingenious show first devised for the Czechoslovakian pavilion at the 1958 Brussels exhibition, which combined projected film images with live performance: characters would appear to emerge from and go back into the screen, filmed dancers would duet with three-dimensional partners and so on. It was the creation of the theatre and film director Alfred Radok, one of the few experimental spirits at work in the Czech cinema of the day; his younger collaborators on the project included the directors Milos Forman and Ivan Passer, both of whom are now considerably better known than their mentor. Radok left the Laterna Magica after a film he made for its second programme was banned, and in 1968 emigrated to Sweden. The Laterna itself continued to be popular, but its work became less inspired.

Latham loops   the early, and – pedantically speaking – still the correct full name of the small loops of film that can be seen on either side of a camera or projector aperture, and which allow the film to switch from continuous to intermittent movement and back again; see *loop*, *Panopticon*.

latitude   (from L *latitud-o*, from *latus*, 'broad, wide'; known in English from late 14th C) the range inside which a film can be exposed so as to produce an adequate image – that is, so that the results will be neither underexposed (too little light) nor overexposed (too much). Also called *exposure latitude*.

lavalier, lavalier microphone   a small microphone that hangs from the performer's neck rather like a decorative pendant; the term is derived from the world of fashion and jewellery, and therefore, ultimately, from the French courtesan Louise de la Vallière (1644–1710). Unlike a necklace, however, the lavalier microphone is carefully hidden under the performer's clothes. The use of lavaliers is more common in documentaries than features.

lavender, or **lavender print**   the colloquial term used in both black and white and colour cinematography for the fine grain master positive used to strike prints. Though well known in the US, the term seems to be somewhat more common in the UK, and dates back to the period from 1929 to 1940 when the high quality positive stock from which *dupes* were made did indeed have a distinct lavender tint. Hence C.B.

De Mille in 1936: 'A "lavender" is something often spoken of in the industry . . .'

lay, lay-in, lay down   standard editing jargon for the process of adding or cutting something in to a workprint, but particularly for matching sound-tracks to picture, or *track-laying*. Hence John Baxter's mischievous play on words in his biography *Fellini* (1993): 'By the mid-thirties Roberto [Rossellini] was in the movies, laying sound effects and just as vigorously laying Assia Noris.'

lead   as in the theatre: the principal actor(s) or actress(es) of a production; or the major parts played by those performers; an abbreviation of 'leading role', a term in common theatrical use since the 18th C. As a verb, to lead is to compose a shot in such a way that there is more room in front of a moving subject than behind; if this convention is not observed, the audience may gather the subliminal impression that the subject is about to crash into the edge of the screen, or into something just off-screen. *Lead man*, the chief of the *swing gang* in the set dressing department. *Lead sheet*, a kind of graph or diagram illustrating the relationship between a music and/or sound track and the visual action of a film, particularly in animated films. Also known as a *bar sheet*. *Lead time*, the period between the start of a production and its agreed delivery date.

leader   the blank or black film used at the heads and tails of release prints which make it possible to thread the film into the projector without damaging or losing the images or, at reel changes, interrupting the dramatic flow of the movie. (C.N. Bennett, *Guide to Kinematography*, 1917: 'Refrain from . . . cutting or punching holes in the film leaders.') The same type of film is used to stand in for missing shots when assembling a work print. The leader used at the beginning of reels will usually have countdown numbers, set at intervals of 16 frames, to help the projectionist time his change-over; this is known as *Academy leader*, since it was designed by the *Academy* of Motion Picture Arts and Sciences.

leaf shutter   a rotating blade set inside a camera or projector; when spinning, it helps reduce flicker and visible frame lines.

Legion of Decency   from its foundation in 1934 until 1968 (when it changed its name to the National Catholic Office for Motion Pictures), the Legion of Decency would draw up an ethical rating for Hollywood films and ask the pious to boycott those it judged unacceptable. See *censorship*.

legs   (a) as in the theatre: a production which can not only draw audiences, but keep drawing them week by week, is said to have 'legs'. (b) Less commonly, another term for *tripod*.

lens   from L *lens*, 'lentil', since the shape is so similar to an optical lens; the word enters English in the late 17th C, and is used in connection with photography from the beginning of the art (OED has a quotation from Fox Talbot in 1841): the translucent (usually glass, usually disc-shaped) object used to focus images onto film stock in a camera, onto a screen from a projector and so on. Lenses fall into three principal categories, according to their focal length: normal, wide angle and telephoto; a *zoom* lens combines all three focal lengths.

Among the many pieces of equipment and terminology associated with lenses are the *lens adapter*, which allows a lens with one type of mount to be used on a camera that usually takes a different type of mount; *lens aperture* (also *lens opening*, *lens stop*), the adjustable opening that determines how much light reaches the film; see *f-stop*; the *lens barrel*, which houses the various parts of the lens apparatus; *lens cap* (or *lens cover*), which protects it when not in use; *lens coating*, a transparent chemical (usually magnesium fluride) layer that allows more light to reach the film by cutting down reflection; *lenser*, which is *Variety*-speak for the cinematographer or Director of Photography; *lens extender*, which moves the lens away from the camera and towards the subject; *lens hood* (or *lens shade*), which shields the lens from light; *lens markings*, the indications of f-stop, depth of field and so on; *lens mount*, the device which hold the lens in place; this can be a *bayonet mount*, a *C-mount* or a *turret mount*; *lens speed*, the measurement of a lens's capacity to accept light: the greater the aperture, the faster the lens, and so the greater its capacity to produce acceptable images from dark, inadequately lit subjects; *lens stop*, see *f-stop*; *lens turret*, the rotable disc on the front of a camera holding several different lenses which can be moved into place as required.

letterbox   the admirable practice of showing a film on television in such a way as to preserve its original aspect ratio, rather than scanning and cropping it; so called because of the similarity between the horizontal, rectangular image and the slot of a letterbox. The letterbox effect, with black margins at top and bottom of the screen, is particularly striking in the case of a film which exploits every corner of its wide-screen aspect ratio, such as *2001: A Space Odyssey*. Hence *letterboxing*.

lettrisme   a post-war avant-garde movement in French literature, art, film, politics and life, founded by Isodore Isou, of which the leading lights were Gil J. Wolman and Guy Debord. Dedicated, according to its founder, to liberating language by emphasising its primary component units (letters, signs, sounds) rather than words, and broadly applying the same principles to other arts, *lettrisme* produced a number of extraordinary films or film-type objects and events, including (in 1952) one made by François Dufresne without any celluloid, consisting simply of the flickering light from a projector played over a range of objects and accompanied by noises. Guy Debord's *Hurlements en faveur de Sade* (*Howls for de Sade*), first shown at the Musée de l'Homme on 30 June 1952, created a public disturbance and had the plug pulled on it after 20 minutes; it consisted of a blank screen, alternating between black when the soundtrack was silent and white when it was filled with the monotone dialogue of a quintet of *lettristes*. The story of Isou's own, marginally more conventional début film, *Treatise on Slime and Eternity*, is even more engaging: the *lettristes* took this work to the 1951 Cannes film festival and, after creating any amount of ruckus, finally managed to screen it, or at least play its soundtrack. Most critics were horrified, though the young Maurice Scherer (better known in his later incarnation as the director Eric Rohmer) made a valiant attempt to defend it in the pages of *Cahiers du Cinéma*, and the Festival authorities, largely swayed by Jean Cocteau, awarded Isou the *Prix de l'Avant-Garde* – an award invented specially for the occasion. For an eloquent account of these and related matters, see Greil Marcus, *Lipstick Traces* (1989). Incidentally, *lettrisme* had another, curious (and largely unremarked) brush with the cinema, when Orson Welles included an encounter with some *lettristes* in a chatty travelogue he made about Paris for British television; they were treated as one of the town's characteristic novelties.

level   either (a) the act of setting a camera at a perfectly horizontal angle, or the adjective applied to a camera thus set; or (b) the volume of a sound recording; or the decibel range within which the best results can be achieved.

LFOA   abbreviation for *Last Frame of Action*; in other words, the final frame before the leader at the end of a reel.

library footage, library shots (or **stock footage** or **archive shots**)   scenes and sequences called up from a film archive (also quite often known as a *library*) rather than specially shot for a production; particularly those from a period or event which it would be difficult or forbiddingly costly to stage. Most of the First World War sequence in Truffaut's *Jules et Jim* is made up of library footage; Philip Kaufman's *The Unbearable Lightness of Being* intercuts black and white archive of the Soviet invasion of Czechoslovakia in 1968 with shots, filmed and processed to look like newsreel footage, of the principal actors caught up in the demonstrations.

light, lighting   One technical definition states that light is radiant energy in the range of 3800 to 7000 Angstrom units – the range, that is, visible to the human eye; *lighting*, in the cinematic sense, is the process and technology of illuminating sets and action in the shooting of a film. Unless shooting on *natural light* (the sun and moon) or *available light* (candles, say, as in the famous scene in Kubrick's *Barry Lyndon* which required special lenses), there are four principal types of electrical light with which the cinematographer can establish the lighting of a particular scene; the *key lights* (basic illumination), the *fill lights* (which reduce contrast, lighten shadows etc), the *back lights* (for adding depth) and the *kick lights* (to make details stand out).

Most of the subsidiary and associated terms terms are fairly straight-forward: *light-balancing filter*, a mildly tinted camera filter that adjusts the colour temperature of the light reflected from a subject; *light batten* (also *lighting batten*), a length of pipe with electrical outlets into which luminaires can be plugged; the batten is then suspended above the set;

light board, the control panel that regulates the supply of electricity to luminaires; *light boom*, a pole used to suspend a single lamp; *light-change*, either (a) a deliberate alteration in lighting during a shoot to suggest a different time, mood etc., or (b) a deliberate alteration in the intensity of light during printing; *Lightflex*, the trade name for a light that fits on top of the camera, acting as a fill light for close-ups and so on; *light level*, the intensity of illumination from a given source, or within a particular scene, usually measured in *foot candles* or sometimes in *lux* units; *light meter*, a photosensitive instrument for measuring light levels; *light piping*, see *halation*; *light plot*, a diagram showing the layout of lights on a set or location; *light-struck*, film that has been inadvertently exposed to light, and so become fogged (though sometimes the exposure is deliberate, and the fogged film used as leader: *light-struck leader*); *light-tight*, any area or piece of equipment that does not admit light; *light trap*, the revolving or double door to a darkroom; or any covering, device or part of a camera that shuts out light; and so on.

Among the terms associated with *lighting*: *lighting balance*, the relationship between light and shade in a scene; *lighting cameraman*, the term often used on British productions for the *cinematographer* or *director of photography*; *lighting contrast*, the degree of difference between the darkest and brightest parts of a set or image; *lighting control console*, another term for *light board*; *lighting cradle*, a platform that holds lights, and can be hung over a set; *lighting grid*, a set of bars mounted above a set on which lights are fixed; *lighting mount*, any device used for holding a light; and many others.

lily   a set of colour bars (or a grey scale) shot at the beginning of a roll to help the lab in establishing true colour values. Also known as a *colour lily*.

limbo; limbo set   a set which has few or no distinguishing details; the effect is often created with a *cyclorama*. It is used either to concentrate attention solely on a performer, especially in close-up, or to create an eerie, disconcerting atmosphere, as in a dream sequence. 'Limbo' is originally the ablative singular form of L *limbus*, 'edge, border': in medieval L, it came to mean 'a region on the border of Hell'. This theological sense appears in English by the end of the 14th C; by the mid-17th C (in Milton, for example), it had also come to mean any unfavourable place or condition, especially one of neglect or oblivion.

limiter   the system inside a sound recorder that prevents sound amplitudes from rising too high.

limpet   a mount supplied with suction cups, used for fixing equipment to smooth surfaces; also known as a *suction mount* or *sucker*. Named after the tenacious gasteropod mollusc.

line producer   the person who is oversees the running of a given production, and to whom the production manager reports.

lines   as in the theatre: the scripted dialogue for a particular character, scene, or whole production.

lining up   in production: (a) positioning the camera, actors and so on immediately prior to a shot; or (b) adjusting a monitor viewfinder to correct for parallax.

linkage   a theoretical term found in the writings of the Soviet director and teacher V.I. Pudovkin; it refers to his conception of the nature and function of editing. See *montage*.

lip sync   a term first recorded by OED, in its unabbreviated form of 'lip synchronization', in 1957: the process in which an actor (a) mimes to a pre-recorded sound-track, particularly of a song in a musical, or (b) re-records dialogue, trying to match each word to the movements of lips on screen. See *sync, loop*.

liquid gate   see *wet gate printing*.

live end   the end of a recording studio where the sound reverberates most satisfactorily; OED's first note of an acoustical sense for 'live' dates from 1931. (The antonym is, of course, 'dead'.) *Live sound*, dialogue, atmosphere and other noises recorded while filming rather than dubbed at a later date.

livestock man   see *wrangler*.

L-KO   a short-lived (1914–19) Hollywood production company of the silent period, which specialised in slapstick comedies. The name was an abbreviation of 'Lehrman Knock-Out'; Henry Lehrman was its founder.

lo mode   in filming with a *Steadicam*: the placing of a camera below the arm instead of above, which results in a knee- or ankle-level shot, suitable for conveying the point of view of a feral animal and so on.

load   to put film into a camera (OED cites a photographical use of the verb in 1902); a large, complex production using a number of cameras will sometimes employ a special *loader* to help the second assistant cameraman with this task; a small darkroom or *loading room* will usually be at hand.

lobby cards   American term for the smallish photographic cards displayed in the entrance halls of cinemas, depicting scenes from the feature being shown or from coming attractions.

local music   music that has an obvious source within the action of a film – a band playing, a radio in the background – and is audible to the characters, as opposed to the soundtrack music.

location   any site used for shooting a film that is not a sound stage or studio lot; a film crew working away from such a studio base is said to be *on location*. The term has been current since the early 20th C: hence *Scribner's Magazine*, March 1914: 'It was his duty ... to pick out "locations", as are called the scenes and backgrounds of a moving-picture play.' In the early years of cinema, many films were shot out of doors since stocks were relatively insensitive and worked best in bright sunlight, but the development of better lighting and other technical resources, and the difficulties of controlling exterior environments gradually brought movie-making indoors. With certain exceptions, it tended to stay there until the 1960s, when changes in technology (such as the production of lightweight cameras, portable lights and wide-angle lenses) and fashion made it at once easier and more attractive to go back on location. Today, most films will combine studio and location sequences.

The business of going on location generally includes most or all of the following: a *location breakdown*, a list of all the equipment and personnel needed for a location shoot; *location camera*, a lightweight camera suitable for hand-held work; *location manager*, the production member whose task is to read through the screenplay, establish the types of site that are needed, search for them in the capacity of (or with the assistance of) a *location scout* and take pictures to show the director and production designer. Next, once the location has been agreed, the location manager draws up a *location budget* and takes charge of the many and various logistical problems created by shooting away from a studio: catering, permits, policing and other security arrangements, payments for the use of property (*location fees*) and so on. One major disadvantage of location filming from the studios' point of view is that the process is not simply more expensive, but much harder to control: see, for example Eleanor Coppola's *Notes on the Making of Apocalypse Now*.

lock   as a verb (a) to fix the position of a camera precisely, often for the purpose of contriving a special effect. The simplest such effect would be to take a shot of a performer in motion, stop the camera, move the performer out of frame, and then film again from the locked camera: when developed and projected, the resulting film will show the performer vanishing. (b) the director's, editor's and/or producer's act of declaring a film *locked* – that is to say, in a state where both the fine cut and the sound track are considered complete, save for the final stages of sound mixing.

log, log sheet   the various technical reports filled out in the course of production, by the assistant cameraman, the sound recordist and so on.

London Film Productions   the production company responsible for many of the British cinema's international sucesses of the 1930s and 1940s, London Films was the brainchild of the Hungarian producer and director Alexander Korda (b.1893), and was in business from 1932 until Korda's death in 1956, with a hiatus for the Second World War. In its first, pre-war period, the company produced such prestige films as *The Private Life of Henry VIII* (Alexander Korda, 1933) – which helped to re-launch British films for the world markets – *Things to Come* (William Cameron Menzies, 1936), *Elephant Boy* (Robert J. Flaherty and Zoltan Korda; this was Flaherty's only commercial fiction film) and *Rembrandt* (Alexander Korda, 1936). From 1936 to 1939, London Films' base was the well-equipped, 160-acre Denham studios, which Korda had built on the Hollywood model (Korda lost control of Denham in 1939 because of financial difficulties, but the studio continued to operate until 1953, when it was sold by the Rank Organisation). After the war, London's principal titles included *Anna Karenina* (Julien Duvivier, 1948) and *The Third Man* (Carol Reed, 1949). The artists who worked for London in the first period included Marlene Dietrich, Graham Greene, Charles Laughton, Vivien Leigh, Lawrence Olivier, Conrad Veidt and H.G. Wells; in the second, David Lean, Launder and Gilliat, Powell and Pressburger.

long   *long focus lens*, see **telephoto lens**; *long pitch*, the fractionally greater distance between sprockets on print stock, which compensates for the fact that print stock is wrapped around the negative when they pass though the printer; *long shot* (*LS*), a shot taken from a reasonable distance away from the subject, which not only shows the main performers from head to toe but also shows something of their environment, and which may sometimes serve as an *establishing shot*: 'A quarter of a mile away, from which distance some of the so-called "long shots" were filmed by the cameraman' – *Scientific American*, 1922 (from the mid-19th C, a 'long shot' has also meant a bet laid against considerable odds; hence the punning title of Maurice Hatton's *Long Shot* (1979), a film about the difficulty of making films in Britain); *long take*, a single uninterrupted shot lasting longer than the usual few seconds to half a minute or so, such as the bravura tracking shots which serve as overtures to Orson Welles's *Touch of Evil* and Robert Altman's *The Player*, or the full-reel takes used by Hitchcock for *Rope*.

loop   (a) one of the basic requirements of both filming and projection is that the continuous motion of the film through camera or projector must be converted into *intermittent motion* at the point where it reaches the aperture, and that this conversion should not tear or damage the film. To achieve this requires a certain amount of slack in the film on either side of the aperture, and these curved lengths of slack are known as loops. (OED notes that the cinematographic sense was well established by 1912.) The loops on a camera were, and sometimes still are referred to as *Latham loops*, after their inventor, Major Woodville Latham; the same term has been applied to the loops on a projector, though it was Thomas Armat who devised those.

(b) a short strip of film, or of recording tape joined end to end so that it will pass repeatedly through an aperture or over a head. (OED notes the term as early as 1931.) This is useful in many ways: to extend a short tape of background noise throughout a long scene; in printing, to run off multiple copies of a short film; or, particularly, in dubbing.

Hence: (c) (as a verb) to replace the dialogue (or, less often, general sounds) recorded during filming with freshly recorded and, with luck, superior versions, as part of post-production. The technique is essentially simple: a scene, or part of a scene is made into a loop, and the performer tries to sync words to lips as it comes up on screen again and again. Hence *looping* and, occasionally, *re-looping*: 'Festival audiences found so much of [Jennifer Jason Leigh's] speech unintelligible that [the director] Rudolph has had to re-loop her performance into a less faithful but more audible version' – review of *Mrs Parker and the Vicious Circle*, *Independent*, 9 March 1995.

loose frame   a shot composed with plenty of empty space between the principal subjects and the edge of the frame; also known as a *loose shot*.

lose   a colloquial verb, often heard in the imperative, meaning to get rid of something – particularly on set, but also during editing ('Lose the opening of the scene, it's boring . . .').

lot   the grounds in which a studio is based, made up of adminstration buildings, sound stages, commissary and so on. Or, more narrowly, an open space within a larger lot on which sets can be constructed. 'The worst of making war, as of acting for the "movies", is the amount of waiting around on the lot' – 'R.West', *Strange Necessity*, 1928.

Louma, Louma crane   a type of compact, lightweight, highly mobile crane, developed in the mid-1970s, that can be operated at a distance, and can therefore be used for shots that would be difficult or impossible to make if the camera operator were riding behind the camera. A video camera mounted on the crane sends back a precise record of the shots that are being filmed to the cameraman's monitor; servomechanisms adjust its movements by remote control. The trade name was arrived at by combining syllables from the names of its inventors, the French filmmakers Jean-Marie LavaLOU and Alain MAsseron.

low   *low-angle shot*, *low shot* a shot taken from close to ground level, facing upwards; *low-budget*, a relative term; at the time of writing, any American film made for less than two or three million dollars can be considered low budget; *low contrast*, an image in which there is little contrast between the light and dark areas; a *low-contrast filter* may be used to achieve this; *low hat*, a mount used to fix a camera at a low height; *low-key lighting*, dim lighting with a great deal of shadow, often used to create an atmosphere of mystery or menace; *low-noise lamps*, lamps designed not to hum; *low-speed camera*, a camera adapted for *time-lapse photography*.

LS   see *long shot*.

Lubin   a pioneering film company, based in Philadelphia and launched by Sigmund Rubin; after a merger with Essenay, Selig and Vitagraph in 1915, it was bought out by Vitagraph in 1917.

lumen   a unit of luminous flux. The term was coined in the French language by A. Blondel in his *La Lumière électrique*, 1894; it is defined as being 'equal to the flux emitted by a point source of . . . one *candela* into a solid angle of one steradian'. It was current in English by the end of the 19th C.

Lumia   a device, invented by one Thomas Wilfred, that throws moving patterns of light across a screen; the result can, it has been suggested, be considered as a type of *absolute film*.

luminaire   a term known in the US since the early 20th C, borrowed directly from Fr *luminaire*: a complete lighting unit made up of the light itself, the housing for the light, an electrical cord and a stand.

luminance   the brightness of a surface, measured in *footlamberts*. See *chrominance*.

lupe   a small lighting unit that can be fixed to a camera and used as a fill light.

lux   a metric unit of illumination; one *footcandle* equals 10.764 lux.

MacGuffin (also **Maguffin, McGuffin**)   a name used (and probably coined) by Alfred Hitchcock to designate a particular kind of narrative device or gimmick often deployed in his thrillers. Essentially, the MacGuffin is something that is of great importance to some of the characters in the film – a stolen document, a stash of uranium – but of little or, preferably, no importance whatsoever to the film-maker and his audience except as a means of setting the plot in motion. In *The Thirty-Nine Steps*, for example, the MacGuffin is the formula for the construction of an aircraft engine, stored not on paper but in the brain cells of 'Mr. Memory'. In *North by Northwest* it is some nebulous 'government secrets'; Hitchcock thought this latter his very best MacGuffin precisely because it was the emptiest, most non-existent, and most absurd. The classic explanation of the term can be found in François Truffaut's book of interviews with the English director, *Hitchcock* (1966; trans., 1968), which also provides a cod history:

'You may be wondering where the term originated', Hitchcock says. 'It might be a Scottish name, taken from a story about two men in a train. One man says, "What's that package up there in the baggage rack?"

And the other answers, "Oh, that's a MacGuffin." The first one asks, "What's a MacGuffin?"

"Well," the other man says, "it's an apparatus for trapping lions in the Scottish Highlands."

The first man says, "But there are no lions in the Scottish Highlands," and the other one answers, "Well then, that's no MacGuffin!" So you see that a MacGuffin is actually nothing at all.'

This and other statements by Hitchcock helped make the term popular; it was used as the title of the title of a comedy thriller made for the BBC in the mid-1980s, starring Charles Dance as a film critic caught up in a criminal conspiracy. When the MacGuffin is an object rather than a concept, it is sometimes referred to as a *weenie*.

machine splicer   see *splicer*.

macrocinematography   the filming of small objects from an extremely close range, using a *macro lens, macro-telephoto lens* or *macrozoom lens*, all of which can focus from very short distances, in some cases, as little as 1mm. The prefix 'macro-' is from Gk *makros*, 'long, large'.

magazine   a word derived from the Arabic *makhazin*, the plural form of *makhzan*, 'storehouse', which enters English by way of the Fr *magasin* around the late 16th C in the sense of 'storehouse, depot'. It acquires its military sense – a place where munitions are kept – shortly afterwards, and comes to mean the part of a gun in which bullets are stored in the mid-18th C. OED's first reference to a 'magazine camera' comes in 1889; in film-making, the magazine is the double-chambered container for film stock which fits on to a camera. During filming, unexposed film is drawn out of the first chamber, passes through the camera for exposure, and is wound into the second chamber.

magic hour   the twilight or gloaming: the brief period between sunlight and full darkness in which shadows are long and the light has a deep, warm tone.

magic lantern   (from the modern Latin *laterna magica*) one of the earliest ancestors of the modern cinema, popular from the late 17th to 19th centuries, the magic lantern projected drawings and, later, photographs onto a wall or screen by means of a candle and a lens. OED suggests that the claim, frequently found in cinema reference books, that a version of the device is discussed in Athanasius Kircher's *Ars Magna Lucis et Umbrae* (1646), is probably incorrect; the author begs to differ. The earliest known use of a device '*sub nomine Laternae magicae*' occurred in Lyons in 1665; four years later, in 1696, an English author wrote of 'a certain small Optical Macheen, that shews by a gloomy Light upon a white Wall, Spectres and Monsters so hideous, that he who knows not the Secret, believes it to be perform'd by Magick Art.' Hence *magic-lanternist*, the ancestor of the modern projectionist. See **Laterna Magica**.

Magiarama   the trade name for a short-lived triple-screen projection process developed late in his life by the veteran French director Abel Gance, in collaboration with André Debrie; it was first shown to the public in 1956.

Magnafilm and **Magnascope**   the brand names from two forms of wide-screen process used by Paramount in the late 1920s and early 1930s. The first method, which employed 56mm film, was rapidly abandoned; the second, which magnified ordinary 35mm images to as much as four times their usual size, produced an unacceptably grainy image and was only used for brief sequences in one or two films.

magnetic   The sound dimension of modern cinema owes everything to the development of magnetic recording technology, and the names for a good deal of recording and playback equipment acknowledge the debt: hence, among many others, *magnetic film*, a film base of the same dimensions as ordinary stock, but coated with iron oxide rather than light-sensitive emulsion, and used for recording sound; *magnetic recording*, sound recorded onto *magnetic tape* in filming; *magnetic stripe*, the iron oxide sound track used on 70mm Dolby film; *magoptical print* (also *magopt print, mag opt, magoptical release print*): a *release print* supplied with both magnetic and optical sound tracks; *magoptical projector*, a projecter that can run both optical and magentic sound films. The word 'magnetic' is derived from the modern Latin *magneticus*, and enters the language in the early 17th C: 'Why doth the stubborne iron prove/ So gentle to th' magnetique stone?' – William Habington, *Castara*, 1634.

main title   the graphic in the *opening credits* which gives the title of the film; or the musical theme which plays with this title.

make-up   the cosmetics (and, in *monster movies* and the like, *prosthetics*) used to enhance or transform the appearance of performers. Hence *make-up artist*, the crew member who applies make-up; *make-up call*, the hour, sometimes well before shooting, at which performers must be on set for make-up; and so on. The earliest theatrical term 'make-up', current from the 18th C and into the 19th C, was rather more general, and applied to every means, including costume, by which a performer might change appearance: hence George Eliot in 1858: 'The Zouaves, with their wondrous make-ups as women.' The narrower sense of 'cosmetics' developed over the same period, but only seems to have been applied to women's facial enhancements in the early 20th C.

Maltese cross mechanism (or **Maltese cross movement**)   the device inside a projector that rotates intermittently, by 90 degrees at a time, to advance each frame of the film in front of the aperture. So called because it is made in the form of a Maltese cross, it was developed from the 'Geneva movement' used in making watches. For a strange fantasy woven on and around this evocative name, see Theodor Rozsak's erudite novel *Flicker*.

M and E track(s)   the Music and Effects track(s); the sound tracks that contain every recorded element except the dialogue.

married print   a positive print in which picture and sound have been joined together; this appears to be mostly a British term, the American industry preferring *composite print* or 'combined print'. Hence *marrying*, the process of putting sound and image into *sync*.

marks   as in the theatre: small pieces of tape (usually *gaffer's tape)* or chalk marks put on the studio or set floor for rehearsals, showing the places to which both the performers and the camera will move in the scene about to be shot.

martini, martini shot   recent US industry slang for the final shot of the day; as soon as it's completed, you can have your martini. In homage or *hommage* to the term, I left this entry to the last when writing *The Language of Cinema*.

mask   either another term for a *matte*, or another term for a *flag* or *gobo*.

master   (a) a *master positive*: the positive version of the completed film from which dupe negatives are made; or (b) a *master shot*, a shot – usually a wide shot – containing the whole action of a given scene, which can either be shown without interruption or (more commonly) edited together with *coverage*: *close-ups*, *reverse shots* and so on. Occasionally called a *master scene*. OED has no citations for 'master shot' before 1953, but it seems likely that the term had already been around for some years by then.

match   (a) to re-stage an action and/or a section of dialogue as precisely as possible, so that shots from various angles and distances can be edited together in such a way that the resulting action appears to be smooth and continuous; this type of cutting is known as *matching action*, though a *match cut* (and, particularly, a *match dissolve*) can also refer to a type of associative *cut* (or *dissolve*) in which one action or object is made to appear connected in some way with another action or object because of a similarity of their shape, direction of movement, colour and so on.

'Match dissolve. That's a film term for a standard motion-picture transition, say from the face of a clock in a police chief's office to the face of another clock in the senator's bedroom' – Wager, *Sledgehammer*, 1971.
Also, to align the final cut of a film up with the original negative; in other words, to *conform*.

matrix, matrices originally, the three individual positives used to build up the final polychrome image in a *subtractive* colour film process; see *imbibition*. More recently, the three emulsion layers, each sensitive to a different primary colour, in *tripack* colour film.

matte (or, though this spelling has been rare since the mid-20th C, **mat**) (a) a technique for producing composite images, and particularly for combining different scenery or actions in the foreground and background; one of the most common forms of *special effects*, The processes involved can be complex, but the essential principle is quite straightforward, and involves the exposure of different areas of film at different times. At its simplest, a *matte shot* is achieved by covering part of the camera or printer lens is with a light-proof sheet, so that only the unmasked areas will be exposed. The unexposed areas are then exposed separately, and a multiple image formed. (b) The matte (also known as a *mask)* itself. Hence such terms as *matte artist*, the member of the special effects department responsible for designing and/or helping to execute matte shots; *matte bleed*, the accidental line or colouring around the edges of figures in matte shots that have been poorly executed; *matte box*, the adjustable structure fitted on to the front of a lens to hold mattes; *matte painting*, a background or scenery painting, either on a glass sheet or photographed and projected from front or rear, that can be combined with live action or animation for a matte shot; and so on.
A *matte screen*, however, has nothing to do with composite images, but is a type of projection screen used in certain cinemas, so constructed that it appears of equal brightness from every angle, and thus is more suitable for wide auditoria than glass-beaded screens which, though brighter, lose much of their brilliance when viewed from seats on the side.

MCS the standard abbreviation for *Medium Close Shot*; *MCU*, the standard abbreviation for *Medium Close-Up*.

meat axe colloquial term for a rod that supports *flags* or *scrims*.

medium close-up (MCU) or **medium close shot (MCS)** a shot somewhere between a medium and a close-up; on a person, this would show roughly the area from chest to scalp. Similarly, a *medium long shot (MLS)* is a shot between a medium and a long shot, where a *medium shot (MS)* (also known as a *mid shot* or *three-quarters shot*) shows a character or characters from about the knee level upwards.

megger a dated and infrequently used slang term for a *director*, which has its origins in the megaphones through which silent film directors shouted instructions at their cast and crew.

Method (or **method**), **method acting** the emotionally intense, indeed often anguished school of performing generally associated with the early careers of Marlon Brando, Rod Steiger, James Dean and Montgomery Clift. The method claims a lineage from the teachings and practice of the Russian actor and director Konstantin Stanislavsky, particularly his book *An Actor Prepares*, and found its way into the American cinema via the theatrical work of *Actors Studio*, founded in 1947 by Elia Kazan and based in New York.

Metro-Goldwyn-Mayer   see *MGM*.

metteur-en-scène   (a) most simply, the older French term for a director: 'one who puts on the stage'. English borrowed it for the theatre around the beginning of the 20th C, and for the screen shortly afterwards. But, though English speakers are on the whole ignorant of the distinction (hence *The Times* for 4 January 1974: 'Murnau's greatness as a *metteur-en-scène* is unimpaired by time . . .'), the term is also sometimes used in a particular critical sense, to distinguish an *auteur* director from (b) a mere journeyman, time-server or hack director.

MGM (Metro-Goldwyn-Mayer)   in the 1930s and early 1940s, the single largest, most powerful and most glamorous of all the Hollywood *studios*. Founded in 1924 by the union of three existing companies (the Metro Picture Corporation, the Goldwyn Picture Corporation and Louis B. Mayer Pictures), it expanded rapidly, partly thanks to its connections with the banking world, partly because of its close relationship with the Loew's cinema chain, and partly because of the leadership of Louis B Mayer (vice-president and head of studio) and the short-lived but – this epithet is inevitable – legendary Irving Thalberg (vice-president in charge of production), the original of Fitzgerald's Monroe Stahr in *The Last Tycoon*, and on most accounts the man who helped make MGM's products the most technically polished and lavish entertainments of their time. 'More stars than there are in the heavens', ran MGM's slogan, and the company's roster was indeed without peer: John Barrymore, Joan Crawford, Clark Gable (*Gone With The Wind* was one of MGM's biggest hits), Greta Garbo, Judy Garland (*Wizard of Oz* was another), James Stewart, Elizabeth Taylor, Spencer Tracy and many others. After Thalberg's premature death in 1936 (he was 37), MGM's output became somewhat less literate and tasteful, and the public did not seem to mind at all: the company continued to dominate Hollywood until the end of the Second World War. Then the commercial and artistic rot gradually set in, relieved now and again by a few high-budget, high-prestige productions and, particularly, by the dazzling succession of *musicals* MGM produced in the 40s and 50s. Afflicted like the other studios by the *Paramount decision*, the defection of audiences to television and other blows, MGM grew weaker and weaker, until in 1969 it was bought out by a Las Vegas businessman, Kirk Kerorian. The new management began a reckless asset-stripping drive, including selling off all MGM's props for just $1.5 million to an auctioneer who made a profit of $12 million. From this point on, the MGM story becomes ever more complex and dismal – a sequence of buy-outs, sell-offs, amalgamations (with *United Artists*, in 1981), firings, hirings and boardroom coups: all of which make the company's famous motto *Ars Gratia Artis* (blazoned beneath the roaring head of Leo the lion – a trademark designed by a songwriter, Howard Dietz) seem grimly inapposite. The company still exists, and occasionally releases hits: *Thelma and Louise* (1991), for example.

micro-cinematography   the filming of extremely small objects, generally for scientific purposes but also for special effects sequences and so on. The prefix is derived from the Gk *micros*, 'small'.

microphone (commonly abbreviated as **mike**, much less often as **mic**)   from Gk *micros*, 'small' and *phone*, 'sound': the term, coined in the late 17th C, originally meant 'an instrument by which small sounds can be intensified'; the modern sense of the word dates from 1878, when two scientists, Prof. Hughes and Dr Ludtge, came up with the same invention almost simultaneously. Thereafter, the microphone became one of the basic components of any sound recording or transmitting process – the instrument which transforms sound waves into electrical signals. Hence a variety of related terms in the cinema, including *microphone boom*, the long pole used to suspend a microphone above the subjects to be recorded (see *boom*); *microphone placement*, the positioning of microphones in the appropriate places; *microphone shadow*, accidental shadows cast on the subject when the microphone blocks a light; and so on. The abbreviation 'mike' has been known since the 1920s, though the verb 'to mike' does not seem to appear in print until the 1960s.

midget   a small *fill* light in the 50 to 200 watt range.

miniature   a small scale model, particularly of a set, used in special effects sequences. *Minature rear projection*, a special effects process which combines *stop-frame* animation with the frame-by-frame projection of live action onto a miniature screen inside a model set. The technique was first used for *King Kong* (1933).

minibrute   a small *brute*, often used to augment natural light on outdoor shoots, or as a *fill* in studio work.

minimal cinema   a school of *underground* or *experimental* filmmaking concerned to strip either content, technique or both down to a minimum – the classic example being George Landow's four-minute epic *Film in which there appear sprocket holes, edge lettering, dirt particles etc* (1966). This distinctly un-minimal title would not have landed Mr Landow in trouble under the terms of the Trades Descriptions Act.

Miramax   the thriving American *independent* production and distribution company, founded by Bob and Harvey Weinstein in 1979, which has specialised in picking up commercial *art house* movies from Europe, China and elsewhere as well as from the United States. Miramax's string of hits include *Cinema Paradiso*, *sex, lies and videotape*, *The Crying Game* and *Farewell My Concubine*. Miramax became a subsidiary of the Disney company in 1993.

mired (or **mired value**)   a name formed from the words 'MIcro REcriprocal Degrees', and designating a unit of colour temperature.

mirror shot   either (a) simply, a shot which includes a mirror and the reflection of a character on its surface (such as the many found in Cocteau's *Orphée*, in which looking-glasses are the doors between this world and the next, or those used in the house-of-mirrors shoot-out sequence from the climax of Orson Welles's *Lady from Shanghai*), or (b) a shot which, as in traditional stage conjuring, mirrors are used to create a particular illusion or special effect. *Mirror shutter*, a camera shutter equipped with reflecting surfaces that permit the cameraman to see the image he is shooting without a parallax effect.

mis-en-cadre, mis-en-shot   terms which originated in (and were occasionally imported by Anglophone writers from) French film criticism, referring to the director's composition of a given shot; which is to say, not merely its organisation into spaces, colours, shadows and forms (that is, all the elements of its spatial composition) but also its use of movement (that is, its temporal composition or rhythms). But both of these terms have largely been absorbed by the looser term *mis-en-scène* (literally, 'putting on stage'), which was borrowed from the theatre where it originally meant the director's arrangement of scenery, lighting and other visual elements. Nowadays, the concept of *mis-en-scène* includes both spatial and temporal composition; to complicate matters still further, it has sometimes been used to indicate a film-making method or ideology that is diametrically opposed to *montage*, notably in the writings of the influential French critic André Bazin and his disciples and epigones. According to this line of thought, a director who emphasises *mis-en-scène* is likely to be closer to *realism* than one who leans on *montage*; for the classic discussion of these matters, see Bazin's collection of essays *What is Cinema?*

mismatch   an accidental (or, less often, deliberate) effect created by editing shots together out of narrative or logical sequence, so that speakers seem to swap places, their actions jump erratically and their surroundings mutate.

Mitchell   the trade name of certain types of large, heavy camera, suitable mainly for studio work. Mitchells were the most widely used camera in Hollywood between the first *talkies* and the early 1960s, when more lightweight cameras – or *self-blimping* models such as the *Arriflex* – became standard.

mix   the act of balancing the sound levels of various recorded *tracks*, combining them all on to a single magnetic tape, and then transferring the results to an *optical* or *mag-optical* track; a process also known as *dubbing*. This process is the job of the *mixer*, or *re-recording mixer*; the mixer on set, whose job is to balance the sound recorded during shooting, is called the *production mixer*. Hence *mixing* and its related terms: *mixing* *console* (which, like the technician who operates it, is also known as the *mixer*), *mixing cue sheet* and the like. The word, ultimately derived from L *mixtus*, the past participle of *miscere*, 'to mix', via Fr *mixte*, acquired this specialist sense in the sound recording industry around the 1920s.

MLS   see *Medium Long Shot.*

model (or **mock-up**)   see *miniature*; though the term can also be applied to a person who substitutes for an actor in shots that require only part of the body – a hand, foot or back – to be seen. A *modelling light* is a light used to dramatise the curvature and surface texture of an object or actor; set opposite the *key* light, it is therefore also known as a *counter key*.

mogul   a term borrowed ultimately from the Persian and Arabic terms (also corrupted into the Spanish and Portugeuse *Mogor*) representing a mispronunciation of the native name *Mongol*, but specifically from the *Great* or *Grand Mogol*, which is to say the standard European term for the emperor of Delhi. It had come to mean 'an autocratic ruler or great personage' by the late 17th C: 'Mr. Limberham is the Mogul of the nest Mansion' – (Dryden, 1678), and this sense continues into the 20th C, when it becomes freely applied to money men, captains of industry and so on. In the movie business, a mogul is any powerful financier, producer or studio head, but particularly those of the silent and early sound eras – Louis B. Mayer, Irving Thalberg, Samuel Goldwyn, Darryl F. Zanuck: see Philip French's brief but informative history of these and other big shots, *The Movie Moguls*. The term is still in fairly common use, at least among journalists and the general public: 'A movie mogul with an ounce of intelligence would sign up Hugh Grant for a remake of *My Fair Lady*': reader's letter to the London *Evening Standard*, 17 July 1995.

money shot   in pornographic films, a shot of a male performer ejaculating. But the term also seems to have been borrowed by the more mainstream film industry, particularly in the field of *exploitation movies*, to refer to any shot which makes the target audience feel that it has had its money's worth: a head being blown apart by bullets, for example, which is the content of the 'money shot' the ghastly producer played by Steve Martin in *Grand Canyon* is outraged to discover missing from the director's cut of his movie.

monitor   from L *monitor*, an agent, and *monere*, to advise, warn, admonish. A common term in broadcasting technology since about 1930, in the cinema it usually means (a) a television or video set, used for viewing relayed or recorded images; or, (b) considerably less often, a loudspeaker (or *monitor speaker, sound monitor* etc). In the course of production, references to the monitor will usually mean the device which shows images filmed by a small video camera mounted on or next to the main camera, so that the director can see roughly how the lighting, performances and so on will eventually appear on screen. Where part or all of the editing is carried out electronically, the monitor will be the set on which rushes and assembled sequences are viewed. (b) verb: to check that pictures and/or sounds are all right during filming and recording.

monochrome   from medieval L *monochroma*, evolved from the Gk adjective *monochromatos*, 'of one colour'; its earliest English meaning, in the 17th C, is a painting executed in different tints of one colour. Thus: (a) any film or image shot in black and white; or, (b) much less commonly, an image shot in shades of just one colour, or just one colour. The purest example of such a film is Derek Jarman's final production *Blue* (1993), the pictures for which consist simply of a rectangle of brilliant blue (a version of the 'International Klein Blue' made famous by the artist Yves Klein). When BBC Radio 3 broadcast the sound-track of *Blue* simultaneously with the Channel Four screening of the film, interested listeners were issued with plain blue postcards at which they could stare, if they so wished, for the duration.

Monogram Picture Corporation   a production company which operated from 1937 to 1953 (when it was incorporated with its classier subsidiary, Allied Artists Productions – founded in 1946 – to become the Allied Artists Picture Corporation) and which specialised in low-budget thrillers, westerns, horror movies and the like, as well as serials. In its heyday, the company made about 30 B-features a year, including the adventures of Charlie Chan, which Monogram took over from Twentieth Century Fox, and of Warner Brothers' Dead End Kids, who were rechristened the East Side Kids and, later, the Bowery Boys. AAPC achieved its first major sucess with *Tickle Me*, the Elvis Presley movie, in 1965, and, despite various ups and downs, managed to produce the prominent (and highly enjoyable) likes of John Huston's *The Man Who Would Be King*. By 1979, however, it was bankrupt, and in 1980 was sold to Lorimar. Jean-Luc Godard was sufficiently fond of Monogram's old thrillers to dedicate *A Bout de souffle* (1959) to the company's memory.

monopack   colour film with three layers of light-sensitive emulsion, each one responsive to a different primary colour; that is, another term for an *integral tripack* colour film.

monopole   a pole used to suspend studio lights from the *rigging*.

monster movie   a sub-category of the *horror film*, in which the horror is derived mainly from the fearsome appearance and unruly conduct of some ghastly, if often sympathetic creature: Frankenstein's unfortunate being, King Kong, Godzilla or the Creature from the Black Lagoon. 'Monster' is from the L *monstrum*, originally meaning a divine portent or warning (from *monere*, to warn); the horrific sense has been known in English since *c*. 1300.

montage   an important and frequently used term with several related but none the less distinct principal meanings. Derived from Fr *monter*, 'to mount', it appears to owe its currency in English to influential discussions in the 1930s of theories developed by early Soviet filmmakers (see definition 'e', below), and particularly those of Pudovkin as translated by Ivor Montagu: 'It is important to gain a conception of the activities embraced here by the word *editing*. The word used by Pudovkin, the German and French word, is *montage*. Its only possible English equivalent is *editing*' (*Pudovkin on Film Technique*, 1929). Chief among the senses of 'montage' are: (a) the whole process of editing a film. (b) In traditional Hollywood films, a short sequence of rapidly cut or dissolved shots which tell a story with great economy, or denote the passage of hours, days, months or years. (c) Any sequence which joins together distinct images rather than following a dramatic action. (d) An ostentatious style of editing narrative material, as opposed to the self-effacing, 'invisible' editing of the classic studio films, that entered the American cinema in the 1960s and has proved both tenacious and contagious. (e) Most specifically, the theories and methods of editing developed by Pudovkin and Eisenstein. Both Soviet directors developed their view from experiments carried out at the Moscow State Film School (see *Kuleshov effect*), where it was held that editing was the basis of film as an art. Pudovkin adhered to a form of montage, sometimes referred to as *linkage*, in which each shot of a film should follow its predecessor as firmly and inevitably as the links of a chain. Eisenstein, on the other hand, argued for the striking juxtaposition of different shots – what he called the 'collision' method of montage – in which meaning was produced not, so to speak, by the thesis of one shot and the antithesis of the next, but by the synthesis or interaction of the two. Entire volumes can, and have, been written on Eisenstein's theories of montage; his own words on the subject can be found in *Film Form* and elsewhere.

moo print   laboratory term for a perfect print. Possibly derived from the early 20th C slang term 'moo', an abbreviation of 'moola' or 'moolah', meaning 'money'?

mood lighting, mood music   standard audiovisual tools for swaying an audience's emotions: according to Manvell and Huntley's *The Technique of Film Music*, volumes of 'mood music' to accompany silent screenings began to appear as early as 1913.

morphing   a recent – late 1980s – coinage from Gk *morphe*, 'form': an increasingly common *special effects* process using *computer animation* to transform or metamorphose one image into the next. Developed by George Lucas's *Industrial Light and Magic* company, the technique was seen at its most spectacular in James Cameron's *Terminator 2: Judgment Day* (1991), in which a cyborg from the future goes about its murderous business, spectacularly modifying its limbs or its whole body into swords, hammers, pools of liquid and the like. Thanks to morphing, the director of live-action films can now achieve the kind of wild images previously reserved for the *animator*: we are at the beginning of a period of cinema history in which anything (even, it has been soberly suggested, the casting of long-dead actors in new films, see *synthespian*) has become possible, given a large enough budget. Whether this proves a great artistic liberation or, as some commentators fear, the eventual death of cinema as a dramatic medium remains an open question.

MOS   a shot filmed without recording any accompanying sound: the letters are said to stand for the fractured half-German phrase *Mit Out Sound*, a cry attributed in myth to the director Lothar Mendes, but more probably coined by an unknown sound recordist in the early days of the talkies when many technicians were of German origin. (An alternative etymology suggests that the initials stand for 'minus optical sound'). Where appropriate, the abbreviation is written on the clapperboard as a guide to the lab, editor and so on.

motion control   an electronic system, used in special effects sequences based on *travelling mattes*, which allows the operator to repeat a camera move (usually across a *model* – one of the spacecraft in *Star Wars*, say) with minute accuracy and as many times as necessary; the earliest such system was the *Dykstraflex*.

motion picture, motion pictures   another term, now felt by most sensible people to be slightly archaic and/or pompous, for a film or, in the plural, the film industry. 'Let us take for our platform this sentence: THE MOTION PICTURE ART IS A GREAT HIGH ART, NOT A PROCESS OF COMMERCIAL MANUFACTURE' (Vachel Lindsay, *The Art of the Moving Picture*). Hence the *Motion Picture Association of America* or *MPAA*, Hollywood's moral watchdog, established in 1921 in the wake of a number of industry scandals, the most notorious of which was the violent death of a young actress at a party given by Fatty Arbuckle (for further sordid details, see Kenneth Anger's *Hollywood Babylon*); and the *Motion Picture Production Code*; see **Hays Code**; and the *Motion Picture Patents Company* (*MPPC*), a short-lived (officially from 1909 to 1917, when it was declared illegal) alliance calculated to monopolise the American film industry, which was proliferating at a giddy rate in the early years of the century. The trust was made up of seven American production companies – *Biograph, Edison, Essanay, Kalem, Lubin, Selig* and *Vitagraph* – the French companies *Pathé* and *Star-Film* and a distributor. Opposition to this attempt to create a monopoly was led by William Fox's Greater New York Film Rental Company; Fox brought an action against the MPPC in 1913, but by this point the efforts of independent producers had already in effect broken the trust.

'Motion' is from L *motionem*, the noun of action from *movere*, 'to move', by way of the 13th C Fr *motion*: 'motion picture' can be found as early as 1891, four years before the Lumière Brothers' Paris screenings: 'A highly composite mechanism which is to be known as the "kineto-graph", or motion-picture': *Leisure Hour* magazine. On most occasions nowadays, the tight-lipped 'motion picture' is abbreviated to the far more familiar *movie*.

motivation lighting   lighting which appears to come from an on-screen source – a bedside lamp, a candelabra – but which is largely the result of off-screen *luminaires*.

mountain film   a German film genre of the 1920s and 1930s, now best remembered as the training ground for Leni Riefenstahl, first as star, later as director – her first film as director was a key example of the form, *Das blaue Licht*, 1932. The *meister* and indeed inventor of the mountain film was Dr Arnold Fanck (1889–1974), a former ski instructor who trained a unit of athletic technicians capable of filming Alpine scenery at its most sublime and hazardous. Though presented at the time as an apolitical form of entertainment combining thrills, scenery and healthy outdoor exercise, mountain films are now generally regarded – thanks to the observations of critics from Siegfried Kracauer to Susan Sontag – as 'anthologies of proto-Nazi sentiments'.

movie   a straightforward abbreviation of *moving picture*, this is a familiar noun and adjective meaning *film*, and is synonymous with it in many phrases; thus *movies* or *the movies* is understood to mean either films in general, a cinema ('let's go to the movies') or the film industry ('he works in movies'), *movie buff* a film enthusiast, *movie director* a film director, *movie star* a film star and so on. But some slight differences in connotation mean that the terms are not entirely synonymous. For example, 'movie' still has a mild but distinct North American inflection, and though the term is universally understood in the UK, it does not sit altogether easily in British mouths, tending to sound a little forced – jocular, mid-Atlantic or affected – in conversation. To judge by the writings of the American literary and cultural critic Paul Fussell, 'film' and 'movie' swap places when they cross the Atlantic. In his comic diatribe *BAD: The Dumbing of America*, Fussell grouches that 'film' is nothing more than the pretentious name for a movie. It is worth noting, however, that though 'film' is on the whole an innocent, unpretentious word in British English, its very neutrality can give it a note of dignity: for example, it could seem unduly familiar, even disrespectful, to refer to Robert Bresson as a 'movie director', but 'film director' is quite dignified.

The decorum of the word appears to have been questionable ever since it was coined. When the word first appears in print, from about 1912 onwards, it is commonly if not always dressed up in inverted commas ('Guiding the wheel-chair through the entrance-gate of the outdoor "movie"' – *New York Evening Post*, July 1913), and H.G. Wells felt obliged to handle the term with tongs as late as 1929: 'It was possible for some of us to forget the crude, shallow trade "movies" we had seen.' North America, as one would expect, became comfortable with the abbreviation long before Britain, and inverted commas dropped away from the term well before the end of the First World War. Thus, in 1918, Carl Sandburg observes: 'There is drama in that point . . . Griffith would make a movie of it to fetch sobs.' Even so, there is a measure of justice in a sardonic distinction offered by the critic Adam Mars-Jones in a review of *The Shawshank Redemption*, which he felt had been unduly drawn-out: 'The simplest explanation of the proceedings is that the director . . . is pushing the material towards being a film rather than a movie. A movie is plot-driven, fits neatly into a genre and lasts less than

100 minutes. A film seeks to make general statements about life, and there is no upper limit of length' (*Independent*, 16 February 1995). Incidentally, OED also notes the alternative spelling *movy*, but cites only one use, in Shaw's *Heartbreak House* (1919): 'Talk like a man, not like a movy.'

Movietone   the brand name for a pioneering form of sound film, developed for Fox in the late 1920s, which rapidly superseded the *Vitaphone* system used by Warners for *The Jazz Singer*, where Vitaphone required a rather clumsy use of discs, Movietone productions used an optical sound method similar to the one still used today. (*Daily Express*, 27 August 1927: 'The "movietone" is an invention with the same technical basis as the "phonofilm"'); 'Movietone' (or 'Movietones') was also the name for the *newsreels* made by Fox from October 1927 onwards; the *Movietone Frame* is the standard frame for sound film with an *aspect ratio* of 4:3 – that is, film with an *Academy* ratio.

Moviola (or, less commonly and in the early days of its use, **Movieola**)   the trade name of a motor-driven viewing device used in editing which runs the exposed film vertically through its mechanism rather than horizontally, as on a *Steenbeck* or other flatbed editing table. (OED's first citation is from *Photoplay* magazine for April 1929.) Like the word 'Steenbeck', 'Moviola' can (though the practice is becoming less common) also be used generically, usually with a lower-case 'M', to designate any similar viewing device, no matter its manufacturer.

moving shot   see *dolly*, *travelling shot*.

MPAA   the *Motion Picture Association of America*, the body which gives theatrical releases their ratings, issuing a certificate (or *MPAA Code Seal*) to approved productions. See *Hays Code*.

MS   the standard abbreviation for *Medium Shot*.

multicamera, multicam   from L *multus*, 'much, many': a sequence shot by two or more cameras simultaneously, both to allow for a good variety of shots and as an insurance measure when filming extremely expensive and unrepeatable scenes, such as the massive explosion in Boston Harbour in *Blown Away* (1994); *multi-head printer*, a printer that can strike more than one copy of a film at a time; *multi-image*, a synonym, or near-synonym for *split screen*, meaning a projected image that is divided into two, three or more distinct sections; strictly speaking, a split screen is divided into just two smaller images, where a multi-image can contain any number. The technique is often used in films of concerts, such as Mike Wadleigh's *Woodstock*, or to show the two speakers in a telephone conversation simultaneously; Oliver Stone's *Wall Street*, for example, includes a multi-image sequence which conveys the feverish activity of the stock markets as a rumour spreads throughout America's financial centres; *multi-layer film*, see *monopack*; *multiplane*, a type of animation which gives the effect of three-dimensional space, an effect achieved by stacking a number of transparent cels, painted with scenery and the like, at intervals one above another and filming the composite image thus produced. The technique was invented by Ub Iwerks, and first used by the Disney studios; *multiple exposure*, the deliberate super-imposition of several images, achieved either in shooting or in printing; *multiple printing*, either the simultaneous printing of several images from the same negative, or the printing of one film from several negatives to achieve a *multiple exposure* (*multiple frame printing*, however, means the repeated printing of a single frame to achieve a *freeze-frame* effect); *multiplex*, a cinema containing several, usually fairly small-scale screening rooms rather than the one large space which was the rule before the 1970s; older filmgoers tend to dislike them intensely, not only because they dilute the essential experience of cinema (a large crowd, cavernous darkness, vast images) but because of their limited and unadventurous, not to say commercially servile programming policies; *multiscreen*, in projection, a system which uses several synchronised cameras and two or more screens, such as the three-screen process *Polyvision*, devised by Abel Gance for his film *Napoléon* (1927), or by the Australian avant-garde film-maker Don Levy, whose *Sources of Power* was shown at the Expo '67 in Montreal; or one which uses several projectors to form a wide-screen image on a single screen such as the *Cinerama* process; *multi-track sound*, the deep and complex sound made possible by the use of several sound tracks or channels.

'Murder Your Wife' brick   a fake brick, named in homage to *How to Murder Your Wife* (1965).

music   from Fr *musique*, L *musica* and Gk *mousike*, 'the art of the Muse'; it comes into English in much its modern sense as early as the mid-13th C: 'Wit of musike, wel he knew.' The music in a sound film may be of two main kinds: either (a) the soundtrack music (or *score)*, or (b) that which is part of the action, performed in full sight by a band, orchestra, soloist or singers, or is heard from some on-screen or just off-screen source – a television, a radio, a marching band in the street below, elevator or supermarket muzak and so on; this latter type is known as *direct music* or **source music** (*musicals*, of course, tend to blur the distinction between these categories); *music bridge*, a musical passage which helps to smooth the transition between scenes; *music department*, the division of a studio that has the job of composing, buying or otherwise acquiring the music for productions, as well as for hiring musicians, arranging recording sessions and the like; *music editor* (or *music mixer*), the person who collaborates with the composer and, often, the director in fitting soundtrack music to the film's images; *music track*, the sound channel that contains the music.

musical   since the early 20th C (though the earliest examples cited in OED are from 1938 and 1940), the near-universal abbreviation for *musical comedy*, a theatrical entertainment introduced to the American stage in the 1860s or thereabouts, and taken up enthusiastically by the cinema with the introduction of sound technology. Indeed, the very first sound picture or *talkie* was a musical of sorts, *The Jazz Singer* (1927), though purists have argued that the mere presence of ten songs in that film is not enough to qualify it as a true musical, in which the elements of song, dance and spectacle must be the essence of the film rather than a pleasing decoration of non-musical activities. Such purists would also deny that the various operettas of the late 1920s and early 1930s, such as Ernst Lubitsch's *The Love Parade* (1929), starring Maurice Chevalier and Jeanette MacDonald, deserve to qualify as musicals. On such strict reckonings, the first authentic example of the 'all-talking, all-singing, all-dancing' movie is *The Broadway Melody* (1929) – a film which also founded the lively tradition of the 'backstage' musical, in which the lives and loves of stage performers offer an ideal pretext for launching into production numbers. Whatever its real point of origin, the musical film soon became something much more ambitious than a simple reproduction of the theatrical musical in another medium, and blossomed into extravagant and distinctive new shapes that were far beyond the resources of any stage production. One of the artists responsible for this flowering was the shamelessly baroque choreographer Busby Berkeley, whose hallucinatory, kaleidoscopic arrangements of limbs and torsos shot with a single highly mobile camera were the main attractions of the Warner Bros productions *42nd Street* (1933), *Gold Diggers of 1933* (1933, of course) and its successors. Some commentators have suggested that the musical is, with the *western*, at once the most important and the most quintessentially American of Hollywood's gifts to the art of cinema. The latter claim, at least, is hard to dispute: most of the classics of the genre were those made by Hollywood between 1930 and the late 1950s, when a combination of increasing costs and declining audiences made the musical a less attractive proposition for studios, and it ceased to be a staple of production. Among the landmarks of the screen musical in its great days: Vincente Minnelli's films for MGM, including *Meet Me in St Louis* (1944), *An American in Paris* (1951) and *The Band Wagon* (1953); Stanley Donen's enduringly popular collaborations with Gene Kelly *On the Town* (1949) and *Singin' in the Rain* (1952), and, without Kelly, *Seven Brides for Seven Brothers* (1954) and *Funny Face* (1956); Rouben Mamoulian's *Summer Holiday* (1948) and *Silk Stockings* (1956); the various films starring Fred Astaire and Ginger Rogers, notably *Flying Down to Rio* (1933), *Top Hat* (1935) and *Swing Time* (1956); and – an essential, though in some ways rule-breaking example – *The Wizard of Oz* (1939), directed by Victor Fleming. By the early 1960s, the expense of shooting a musical had become sufficiently daunting that most of the films which made it into production were those with an established track record on the stage, and though a few of these made handsome profits – *West Side Story* (1961), *My Fair Lady* (1964), *The Sound of Music* (1965) – the decade ended with a series of financial and artistic flops that appeared to kill off the form for good: *Star!* (1968), *Paint Your Wagon* (1969) and *Dr Dolittle* (1967). A few American directors have subsequently made some interesting attempts at or revisions of the form, including the choreographer Bob Fosse with *Cabaret* (1972) and *All That Jazz* (1979), Robert Altman with *Nashville* (1975), Martin Scorsese with *New York, New York* (1977) and Francis Ford Coppola with the financial disaster of *One From the Heart* (1982) and *The Cotton Club* (1984), both of them representing a triumph of hope over experience: one of Coppola's first films as a director was *Finian's Rainbow* (1968), which also flopped. The years during which the classic film musical went into decline coincide almost exactly with the ascendancy of rock and roll music and its myriad offshoots, and it might be argued that quite a few of the films which employed rock music and musicians – from Elvis Presley's largely undistinguished, often indistinguishable star vehicles between 1956 to 1969 to David Byrne's charming and frequently inspired essay on small-town America *True Stories* (1986) – can or must be regarded as musicals; see **rock films**. Few musicals made outside the United States have rivalled the Hollywood products for invention, wit and popular appeal, though the French cinema has produced a handful of poetic variations, such as Rene Clair's *A Nous la liberté* (1932) and Jaques Demy's *Les Parapluies de Cherbourg* (1964), in which all the dialogue was sung, and *Les Desmoiselles de Rochefort* (1967), in which Demy's admiration for Hollywood musicals was underlined by his decision to cast Gene Kelly in a leading role. Jean-Luc Godard's *Une Femme est une Femme* (1961), though it defies ready categorization (save perhaps as an early Godard film), was a kind of eccentric, knockabout tribute to the MGM musical. On the whole, the tradition of the screen musical in Britain is best passed over in awkward silence, though there are notable exceptions, particularly if the engaging and commercially successful films made by Richard Lester with the Beatles (*A Hard Day's Night* and *Help!*) may be classified as musicals rather than rock films. A brief roll-call of notable British musical films would have to include the showcases, immensely popular with British audiences of the time, for the singing talents of Gracie Fields (*Sing As We Go*, 1934), Jessie Matthews (*Evergreen*, 1934) and George Formby (*No Limit*, 1935); various adaptations of stage shows including Lionel Bart's *Oliver!* (1968), directed by Carol Reed; Ken Russell's surprisingly restrained *The Boy Friend* (1971) and his wholly embarrassing, indeed humiliating *Tommy* (1975), adapted from the 'rock opera' by The Who; and Julien Temple's *Great Rock'n'Roll Swindle* (1979), featuring the Sex Pistols, and the catastrophic *Absolute Beginners* (1986). But if the British film industry has not tended to excel at musicals, British television produced at least one extraordinary talent whose work was simultaneously an imaginative elaboration from and a withering condemnation of the form: the playwright Dennis Potter, author of the series *Pennies from Heaven* (1978, made into an unsuccessful American film, directed by Herbert Ross and starring Steve Martin, in 1981), *Lipstick on Your Collar* (1993) and – by general consent his finest work – *The Singing Detective* (1986).

mute   a print or negative with no sound track; this term is mostly used in the UK.

Mutograph, Mutoscope   the trade names for two complementary devices said to have been invented by the former Edison employee W.K.L. Dickson, that were immediate forerunners of the technology of cinema, and similar to Edison's *Kinetoscope*. According to *Scientific American* for 17 April 1897, however, 'The "mutograph" and "mutoscope" are the inventions of Mr Herman Casler . . . The machine with which the original pictures are taken . . . is known as the "mutograph", nearly following the Latin and Greek words signifying "changing delineation".' (The Latin *mutare* means 'to change'.) The Mutograph was used to take a sequence of still photographs, 2 x 2¾ inches in size, which were then installed in a peep-hole machine – the Mutoscope – installed in arcades. The customer would deposit a penny, look into a slot and crank the handle so as to riffle through these photographs quickly enough to create the effect of motion. The American Mutograph Company, established in 1895, later went on to develop a true form of cinema with their *Biograph*. It could be argued that the Mutoscope created the first 'movie star' – the actor Joseph Jefferson, who posed for brief Mutoscopic extracts from his successful stage play *Rip Van Winkle*. The Mutoscope 'film' of a boxing match in 1897 was filmed under artificial lights by Billy Bitzer (1874–1944), now remembered for his pioneering work as a cinematographer on D.W. Griffith's films from 1908 to 1924. The Mutoscope enjoyed a second lease of life in the late 1940s, when the American experimental film-maker Douglas Crockwell began to play around with its possibilities. Crockwell went on to modify the original design, and made a number of abstract 'films' that could be viewed on the machine.

Mutual Film Corporation   the early American production company, founded in 1912, chiefly remembered for the slapstick efforts made by its subsidiary *Keystone* and for producing some of Charlie Chaplin's best comedies. After a tangled corporate history, the remains of Mutual were eventually taken over by the company which became *RKO*.

Mylar   a strong plastic manufactured by du Pont and used as the base for audio and video tape. *Mylar splice*, a splice in a workprint made with transparent Mylar tape rather than with cement.

mystery film   any film concerned with the discovery, investigation and, usually, resolution of some mysterious event or circumstance; generally a *thriller* or *detective film*, though the term would also apply to some *science fiction* or *horror movies*.

Nagra   the trade name of a small sound recorder of extremely high quality, developed by Stefan Kudeslski and now widely employed by film-makers throughout the world; it uses quarter-inch reel-to-reel tape. The introduction of the Nagra was one of the technical factors that helped liberate film-making from the studio, and was particularly important for the development of *cinema verité* and *direct cinema*.

narration   from the 12–13 C Fr *narration*, and L *narration-em*, the noun of action from *narrare*, to tell, narrate (the word enters English in a variety of spellings, but much the modern range of senses in the early 14th C: 'the ordre of the narracion of stories requirethe that the gestes of the worlde scholde be describede also' – *Higden*, 1432–50). In the cinema, an alternative term for the *voice-over* – often, though not always, spoken by the leading character – used in some feature films, either throughout the narrative or just at one or two important moments, such as the beginning and end. For example, *Sunset Boulevard* (the narration of which is spoken by a corpse), *Kind Hearts and Coronets* (Dennis Price's elegantly murderous musings as he wipes out the d'Ascoyne family), *A Clockwork Orange* (the sardonic retrospect of its barbarous protagonist Alex, who speaks in a colourful teenage argot called Nadsat; this was invention of the novelist Anthony Burgess, who drew on the Russian dictionary), *Taxi Driver* (where it represents the inner monologue of, or pages from the obsessive diary written by the anti-hero, Travis Bickle), *Apocalypse Now* (Willard's ruminations as he proceeds upriver), *Full Metal Jacket* and so on. In Scorsese's *The Age of Innocence* (1993), the narration, spoken by Joanne Woodward, represents the authorial voice of Edith Wharton. Narrations, or *commentaries*, are on the whole a more standard component of documentaries than of features, generally serving as an unobtrusive means of leading the audience through an argument or supplying information that cannot easily be given by any other means. Some documentary or semi-documentary film-makers have used the device in more complex ways: to raise questions about the status of the images that are being displayed (as in Chris Marker's *The Last Bolshevik*) or to create a kind of unseen dramatic character meditating on what is seen (as in Patrick Keillor's *London*). Hence *narration script*, a text which usually contains both the words for the voice-over and some indication of the points at which it occurs in the film, and *narrator*, the character or performer who speaks the voice-over.

narrative film   a conventional story-telling film, whether dramatic or documentary, as opposed to the kind of poetic or *abstract* film characteristic of the *avant-garde*.

narrow-gauge film   all films with a gauge lower than 35mm, the standard gauge for feature-film making, and particularly for 16mm and 8mm or *Super-8*.

National Board of Review   the American body dedicated to the advancement of those productions it holds to be of high aesthetic merit; it has an annual prize-giving event, the D.W. Griffith awards. It was founded in New York in 1909 as the National Board of Censorship, which, despite its tight-lipped name, was in fact a fairly liberal organis-ation, backed by the film industry, and designed to pre-empt a system of government censorship. It changed its name and function in 1921, after New York State introduced a film licensing law.

National Film Archive   the principal film *archive* of the United Kingdom was founded as the National Film Library, a sub-divison of the *BFI*, in 1935, under the direction of Ernest Lindgren. The *NFT* and *MOMI* frequently screen prints from the collection under the series heading 'Treasures from the Archive'.

National Film Theatre (NFT)   also founded by the BFI, which took over a building on the South Bank of the Thames known as the Telekinema (one of the fruits of the Festival of Britain, 1951) and rebuilt it into more or less its present form. With the almost complete collapse of *repertory* cinema in Britain over the last couple of decades, the NFT remains one of the very few places where it is possible to see the classics of the medium, or indeed just about any film outside the realm of *multiplex* fodder, in the form their makers intended.

NATO   lest there should be some confusion with the slightly better-known military alliance, the acronym also stands for the American National Association of Theatre Owners, Inc.

naturalism   Despite the highly complex history of this critical term, in general cinematic use it is taken as pretty much a synonym for 'realism' and an antonym for 'stylisation'; that is to say, it is applied to films, or sequences within films, that are shot without any of the conspicuous artifice of lighting, editing, set design, acting technique and the like that are used to make human actions seem more interesting, dramatic, funny or enticing than they would be without such adornments. Much less often, it is put to rather more precise or pedantic use, and refers to those films which follow the example of the literary naturalists of the late 19th C–early 20th C, such as Emile Zola, who appears to have given currency to the term in his preface to *Thérèse Raquin*, where he described himself as a *naturaliste*. Briefly, literary naturalism of the Zola kind is a school of writing which takes pride in a quasi-scientific appoach, more or less vaguely inspired by Darwin and Comte. Concerned to stress that human existence is dominated by environment and heredity rather than by the free spirit, its characteristic settings are harsh or sordid, its typical mood relentlessly gloomy. Zola's work has been filmed a number of times (*La Bête Humaine*, for example, by Jean Renoir in 1938, and, with the title *Human Desire*, by Fritz Lang in 1954), but the most famous naturalistic film is probably Erich von Stroheim's mutilated epic *Greed*, adapted from Frank Norris's novel *McTeague*.

natural lighting   the light given by the sun, moon and reflecting surfaces, or from candles, blazing heaths and the like, as opposed to the controlled light created by *luminaires*; see *available light*.

natural wipe   a *wipe* created with live action rather than in printing, and achieved by having a person or object pass briefly in front of the camera, thus blocking out the first scene and then allowing its successor to appear.

nature film   a documentary about fauna, flora and other aspects of the natural world, such as the popular wildlife series presented by David Attenborough for BBC television (*Life on Earth*), or, for the cinema, the well-regarded Swedish feature *The Great Adventure* (1953), directed by Arne Sucksdorff, and the American real-life shark drama *Blue Water, White Death* (1971).

NC17   an abbreviation for 'No Children under 17 years of age', the recent American classification for films which have a marked erotic content but are not deemed to be pornographic (and thus liable to the X rating); see *rating*.

ND   an abbreviation, either for (a) 'nondescript' or (b) for *Neutral Density Filter* (or *Gel*), a filter which produces an even reduction in exposure and contrast without distorting the colour balance.

negative   from 13th C Fr *negatif* or late L *negativ-us*, from *negat-*, the participle stem of *negare*, to deny; in the sense of a prohibition or negative command, it can be found in English from the late 14th C; OED's earliest citation for the photographic sense of the word is from 1853. In the cinema, *negative* usually means either (a) film that contains an inverse image of the scene that has been photographed; in other words, the state of the film after it has been exposed and processed, and is ready to be used for printing positive images, or (b) film that has not yet been exposed or processed (that is, *raw stock*) or (c) any negative image. Hence various related terms: *negative cost*, the total amount of money spent to bring a production to the stage where a final cut of the negative is ready; this does not, therefore, include the considerable costs of making projection prints, publicising, distributing or exhibiting a film; *negative cutting* (or *negative matching*) is the process which takes place when editing is complete, and which consists of *conforming* the negative to the *work print*, using *key numbers* (*edge numbers*) as guide – in other words, of producing a clean and undamaged negative version of the completed film, using the generally rather scratched and worn edited footage as a guide (the person who carries out this task, if it is not the *editor*, is referred to as the *negative cutter* or *neg cutter*); *negative numbers*, another term for *key numbers* or *edge numbers*; *negative perforation*, the rectangular sprocket holes on 35mm negatives; *negative splice*, the cemented line at which two strips of negative are joined, narrower (and therefore less secure) than a *positive splice* because they do not have to stand up to the strain of passing through a projector.

negative pick-up   a common term in film financing. It refers to a deal between a distribution company or studio and a producer, in which the studio or company guarantees to buy ('pick up') distribution rights to a film for an agreed sum on presentation of a completed negative. With this guarantee, the producer can then approach backers to raise the sum needed to shoot and post-produce a feature. In other words, a negative pick-up is the opposite of the more traditional type of film financing, in which the studio will fund a movie from the pre-production stage all the way through to its final release.

neorealism (also **neo-realism, Neorealism** etc.)   'The earnest talker on films, the *cineaste* [sic], finds his brother in the balletomane and his cousin in the first-nighter . . . and his conversation is full of words like montage, neo-realism, and audio-visual correspondence' – *The Times*, 4 July 1955. Neorealism was a short-lived but widely admired and exceptionally influential movement of the Italian cinema during the years immediately following the Second World War; among the defining features of the movement (many of them determined more by the extreme poverty of the film-makers involved than any point of principle) were the use of non-professionals as actors, location rather than studio shooting, a concentration on social and political issues and a raw, sometimes almost semi-documentary approach to storytelling. Although some historians have traced the movement's orgins back as far as the period 1913–16, when Italian film-makers experimented with a *verismo* style, the term 'neorealism' seems to have been coined in 1942 by Antonio Pietrangeli in an article for the Italian film journal *Cinema*, and was also used at around the same time by Pietrangeli's fellow critic Umberto Barbara. Pietrangeli was the screenwriter for a film now regarded as the principal harbinger of the movement, Luchino Visconti's *Ossessione* (1942); his script was based on James M. Cain's hard-bitten crime novel *The Postman Always Rings Twice*, which would subsequently be filmed in America by Tay Garnett in 1946 and by Bob Rafelson in 1981. But most authorities agree that the first true neorealist film was Roberto Rossellini's wonderful, intensely moving account of the last days of fascist Italy, *Rome, Open City* (1945); this was also the film that introduced neorealism to the international audience, which had not been able to see Italian films made during the war. Other outstanding productions of the period include several more films by Rossellini, including *Paisa* (1946) and *Germania Anno Zero* (1947); De Sica's *Ladri di Biciclette* (1947); and Guiseppe De Santis's *Riso amaro* (1949), a film sometimes regarded as the first sign of the movement's decadence, since, despite the title, it began to sweeten and prettify its conventions (particularly by drawing attention to the conspicuous charms of Silvano Mangano). Neorealism petered out in the early 1950s – the last film usually ascribed to the movement is De Sica's *Umberto D* – though its leading lights went on to make very different kinds of films that could be no less fascinating in their own ways; it has inspired many subsequent film-makers from Pasolini and Satyajit Ray to Ermanno Olmi and Ken Loach; and it remains a landmark for most lovers of the cinema – the doomed screenwriter in Altman's *The Player*, for example, goes to see *Ladri di Biciclette* on the evening of his death. The Spanish director Pedro Almodóvar has recently suggested that 'For me, Italian neo-realism is a sub-genre of melodrama which specifically deals not just with emotions but also with social conscience. It's a genre which takes the artificiality out of melodrama, while retaining its essential elements.'

net   a type of *diffuser* or *scrim*.

Neubabelsberg   the huge studio complex, founded in 1911 on the outskirts of Berlin, which was so well-equipped (with rivers, lakes, railways, a zoo . . .) that it became known as the 'German Hollywood'. From 1938 to 1940 it was the home for a film school; heavily damaged during the war, it was taken over by East Germany in 1946. See *UFA*.

neutral angle   a unobtrusive shot taken from about eye-level and facing the subject or action head-on; *neutral density filter*, a grey filter that cuts down the amount of light passing through the camera, so that the depth of field can be reduced without having to close down the aperture.

New American Cinema   the critical label sometimes applied to a particular school of *avant-garde* film-making that flourished in the United States in the 1960s, though its roots may be found much earlier – in, for example, the extraordinary short films of Maya Deren, director and scholar (and, indeed, priestess) of Voodoo, made during the Second World War. The label is derived from the New American Cinema Group, and was given currency by the director and critic Jonas Mekas through his journal *Film Culture*. The New American Cinema Group was an alliance of semi-commercial film-makers with those of the emerging *underground*, founded on 28 September 1960 at the New York office of the producer Lewis Allen. The (inevitable) manifesto drawn up by members of the Group proclaimed their commitment to the idea of film as a means of personal expression, announced plans for a co-operative scheme of finance and distribution, and condemned censorship. It ended with the ringing declaration, 'We don't want false, polished, slick films – we prefer them rough, unpolished, but alive; we don't want rosy films – we want them the color of blood.' One practical consequence of this alliance was the creation of the Film-maker's Cooperative in 1962, under the direction of Jonas Mekas. This body ensured that the work of its members would receive at least some public exhibition. According to Sheldon Renan's *An Introduction to the American Underground Film* (1967), the term 'New American Cinema' can be used 'interchangeably' with 'the underground film'. However, he adds, 'The New American Cinema takes in the underground film, but is broader than it. It is the total rebellion in the United States against the domination of film by Hollywood and other commercial factors'. But the term is now relatively uncommon.

new angle   in a script: a direction from the screenwriter indicating that a change of angle is needed at that point.

New Line   the commercially succesful (it made the *Nightmare on Elm Street* series and *Teenage Mutant Ninja Turtles*) and, usually via its up-market sibling Fine Line, artistically respected independent production and video distribution company, responsible among other notable movies of recent years for Gus Van Sant's *My Own Private Idaho* and Robert Altman's *Short Cuts*. It is now a subsidiary of the Turner Broadcasting System.

newsreel   a short film carrying news or other current affairs matter: an immensely important form of cinema that has been almost wholly superseded by the news-gathering agencies of television stations and companies around the world. The genre began almost as soon as the cinema itself, when the Lumière brothers sent their cameramen off to shoot brief films about happenings in Europe, the Middle East and the United States. Others soon followed suit, recording, for example, the coronation of Tsar Nicholas II in 1896, the Derby of 1897 and the funeral of Queen Victoria in 1901; reconstructions, or wilful fake-ups of topical events were also quite common. The newsreel as we think of it today – a group of several short films put together much in the manner of those television news bulletin of which they are the ancestor – was introduced by Pathé in 1908; the first true British newsreel, *Pathé Gazette*, was launched in 1909, and most of the world's leading nations had comparable institutions by 1910 or thereabouts. The form excited intellectuals as well as hacks; Dziga Vertov's *kino-pravda* series of 1922–5 are still of more than merely historical interest. Newsreels flourished in the 1930s and 1940s, when most cinemas would change their programme every three or four days, when audiences were hungry for the spectacle of international crisis and war, and when light-hearted or even frankly comic material (the precursors of today's 'and finally . . .' news items about skateboarding ducks) became a fixed part of the format; the American *March of Time* series, launched in 1934, is probably the best-known newsreel of the period. Cinemas yielded rapidly to the onslaught of television in the 1950s, and though *British Movietone* manged to struggle on to the 1970s, there are now a couple of generations of film-goers who have probably never seen newsreels except in period documentaries. OED's earliest citation of the word, pleasingly, is from a 1916 edition of the *Wells Fargo Messenger*.

Newton's Rings   in the cinema, circular flaws that appear on film because of light bouncing between shiny surfaces; Sir Isaac Newton discovered the phenomenon when, as the transactions of the Royal Society for 1807 put it, he noted 'coloured concentric rings . . . between two object-glasses laid upon one another.'

New Wave   the standard English translation of the French *Nouvelle Vague*, widely used in journalism, criticism and so on since about 1960 either to designate the *nouvelle vague* itself, or, by analogy, to categorise some innovative movement in another field of endeavour.

NG   standard abbreviation for 'No Good' – the mark logged against a bad take, indicating that it is not to be used.

nickelodeon   the earliest forms of commercial cinema in the United States, so called because the price of admission was originally a nickel – five cents; the '-odeon' suffix is derived from Gk *odeon*, 'building for musical performances' or 'theatre'. According to some sources, the word was coined by the showman John P. Harris. The first nickelodeon was opened in 1905 in Pittsburgh, and proved so successful that five years later there were some ten thousand of them throughout North America. In Britain, the equivalent institution was known as a *penny gaff*. See also *Odeon*.

night filter   a filter used to create the effect of nocturnal lighting for scenes shot in daylight or by artificial light; see *day for night*; *night for day*, the opposite – that is, scenes that are shot at night-time with enough artificial illumination to create the illusion of day; *night for night*, as one would expect, denotes nocturnal scenes that are actually shot in the hours of darkness.

9.8mm   a *narrow gauge* film stock, used mainly by amateur film-makers; it was manufactured in France from 1922 onwards to replace the earlier 11mm film, but was itself rapidly superseded by *8mm* and *Super-8*.

nit   a metric unit of luminance, established as one *candela* per square metre. Taken from Fr *nit* and L *nit-ere*, 'to shine', it was adopted for international use in 1948 at the 11th meeting of the Commission Internationale de l'Eclairage.

nitrate film, nitrate, nitrate base   the standard abbreviated or colloquial forms of 'cellulose nitrate base' – that is, the usefully flexible but, unfortunately, highly flammable base used for much of the first half-century of film-making; it was developed by George Eastman in 1899. Since about 1950–1, it has been superseded by *safety film* in its various manifestations, and *archives* around the world are engaged in transferring nitrate films to safety since they are not merely dangerous to store but are given to rotting.

noiseless camera   a *self-blimping* camera – one that is set in a soundproof case so that the noise of its engine will not be picked up by the microphones.

noncamera film   a type of *avant-garde* film produced without the use of a camera or other photographic techniques, but rather by making marks directly on to celluloid. See *direct film*.

nondirectional microphone   a microphone that can pick up sound from all directions; also known as an *omnidirectional microphone*.

nonfiction film   generally speaking, a less common term for *documentaries*, though it also applies to short instructional or educational films, *newsreels* and so on as well as more standard documentary formats.

nonsynchronous sound   sound that is not matched to the image, also known as *wild sound*.

Nordisk   though its name will not be familiar to the average movie-goer, this Danish production company is not only the world's oldest such body (it was founded in 1906 and is still in operation), but in the years before the First World War was a major force in world cinema, pouring forth a steady stream of undemanding but highly successful movies from its exceptionally well-furnished studio in Copenhagen.

normal lens   a type of lens designed to create an image which appoximates to what is seen by the unaided human eye – in technical terms, this means that a normal lens for a 35mm camera will have a focal length of 50mm.

north   the top part of an animation stand or drawing (as of a map); or, less often, the top part of any image.

notch   a small nick made on the edge of a negative, which, when it passes through a printer, sets off a mechanism that adjusts the amount of light reaching the film, and thus its degree of exposure.

***Nouvelle Vague, nouvelle vague*, New Wave**   a term coined by French journalists to pin down one of the most remarkable episodes in the history of cinema, and possibly of any art form: the sudden uprising, invasion, palace *coup*, revolution or what you will staged in Paris in 1958–9, when a group of young, passionate, intense, gifted and some-times downright cranky film critics writing for *Cahiers du Cinéma* and related publications (Claude Chabrol, Jean-Luc Godard, Jacques Rivette, Eric Rohmer, François Truffaut and the nowadays somewhat less renowned Jacques Doniol-Valcroze) not only managed to quit their day jobs and set up as film directors virtually overnight, but created a whole style of cinema – or what seemed like one, anyway – into the bargain. These young turks rapidly became known as the *Nouvelle Vague*; by 4 September 1959 word had crossed the Channel clearly enough for *The Times* to explain of a film that it was 'made by one of the old guard rather than by a member of the *nouvelle vague.*' (The term also proved popular enough to be applied to other forms of innovation, from mathematics teaching to cookery.) Many factors helped make this extraordinary feat possible, but perhaps the most important was a state of crisis in French film production which made producers willing to take risks on low-budget productions: the impact of the *nouvelle vague* was the most highly publicised aspect of a sudden flood of first-time directors (24 in 1959, 43 in 1960), and other important film-makers who were not really part of the *Cahiers* group, including Alain Resnais and Louis Malle, also enjoyed breakthroughs in the same period. But this *vague*, for all its worship of certain aspects of the cinematic past (Hitchcock, Hawks, Rossellini, Bresson), was in certain regards genuinely *nouvelle*. As critics, these ardent fellows had argued the need for a personal cinema, an *auteur*'s cinema, and it can be maintained that in their very different ways they achieved it: in Chabrol's *Le Beau Serge*, in Truffaut's *Les Quatres Cent Coups* (garlanded at Cannes), in Godard's *A Bout de souffle*, in Rohmer's *Le Signe de Lion*, in Rivette's *Paris nous appartient*. *Nouvelle vague* films were generally recognisable by their neglect or deliberate violations of standard industry practice (the *jump-cuts* in Godard's *A Bout de souffle* are the best-known example of such mischief), by their vivid use of locations (a practice made easier by their use of lightweight, easily portable *Arriflex* cameras) and by their habit of alluding not only to classic films but to each other's efforts, as well. Some critics feel that the *nouvelle vague* broke around 1962–3, at which point Truffaut, Chabrol and others went on to have much more conventional industry careers, leaving the increasingly hermetic and, later, revolutionary Godard as the movement's ancient mariner. Whether or not one agrees with this vision of betrayal and decline, however, there is no doubt that the example of the *nouvelle vague* fired up young film-makers around the world, and that even Hollywood came to pick up their tricks – in *Bonnie and Clyde*, for example, a film its writers originally intended as an American project for Godard or Truffaut. And some of its films still look wonderful.

nudie   a rather dated, indeed quaint slang term for a pornographic film or *blue movie*.

number board   another term for a *slate*.

numbering machine (or **encoding machine**)   in editing, a device used to print code numbers along the edge of the work print.

O **ater** *Variety*-speak: a *western*; so called because the equine performers in these productions are fuelled with oats. Other jocular terms include *horse opera* (by analogy with *soap opera*) and *sagebrusher*.

Oberhausen festival a festival specialising in films of a social or political nature, particularly shorts, founded in 1955 by Helmar Hoffman, a former POW in Scotland and idealist. It was at the 1962 festival that a group of 26 young German writers and directors drew up the *Oberhausen Manifesto*, an act of rebellion against the stale and trashy domestic productions of the post-war period, and thus the origin of the *Junger Deutscher Film* movement. The federal government was slow to respond to their demands, but gradually began to set up a system of grants and other financial aid for film-makers, so that – with more than a little help from German television – by the end of the 1960s the revolution was in full swing. Volker Schlöndorff, Edgar Reitz and Jean-Marie Straub were in the advance guard, to be followed in the 1970s by the likes of Fassbinder, Herzog, Syberberg and Wenders, whose films brought German cinema a degree of international attention and respect it had not enjoyed for the best part of half a century.

obie a small spotlight of some 250 watts.

object animation another term for the three-dimensional form of *animation* usually referred to as *stop-motion*.

objective a term for the principal lens in a camera or other apparatus that brings images to definition on a focal plane; 'objective', an abbreviation of 'objective glass', has been used in the optical sense from the mid-18th C: 'An heliometer: which is an instrument, consisting of two objective glasses, for measuring the diameters of the planets' – Short, *Philosophical Transactions*, 1753.

objective camera a neutral, dispassionate, self-effacing camera style, either in documentary or in fiction films, that is calculated to give the illusion that what is being shown to the audience is unmediated reality. Characteristics of this style include a camera placed at ordinary eye level, relatively little camera movement and unobtrusive, infrequent cutting.

obligatory scene in film marketing terms, a scene which must be included to satisfy the demands of the genre and the appetites of the audience: a graphic sex scene in soft pornography, a shot of the hero blowing out the entrails of the villain in a violent thriller. Less cynically, the term can also refer to a *denouement*, or any other scene which must be included if the narrative is to seem coherent and satisfying.

oblique angle (oblique frame) a tilted camera angle; see *Dutch angle*.

OC see *off camera*.

Odeon the trade name for a chain of British cinemas, launched in 1933 by Oscar Deutsch with financial backing from his shareholders *United Artists*. Though in fact derived from the Gk *odeion*, 'a building for musical performances', the name was reputed to be an acronym for

'Oscar Deutsch Entertains Our Nation'. J. Arthur Rank became a member of the Odeon board in 1939, and soon after Deutsch's death in 1941, the chain was taken over by the Rank Organisation. All Odeon cinemas were built on the same model, boasting a rectangular tower with the name spelled out in illuminated letters, and satisfyingly lavish interior decor. It was noted in 1952 that timid or homesick holidaymakers would often seek out the Odeon in their resort town because it reminded them of their local cinema. Indeed, the chain proved so sucessful in its first decade that the word 'Odeon' not only became a near-synonym for 'local cinema', but, as Rank's biographer suggested, seemed to sum up the British way of life in the 1930s.

Odorama   a crude but memorable gimmick invented by the director John Waters to help promote his scabrous feature *Polyester* (1981): in response to an on-screen cue, audiences would scratch at a new panel on the cards they had been given on entering, and sniff the resulting smell – of dirty tennis shoes and worse. Curiously, Odorama was far from being the cinema's first attempt to escalate from sight and sound to smell; see *Aroma-Rama*, *Smell-O-Vision*.

off-camera   anything outside the camera's field of vision; hence *off-camera turn*, a performer's turn away from the camera, the opposite of an *on-camera turn*; *off-line*, in video editing, the preparatory and sometimes experimental cutting that takes place before the true, or *on-line* edit; *off-mike*, a sound that is out of microphone range, or directed away from the microphone; *off-register*, the accidental or deliberate wobbling of a camera in genuine or apparent response to vibrations, tremors or shocks (such as explosions); *off scene, off-screen* (*OS*), an action, sound or (particularly) piece of dialogue that comes from some off-camera area; in a screenplay, such dialogue is marked by an (OS) immediately next to the name of the character speaking.

old-timer   a flexible pole that supports *flags* or *scrims*.

OK, OK takes   marks of approval which indicate the range of satisfactory takes that the editor can call on when assembling sequences; the opposite, that is, of *NG takes*.

omni-directional microphone, omnidirectional microphone   a microphone that registers sounds from all directions. Also known as a *non-directional microphone*.

Omnimax   the trade name for a wide-angle camera lens system, designed to be used in *Imax* film-making.

on-camera   anything recorded by the camera; *on-camera turn*, a performer's turn towards the camera; *on-line*, in video editing, the final tape-edit, based on the work done in preparatory *off-line* editing; *on location*, shooting away from the studio; see *location*.

one hundred and eighty degree rule, 180 degree rule   see *imaginary line*.

one-light print   a print exposed at a single lighting level, usually because it is being made from a *dupe negative* that has already been corrected.

one shot   a shot of a single person; also known as a *single*.

opaque leader   any non-transparent film used as *leader*, particularly in *A and B roll* editing.

open call   a large-scale audition for actors; the more polite term for a *cattle call*.

opening credits   the *credits* shown at the beginning of a film, usually containing the film's title and the names of the producers, directors, writer and principal actors; *end credits* are more complete.

open up   either (a), to increase the lens aperture by choosing a lower *f-stop* number on the *calibration ring*, or (b) in the process of adapting a play for the screen, to add the kinds of action, setting and detail that will make for an appropriately cinematic spectacle, and so disguise the movie's origin within the confines of the proscenium stage.

opera film   any filmed version of an opera, whether as a more or less straightforward record of a stage production or re-interpreted in cinematic terms; or any film which takes the story-line of an opera as the basis of its own narrative; or any film, particularly a *biopic*, about the lives of opera composers or stars. There are countless examples are of each type, including many made for the silent cinema: *Carmen* (1915, 1918, and many remakes ever since), *The Flying Dutchman* (1923), *La Boheme* (1926), *Der Rosenkavalier* (Robert Weine, 1926, with the participation of both Strauss and von Hoffmanstahl). The advent of sound opened the floodgates, and the waters have yet to recede: consider *La Boheme* (Comencini, 1988), *Carmen* (Carlos Saura, 1983, and Francesco Rosi, 1984), *Don Giovanni* (Joseph Losey, 1979), *The Magic Flute* (Ingmar Bergman, 1974), *Otello* (Franco Zeffirelli, 1986), *Parsifal* (Syberberg, 1982), *The Tales of Hoffman* (Powell and Pressburger, 1951) ... The close relationship between opera and film has frequently been remarked, and it is something of a cliché by now to observe that cinema may have been the true *Gesamtkunstwerk* adumbrated by Wagner. It is rather less of a cliché to note that many films that at first sight have nothing to do with opera may show certain affinities with the older form – Coppola's *Apocalypse Now*, for example, not only uses Wagner's 'Ride of the Valryries' to unsettling effect but begins with a kind of hallucinatory overture, in which the film's visual themes are declared to the melodramatic strains of The Doors.

operator   the member of the camera crew who actually manipulates the camera; see *camera operator*.

optical   derived, by way of Fr *optique* and the medieval L *opticus* from Gk *optikos*, and found in English from the late 16th C onwards, the adjective 'optical' qualifies (as one might expect) a number of significant cinematic tools and concepts. These include: *optical axis*, a hypothetical line drawn through the focal point and physical centre of a lens and extended into infinity; *optical composite*, a multiple, special-effects shot composed of a number of separate images; *opticals* or *optical effects*, the effects, including *dissolves, fades, matte shots*, and *special effects* – that can be achieved with an *optical printer*: a sort of combined camera and projector that can add images to film that has already been processed (though a number of opticals, particularly special effects, are now computer-generated). 'Opticals' has been a common abbreviation from the mid-20th C; hence *Punch*'s quip in 1959: 'Many amateurs are clearly of the opinion that this [i.e. the subject-matter of their film] is of minor importance, their chief concern being to demonstrate their skill at devising star-burst wipes and other trick opticals.' Optical printers are also used to transfer film from one *gauge* to another – that is, to enlarge or reduce film, say from 16mm to 35mm. *Optical flip* (or *optical flop*), the use of an optical printer to spin an image over like a coin, to reveal a new scene on, so to speak, its other side; *optical house*, a laboratory which carries out *optical printing*; *optical reduction*, the use of an optical printer to reduce a larger gauge to a smaller; *optical sound, optical sound track*: the sound track on film that can be converted into sound impulses when it passes over an *optical sound reader*; the alternative to a *magnetic sound* track or a *digital sound track*. The basis of optical sound is a *variable density* track running along the side of the film which registers sound signals as a series of jagged horizontal stripes; the development of this technology made it possible to create *married prints*, in which image and sound were in permanent sync, and to do away with the previous, unreliable sound-system based on separate discs. *Optical viewfinder*, a *viewfinder* using an optical system separate from the camera; *optical zoom* a *zoom* created with an optical printer, rather than (as is more common) with the camera in the course of shooting; the printer's camera is moved closer to (or away from) the film.

option   an agreement in which a producer, studio or other buyer pays a fee for the rights to represent an artist or, more often, a screenplay or other *property* for a given period of time.

order of appearance   a list of performers, usually in the *end credits*, that gives their names not in alphabetical order or in descending order of fee, but simply according to when their character first appears on screen.

orientable viewfinder   a type of *viewfinder* which allows the camera operator to view what is being shot, regardless of the position the camera might be in, and is therefore extremely useful when shooting in cramped or otherwise difficult circumstances.

orientation shot   a particular type of *establishing shot*: a shot which lets the audience see not only where the action is set and but also the logic of what exactly is happening there.

original   the fully cut original negative of a film; *original screenplay*, any *screenplay* written expressly for the cinema, and not adapted from some other source material, such as a book, play or article.

Orion   the American production and distribution company, founded in 1978 by a quintet of former *United Artists* executives which flourished in the 1980s but fell into financial difficulties in the early 1990s after suffering a number of major box-office flops. Among the hits of its happier years: *10* (1979), *Arthur* (1981), *Amadeus* (1984), *Platoon* (1986), *Robocop* (1987), *Dances With Wolves* (1990) and *The Silence of the Lambs* (1991).

orthochromic film, orthochromatic film, ortho film   a type of relatively fast *black and white* film that is sensitive to blue and green but not red. The name, taken from Gk *orthos* 'straight, right' and *chromatikos*, 'of colour', and thus meaning 'correct colour', implies that it was seen as an improvement on earlier stocks which had only been sensitive to blues. 'The colours were purposely selected to test as severely as possible the capacity of the plate used – a Dixon's orthochromatic': *Athenaeum*, 26 March 1887. It was rapidly superseded by the yet more sensitive *panchromatic* film after 1926, but did have certain virtues: for example, its speed enabled cameramen to use small lens apertures and thus achieve a fair measure of *deep focus*.

Orwocolor   a brand of colour reversal film, related to *Agfacolor*, and made at the Wolfen factory in the former DDR: the name abbreviates 'ORiginal WOlfen'.

OS   see *off-screen*.

Oscar   the familar name for the gold statuette, thirteen and a half inches high, handed out at the *Academy Awards* from 1929 onwards, and so for the Award itself. The original statuette was made by George Stanley from designs by MGM's supervising Art Director, Cedric Gibbons, There are many versions of the legend of Oscar's christening; the most widely repeated one attributes the act to the Academy's librarian, Margaret Herrick, who on seeing the figurine for the first time in 1931, said, 'Why, he looks just like my uncle Oscar!' – that is, Oscar Pierce. Other rumours credit Bette Davis and the journalist Sidney Skolsky with christening Oscar. OED notes that the award soon became so well known that 'Oscar' became a kind of all-purpose name for awards, real or hypothetical, or for outstanding achivements in any field: it cites the examples of company reports, fashion shows, goal-keeping and so on.

OTS   an abbreviation for an *over-the-shoulder shot (OSS)*.

out of focus dissolve   a type of *dissolve* in which the first or *outgoing* scene grows brighter and more blurry before giving way to the new or *incoming* scene; *out of frame*, either (a) any person, action or thing outside the rectangle which frames the filmed action, or (b) film which has been clumsily threaded into a projector, so producing an image which is split or not centred; *out of sync*, film in which the sound and image do not match correctly; *out-take*s, exposed and processed footage not used in the film's final version, also known as *outs*; *outgoing scene, outgoing shot*, the scene or shot which leaves the screen at the beggining of a dissolve or other transition, to be replaced by the *incoming* shot.

outline   a brief synopsis for a film, drawn up to give producers some idea of its general plot and characters.

overage   production costs that are higher than those allowed for in the production budget; *overcoat*, a transparent protective layer coated over the *emulsion*; *overcrank*, to run film through a camera more quickly than usual (at speeds faster, that is, than 24 frames per second), so as to achieve slow-motion effects when it is projected at normal or slower speeds (hence *overcranked*, etc., and the converse, *undercranked*; see *accelerated motion*); *overdevelop*, if deliberate: to process film for longer than usual, so producing high-contrast images, a technique also known as *cooking* or *forced development*; if accidental, to produce an unacceptably foggy or grainy image; *overexpose*, to allow too much light into contact with stock, thus creating a bleached-out image; *overheads*, as in other industries: the basic costs to a studio or production of renting offices, keeping staff on the payroll and so on; *overhead cluster*, a group of lights suspended from a rig; *overhead shot*, a shot looking directly down on the action; *overlap*, (a) a moment in which the activities of one scene, usually its dialogue or sound track (hence *overlap dialogue, sound*, etc.) bleeds over into the subsequent or – less often, since the effect can be slightly bewildering – the preceding scene; (b) a moment or scene in which two or more actors speak their dialogue at the same time, as in the films of Robert Altman; *overlap splice*, joining two strips of film together by scratching the emulsion from one piece and gluing it to the end of the other *overs*; *over-the-shoulder shot* (*OSS*), a shot which in which the camera takes the position of a person peering at the action over the shoulder of an actor, the back of whose head and shoulder remain in shot; *overshoot*, to film too much footage, either for a particular scene or throughout an entire production. For a memorable account of overshooting in action, see Steven Bach's memoir *Final Cut: Dreams and Disasters in the Making of Heaven's Gate*.

P an initial written on a camera report to indicate that a shot should be printed.

PA standard abbreviation for *production assistant* – a junior member of a production, responsible for a wide variety of minor (and sometimes not so minor) errands.

pace, pacing the speed – or rhythm – of dialogue, or of editing, or of narrative exposition. David Lean, when asked to name the hardest part of the director's job, is said to have answered 'Knowing how fast the actors should talk.'

package a business term, both noun and verb, meaning (a) to put together two or more of the components – a director, a star or stars, a property – into a team that will make a production seem commercially attractive, and thus (b) the resulting commercial unit.

page a rough measurement of day-by-day progress on a film, based on how many pages of the screenplay have been satisfactorily put on film; given that the average screenplay is somewhere between 90 and 120 pages and the average running time for a feature somewhere between 90 and 120 minutes, this ought to mean that every page shot will result in one minute of the finished film. In reality, since even the most economical production will usually shoot more scenes than will eventually be used, the equation is not quite so neat. Incidentally, Gore Vidal recalls – as part of his long-playing joke against proponents of the *auteur* theory – that in the high period of the studio system executives would congratulate each other while watching by saying that the unit had got some 'good pages' done that day – not, that is, good scenes or good footage. (See 'The Top Ten Best Sellers', in *Matters of Fact and Fiction*, 1977.)

paint box an electronic image generator used to manipulate video footage.

painted matte shot a *matte shot* in which the live action image is adapted or modified by a matte on which other images – usually of buildings or scenery – have been painted.

pan in contemporary use, 'pan' has two principal meanings: (a) as a verb, to turn the camera horizontally on the axis of its mount or tripod (though it is sometimes used more carelessly to indicate any type of camera movement on an axis); and hence (b) as a noun, (i) that camera movement itself or (ii) its on-screen result – an abbreviation of *pan shot*. According to the OED, the verb also originally meant 'to follow or pass along (a person or object) with a camera' – movements, that is, which would now be described as *tracking*, *travelling* or *follow* shots – and could be used both transitively ('We'll "pan" you down the middle of the picture to the raft' – *Saturday Evening Post*, 1 November 1913) and intransitively ('The camera "pans" around the room, bringing to view the shabby furniture' – A. Buchanan, 1932). Self-conscious inverted commas around the word in the 1910s and 1920s seem to indicate that the verb had only recently been abbreviated and adapted from 'panorama' or 'panoramic', and it tends to retain the inverted commas until the late 1930s. The less truncated form *panoram* also crops up in the early literature: 'The tilting handle ... is used to panoram down into valleys ... It is also used to "pan" up the cathedral spire' (*Amateur Cinematographer's Handbook*, 1931); but note that the kind of horizontal movements described here, and in other examples of the period, would now be called a *tilt*. The noun appears in print in the early 1920s, usually to indicate the direct manipulation of the camera; the related sense of 'pan shot' follows a little more slowly, but was clearly established by 1960: 'The opening shot of *Exodus* is a huge 200-degree pan across the landscape and coastline of Cyprus' – *Listener*, 5 April 1962. Apart from 'pan shot' itself, which generally occurs in its full form into well into the 1950s – John Steinbeck and the immortal Ed Ricketts, for example, use it in their oceanographical adventure *Sea of Cortez* in 1941 – the most common terms incorporating 'pan' include: *pan and scan*, a technique used in preparing films to be shown on television, which has a narrower aspect ratio: see **letterboxing**; *pan head, pan and tilt head* a type of camera mount which allows the camera to be panned or tilted (the term became current in the late 1930s); *pan focus*, a focus setting with sufficient *depth of field* to keep a large area in sharp focus.

Pan can also be an abbreviation of *panchromatic*; a *pan glass* is a coloured filter (blue-green or brown-yellow) used by the director and/or cameraman to judge how the resulting images will look on particular stocks.

Panaglide   the brand name for *Panavision*'s equivalent of the **steadicam** – a body frame which allows for the smooth manipulation of a hand-held camera.

Panavision   the trade name of a widely used 35mm, anamorphic wide screen system; the corresponding 70mm process is called *Super Panavision* or *Panavision 70*.

pancake   (a) as in the theatre: the usual kind of opaque make-up base; the term is American in origin, and seems to be derived from the slang term 'pan', meaning 'face'.

(b) The smallest kind of *apple box*, just two inches high, and hence 'flat as pancake'; OED notes that the word 'pancake' has been applied to any thin, flat object since the 1870s.

panchromatic film, panchromatic   the term, which appears in print around the turn of the century, generally refers to a type of black and white film stock that produces shades of black, white and grey corresponding to all the colours visible to the human eye; an improvement on *orthochromatic film*, which was insensitive to hues of red. 'My darkroom lamp has three interchangeable safe-lights, ... one a dark green for panchromatics' – *Glasgow Herald*, 6 April 1921. Hence *panchromatic master positive*, a black and white master positive made from a colour negative.

Panopticon   the trade name for a short-lived form of 70mm combination camera-projector, developed by Major Woodville Latham (see also **Latham loop**), first demonstrated in 1895, but abandoned because its images tended to wobble. Latham was presumably unaware that the term 'panopticon' had previously – from 1791, when the philosopher published a book with that title – been the name for Jeremy Bentham's ideal prison, which has been brought back to a degree of public notice in recent years by the pages of M. Foucault's *Discipline and Punish*. 'Panopticon' is derived from Gk *pan*, 'all', and *optikon*, the neuter form of *optikos*, 'of, or for sight'; hence, 'all-seeing'. Bentham's prison would have been circular, with its cells exposed to the gaze of warders in a central cell. Earlier still, in the mid-18th C, 'panopticon' had been the name of a type, or several types, of optical toys; it also came to mean, by the mid-19th C, a kind of show-room for novelties and curiosities.

paper prints   an early form of film copyrighting in the United States, used until 1907 when new legislation came into force: prints, with a paper base, were deposited in the Library of Congress.

parallax   (from Fr *parallaxe*, and ultimately Gk *parallaxis*, 'change, alteration' etc; various technical senses of the word, particularly the astronomical, have been current in English since the late 16th C.) A term taken over from optics, which in filming applies to the slight but significant difference in framing between what is seen through the viewfinder and what is seen by the camera. Failure to correct for this results in *parallax error* – faulty framing; the device used for such correction is a *reflex viewfinder*.

Parallax is also the name of the British independent production company, originally founded in the early 1980s, which now produces films by Ken Loach – *Raining Stones, Ladybird, Ladybird, Land and Freedom* – Les Blair (*Bad Behaviour*) and others, generally of an overtly or implicitly radical political cast. It derives its name, as the producer Sally Hibbin explained to the author, from the partnership's ambition 'to see things from a different angle'.

parallel   from the French *paralelle*, the Latin *parallelus* and, ultimately, the Greek *paralellos*, 'side by side': in shooting: a platform constructed some distance above floor or ground level on which the camera can be mounted for high angle shots; *parallel action*, two (or more) sets of action, usually taking place at the same time but in different locations, brought together by *intercutting* – more exactly, *parallel cutting*. The classic example would be a sequence cutting between the heroine tied to the rail as the train approaches and the hero racing frantically towards her on horseback. Most textbooks agree that the technique was used as early as 1903, in Edwin S. Porter's *The Great Train Robbery*, but was refined into more or less its present form by D.W. Griffith in the following decade. *Parallel sound* usually means a type of non-synchronous use of soundtrack, in which there is none the less some clear logical or narrative connection between images and sounds: for example, a character's voice describing or commenting on an action which is being shown in flashback.

Paramount, Paramount Pictures Corporation the major American production company, which grew from a merger between W.W. Hodkinson's distribution company Paramount Pictures (est. 1914) and Famous Players-Lasky, the production company originally founded in 1912 and owned by Cecil B. De Mille, Jesse L. Lasky and Adolph Zukor, a former furrier. In 1927 the merged company became known as the Paramount Famous Lasky Corporation; in 1930, after buying the chain of cinemas belonging to the Publix Corporation, as the Paramount Publix Corporation; and in 1933, after various financial problems and considerable restructuring, as Paramount Pictures Corporation. Paramount advertised its wares with the slogan 'If it's a Paramount Picture, it's the best show in town', and the claim was not always so far from the truth, especially if the picture in question were a comedy or an historical spectacle such as De Mille's *The Ten Commandments* (1923, remade 1956). Apart from De Mille himself, the directors employed by Paramount in its early years included Lubitsch, Mamoulian, Von Sternberg and Von Stroheim, to be followed in later years by the estimable likes of Frank Capra, Preston Sturges and Billy Wilder; the players included Marlene Dietrich, Mae West, Gloria Swanson, Barabara Stanwyck, John Wayne, Bob Hope and Bing Crosby (for the 'Road' series, one of which contains a neat visual joke about the Paramount title logo, a snow-covered peak surrounded by stars), Montgomery Clift and the Marx Brothers. After 1948 (see *Paramount decision*), Paramount lost its cinema chain, and its losses from this area were exacerbated by the drift of audiences towards television. But the studio still managed to thrive, thanks to a careful balance of crowd-pleasers – such as the Jerry Lewis/Dean Martin comedies – and more distinguished fare, including several films by Alfred Hitchcock (*Rear Window, Vertigo, Psycho*); the company also developed its own wide-screen process, *VistaVision*, in response to Fox's *CinemaScope*. In the 1960s (when it was taken over by Gulf & Western) and early 1970s, the studio suffered much the same difficulties as its rivals, and despite some outstanding commercial successes, including *Love Story* and Coppola's first two *Godfather* films, the studio appeared to go into terminal decline, but bounced back triumphantly in 1978, when it broke industry records with box office returns of $290 million, thanks mostly to the appeal of *Grease* and *Saturday Night Fever* to juvenile audiences. Paramount continued to be a major player throughout the 1980s and early 1990s, producing Spielberg's 'Indiana Jones' series (the first of which includes another visual pun on the Paramount logo), the *Star Trek* movies, *Beverly Hills Cop* and its sequels, *Top Gun*, *Fatal Attraction* and so on. In 1989 the company's name was changed to Paramount Communications; in 1994, after many months of well-publicised negotiations and tussles, the media company Viacom took control of Paramount.

Paramount decision sometimes referred to as the *Paramount decrees*, a momentous legal judgment of the United States' Supreme Court in

1948, which, after a two or three years of fruitless appeals by the major studios – Paramount, MGM, RKO, Twentieth-Century Fox, Warner Brothers – put an end to their almost complete monopoly over the distribution and exhibition of their films, which were held to be in violation of anti-trust laws. (See *vertical control*.) The long-term consequences of allowing American cinemas to show any films they wished were various: the market became open for independent producers and the distributors of foreign movies; the *B-movie*, which had previously helped fill out programmes, dwindled away; and the *studio system*, assailed by rising production costs and the growth of television, perished.

parent roll   the large, wide roles of film stock out of which different gauges are sliced by the manufacturer.

PAR light   a type of spotlight, the beam of which is adjusted by means of a parabolic reflector. It was developed by one Clarence Birdseye, and is thus sometimes referred to as a 'birdseye'.

parody   as in literature and the other arts: a film which mockingly imitates the main characteristics of another, more serious film or film genre. The word appears to come into English in the late 16th C, either from Fr *parodie* or L *parodia*; both of these descend from Gk *paroidia*, 'a burlesque poem or song'. Among the most succesful movie parodies of the past couple of decades: Carl Reiner's *Dead Men Don't Wear Plaid*, a parody of *film noir*; Rob Reiner's *This is Spinal Tap*, a parody of the *rockumentary*; *Porklips Now*, a bargain-basement spoof of *Apocalypse Now*; and the major part of the filmography of Mel Brooks, including *Blazing Saddles* (the Western), *Young Frankenstein* (the Universal horror movies of the 1930s), *High Anxiety* (Hitchcock's films), *Spaceballs* (the *Star Wars* trilogy) . . .

Pasadena, They took a   recent Hollywood screenwriter's slang, meaning 'They turned it down': Pasadena, in this slur, being considered the most remote, suburban and *passé* of all Los Angeles's satelite towns.

pass, passing shot   (a) a shot which passes (or appears to pass) over something rather than following it; achieved either by keeping the camera fixed and having the performer move across the field of vision, or by moving the camera to create the same effect.

(b) In industry slang, 'pass' also means to turn down or reject a proposed script or other project.

Pathé Frères   the well-known early French production and distribution company, founded in 1896 by the industrialist Charles Pathé (1863–1957) and his brothers Emile, Jacques and Théophile. Charles had already developed his own form of *kinéstoscope*, but the device on which the early fortunes of his company were based was a version of the Lumière *cinématographe*, which showed short films largely imitative of the Lumières' productions. In 1902, the *frères* built their own studios in Vincennes and began to turn out films at a prodigious rate; the best known of these today are the 400-odd comedies made by Max Linder.

By 1908 they were the world's largest production company, with branches as far afield as Calcutta and Singapore, and even in the United States their films far outsold all the domestic productions put together. For a few years they appeared unstoppable, expanding into the manufacture of film stocks (so breaking Eastman's monopoly) and equipment, building laboratories and cinemas, introducing the weekly newsreel *Pathé Journal* to the world and the convention of the adventure serial to the United States, and devising a colour process. But the First World War put a stop to this rise. French production was disrupted or shut down, and when Charles returned from the United States in 1917, he found chaos: escalating production costs, a domestic market flooded with American films and a sharp decline in overseas orders. He began to break up and sell off the company by stages, and gave up his last interest to Bernard Natan in 1929. The surviving company, Pathé-Natan, eventually collapsed in 1939, and was partially revived in 1944 as the Société Nouvelle Pathé-Cinéma, which concentrated on distribution.

Patsy Awards the zoological counterpart to the Oscars, awarded to an animal performer each year by the American Humane Association. The name is an acronym for Picture Animal Top Star of the Year; the Patsy was first awarded in 1951, to Francis the mule.

pay or play Hollywood industry jargon: a type of contract that guarantees that a performer, director or writer will be paid by a studio whether or not his or her services are called on or the production is completed (or indeed, begun).

peanut fixture a very small *luminaire*, fixed to objects so as to make them seem to radiate light.

penny gaff the British equivalent of the American *nickelodeon*, so called because the price of admission was a penny.

perambulator the wheeled platform used to move around the microphone *boom* and its operator.

perforations (or **sprocket holes**) the small, evenly spaced holes at the edges of film stock; miniature teeth or claws engage with these holes and draw the film forward a frame at a time through the camera or projector. See *intermittent movement*.

performer any actor with a speaking part in a production; also any performing singer, dancer, acrobat, ventriloquist, conjurer, juggler etc. The term is not usually, however, applied to extras or walk-ons. *Perform*, *performance* and *performer*, with their various meanings all come into English from OF *performer*, or *parfourmer*; 'perform' in the 14th C, 'performance' and 'performer' in the 15th C; show-biz senses seem to be well established by the early 17th C: 'In Theatrical Speaking, if the Performer is not exactly proper and graceful, he is utterly ridiculous' – Steele, *The Spectator*, 1711.

period film any film set largely or wholly in a period significantly earlier than the present, but particularly to *costume dramas* that take place at any time from the dark ages to the early twentieth century. So, for example, *The Age of Innocence* is the only film directed by Martin Scorsese that would usually be described as a 'period drama', even though several of his other films are set in the recent or remote past – *Raging Bull* (the 1950s, mostly), *Boxcar Bertha* (the Depression), *GoodFellas* (the 1960s and 1970s, mostly) and *The Last Temptation of Christ* (the first century AD). The British-based production company Merchant-Ivory has made such a speciality of period dramas, drawing particularly on the novels of E.M. Forster, that one cruel soul (the director Alan Parker) notoriously described them as 'the Laura Ashley school' of film-making.

persistence of vision   the physical phenomenon which makes cinema possible. Since the human retina has the property of retaining any images that meet it for as much as a third of a second after they disappear, a succession of static images presented to the eye with sufficient rapidity will appear to move. The man who formally identified the phenomenon in 1824 was Peter Mark Roget, M.D., who must therefore be credited with inventing no fewer than three useful devices – the *Thesaurus*, the slide rule and the cinema. (For a slightly fuller account, see the Introduction to this book.) A somewhat less theoretical grasp of such persistence would presumably have been available to the first cave dweller who waved a burning stick around in the dark and noticed that it left a glowing line. The fuller illusion of continuous movement created by films is sometimes known as the *Phi effect* or *Phi phenomenon*, though strictly speaking this latter term refers to a psychological effect, occuring in the brain, rather than a physical phenomenon, occuring in the eye. A rate of 16 frames per second is sufficient to create the appearance of normal motion, and this continues to be the standard speed for silent films. For sound films, the standard rate of frames per second is 24; hence Jean-Luc Godard's dubious maxim, 'the cinema is truth 24 times a second.'

PG   an abbreviation for *Parental Guidance* – the phrase used for cinema certification in both the UK and the USA to indicate that a given film, though broadly suitable for younger viewers, may contain one or two scenes that an anxious parent might not wish young children to see.

phasing   a type of audio distortion, sounding something like a cross between an echo and a rushing wind, created by having two or more sources giving out the same sound at fractionally different intervals. In the 1960s, quite a few pop and soul records (including 'Itchycoo Park' by the Small Faces) used the effect deliberately for its supposedly 'psychedelic' effect.

Phenakistiscope (also **Phantascope, Fantascope** or, simply, **Magic Disc**)   an optical novelty devised or adapted in 1832 by the Belgian physicist Joseph Antoine Ferdinand Plateau (1801–83), made up of a disc with thin notches cut into its circumference and small figures drawn across its surface. (Such experiments were in the air, thanks to Roget's recent discovery of *persistence of vision*: an Austrian physicist came up with a similar device at about the same time, see *stroboscope*.) By spinning the disc and peering through the notches at its reflection in a mirror, the viewer would see the figures appear to spring into motion. Its name was coined from the Gk *phenakistes*, an imposter or cheat. 'The phenakistoscope ... was, we believe, originally invented by Dr Roget, and improved by M.Plateau, at Brussels, and Mr. Faraday' – *Encyclopaedia Brittanica*, 1838, which may be wrong about Roget (himself a notable contributor to the *E.B*). The toy was put to more serious use later in the century when Eadweard Muybridge used a variant of it as a component for his early photographic projector, the *Zoopraxiscope*.

phi phenomenon   see *persistence of vision.*

phone in   industry slang: for an actor to give a passionless, routine, non-committal or otherwise perfunctory performance, as though mentally at a great distance from the set.

phone monkey   abusive slang for the type of Hollywood studio executive who spends an inordinate amount of time being sycophantic, manipulative, self-advancing and/or ruthless on the telephone. The coining of this insult has been attributed to the actor Alec Baldwin, who became particularly annoyed with one such executive when making *The Marrying Man.*

Phonofilm   (from Gk *phone*, 'voice, sound', plus *film*) the trade name of a prototype optical sound system, invented by Lee De Forest in 1922, and used in cinemas for a thousand or so short films until 1927.

Phonoplay, see *photoplay*

photo   the near-universal abbreviation for *photograph* or *photography*, a word devised in the early 19th C from Gk *phos, photo-* 'light', and -*graphos,* 'written, delineated': 'Pure water will fix the photograph by washing out the nitrate of silver' – Sir John Herschel, *Proceedings of the Royal Society,* March 1839. Hence the various associated terms in the cinema, including: *photo double,* a double with a strong enough resemblance to the star to be a good substitute in all but close-up or speaking scenes; *photoflood,* a powerful tungsten bulb; *photogenic,* attractive to the camera – a term which originated in the United States in the 1920s. 'An actor may be "photogenic" and have personality and appearance, but that is not enough' – Sam Goldwyn, *Saturday Review,* February 1931. The word had quite a different sense in the mid-19th C, when it meant either 'produced by light' or was synonymous with 'photographic'. Fox Talbot, for example, referred to his earliest photographs as 'photogenic drawings'. *Photokinesis,* any use of still photographs to make part or all of a film, usually in the form of a rapid montage, camera movements over stills, dissolves and the like; see *kinestasis; photo matte,* a still photograph combined with live action in a *matte* shot; *photometer,* an instrument similar to a light meter, used for measuring brightness. *Photoplay,* an early synonym for 'motion picture' or 'movie': 'We go to the photoplay to enjoy right and splendid picture-motions, to feel a certain thrill when the pieces of kaleidoscope glass slide into new places. Instead of moving on straight lines, as they do in the mechanical toy, they progress in strange curves that are part of the very shapes into which they fall' – Vachel Lindsay, *The Art of the Moving Picture*. Lindsay was one of the theorists who believed that the silent cinema of his day represented the film medium in its perfect form, and that the then-hypothetical 'talking moving picture' would inevitably caricature or dilute the art: 'If the talking moving picture becomes a reliable mirror of the human voice and frame, it will be the basis of such a separate art that none of the photoplay precedents will apply. It will be the *phonoplay*, not the photoplay.'

pick-up   (a) as a noun: additional scenes that may have to be filmed after principal photography has been completed, to help the editor overcome problems in establishing continuity, or generally to cover up problems that were not spotted during the shoot; (b) (as a verb) to retake a small part of a shot rather than repeat the whole take from the top (this is also known as a *print and pick up*), or (c) the action of a studio in accepting a project that has been initiated elsewhere; see *negative pick-up*.

picture   either (a) a film or (b) the filmed image, especially as distinguished from the sound. OED records both senses from early 20th C onwards: 'The pictures one sees nowadays are . . . in much better taste than those of a few years ago' – *Home Chat*, 20 September 1913; 'In order to get a picture of the sacking of a village, an actual village was some time ago purchased and fired' – ibid., 25 May 1912. The plural *pictures*, as a familiar term for the cinema in general ('Honey, you should be in pictures!') or – though this is less common today – as the similarly colloquial term for a local cinema ('Let's go to the pictures!') starts to appear from 1915 onwards, though nowadays the latter sense in particular often sounds a little faux-naif, as in the slightly too chummy title *A Night at the Pictures* – a short history of the British cinema by Gilbert Adair and Nick Roddick (1984; this volume is actually more distinguished than the browser might assume). *Picture car*, a car or other motor vehicle which will be used on camera, rather than being part of the production's transport pool; *picture negative*, see *negative*; *picture print*, a positive print without matching sound track, also known as a *silent print*.

pilot pins   the teeth inside the gate that slot into the sprocket holes of film as it passes through a camera, printer or projector; hence *pilot pin registration*, the system or technology of drawing a film accurately through a camera, printer or projector, frame by frame, using pilot pins and sprocket holes.

pincushion distortion   a lens aberration which makes images appear to buckle inwards under pressure, like the surface of a pincushion.

Pinewood   the well-known British film studio, opened in 1936 by J. Arthur Rank's Pinewood Studios Ltd. The studio's early years were disrupted by war, and from 1941 to 1945 it became a production base for the *Crown Film Unit* and the Royal Air Force. Among Pinewood's most notable productions of the immediate post-war years were Powell & Pressburger's *Black Narcissus* (1947) and *The Red Shoes* (1948), David Lean's *Great Expectations* (1946) and *Oliver Twist* (1948). From 1960 onwards, Pinewood began to rent its facilities and staff to independent producers: the James Bond films were made at the studios, for example.

pitch   (a) the distance between individual sprocket holes on a strip of film; (b) as in salesmanship: to suggest or 'sell' a possible project to a producer, director or some other influential figure.

pix   *Variety* slang for 'pictures' – films, or the film industry in general.

pixel   compounded of *pix* (pictures, picture) and *-el* (i.e. element), *pixel* has been in use since the late 1960s, to denote the tiny dots that compose a television or video image; the greater the density of pixels, the sharper the definition.

Pixelvision   a term coined by the director Michael Almereyda for the unconventional, indeed unique process he used in making his film *Another Girl Another Planet*: he shot the entire production on the Fisher-Price PXL 2000, a child's toy camera first manufactured in 1987, discontinued three years later, and retailing in more or less adequately repaired form at $45 dollars. For a fuller and more rapturous account of the properties of the pixelvision image, see Almereyda's article 'My Stunning Future: The Luxuries of Pixelvision' in *Projections 3*, ed. Boorman and Donohue (Faber, 1994).

pixilation (sometimes, rarely, **pixylation**)   a special visual effect, created either by stop-motion photography or by selective editing of frames from a normally shot sequence. In both cases, the result is jerky, accelerated motion, which tends to look either comical and cartoon-like or eerily disorienting, according to context. 'We call it pixilation, Dracula's fast-moving POV. It's something like animation, and is produced by a device inside the camera that takes individual images. The trick is to click off frames erratically – single frames and then a burst of several per second – giving the effect of an animal-like sensory perception, something primordial' – Roman Coppola, Visual Effects supervisor on *Bram Stoker's Dracula*, 1992. OED notes the earliest use, as *pixlation*, in *Punch* for 1947, where it refers to a special lighting effect used in the theatre to make the performers seem like cartoon characters; the earliest cinematic use is from 1953: 'McLaren feels this kind of live-actor animation has considerable creative potentiality, though he refers to its slightingly as the 'pixilation' technique.' The word is compounded of *pixilated* – a US dialect word, known since the mid-19th C, meaning 'whimsical, insane, fey' – and *animation*. (Pixilated, in turn, comes from *pixie* and *-lated*, as in 'elated'; *pixie* – also *pixy*, *pisky* etc. – meaning a small supernatural creature indigenous to the Western counties of England, is recorded in print since the early 17th C; its origins are unknown.) See also *kinestasis*.

plan-sequence   a term coined by French film critics and sometimes borrowed by their Anglophone colleages, since there is no exact English equivalent. It refers to the type of extended shot, such as those in the films of Jean Renoir, in which the narrative is advanced by movement within the frame rather than by the more conventional method of cutting from action to action; thus, it may be argued, such shots allow or encourage the viewer to work out the significance of the shot independently, rather than have it served up whole by the editing.

play as a verb: (a) for an actor: to act a role in a film (the verb enters English in the 14th C); (b) for a screenplay, action, scene or film to seem convincing, exciting, appealing and so on, or to show commercial potential: hence, for example, such an exchange as 'This flagellation scene really plays!' (meaning: it is vivid, highly charged, persuasive . . .) 'Maybe, but will it play in Peoria?' (meaning: will it prove acceptable to unsophisticated or conservative viewers, such as those who live in the less stimulating towns of the American heartland?).

player either (a) an actor (the synonym is known in English since the early 15th C), or (b) in relatively recent slang: an important and influential figure in the Hollywood heirarchy. Hence the title of Michael Tolkin's satirical novel *The Player*, and the subsequent film version, directed by Robert Altman from Tolkin's own screenplay. Altman's career had been in the doldrums for some years, and the happiest irony of *The Player* (1992) is that it helped re-establish him as a 'player' once more, though the more recent flop of *Pret à Porter* may have put him beyond the pale once again.

playback either (a) the process of listening to a recording as soon as it has been completed, or (b) a production technique used in filming *musicals* and rock *videos*, in which a pre-recorded track of a song or other music is played at high volume to actors, musicians, dancers and so on so that they can dance or lip-sync to it as they are being filmed.

plugumentary derisive slang term (from the late 1980s) for a film that is essentially an extended advertisement or trailer, but which tries to pass itself off as an objective documentary. Though the term can be applied to any boosting film, the commonest form of plugumentary is the uncritical 'making-of' video, which interviews stars, director and others about the film they are in the process of making: a particularly inflated example was produced for Mel Gibson's *Braveheart* (1995). See also *press kit.*

poetic cinema see *New American Cinema.*

poetic realism a critical term sometimes applied to a loose grouping of French films made between about 1934 and 1940, which, as the term suggests, managed to combine realistic subject matter with a poetic style: a roll-call of such films would usually include Renoir's sublime *La Regle du Jeu* (1939) and *La Grande Illusion* (1937), as well as the almost equally celebrated collaborations between Marcel Carné and the poet-screenwriter Jacques Prévert (*Quai des Brumes*, 1938, *Le Jour se Leve*, 1939, *Les Visiteurs du Soir*, 1942 and *Les Enfants du Paradis*, 1945). The term seems to have been coined by the critic and historian Georges Sadoul.

points   the percentage of the net or gross profits which a director, writer or star is contractually entitled to achieve from a given film.

point of view, point-of-view shot, (POV)   usually (a) a shot taken as though it were being seen through the eyes of a specific character. But the term is also used – particularly in film criticism and screenwriting classes – much as it is in literary discussions, to indicate the way in which the film's narrative is arranged; that is, which character's perspective on the action is shared by the audience, either from scene to scene or throughout the film. Point of view is, then, one of the elements that may help determine the *genre* of a film: the story of a murder seen from the point of view of the investigating policeman will usually be a *detective* or *mystery* film, whereas the same story as seen by the murderer might well be a more serious *psychological thriller*, and so on.

polarize   (from the modern L *polaris*, 'polar'; a verb known in English from 1811 onwards) to treat light – usually by passing it through a special lens – in such a way that it ceases to cause glare and unwanted reflections; hence *polaroid filter* (or *pola screen*), a filter that cuts down glare by polarizing light.

Polaroid   the brand name of the well-known stills camera which produces small, fully-developed photographs within seconds of shooting, and is used on sets as a kind of visual notebook by the *continuity* person.

polecat   a telescopic bar ('pole') that can be wedged between two surfaces to act as a support for lamps.

polish   as a verb: to rewrite a screenplay, particularly on the eve of production. As a noun: in Hollywood, the standard contractual term for a relatively minor revision of screenplay, less substantial than a *revision*.

polyester   an abbreviation for polyethelene terephthalate, a substance widely used in the manufacture of film *bases*, under a variety of trade names: *Cronar* (du Pont), *Estar* (Kodak).

Polyvison   a triple-screen projection system developed by Abel Gance (in collaboration with André Debrie) for the climax of his *Napoléon* (1927); see *multi-screen*.

popping   the irritating noise made when an actor makes 'p' sounds too loudly, or too close to the microphone; a *pop filter* is used to limit the effect.

pornography   from Gk *porne*, 'harlot', and *graphos*, 'writing, writer'; the generic term may have been derived from the signs displayed outside brothels, or – as Webster suggests – from the erotic murals found in rooms dedicated to Bacchanalian orgies, such as those uncovered in Pompeii. (The word enters English in the mid-19th C.) A film described as pornographic will generally be either (a) a *blue movie*, *stag movie*, *skin flick* etc: that is, a low-budget sex film made outside the mainstream industry, or (b) a mainstream erotic film of which the speaker or writer disapproves.

positive   either (a) film that has been exposed, developed and processed so that the resulting images are suitable for editing or projection, or (b) a projection print made from a master or some other negative. 'In order to avoid circumlocution, the author employs the terms *positive* and *negative* to express respectively pictures in which the lights and shades are the same as in nature ... and in which they are opposite; that is, light representing shade, and shade light' – Sir John Herschel, *Proceedings of the Royal Society*, 1840. The positive/negative opposition had been used in various fields (algebra, logic) since the early 17th C; 'positive' comes from ME *positif*, and the 13th C Fr *positif*, 'characterised by laying down or being laid down'. *Positive drive*, the mechanism which draws positive film through a projector; *positive perforation*, the rectangular perforations with curved edges used found in positive 35mm film, known as *KS* (Kodak Standard) *perforations*, as distinct from the less robust *BH* (Bell and Howell) *perforations* found on negative film; *positive splice*, the glued overlap between two pieces of positive film.

post-production   the period and the processes which come between the completion of principal photography and the completed film: that is to say, *editing*, *looping*, *mixing* and so on. *Post-synchronization*, *postsync*: adding dialogue and other sounds to scenes that were shot silently, or (much more usually in the USA and UK), re-recording unsatisfactory dialogue and matching the new performances to the action on screen. See *dubbing* and *looping*.

POV   a point-of-view shot; the abbreviation in a script indicating that a given scene is to be shot from a particular character's *point of view*.

powder man   slang name for the crew member in charge of explosives.

power zoom   either (a) a *zoom* executed electronically rather than manually, or (b) the electrical mechanism that makes such zooms possible.

practical   a working prop, such as a gun that actually fires bullets, as opposed to a mere imitation or dummy. A *practical set* is a real-life location rather than a specially constructed set.

Praxinoscope   a development of the *Zoetrope*, invented by Emile Raynaud in 1877, who took the name from the Gk *praxis*, 'action'. Like the Zoetrope, it used a rotating strip of drawn pictures; but Raynaud adapted it into a kind of *magic lantern*, and projected the resulting animation onto a screen. From 1892 to 1900, he put the results on show at his Théâtre Optique in Paris, but was eventually driven out of business by the early products of the cinema.

predub, premix   the preliminary stage of making a composite sound track, during which a number of different sound-tracks are combined.

première   in the USA, sometimes spelled *premier*, and pronounced pre-MEER, as a British observer noted in the early 1940s: 'The movie première – pronounced pre-meer, with heavy emphasis on the second syllable – is a national phenomenon' – *Commonweal*, 10 January 1941; indeed, there is also a rare form spelled *premeer*. Either (a) the first showing of a completed film to any public audience, usually at one of the major festivals, or (b) the opening night of a film, attended by an invited audience which will usually include its cast and principal makers as well as members of royalty, models, rock musicians and the like, or (c) more loosely, the first run of a film, usually at a single cinema – in the UK, usually one of the large cinemas in London's West End. It is taken over by the film industry directly from theatrical circles, who borrowed the term from French in the 19th C: it was originally an abbreviation of *la première* [i.e., *première nuit*] *d'une pièce*; *Premiere* is also the title of a popular American magazine about movies, and its modified British counterpart.

preproduction, pre-production   the whole range of preparations that are made for shooting once a production has been given the *green light*, including drawing up budgets, contracting actors and crew, building sets and so on. Films are only said to be *in pre-production* when this process is under way; it does not apply to more speculative activities.

prequel   by analogy with 'sequel': a film made and released in the wake of a successful feature, and generally using some or all of its main characters, telling a story that takes place at some earlier period. For example, *Indiana Jones and the Temple of Doom* takes place a few years before the main action of the first Indiana Jones adventure, *Raiders of the Lost Ark*.

presence   the general sound quality of a given location; its *atmosphere* or *ambient* noise.

presentative blocking   placing a character head-on to the camera so that he or she appears to be addressing the audience directly. Sometimes this blocking provides the content for a dramatic point-of-view shot; sometimes, particularly in comedies, it suggests a character confiding in the viewer – *Alfie* is a famous example, but the device is repeated in *Ferris Bueller's Day Off*, *Wayne's World*, and, at the other end of the artistic spectrum, Fellini's *And the Ship Sails On*, in which an ageing journalist (Freddie Jones) acts as on-screen narrator. It may also be used to indicate a particular form of speech or writing. In Scorsese's *The Age of Innocence*, for example, letters written to the hero by his fiancée (Winona Ryder) and his lover (Michelle Pfeiffer) are represented by having the actresses speak them to the camera.

press kit   the package of stills, production notes, advance reviews and related material sent out to journalists and critics when the film is released; an *electronic press kit* or *EPK* is a short video, featuring interviews with the director and leading actors as well as selected clips and footage of the film being shot; this may either sent both to the press or shown on television. See *plugumentary*.

pressure plate   a device used to hold the film steady and in correct relationship with the lens in a camera, projector or printer.

preview   (a) a screening held in advance of a film's release, either to the press and other members of the film industry, or to see how representative or random groups of the general public react. (See *sneak preview*.) In the USA, it is fairly common for films to be re-edited to take such reactions into account. (b) Another term for a cinema *trailer*.

prime lens   a lens with a set, rather than adjustable focal length.

principal focus   the point at which light comes into focus after being refracted through a lens; *principal photography*, the main period of shooting on a production, including all the dialogue scenes, but not, usually, the material shot by the *second unit* or any *pick-ups*; *principal players*, the main actors.

print   (noun) a positive version of a completed film that is ready for projection, struck from either an *original* or a *dupe negative*; (verb), to create a positive from a negative, or vice versa. Hence *printing*, etc. *Print it!* is the director's order that the lab should make a print of a particular take; *print-up*, to blow up film from a smaller to a larger gauge; *printer*, the machine used to make prints from positives or negatives; *print stock*, the film stock used to manufacture prints.

prism lens   a lens used to split a single image into a number of smaller duplicate images.

Prizma, Prizmacolor   an early, two-colour *additive* process, first used in 1918; the most notable film shot in Prizmacolor was James Stuart Blackton's *The Glorious Adventure* (1921).

procedural   a type of drama which owes some of its entertainment value to showing, with a reasonable degree or realism and accuracy, how a particular institution – a hospital, a court, a police department – functions, as well as to the dramas which take place within that milieu: Humphrey Jennings's *Fires Were Started*, for example, which shows the workings of London's fire services during the Blitz, or Ron Howard's *The Paper*, about the struggles of journalists and editors to produce a daily tabloid. Though fairly self-explanatory, the term appears to be derived from 'police procedural', a modern sub-genre of the detective story which runs, roughly speaking, from Laurence Treat's *V is for Victim* (1945) to Ed McBain's 87th precinct series, and follows criminal investigations from the point of view of professional policemen.

process, processing   the developing and printing of film; in other words, the chemical and mechanical procedures employed to bring out the latent images in exposed film.

process body   the mock-up of a car or some other vehicle, parts of which can be removed to allow the camera to film interiors from different angles, generally used for sequences of simulated movement – that is to say, of *process shots*. In a process shot, film of a moving background is projected on to a transparent screen while the actors sit inside a process body. (See *rear projection*.) Hence various more or less self-explanatory associated words: *process camera*; *process photography*; *process projection*; *process screen*, etc.

producer   a complex, indeed vexed title that can be defined in a wide variety of ways, from the relatively humble to the preposterously exalted. The broadest and most useful description of a producer's role nowadays would probably be that he or she is the person responsible, either wholly or in collaboration with other producers, for all the financial and logistical aspects of making a film – these can include raising funds, casting, and controlling day-by-day expenditure in the course of a shoot (including sacking the director) – and for its more general creative aspects. Unless assigned to a particular project by a studio or company, the producer will usually be the person who comes up with the idea for a film, and puts together the *package* of stars and director; he or she will almost certainly be the person who then oversees every aspect of its making, up to and including its distribution. Note, however, that there are different grades and kinds of producer, from *line producer* (the most hands-on kind) to *executive producer*, which may either mean the person within a large company to whom other producers report, or the person in charge of the budget, or simply be a vanity title. Popular usage persists in treating the terms 'producer' and 'director' as synonymous, and though strictly speaking this is wrong, the confusion is understandable, since the earliest film directors often acted as their own producers, and even today directors will sometimes take a production role, generally to secure their status. Note, too, that television terminology has muddied the definitions still further. Though BBC drama producers do a job similar to their counterparts in the film industry, some BBC documentary productions (including a couple made by the present author), give the credit 'producer' to the person who would in any other circumstance be credited as director.

In the film industry, however, the beginnings of a clear division of labour between directors and producers can be found in the century's late teens to early twenties, and are sometimes ascribed to the huge losses incurred by *Intolerance* (1916), which seemed to demonstrate that artists could not be trusted to look after budgets; the development of studios along standard industrial lines made the division still more rigid. 'Producer', ultimately derived from L *producere*, 'to lead or bring forth', seems to have been adopted by film-makers directly from the theatre, where it had been in use since the late 19th C to mean (usually) manager or what we would nowadays call, following the American example, director. The first cinematic uses cited by OED are from 1911 ('The producer is in charge of the studio') and 1912 ('There is every indication that the British producers are making up headway'). Another reason for the frequent confusion between director and producer in the public is that the most famous producers of the studio days – Samuel Goldwyn, Louis B. Mayer, David O. Selznick and Irving Thalberg (the original of F. Scott Fitzgerald's Monroe Stahr) – were not only better known to the public than many directors, but helped establish a popular mythology of the producer's role, as a kind of latterday Renaissance prince. Though the rise of the *auteur* theory removed some of the lustre from these names, critics hostile to such pantheons have argued that it makes a lot more sense to look for similarities of style, thematic continuity and narrative technique in the films of a given producer than those of the directors he employs; in other words, that the true *auteurs* of the studio system were the producers. Names cited in support of this view are those of Val Lewton, whose wonderfully atmospheric low-budget horror films for RKO obviously exhibit similar virtues no matter who was directing, and Arthur Freed, who was responsible for MGM's musicals in the 1940s and 1950s. Another way in which today's Hollywood producers have regained some of their former power is that they now tend not to be salaried employees but work as more or less independent partners who offer projects to potential backers in return for a percentage of the eventual profits. Despite the best efforts of humble lexicographers, the popcorn-eating public will, one suspects, continue to be vague about precise job demarcations between director and producer for many years to come.

production   either (a) a particular film, or (b) the period of weeks or months during which a film is made or (c) all the activities involved in making a film. The word, ultimately derived from L *producere* by way of *productionem*, 'a lengthening', first appears in English at the end of the 15th C ('God is the unyuersal commaundour of all our production': Caxton, *Cato*, 1483), meaning 'the action of bringing forth, making or causing'. By the mid-17th C, one of its major senses denotes any product of human activity or effort, but especially literary or artistic works: 'We lay a partiall estimate upon our own productions' – Hobbes, 1651. According to OED, the word acquires its common theatrical senses in the late 19th C, when it comes to mean (a) the process of mounting a play, and (b) the play itself. The cinema adopted the word some time in the early 20th C, presumably well before the date of first example given (1932), as did radio and television in their turn.

There are many associated terms, of which the most important include: *production assistant* (*PA*); a menial but valuable member of the crew, who carries out minor tasks for the director, producer or production manager; *production board* (or *production strip board*), a kind of chart or schedule used by the production manager and others to work out the most efficent and economical sequence in which to shoot a film; strips are marked up with details of interior and exterior scenes, day shoots and night shoots and so on, and then fixed to a large board representing the number of days' shooting permitted by the budget; *production buyer*, person in charge of buying props, materials and the like; *production company*, the company responsible for seeing a particular project through to completion, sometimes formed for the purpose of making just one film (for example, Grain of Sand Productions, founded by the director Paul Schrader to make his film *Light Sleeper*), more often a more durable association; *production designer*, the person who co-ordinates costumes, sets, make-up and the like and who, in collaboration with the director and cinematographer, creates the overall 'look' of a film; this is a title sometimes given to the *Art Director*; *production editor*, the editor who assembles *rushes* or *dailies* as a film is being shot; *production house*, a company which provides various technical facilities for the film industry;

production manager (or *unit production manager*), the person responsible for the day-by-day technical and financial aspects of a production, and who usually reports directly to the *producer*; *production number*, in a *musical*: one of the set pieces of singing and dancing, particularly those which take place on a suitably grand scale, involving many performers and lavish sets; *production report* (also known as *production notes*), a list drawn up at the end of a day's (or night's) shooting which gives details of which scenes were shot, which members of cast and crew were employed, how much footage was exposed and so on. On a large production, this will be filled out by an Assistant Director, approved by the Production manager and sent to the director, producer and anyone else involved in monitoring costs; *production schedule*, a break-down of the requirements for each day's shooting, often drawn up by the production manager; *production script*, the version of the script that is prepared, and sometimes published, once the film has been completely shot and edited; *production still*, a photograph taken on set or location during filming, and, usually, issued to the press for publicity; *production unit*, all the technical staff involved in a shoot – the director and all the crew members, but not the cast; *production values*, the visual (or, less obviously, sound) elements which make a film appear either lavish or impoverished: the quality and/or dimensions of its cast, sets, special effects and so on. These are generally spoken of as either *high* (when the film looks expensive) or *low* (when it looks cheap) *production values*.

Production Code   a system of voluntary censorship operated by the Hollywood studios from the early 1930s to the late 1960s, more formally known as the *Motion Picture Production Code*, informally known as the *Hays Code*.

programmer   industry jargon: a low-budget film of limited commercial potential; see *straight to video*.

progressive angles   a short and usually quite rapid sequence of shots taken from sharper and sharper angles; *progressive shots*, similarly: a short and usually quite rapid sequence of shots which close in on the subject stage by stage – from a *master*, say, to a *medium*, a *close-up* and an *extreme close-up*.

project, projection   (a) for an actor, to project is to speak in a forceful manner so as to be audible at a much greater distance than usual; (b) as a movie business term, *projections* are estimates of a film's likely performace in the market-place; (c) in cinemas, projection is the process of casting moving images onto a screen by means of a *projector*; this device passes film between a light source and a lens, generally at the rate of 24 frames per second; the projector is housed in a *projection booth*, the small room at the back of a cinema or screening theatre; the person who operates the projection equipment is called a *projectionist*. OED notes a pre-cinematic use of the verb 'project' (derived from the Latin participal stem *project-*, from *proicere*, 'to throw forth', by way of OF *purjeter* and later forms) and its various forms in the mid-19th C: 'The impresssive character of the image projected [by a magic lantern] being often stereoscopic in aspect' (1865). Fully cinematic senses appear hard on the heels of the Lumières' first screenings, and there is an application to the British Patents Office in 1896 in which the hopeful inventor of an 'improved apparatus for producing representations of moving scenes' uses the word as we continue to use it. By the second decade of the 20th C, 'project' and its associated terms were firmly established: 'The film to be projected is carried upon a spool mounted on an arm or bracket above the mechanism' – F.A. Talbot, *Moving Pictures*, 1912. (A reasonably accurate technical definition of 'projector' is recorded in 1884: 'A camera with electric, magnesium, or oxy-hydrogen light, for throwing an image upon a screen.')

Associated terms include: *projection leader*, the **leader** used in projection reels, marked with a count-down of numbers to the first true image; *projection lens*, any of the lenses designed to be used in projectors; *projection speed*, the rate at which film must be run through a projector to create a satisfactory image: 24 frames per second in modern sound films, about 16 frames per second in the days of silent cinema; *projection sync*, the slight space between the sound-track and the pictures to which it corresponds: in 35mm film, the sound track sits 21 frames in *advance* of the picture.

promo, promotional film   any (usually short) film made to boost or publicise a product, cause or person, whether in the form of a *plugumentary* or a rock *video*.

prop, props   (less commonly in its fuller form, *property*, hardly ever in its fullest, theatrical form *stage property*) generally: any movable object that appears on screen, but particularly those which are used by actors (guns, glasses, gadgets) rather than those which form part of the decor or set dressing (chairs, curtains). The term comes from ME *proprete*, a modification of OF *propriete* (12C), itself from L *proprietatem*, the noun from *proprius*, 'own, proper'. The theatrical sense is found as early as *c*.1425, and Shakespeare seems to have found it useful in his line of work: 'I will draw a bill of properties, such as our play wants' – *A Midsummer Night's Dream*, 1590. Hence *prop* or *property department*, *prop handler*, *prop maker* (the member of the construction department who makes any special props), *prop man* or *prop master* (the person responsible for the care and placing of props), *prop sheet* (the list of props needed for that day's shooting, or for the whole production), and so on.

propaganda   a term originally derived from the modern Latin title *Congregatio de propaganda fide*, 'congregation for propagating the faith' – a committee overseeing foreign missions founded by Pope Gregory XV in 1622. By the mid-19th C, the term as taken over into English had come to designate, often pejoratively, any scheme or association dedicated to spreading a given doctrine or practice; but the more modern senses of the word, both as noun and adjective, also came into use at around the same time, and were firmly established by the end of the century: 'We would rather see our money spent in propaganda work than in paying election expenses' (*Westminster Gazette*, 1898). Thus, as in print and other more traditional media, *propaganda* films are those calculated primarily to advance a particular national or political ideology or cause (especially in time of war), rather than those which are a more or less unwitting expression of the values of the persons and institutions which make them. The power of the cinema as a propaganda tool – particularly among the illiterate urban proletariat and peasantry – was quickly recognised by politicians and rulers of all stripes. Lenin, for example, declared that 'For us, the cinema is the most important of the arts'; and the enduring power of many of the films produced in the early Soviet period by the likes of Dovzhenko, Eisenstein, Pudovkin and Vertov (see *kino-pravda*), suggest that there is no necessary contradiction between propagandist intentions and artistic accomplishment. This thought tends to create rather more queasiness and soul-searching in the case of Leni Riefenstahl (b.1902), whose *Triumph des Willens* (a grandiose record of the 1934 National Socialist party rally in Nuremberg) and *Olympia* (1938) have been known to stir even the most resolutely antifascist breasts, though it is also possible to regard these strenuously aestheticising movies not only as profoundly evil but as hopeless kitsch to boot. The film section of Dr Goebbels's Propaganda Ministry, the *Reichsfilmkammer*, was particularly accomplished at mingling Nazi values with box office appeal; it is revealing to note that the only Nazi filmmaker ultimately brought to trial by the Allies was Veit Harlan, director of the anti-semitic drama *Jud Süss*, though Fritz Hippler's documentary *Der Ewige Jude*, made in the same year (1940), was an even more repellent piece of work. Allied logic, if debatable, is clear enough: sweetened by fiction and other modes of entertainment, propaganda not only reaches a larger audience than it would in less beguiling documentary forms, but may affect its audience more profoundly. Propaganda films are almost as old as the medium itself – Méliès, one of cinema's founding fathers, made his *L'Affaire Dreyfus* as early as 1899 – and they continue to be made to the present day. Among influential examples of the form: Abel Gance's pacifist *J'accuse* (1919); Pare Lorentz's *The Plow that Broke the Plains* (1936), about dustbowl America; the work of John Grierson and the *Crown Film Unit* in Britain, notably the poetic documentaries of life on the Home Front directed by Humphrey Jennings; Howard Hawks' interventionist drama *Sergeant York* (1941), starring Gary Copper as a conscientious objector who none the less became a hero of the First World War, and William Wyler's *Mrs Miniver* (1942), a weepy tribute to the British way of life; the *Why We Fight* series, produced by Frank Capra for the United States' armed forces between 1942 and 1945; and several films about America's war in Vietnam, from the John Wayne vehicle *The Green Berets* (1968) to the radical compilation film *Loin du Viet-nam* by Chris Marker and others.

property   (a) a more formal synonym for *prop*; (b) the copyrighted text – anything from a novel via a magazine article to a song title – that provides the basis for a production. 'In the new vocabulary he [William Faulkner] was learning, a "property" was anything that might be turned into a motion picture: an idea, a synopsis, an original story, an adaptation of an existing work, a movie-style "treatment" of one of these, or a script with dialogue and directions' (Joseph Blotner, 'Faulkner in Hollywood').

proposal   a short written or oral description of an idea for a film. See also *pitch*.

protection shot   a shot, usually a *master*, taken by the director as a safety net in the event that a sequence should prove hard to edit; also known as a *cover shot*.

proximity effect   a minor sound distortion that may occur when a directional microphone picks up the low frequencies of a voice or other sound.

psychological thriller   a form of *thriller* in which the focus of interest is not solely danger, violence and pursuit but the convoluted, tortured mentality of criminals, victims, investigators or all three: Hitchcock's *Vertigo* is a classic example.

publicist, publicity department   the person or team responsible for interesting newspapers, magazines, radio and television in particular productions, and so contriving a kind of unpaid advertising campaign; the publicist assigned to a given film is usually called the *unit publicist*. A *publicity still* is a photograph made available to the press, showing either a scene from the completed film, or some aspect of its production (typically: the director giving instructions to the leading players).

pull back or **pullback**   the reverse movement of a camera away from the subject which turns a close-up into a medium shot or the like; this can sometimes function as a type of *reveal*, in which the original meaning of the shot changes as its subject is shown to be in an unsuspected context; such a movement can also be known as a *pull-back dolly*, and the resulting image, whether achieved by dolly, crane, or lens adjustment, may be called a *pull-back shot*. The *pull-down claw* is the device which slots into the sprocket holes on film to draw it through the camera or projector; in other words, the business end of the *pull-down mechanism* used to achieve *intermittent movement*.

pull focus, pulling focus   to adjust the focus of a lens in the middle of a scene so that the hazy foreground suddenly becomes sharp and the sharp background becomes hazy, or vice versa. Also known as *racking focus*.

pull-up   the slack loop of film necessary to achieve a transition from intermittent to continuous movement; see *Latham loops*.

pulsed lamp   a type of carbon arc lamp used in some projectors, which flashes on and off in synchronization with the intermittent movement of film through the *gate*.

punch   in early Hollywood, industry slang for a sudden emotional shock or pay-off: 'Then comes what the photoplay people call the punch . . . It is a kind of solar plexus blow to the sensibilities, certainly by this time an unnecessary part of the film. Usually every soul movement carefully built up to where the punch begins is forgotten in the material smash or rescue' (Vachel Lindsay, *The Art of the Moving Picture*). (b) a small hand punch used to pierce marker holes in *leader*.

pup   a 500-watt lamp.

puppet   the generic term for any kind of model – of man, beast or monster – used in film-making, from traditional marionettes to *animatronics*, and sometimes including the semi-automated creature suits worn by actors in science-fiction or fantasy films. Thus, the tiny model of the giant ape used in the *stop-motion* animation of *King Kong* (devised by Willis H. O'Brien), the fairies of Jiri Trnka's *A Midsummer Night's Dream* (the 1935 Czech production) and the dinosaurs and saurian limbs of *Jurassic Park* may all be described as puppets.

pure cinema   a movement of the French *avant-garde* cinema of the 1920s, similar to, if not indistinguishable from, *absolute cinema*; see *cinéma-pur*.

push   to increase the speed of film during shooting, and/or to overdevelop it, usually (a) to 'rescue' film that has been shot with too little light, or (b) to boost contrast or give the effect of graininess. Presumably derived from the older sense 'to impel [a horse, etc.] to greater speed', known from the early 18th C and current into the present century ('The steeds with urgent speed were push'd/ Till lost in distance all was hush'd' – Standish, *Maid of Jaen*, 1832). Also known as *uprating*. *'Push in!'*, the director's order to move the camera closer to the action; *push-over wipe*, a form of lateral *wipe* in which the incoming image appears to elbow the outgoing image off the screen.

pyrotechnics   all the explosive devices used in action films, controlled by the *pyrotechnist*. A compound of Gk *pyro*, 'fire', and *technikos*, from *techne*, 'art', coined some time in the early 18th C to apply to any use of fire in chemistry, gunnery and the like, and applied more narrowly to the manufacture and display of fireworks from the early 19th C onwards.

Quad-8   a film stock used in the mass printing of *Super-8mm*; four separate strips of 8mm can be processed on the quad-8 side by side. An abbreviation, of course, from the L stem *quadr-*, 'four'. Hence, among other terms, *quadlite*, a unit made up of four floodlights.

quarter apple   an *apple-box* that is as long and wide as the conventional kind, but only a quarter the height.

quartz bulb   a light bulb made of quartz (which can withstand high temperatures without shattering), with a tungsten filament inside a halogen gas. The word 'quartz', meaning a mineral composed in its purest state of silica or silicon dioxide, is taken from the German *quarz*, itself of unknown origin; it can be found in geological and other accounts from the mid-18th C onwards. Quartz bulbs have a number of advantages: they are small, lightweight and easily transported; they burn with an even intensity; and, unlike some bulbs, do not blacken, since the tungsten that is burned off combines with the halide and settles back on the filament. *Quartz light*, a light using a quartz bulb.

Queer Cinema (or sometimes **New Queer Cinema**)   a journalistic and/or critical tag, which has been fastened to a number of films made in the late 1980s and early 1990s by homosexual directors and addressing homosexual themes. It marks a notable shift in the connotations of the epithet 'queer'. For much of this century a harsh insult directed at homosexuals (particularly men), the word 'queer' has now been defiantly embraced by a number of politicised gays – who, indeed, prefer its determined abrasiveness to the more familiar and anodyne 'gay' – and has become either a neutrally descriptive or an honorific term. OED suggests that 'queer' originates as a slang term for the adjective 'homosexual' or the noun 'homosexual man' in the USA, some time during the early 20th C ('A young man, easily ascertainable to be unsually fine in other characteristics, is probably "queer" in sex tendency' – Children's Bureau, U.S. Department of Labor, 1922) and had been imported to Britain by the late 1930s: Christopher Isherwood's *Goodbye to Berlin* (1939) uses 'queer' in this sense. But the term 'queer fellow' had been used since the early 18th C, especially in Ireland and the Navy, to designate a man who did not conform to the usual type, an eccentric or individualist, and the homosexual sense may well be derived from such uses. Amusingly enough, OED says that 'queer' itself is 'of doubtful origin'; it enters the language, in a variety of different spellings (*queir*, *queyr* etc.) around the early 16th C.

Whether or not this new militant usage proves to be long-lived or popular, the term 'Queer Cinema' is certainly useful as a way of distinguishing this recent tendency of the independent cinema from the countless earlier films made by or starring homosexual artists, or from those films which have traditionally been the favourites of gay audiences. (See *gay films*.) Often formally innovative, perhaps by way of underlining the position that gay artists perceive the universe differently, some products of Queer Cinema have also proved strikingly successful with straight audiences – Gus Van Sant's *My Own Private Idaho* (1991), for example, or the extravagant films of Pedro Almodóvar, though purists might deny that either of these directors quite fits the New Queer bill. Among the more notable productions that even purists would admit into the Queer canon are *Edward II* and *Wittgenstein* by the late Derek Jarman; Tom Kalin's *Swoon*, which returns to the Leopold and Loeb murder case that also inspired Hitchcock's *Rope*; Todd Haynes's *Poison*; the lesbian romance *Go Fish*; Jennie Livingston's documentary about transvestites *Paris is Burning*; and many others, including productions by avant-garde film-makers such as Sadie Benning working mostly in video.

quick cut   another term for a *jump cut*.

quickie   a low-budget production – usually an *exploitation* film, or *Z picture* – generally made in extreme haste. 'Motion pictures which are ground out wholesale by the studios at the rate of one a week are called *quickies*' – *American Mercury*, December 1926; see *quota quickies*.

quiet or **quiet on the set!**   the command given by the assistant director before the cameras turn over and shooting can begin.

quota quickies   the generic name for a number of films produced in Britain from the late 1920s onwards, in reponse to the 1927 Cinematograph Act. This required that about 30 per cent of films shown on British screens should be of domestic origin; the results, as one might expect, did little to enhance the standing of our national industry. Quota systems have also been operated at various times since the 1920s, almost always against the global domination of Hollywood, and almost always by countries which lacked either a nationalised industry (such as the former Soviet Union and its satellite states) or a sufficiently lively local industry.

R in the USA, the *rating* given to films that can only be seen by viewers under the age of 17 if they are accompanied by a parent or guardian; an abbreviation of the word 'Restricted'.

race movies a term for the films made for black audiences, with all-black casts, in the United States between the silent period and the end of the 1940s. (Cf. the term 'race records', applied to blues and other African-American music of approximately the same period; OED's earliest citation of this label is from 1926.) Though many of the producers and directors of race movies were white, the form did allow for the emergence of Hollywood's first generation of black directors (George and Noble Johnson, Oscar Micheaux) as well as providing considerably less demeaning roles for black actors than the industry was offering at the time.

rack (a) to thread film through a projector or editing table; (b) to line up a frame on such a device; or, most commonly of all (c) an abbreviation of the verb to *rack focus* – that is, to adjust the camera lens during a shot so that the background becomes sharp and the foreground blurry, or vice versa; or, in more subtle racks, to make an adjustment that redirects the audience's gaze from one part of the image to another; see *pull focus*, (*Rack* is also the term for the stand from which film is suspended in a cutting room.)

rackover, rackover viewfinder a device found on some cameras for overcoming problems of *parallax*. It permits the camera operator to move ('rack') the body of the camera to one side so that a viewfinder can be lined up directly behind the lens and the correct *framing* established; for actual shooting, the camera body has to be racked back into place.

racket cutting a technique sometimes found in avant-garde film-making, in which a few frames of one shot are intercut with a few frames of another, producing a dazzling, disorienting effect of the kind that used to be called 'psychedelic'.

Radio-Keith-Orpheum see *RKO*.

rain cluster a group of *rain standards* – movable water sprinklers mounted above the set or field of action to give the illusion of rain; rain clusters are used when a large area has to be covered; a *rain hat*, however, is simply what its name suggests – a cover used for microphones when it's raining.

range is the distance between the camera and its subject; a *range extender* a device used to increase the focal distance of a camera lens by increasing its magnification; a *rangefinder* (or *telemeter*) an optical device used for measuring range. Range, from OF *range*, 'row, rank, file', is found in English as early as 1300; the photographic sense of the term seems to be developed from its applications in ballistics (which occur from the late 16th C onwards), possibly with some additional shading from the sense 'sphere or scope of operation or action', which is found from the 17th C ('He would not suffer them to fall without the range of Mercy' – Bunyan, *Grace Abounding*, 1666).

Rank, Rank Organisation the well-known British production, distribution (through Rank Film Distributors) and exhibition company, officially incorporated in March 1946 under its full name, the J. Arthur Rank Organisation. Its founder, J. Arthur Rank (1888–1972), a patriotic and pious gentleman (he was at one time a Methodist Sunday School teacher) who thought that the British cinema could be at once a means for spreading the gospel, a dam against the tide of imports from Hollywood and a splendid way of making money, began his serious film career as a distributor in 1935 with General Film Distributors, dealing with *Universal*'s products, and expanded rapidly into all other areas of the business. By the late 1940s, the time of its greatest prosperity, Rank was more or less a monopoly, controlling virtually all the major studio facilities in Britain, including *Denham* and *Pinewood*, a good number of smaller production companies including *Gainsborough* and more than 1,000 cinemas. As all trivia buffs know, the man who strikes the gong for Rank's trademark opening credit is Bombardier Billy Wells; the resulting crash was dubbed by James Blades. The *Rank Charm School* was the company's in-house facility for producing British *starlets* such as Joan Collins; the *Rank Cintel* is the trade name for that company's *telecine* machine.

rating   the system of rating or certification of feature films and their trailers, and of pre-recorded videotapes in the United Kingdom now looks fairly similar to that of the *MPAA*'s rating system for the United States, though there are a couple of significant differences. In the UK, the present ratings are U, PG, 12, 15 and 18 (see *certificate*); in the US, G, PG, PG13 (introduced in 1984 after a campaign by Steven Spielberg, and designating movies which, though generally wholesome enough, might include sequences alarming to pre-teens), R and X, the last of these indicating that no one under the age of 17 may see the film; and, since 1990, the NC17, also meaning 'No children under 17 admitted'. This new rating came into force when it became apparent that the X rating, originally intended solely for pornographic films, was being slapped on art-house movies with erotic or otherwise risky content: Peter Greenaway's *The Cook, The Thief, His Wife and Her Lover,* Pedro Almodóvar's *Tie me up! Tie me Down!* and so on. The turning point came when Universal fought the X certificate awarded to Phil Kaufman's *Henry and June,* and, with the help of the celebrated (or notorious, depending on one's sympathies) Alan M. Dershowitz, won. (American trailers are classified as either All Audience or Restricted.) The British rating conventions have undergone a number of changes since the British Board of Film Censors was set up in 1912. The two original ratings of 'U' for Universal and 'A' for adult became increasingly unsatisfactory in the light of the more violent, erotic, frightening or otherwise disturbing content of films. An 'H' (for Horror) certificate was introduced in 1937 to keep children out of horror films, and dropped in 1942 when all such films were banned. The 'X' certificate came into force in 1951. See *censorship*.

ratio see *aspect ratio*.

raw stock film stock that has not yet been exposed; sometimes referred to as *negative*.

reaction shot a close-up or medium close-up of an actor responding to what has been done or said in the previous shot (or, less commonly, to something that is happening off-camera); hence *reaction pan*, a slower version of the same effect done with a single camera movement rather than a cut, and often used for comic effect: parents enter house where their children have been throwing a wild party: shot of devastation; slow reaction pan to the horror on their faces. Though it cross-refers to *off-screen*, the OED chooses as its principal citation, curiously, a televisual rather than cinematic example – a report in the *Guardian* for 11 August 1966 that Members of Parliament were worried that television producers might make mischievous use of '"reaction shots", by which the committee meant pictures not only of the member addressing the House . . . but of other members reacting to his speech.'

read (a) as a verb: to be literally or metaphorically legible to the viewer – that is, for an object to be large and clearly defined enough to be easily made out – or to be bright enough to register on a light meter; or (b), as in the theatre, to hold or attend auditions for a role (this appears to be a 20th C coinage). A *reader* is – much as in the theatre, where the professional term has been current since the early 19th C – the person who reads, summarises and assesses various unproduced screenplays and other properties for producers and directors who are too busy to cope with the torrent of scripts that arrive on their desks every week; the critical synopses drawn up by readers are often referred to as *coverage*. In Hollywood, the reader will usually be an employee of a *Story Department* or an agency. *Reading* (or *read-through*), (a) a preliminary rehearsal, in which the cast members sit around reading the screenplay out loud so as to make themselves familiar with the plot and characters and to work out any problems it may pose for them; (b) an indication of brightness or sound levels, given by an *exposure meter* or *VU*.

réalisateur one of the standard French words for a film director, occasionally found in affected English prose.

realism much as as in other arts: (a) the impulse, struggle, attempt, hope or vain aspiration towards – or triumphant achievement of – a true *mimesis* of the physical and material world within the artifice of the cinema, and the various overt and covert beliefs bound up with such efforts. The aesthetic sense of the word begins to be used in English around the middle of the 19th C; hence Ruskin: 'To try by startling realism to enforce the monstrosity that has no terror in itself' – *Modern Painters*, 1856. (b) The self-effacing and thus highly plausible film style that stands in opposition to artifice, stylisation, fantasy, surrealism and any form of self-advertising flourish. Theoretical debates about the issue of realism in the cinema have been predictably copious and occasionally vehement. See *neorealism*.

rear projection, rear screen projection (also **back projection**)   one of the simplest and most common forms of cinema fakery, in which actors are filmed in a studio against a background (usually an exterior) that is projected onto the back of a translucent screen. So, for example, the actors may sit in a mock-up of a car; moving images of the road they are supposedly taking will be projected behind them; and the camera, synchronised with the projector to prevent flickering, will record their illusory journey. The result is usually known as a *process shot*. See also *matte shot*.

reciprocity law   a term derived from the physics and chemistry of processing: the general rule (not applicable either for very long or very short exposures) is that the degree of photographic exposure is a product of the length of exposure and the intensity of the light source.

record   from OF *recorder* and L *recordare*, from *cor*, 'heart': the verb, which appears very early (early 13th C) in English, originally meant 'to get by heart', or commit to memory. Hence its application to all our surrogates for and aids to personal memory, including print and more recent technologies.

In the cinema, the verb applies to the electronic registration and fixing of sound on tape or some other medium: hence a variety of associated terms, including *recorder*, the machine used to preserve sounds; *recording level*, the point on the volume control at which a recorder is set for use; *recording studio*, a soundproof room where sounds can be recorded or re-recorded; the *recordist* or *sound recordist* (or *production mixer* or *recording supervisor*) is the crew member responsible for sound recording.

red light   the warning light set outside a sound stage to alert passers-by to the fact that shooting is in progress, silence must be observed and the studio may not be entered.

reduction print   a print made on a smaller gauge from an original on a wider gauge – a 16mm from a 35mm, for example.

reel   from OE *hreol*, an instrument on which thread is wound, in the cinema means either (a) the metal or plastic wheel around which printed film is wound for projection or storage, or (b) the wound film itself, considered either simply as an object or as a unit of measurement: 'In the last reel the good brother has to be killed off so that the bad brother can be regenerated' – Budd Schulberg, *What Makes Sammy Run?*, 1941. Her Majesty Queen Victoria, no less, made reference in her journals to 'the new cinematograph process, – which makes moving pictures by winding off a reel of film' (entry for 3 October 1896; the monarch was admirably quick on the uptake, since Britons had witnessed the device for the first time only seven months or so earlier). Since the standard 35mm reel holds up to 1,000 feet of film, which would run for about 10 minutes at a speed of 90 feet a minute for sound film, or 15 minutes at 60 feet per minute for silent film, 'reel' is generally understood to mean a running time of roughly ten minutes. In the early days of cinema, films were designated as one-reelers, two-reelers and so on. *Reel change*: the smooth hand-over from one projector to the next in a theatrical screening; the projectionist is warned of the imminent end of the first reel by a series of unobtrusive marks at the top right-hand side of the screen, and starts up the second projector so that, in ideal circumstances, the film continues without apparent interruption.

reel-to-reel   a form of tape recorder, such as a *Nagra*, which uses large open reels of quarter-inch tape rather than cassettes.

reference print   a high quality print which serves as the standard against which subsequent prints may be checked.

reflectance   a term taken over from physics: a measurement of the relationship between the intensity of light striking a surface and that reflected by the surface; *reflected light meter*, an exposure meter that measures reflected rather than incident light; *reflector, reflector board*, a sheet or panel with a shiny surface, usually silver in colour, used to direct natural or artificial light; they are supported by *reflector stands*, usually made of metal. The white cards used as reflectors are sometimes called *bounce boards*.

reflex camera   a camera designed to allow the operator to see through its viewfinder exactly what the lens sees; in other words, which does away with the difficulties of *parallax* by the use of a series of mirrors; the device, and therefore the word, was in fairly wide use by the 1890s. A *reflex screen* is a type of screen, made out of tiny glass beads, used in the *front-projection* process; a *reflex viewfinder* is a type of camera viewfinder which, usually by means of a mirror and prism system, allows the cameraman to see the images that are entering the lens. When built into the camera (as such systems usually are), it is also called an *integral reflex viewfinder*.

refraction   the change in direction that takes place when light passes from a less dense to a denser medium or *vice versa*. From L *refract-*, from *refingere* and ultimately *frangere*, 'to break'. 'By . . . rash collecting (as it were) from visual beams refracted through another's eye' – Selden, 1612.

reframe   to move the camera so as to adjust the composition of an image.

registration pins (or **register pins**)   the small teeth in a gate of a projector or camera which slot into the sprocket holes of the film (*pilot pins*). *Registration* usually means the precise positioning of a frame inside a camera or projector so as to produce a steady image; a *registration shot* is a type of shot which begins as a still, or drawing, and then jumps into action.

regressive angles   a sequence of shots which start with a very sharp angle (such as an *extreme high shot*) and work their way down to a low angle, usually coming in to rest on a character or characters; not to be confused with *regressive shots*, a sequence of shots which jump further and further away from the subject, reducing it to a tiny point in the landscape.

Reichsfilmkammer, 'Reich Chamber of Film'   the cinema division of Dr Goebbels' Propaganda Minstry, founded in June 1933 with the long-term intention of taking over the whole German film industry, a goal which it achieved by 1942. From September 1933 it became part of the *Reichskulturkammer* under the presidency of Dr Fritz Scheuermann; from 1934 onwards it began to exercise a strict system of censorship, blocking the productions of non-member producers and rewarding ideologically sympathetic films with prizes and the like.

relation editing   a term coined by Pudovkin to desigante the type of editing or *montage* which establishes some thematic relationship between two or more different subjects – a technique also, and somewhat more commonly known as *associative editing*.

release   (a) the first major distribution of a film to cinema chains – *general release* means distribution across a whole country or other large marketplace; or (b) the released film itself ('An Essanay release called "Sunshine"': *Motion Picture Annual*, 1912). The term *re-release* or *rerelease* indicates any subsequent process of distribution, whether across the country or to a limited market: re-releases of art films are fairly common (in the week of writing this entry alone, Volker Schlöndorff's *The Tin Drum* and Kurosawa's *Seven Samurai* have both been re-released in London), those of more mainstream films less so, especially in the age of video, though the fad for *director's cuts* (Ridley Scott's *Blade Runner*, David Lean's *Lawrence of Arabia* and the like) has changed matters somewhat. Also an abbreviation for *release form*, a legal document which grants the production company various rights, chiefly the right to show the cinematic image of a person to the paying public. A *release negative* is the master negative from which the *release prints* – the composite print used in cinemas – may be struck.

remake   a film more or less closely based on an earlier film or films, such as Sydney Pollack's rather sorry 1995 updating of Billy Wilder's romantic comedy *Sabrina* (1954). The term is also applied, though with less obvious justice, to movies which return to a favourite story or character from some literary or otherwise non-cinematic original – the many adventures of Dracula or Sherlock Holmes, for example. In recent years, Hollywood has shown a penchant for seizing on succesful (and often poor) French films and remaking them in Americanised (and often still worse) versions; thus *Cousin, Cousine* becomes *Cousins*, *Trois Hommes et une couffin Three Men and a Baby*, *Nikita* (known in the United States as *La Femme Nikita*) *The Assassin*, and *Mon père ce héros My Father the Hero*. But there have been some worthwhile remakes, too, from Howard Hawks's *His Girl Friday* (1940), a remake of Lewis Milestone's *The Front Page* (1931) to Philip Kaufman's *Invasion of the Body Snatchers* (1978), a remake of the Don Siegel original of 1956.

Rembrandt lighting   a term said to have been coined by Cecil B. De Mille in a telegram to his irate producers (who wondered why the actors' faces were wrapped in shadows), denoting a tenebrous lighting style notionally influenced by – or at any rate roughly approximating to – the dark painterly style of Rembrandt.

rental   the process or agreement by which an *exhibitor* hires a film from a *distributor*. *Rentals* are the sums of money paid by the exhibitor, either as a percentage of the box-office takings or as straightforward fees.

repertory cinema   a cinema, such as the Everyman in Hampstead or the National Film Theatre, which specialises in showing a wide variety of old and new films from around the world, rather than the far more restricted fare of first-run Hollywood releases, lightly seasoned from time to time with the odd unthreatening *art-house* import from France, that is to be found in the great majority of commercial cinemas. London used to be rich in such cinemas (RIP the Electric, Notting Hill); now the breed is all but extinct.

reprise shots   shots that are repeated for some narrative purpose from an earlier sequence in a film, such as the replayed shots of a couple engaged in quiet colloquy – apparently the potential victims of a murder conspiracy, in fact conspirators themselves – in Coppola's *The Conversation* (1974).

report sheets   (or *production reports*) forms filled out at the end of a day's shooting by the camera and sound crews. They show details of each take, and indicate which takes are suitable for printing.

Republic   an efficient factory studio, which specialised in churning out *B-movies* and *quickies*, especially *Westerns*; its trademark, still occasionally to be seen on television in off-peak hours, was an eagle on a mountain peak. Republic was a lively force in the film industry from its foundation in 1935 until the 1950s, when it turned to producing television shows. Its earliest stars were John Wayne and Gene Autry – cowboys later joined by Roy Rogers; Duke Ellington and Cab Calloway both lent their talents and orchestras to Republic's musical productions. The company's most distinguished productions came in its last years: John Ford's *Rio Grande* (1950) and *The Quiet Man* (1952), Nicholas Ray's *Johnny Guitar* (1954). Erich von Stroheim, it appears, would refer to the company as 'Repulsive Pictures'.

resolution (or **resolving power**)   the degree to which a particular film stock or lens can record sharp images; the higher the resolution, the sharper the image. OED records an optical sense ('the effect of an instrument in making the separate parts of an object distinguishable to the eye') of the word from the mid-19th C onwards.

retake   to shoot a scene or scenes again, usually because earlier takes were not good enough. 'Directly on finishing the scene it is filmed again, the second exposure being called a "retake"' – H. Croy, *How Motion Pictures are Made*, 1918. The term passed into general use quite quickly, and soon became widely applied in metaphorical senses to acts or events that were more or less precisely repeated, such as sporting occasions.

reticle, reticle lines   the guidelines etched or printed inside a camera *viewfinder* that help the cinematographer compose the image; these will

usually show the *safe area* or *TV-cutoff* area and so on. 'Reticle', from
L *reticulum*, the diminutive form of *rete*, 'net', took on its optical sense in
the early 17th C, when it came to mean the set of parallel and intersecting
threads placed in the object-glass of a telescope.

retrospective   as in the fine arts: a series of screenings devoted to the
career of a particular director, actor or writer; in Britain, such series are
often held at the National Film Theatre, at festivals in Cambridge,
Edinburgh etc., or in local arts centres.

reveal   from OF *reveler* and L *revelare*, from *velum*, 'veil': a shot which
moves backwards, or sideways, or upwards, to show something that was
not initially visible to the audience, the presence of which generally alters
its meaning – showing, for example, that a woman apparently having a
nervous breakdown is actually auditioning for a famous director; a *pan*
which serves this function is sometimes known as a *revelation pan*.

reverse (or **reverse angle, reverse angle shot**   a shot taken from a
position that is the opposite of that in the preceding shot – for example,
the first shot shows a character approaching a door; the reverse shot,
filmed from inside the room, shows him entering. Using a series of
alternating reverse angles (this sometimes referred to as *shot/reverse shot*
technique) is a common way of filming dialogue between two characters.

reversal film   a film stock which, once exposed, can be processed to
bring out its positive images with no intermediate negative stage. The
material, and the word, have been current in photography since at least
the late 1870s. Thus, a *reversal dupe* is a positive made from a positive;
this technique is known as a *reversal process*.

reverse motion (or **reverse action**)   a simple form of special effect,
achieved by running film backwards, so that fallen bodies leap magically
into the air, shattered glass reconstitutes itself and the like. Though the
resulting effect can be comical, and even a little childish, the device has
been used to great effect in, among other notable films, Cocteau's *Orphée*
and *La Belle et la Bête*, and in Jean Renoir's early film *La Fille de l'eau*;
reverse scene, a scene that has been *flipped* during printing so as to create
a kind of mirror-image effect.

revision   in the term recognised by the Writer's Guild of America, and
used in contracts, a revision is a script alteration that is more radical than
a mere *polish*, but less radical than an entirely new draft. When revisions
are made to a screenplay after it has been distributed to the cast and
crew, the first changes are indicated by being printed up on blue paper;
subsequent changes are signalled by the use of pink, yellow, green,
'goldenrod' and finally white paper.

rewind   noun; the geared machine used to feed film back onto its
original reel after projection, or in the process of editing; OED's earliest
example is from 1938, but it was almost certainly common before then.
Hence the verb forms 'rewind' and 'rewinding'.

ribbon microphone   a sensitive microphone, originally developed for radio, and often used for recording *voice-overs*, since it produces an intimate effect.

rifle mike   a directional microphone that is aimed at sound sources much as one would aim a rifle; *rifle spot*, a spotlight designed to project a long, narrow beam.

rig   the scaffolding that is put up around and over a set, chiefly to hold lights; the workers who construct this scaffolding and arrange the lights are known as *riggers*; *rigging* means either (a) the rig itself, or (b) the business of setting lights in place before filming begins. 'Rig', which begins its career in English around the late 15th C as a nautical term meaning 'to make a ship ready for sea, to fit out with tackle', is of obscure origin, since its cognate words in Danish (*rigge*) Swedish and Norwegian (both use *rigga*) appear to be borrowed from our language. The theatre appears to have adopted the term for its above-stage machinery in the 18th C.

rim lighting   lighting which creates the effect of a halo around the subject.

ripple dissolve   a once-popular transitional device in which the screen wobbles and dissolves from one scene to another, often used for movement into and out of dream sequences and narrated memories. Nowadays it is confined almost exclusively to comedies, such as *Wayne's World*.

riser   another term for an *apple box*; or a platform device (also called a *bridge plate*) for raising the camera.

RKO   an abbreviation for *Radio-Keith-Orpheum* or *RKO Radio Pictures Incorporated*, the American production company founded in 1928 from a complex tangle of merged, expanded and taken-over bodies that appears to have grown from a single Milwaukee **nickelodeon**, itself founded in 1909. Its trademark emblem – a giant pylon transmitting from atop the planet Earth – is as instantly recognisable to amateurs of 1930s and 1940s Hollywood as the MGM lion: during this period, it produced films as successful and various as *King Kong* (1933), the Fred Astaire–Ginger Rogers musicals from *Flying Down to Rio* (1933) onwards, all of Katherine Hepburn's early films including the wonderful screwball comedy *Bringing Up Baby* (1938), Hitchcock's *Suspicion* and *Notorious* (1946), the superbly atmospheric horror films produced by Val Lewton and, of course, *Citizen Kane* (1941). Howard Hughes bought out the troubled company in 1948, but his eccentric management style soon brought about its death: RKO ceased production altogether in 1953, and the studio itself was sold to Desilu Productions in 1957. The rights to many RKO films are now owned by Ted Turner.

road movie   in many respects the cinematic equivalent of the pica-resque novel, the road movie in its most typical form involves a couple of young(ish) men driving around the landscape either in quest of something or, as Chuck Berry put it, with no particular place to go: characteristic examples include *Two-Lane Blacktop* (1971), *Vanishing*

Point (1971) and *Easy Rider* (1969). Though essentially an American genre, inspired by the vastness of the continent, the low price of petrol and (more speculatively) elements of restlessness and urges towards male comradeship in the American psyche of the kind Prof. Leslie Fiedler has expounded upon, the form was taken up eagerly in the former West Germany by Wim Wenders (whose production company is still called Road Movies) in such films as *Kings of the Road*, *Wrong Movement* and – probably the most extreme and, with any luck, the most decadent instance of the form – *Until the End of the World*, a science-fiction road movie on a global scale, and a spectacular critical and commercial flop. There have been several British attempts at road movies, notably Chris Petit's *Radio On* and, more recently, Michael Winterbottom's *Butterfly Kiss* (a cross-breed, this, with the serial killer and lesbian romance genres), both of which owe something to Wenders' example. Even those who admire such films, however, will tend to concede that the cramped and profoundly unromantic nature of the British motorway scene seems to put a damper on proceedings. Ridley Scott's *Thelma and Louise* is far and away the most successful attempt so far to put a feminine, if not feminist spin on this otherwise clannishly male genre.

road show the American term for a marketing strategy whereby a feature will be shown at a limited number of cinemas (usually with higher ticket prices) for a period of some weeks or months before being put on general *release*.

rock and roll a widely-used colloquial term for the process of roll-back sound mixing, which allows sound tracks and picture to be 'rocked' forwards and 'rolled' backwards without going out of synch; in this way, new tracks may be added or existing tracks re-recorded. The technique first became widely used in the 1960s.

rock film any film, including concert films such as *Stop Making Sense* (Talking Heads on stage) or *rockumentaries* such as *Don't Look Back* (Bob Dylan touring an extraordinarily drab-looking England), which makes extensive use of rock (or pop, rap, reggae, soul, R&B, heavy metal, punk . . . .) and/or which appeals to the audience for such music – including, it may be argued, films which have a relatively slight musical content but appeal to the rock audience because they star rock musicians or portray some theme or milieu attractive to the conventional rock audience. *Performance* (directed by Donald Cammell and Nicholas Roeg, and starring Mick Jagger), for example, boasts only one fully staged musical number, but has long been a favourite among several generations of rock fans.

rockumentary a documentary about rock music and musicians, which will generally combine backstage footage and interviews with concert sequences. 'The rockumentary is a discredited form, but if anyone can rescue it it's Christy Moore' (Jasper Rees, *Independent*, 3 June 1995). The term appears to be have been invented by Rob Reiner for his opening monologue in *This is Spinal Tap*, a brilliantly observed spoof (or *mockumentary*, if you will) about a fictitious British heavy-metal group on tour in America. It has since been taken up and used without any obvious satirical intent, particularly by MTV (Music Television), the international rock video network. MTV has also produced a number of mutant forms of the term, notably *rapumentary* (for a documentary about rap acts) and *Bedrockumentary* (about the making of the live-action version of *The Flintstones*).

roll a length of film wound around a core; the term has been in general use for photographic purposes since the late 19th C: *roll camera!* (or *roll it!*, etc.: a cue for the camera operator to start the motor running for a take, and, thus, also a warning to the cast and crew that a take is about to begin; *rolling titles*, the **credits** (almost always the end credits) that move up from the bottom of the screen and disappear through its top; these are also known as *crawls*, *creeping titles* or *running titles*; titles which move in the opposite direction are known, logically, as *roll-up titles*; *roll-off* is a term from sound recording, indicating a gradual reduction in frequency.

romantic lead the *lead* in a movie about romantic love: Hugh Grant in *Four Weddings and a Funeral* or *Nine Months*, say.

room tone the low-level, ambient noise of a quiet room, recorded separately from the dialogue track and mixed later, either to cover sound edits or simply to create a more satisfactory acoustic effect; see *wild track*, *atmos*. Tom DiCillo's *Living in Oblivion* (1995) ends with a sound recordist taking half a minute of room tone while the film's leading characters drift off into silent private reveries.

rostrum from L *rostrum*, 'beak', but more directly and obviously from the name of the platform for public speakers in the Roman Forum, so called because it was decorated with the 'beaks' of ships taken from the Antiates in 338 BC; the word has been used to mean 'platform', etc., in English since the mid-18th C. (a) a type of adjustable platform used to mount a camera (or, less often, a light); or (b) the machine that holds a camera above an animation board for animation work – another term, that is, for *animation stand* (c) particularly in British documentary work, an abbreviation for *rostrum shots*, *rostrum sequences*, *rostrum footage* and so on – that is, the shots of still photographs, objects and other material produced, with the use of a mechanism similar to an animation stand, by a rostrum team; or sometimes, less often, (d) that team itself. The most famous rostrum cameraman in the United Kingdon is Ken Morse, a credit which will have been noted (if only subliminally) by anyone who has watched much British television over the past decade or so.

rotary movement an effect, now rather outdated, in which the image goes into a rapid spin (montages of whirling newspaper headlines were the outstanding cliché); this can be easily contrived with an *optical printer*. A *rotary printer*, however, is a simple type of continuous-contact printer, in which negatives and stock are brought surface-to-surface from their respective reels by a rotating sprocket.

rotoscope   a device used for projecting individual frames of film, particularly for *matte* sequences including animation.

rough assembly, rough cut   the version of the film produced by the earliest stages of editing, made up of all the principal scenes put in more or less the intended sequence so that the narrative is coherent. 'The only demands we have made on the producers as a Guild were to have two weeks' preparation time for "A" pictures, one week preparation time for "B" pictures and to have supervision of just the rough cut of the picture' – *New York Times*, 2 April 1939. A rough cut is usually a good deal longer than the final cut.

run-by   a shot of a moving vehicle passing before an immobile camera; *runners*, (a) junior production assistants or *gofers*, employed to run minor errands; (b) another term for the *rigging*; *running shot*, a shot which runs alongside a moving actor or vehicle; *running speed*, the rate at which film (or tape) passes through a camera, projector or recorder; the passage of film is measured in frames per second (*FPS*), that of sound tape in inches per second (IPS); *running time*, the duration of a completed film; *run out*, the short length of blank frames that come between the end of the picture frames and the tail *leader*; *run-through* (or *walk-through*), as in the theatre: an actors' rehearsal prior to shooting.

rushes   (also known as *dailies* – the more common term in the United States) positive prints of each day's shooting, with or without synchronised sound, which are watched by the director, producer and others late in the evening or early the following morning. 'Isidor Iskovitch sat very cockily exhibiting to his friend and boss . . . some thousands of feet of "rushes" on his pet picture . . .' – G.R. Chester, *On Set & Off*, 1924.

S **afe-action area** the central part of the film image that will remain in sight and uncropped when the film is shown on television, which has a narrower *aspect ratio* than films; hence *safe-title area*, the area within which titles must be printed if they are not to be cropped at the sides in television broadcasts.

safelight the low-intensity bulb, often yellow in colour, used in dark-rooms when photographs are being processed.

safety base (or **safety film**) the type of film base, usually made of cellulose, that has been in common use since supplanting *nitrate stock* in 1950/51 or thereabouts; nitrate stock was highly flammable, but safety film is very slow-burning. It was originally developed before the First World War as a stock suitable for amateur use, and seldom produced in 35mm formats for professionals until the late 1930s.

safety shots additional shots of a scene made either as insurance against camera faults or to provide the director and editor with alternative angles.

SAG see *Screen Actor's Guild*.

salad slang: film stock that has become tangled up inside a camera or projector after jamming.

sample print also known as a *final trial composite* or *check print*, the final version of the edited and mixed film; once this version has been approved, *release prints* can be printed.

saturation the degree to which a colour is pure, and undiluted by white light. The term, from L *saturat-*, a stem of *saturare*, itself from *satur*, 'full, satiated', antedates the cinema by a couple of centuries in its earlier form of 'saturate': 'It would yeild a deep saturate green tincture', 1669. Which is to say that highly saturated colours are extremely rich and vivid; *desaturated* colours are pale and watery.

saturation booking has nothing to do with colour, but is a marketing term, meaning the intensive distribution of a film in a particular market.

scale in Hollywood productions, the minimum wage paid for jobs recognised by the various film industry unions. When it is said that stars worked on a production 'for scale', therefore, the meaning is that these performers agreed to work for a small fraction of their usual fees, usually because they had some personal or ideological commitment to the project.

scanned print a wide-screen film that has been squeezed down to fit the narrower aspect ratio of television by the simple, not to say brutal measure of re-printing the original film so as to preserve the principal action – that which falls inside the *safe-action area* – and lose all peripheral details. Since this can sometimes produce ludicrous effects (there is a scene in *2001*, for example, in which astronauts talk to each other from either side of the screen; a conventional scanned version of this moment results in a picture without human presence), sensitive broadcasters have begun to show such films in a *letterbox* format. A *scanning beam* is the beam which reads the sound-track as film passes through a projector.

scenario   (a) a synonym or near-synonym, now slightly old-fashioned, for a *screenplay*. 'So many times it comes up in the scenarios and the picture-plots . . . how money don't always bring happiness' – F. Hurst, *Humoresque*, 1919. Hence the similarly dated *scenarist*, a screenwriter. ('You never can tell just what happened to the tale when it fell into the hands of the gifted scenarists' – *New Yorker*, 28 November 1925.) (b) A plot-line or short story used as the basis for a screenplay. 'Scenario', an Italian word from L *scena*, 'scene', was taken over by English in the late 19th C to mean an outline of the plot of a play.

scene   (a) much as in the theatre: the basic dramatic unit from which a film is built, presenting a single action or multiple actions that take place within one location or on one set, usually about a couple of minutes long; less often, (b) an individual shot or take. Like 'scenario', it comes from L *scena*, itself from Gk *scene*, 'tent, booth, stage, scene', via Fr *scène*; various theatrical meanings of 'scene' appear in English from the mid- to late 16th C onwards, including the one closest to the cinematic sense, the sub-division of an act of a play. 'In volewmes full or flat,/There is no chapter, nor no sceane,/That thou appliest like that' – Heywood, *Proverbs & Epigrams*, 1562.

scenery   as in the theatre, the flats, set furniture and so on which are used on set to build up the illusion of a particular space – a bedroom, an office, a morgue and so on. *Scenic artist,* the person who paints up flats and backgrounds, or 'touches up' other parts of the set.

Schüfftan process   an early form of *special effects* photography, which enabled film-makers to combine live action with models: the earliest, and perhaps the most famous film in which it was used was Fritz Lang's *Metropolis* (1927). It was devised by the German architect, painter, sculptor and cameraman Eugen Schüfftan, and was all done with mirrors – semi-reflective mirrors, to be exact. In brief, it required a semi-reflective surface placed between the camera and the film set at an angle of 45 degrees, and a model put off to one side at 90 degrees. Light passed through the mirror all across its surface, except for a small masked-off area which reflected the model; the result was a composite image produced within the camera, rather than by multiple exposures and the use of an *optical printer*. Naturally, the process was extremely time-consuming and soon became superseded by more convenient methods.

science fiction   a popular cinematic genre ever since the days of Méliès's loose adaptation of Jules Verne's *Le Voyage dans la Lune* (1902), but with rare exceptions – such as William Cameron Menzies' *Things to Come,* based on the novel by H.G. Wells – generally a rather disreputable one until well past the mid-century, associated with poverty-row budgets, atrocious acting, laughable special effects and still more risible stories. As late as 1965, in her excellent and highly recommended essay 'The

Imagination of Disaster', Susan Sontag could reasonably write of science fiction films as if they were a particularly naïve and spontaneous form of folk art. But the genre came of age in critical terms towards the end of the 1960s (at the same time as the Apollo space programme) with Stanley Kubrick's *2001: A Space Odyssey*, which, while it has many articulate detractors, regularly finds its way onto Top Ten lists of best films; while the immense success of George Lucas's *Star Wars* trilogy of the late 1970s and early 1980s made the high-budget science fiction film an attractive prospect for studios as well as audiences. So much so, indeed, that the old B-movie staple became the ultimate A-movie (with consequences for the cinema – infantilising, reduction to mere spectacle – that, it can be argued, amounted to a type of disaster quite other than the ones Susan Sontag had in mind). Reliable accounts suggest that some of the most expensive films so far produced have been a science fiction thriller, James Cameron's *Terminator 2: Judgment Day* and Kevin Reynold's notoriously unsuccessful aquatic answer to the Mad Max series, *Waterworld*. Notable examples of this late-century form of science fiction include Steven Spielberg's *Close Encounters of the Third Kind* and *ET the Extra-Terrestrial*; Ridley Scott's *Alien* and *Blade Runner*; James Cameron's *Aliens* and *The Abyss*, as well as his 'Terminator' films; *Independence Day* and *The Fifth Element*; and John Carpenter's *Starman* and *The Thing* (Carpenter also wrote and directed the funniest and most inspired of all science fiction comedies, *Dark Star*, made on a tiny budget, it found humour in both the unassuming conventions of the 1950s space adventures and the metaphysical pretensions of *2001*. Other parodies include the title segment of John Landis's compilation film *Amazon Women on the Moon* and Mel Brooks's *Spaceballs*). But the genre is not only a playground for the special-effects merchants; it has attracted some of the most austere and uncompromising of film-makers, including Jean-Luc Godard in *Alphaville* and his short film *Anticipation*, Andrei Tarkovsky in *Solaris* and *Stalker*, and Chris Marker in *La Jetée*, a time-travel narrative made up wholly (but for a single close-up) of stills – itself the inspiration for a better-known, louder and incomparably more expensive film, Terry Gilliam's *Twelve Monkeys*. Apart from a single freak occurence in 1851 in a book by one W. Wilson, the critical label 'science fiction' does not appear before the late 1920s, and seems to have been coined by the magazine editor Hugo Gernsback (immortalised by the annual Hugo awards for writers) in 1929, when he offered readers of *Science Wonder Stories* prizes of $50.00 for the best letter published each month on the theme of 'What Science Fiction Means to Me'. A coincidence worth noting: the first true science fiction story, H.G. Wells's *The Time Machine*, was first published in 1895, the Lumière year. 'The cinema, which itself must have seemed like a science-fictional device to the first generation which witnessed it, is a medium composed of the representation and manipulation of space and time; and Wells's description of travelling through time may have been inspired by his awareness of contemporary experimentation with the running forwards and backwards of strips of film' – from a lecture on Science Fiction by the author, delivered at London's South Bank Centre in 1996.

scoop   a wide-angle floodlight, which uses a hemispherical reflective surface and a bulb of between 500 and 1500 watts.

scope   the informal term for an anamorphic wide-screen technique, most obviously *CinemaScope*, from which it is derived.

score   as a noun, the soundtrack music for a film; as a verb, to compose soundtrack music. It originally meant the background music and effects produced in cinemas to accompany silent films, and took on its present meaning with the sound period: 'The score composed by Edmund Meisel for *Ten Days*' – Spottiswoode, *Grammar of Film*, 1935. *Scoring stage*, the sound stage, equipped with a large screen, on which the musicians record the score.

scout   person who seeks out suitable locations for filming (a *location scout*), suitable performers (a *talent scout*) etc. Hence *scouting*.

scratch, scratchprint (or **slap print, slash dupe, slash print, slop print**)   (a) a print, often black and white, struck from the completed work print, and used for dubbing and sound mixing; (b) a print that has been scratched throughout its length so that it will not be pirated. *Scratch track*, a rough sync recording used as a guide for actors in *dubbing* or *looping*.

screen   'Of difficult etymology', notes OED forebodingly, going on to discuss the ME *skrene*, Fr *écran* and OF *escran*, and recording various English uses from the late 14th C onwards – 'a contrivance for warding off the heat of a fire or a draught of air', and so on. In the cinematic senses, it means primarily: (1) the opaque, reflective, vertical surface on which film images are projected in a cinema or screening room; or, less often, the similar translucent surface used for rear projection. 'People . . . like to see on the screen what they read about' – *Moving Picture World*, 19 February 1910. (2) Thus, metaphorically, or more exactly metonymically, films or the cinema in general. 'Unlike the legitimate stage, the screen does not have to wait for a dramatist to become inspired before it may present the topic of the hour' – *New York Times*, 15 November 1915. Hence, for example, the title of *Screen*, the British Film Institute's journal of film theory; hence, too, such cliches as 'star of stage and screen' and *silver screen* – a stock phrase that was born in the silent period, when screens really did have a silvery glow, but has proved eerily durable, since sloppy writers still apply it to films of the early colour era and even to present-day films.

There are many, many associated terms and phrases, of which some of the more common include:

Screen Actor's Guild, the American trade union for cinema performers. The corresponding union for extras is the *Screen Extras Guild* or *SEG*; *screen brightness*, a measurement, in *candelas* per square foot, of the amount of light reflected by a screen; *screen credits*, either (a) a synonym for *credits*, or (b) a list of all the films on which a cast or crew member has worked (or is willing to admit to), often drawn up for professional purposes as part of a C.V. or the like; *screen direction* the direction, as seen by the camera and audience, in which a character moves towards the edge of the frame; *screening*, any occasion on which a film is shown to an audience, though the term generally refers to private showings of all or part of a film (such as *dailies* or *rushes*) to small groups of people within the film industry, usually in a medium-sized theatre or *screening room*; *screen ratio*, an alternative, less usual term for *aspect ratio*; *screen test*, a filmed (or, nowadays, taped) audition for an actor or other performer to establish their suitability for a part; *screen time*, a measurement of the actual running time of a film as opposed to the passage of days, weeks, months or years in its narrative.

screenplay   the written outline or *script* of a film, written by a *screenwriter* (also *script-writer* or, particularly within the industry, simply *writer*), and containing the dialogue, descriptions of the principal characters and settings, and sometimes a few basic camera directions; since one page of screenplay represents roughly a minute of running time, the average length of the screenplay for a standard feature is about 90 to 120 pages; hence *screenwriting*, the craft or art of the screenwriter. In the early years of the cinema, 'screenplay' or 'screen play' was a synonym for 'moving picture' – a play for the screen – and OED records this use as late as 1916. 'Anna Held's debut in a screen play' – *New York Times*, 7 February 1916. 'Screenwriter' or 'screen writer' was current by the 1920s: 'A Robertson-Cole picture . . . written by . . . two well-known screen writers' – *Moving Picture Stories*, 12 August 1921.

screwball comedy   one of the jewels of the classic Hollywood film: a phenomenon of the 1940s and early 1940s, short-lived and never quite rivalled, which crackled with Gatling-gun dialogue, sexual electricity, giddy action, florid eccentricity and startling moments of bleakness: think of Howard Hawks's *His Girl Friday* or *Bringing Up Baby* (the textbook example) or *Ball of Fire*, Preston Sturges' *The Lady Eve* or *The Palm Beach Story*, Frank Capra's *It Happened One Night* . . . Hollywood has lost the knack and apparently the taste for such intricate delights, although Peter Bogdanovich made a very creditable stab at reviving screwball a couple of decades ago in *What's Up, Doc?* (1972), the Coen Brothers made a partial pastiche of it in *The Hudsucker Proxy* (1994), and there are reminiscences of some of its classic components – the stuffy, virginal hero, the forceful or anarchic heroine or voraciously seductive heroine – in many other comic films, such as Carl Reiner's *The Jerk* (1978), written by and starring Steve Martin. It's also worth noting that, in its heyday, certain flavours of the form tended to seep over into other genres: Hawks's *The Big Sleep* has a wonderful scene in which Bacall and Bogart make a rapid-fire, prank phone call to a police station that is pure screwball. OED notes that the term began to occur in print from 1938 onwards (*New York Times*, 2 September: 'Metro-Goldwyn-

Mayer ... has popped up with another of those screwball comedies – this one called "Three Loves Has Nancy"'), which would be just a couple of years after the first screwball films were made. Some reference books contend that the earliest comedy to bring together all the key components was a largely forgotten film of 1935, *Remember Last Night?*, directed – incongruously, since he is best known for *Frankenstein* – by James Whale; a more conventional starting point is Howard Hawks's *Twentieth Century*, made in 1934. The word had previously meant and continues to mean 'eccentric' or 'maniac', particularly in the US, and is obviously associated with such expressions as 'to have a screw loose' (used by Trollope in *The Eustace Diamonds*, 1873) and the cricket and baseball slang term of mid-19th C onwards, 'screwball', meaning a ball that has been thrown with a reverse spin: the writers who started applied the term to film comedies were no doubt responding to the near-lunatic behaviour of such characters as Katherine Hepburn's leopard-loving heiress in *Bringing Up Baby* (1938). For a philosophical consideration of these films, which finds affinities between screwball comedy and Shakespearean Romance (particularly *The Winter's Tale*), see Stanley Cavell, *Pursuits of Happiness: The Hollywood Comedy of Remarriage* (Cambridge, Mass.: Harvard University Press, 1981).

scribe   a small metal tool used by an editor to etch directions – *scribe marks* – on film for the lab.

scrim   a translucent screen or *flag* used to diffuse the light from a lamp.

script   another, slightly less common term for *screenplay*, borrowed from the theatre where it has been in use since the late 19th C, an abbreviation for 'manuscript'. Associated terms include: *script breakdown* (or *breakdown*), (a) the process of analysing a screenplay in terms of its various locations and other requirements, so that its scenes can be shot in the cheapest and most efficient order; this task is usually carried out by the production manager; (b) the script supervisor's analysis of the timing for each scene. *Script doctor*, a professional, and usually highly paid screenwriter who is called in to 'rescue' a script that is deemed to be gravely inadequate in some way, usually on the eve of production or even when shooting is actually under way. The script doctor may not always be credited for such rescues, but word will usually get out anyway: Robert Towne, for example, is well known to have doctored many scripts, and in recent years Quentin Tarantino has also made some swift and lucrative house calls, grafting his knowing, pop-cultured dialogue on to more fatty tissue. *Script girl* (*script clerk, script supervisor*); the person, traditionally a woman, responsible for making full and detailed notes on each take – the position of furniture and other props, the actors' words and gestures, the length of ash on a burning cigarette – for the purpose of keeping a tight rein on continuity.

search pan   a type of *pan* in which the camera will appear to hunt around an area until it lights on the character or thing in which it is interested; in most cases, this will be some kind of *subjective shot*, representing, say, the viewpoint of a burglar as he cases a room.

second assistant cameraman   the crew member who loads and unloads magazines, fills out camera reports and, usually, operates the clapsticks; *second assistant director*, the crew member whose main tasks include handling the day-by-day paperwork of a production, such as call sheets, helping the First Assistant Director with crowd scenes and the like; *second camera*, a camera used in tandem with the main camera for scenes that would be difficult to re-stage, such as large-scale explosions; *second feature*, the B-movie in a double bill; *second unit*, a subsidiary crew, run by a *second unit director* – often a cameraman – which shoots sequences that do not involve the main cast, or any performers at all: backgrounds for *process shots*, *establishing shots* of exotic locations, *inserts* and so on. Curiously enough, a number of second unit directors have made modest critical reputations as well as lucrative careers from their specialised work, from B. Reaves Eason in the silent era to the likes of Yakima Canutt (*El Cid*, etc.). Incidentally, an uncredited second unit director of *Lawrence of Arabia* was that extraordinary Hungarian *cinéaste* and man of action, André de Toth; the main credits list only André Smagghe and Noel Howard.

segue   the transition from one scene to another, a passage that is often smoothed by a musical *bridge*. (The word is also used in other industries of mechanical reproduction and communication: in a running order for a live radio programme, for example, it indicates a movement from tape insert to tape insert, or from music to music, without any intervening remark by the presenter.) Pronounced, approximately, 'seg-way', and borrowed from the world of music, where it signifies a movement without pause from one piece to the next, it comes into English from the Italian, meaning 'it follows', in the early 18th C.

self-blimped camera   a lightweight camera, used for hand-held sequences and the like, silenced by its normal housing rather than a bulky sound-proofing container or *blimp*.

Selig   an early American production company, founded in 1896 by the inventor William N. Selig; best known for its one-reel Westerns directed by and starring Tom Mix, and various *serials*, including the first of its kind, *The Adventures of Kathlyn* (1913). After becoming one of the founding members of the *Motion Picture Patents Company* in 1909, Selig went on to merge with *Vitagraph*, *Lubin* and *Essanay* in 1915, thus becoming a key component of *VLSE*.

senior   a 5000-watt spotlight with a *Fresnel* lens.

sensitivity   the measurement of a film's responsiveness to light, usually expressed in terms of an *exposure index* such as an *ASA* number; *sensitometer*, a device used to test the responsiveness of film emulsions to light; hence *sensitometry*, the technology or science of exposure and development.

Sensurround   trade name for an audio gimmick developed by Universal Studios, which added low-frequency vibrations to sound-tracks, and so, in theory, gave the audience the sensation of being shaken by explosions, earth tremors and the like.

sepmag the term for a film which has a separate magentic sound-track, just as a *sepopt* has a separate optical sound-track.

sequel a film which picks up characters, stories or gimmickry that have already proved a success at the box-office and re-packages them in more or less derivative ways, such as the *Jaws* spin-offs, or the *Friday the Thirteenth* and *Hallowe'en* movies. It is often said that sequels are always and inevitably inferior to their originals, though there are some possible or unarguable exceptions: John Boorman's *Exorcist 2: The Heretic*, James Cameron's *Aliens* and *Terminator 2: Judgment Day*, Francis Ford Coppola's *Godfather 2*, *Addams Family Values* and so on.

sequence from L *sequentia*, from *sequent-em* and the verb *sequi*, to follow: 'For how art thou a King/But by faire sequence and succesion?' – Shakespeare, *Richard II*, 1593. In the cinema, a sequence is a group of *shots* that make up a coherent narrative unit, such as a single action: a fight sequence, a chase sequence, an escape sequence and so on. Generally speaking, a sequence will be made up of several *scenes*, though there are are times when it would be difficult to draw a sharp distinction between them – for example, the fight sequences in *Raging Bull* could equally well be termed fight scenes – and in practice the terms 'scene' and 'sequence' are often used as synonyms or near synonyms. 'Until recently, in all talking sequences, the actor has been compelled to be static' – *Morning Post*, 24 May 1929.

Sequence the short-lived (14 quarterly issues between 1946 and 1952) but disproportionately influential magazine of the Oxford University Film Society. Its editors included Lindsay Anderson, Penelope Houston and Gavin Lambert; its contributors included the famous (William Wyler, John Huston) and those on the brink of fame (Satyajit Ray, Karel Reisz); and it played something of the same role in British film culture as *Cahiers du Cinéma* did in French, serving as the first outlet for the ideas and beliefs which later found expression in the *Free Cinema* movement.

serial now rarely seen in the cinema, though still a staple of television production, the serial or *chapter play* – an extended narrative cut up and presented to the public in small chunks, week after week – thrived in the first half of the century, both in Hollywood and around the world. 'Serial', from L *serialis*, was the term applied to literary works which appeared in sucessive installments from the early 19th C; the cinema takes on the word a century later. Many of the more successful of these serials were inspired by comic book characters (Batman, Flash Gordon, Buck Rogers); the earliest comic strips began to appear in 1896, which means that the two popular art forms are almost exactly the same age. Almost all had what might be called a comic-book sensibility, relying on simple, fast-moving plots with clearly defined heroes and villains, each episode culminating in a *cliff-hanger* that would be resolved the following week thanks to shameless re-staging of each dilemma. Though long gone, these old serials are far from forgotten by film-makers, as the present-day phenomenon of the Batman films indicates: they have proved the direct inspiration for such crowd-pleasers as *Raiders of the Lost Ark* and the *Star Wars* films. Not all serial products were aesthetically negligible: the immensely popular serials made by Louis Feuillade (1873–1925) in France before and during the First World War – especially *Fantômas* (1913), *Les Vampires* (1915–16) and *Judex* (1916) – were enthusiastically admired by the Surrealists, and are still held in high esteem by many *cinéphiles*. The first true serial is said to have been *The Adventures of Kathlyn* (1913), produced by the *Selig* company, though it was the tremendous success of Pathé's *The Perils of Pauline* (1914) which really brought the serial to the fore of production. The decline of the serial in the years after the Second World War was largely due to the rise of television; it was pretty much defunct by the early 1950s. Compare:

series   a succession of short or feature-length films featuring the same character. The cinema series both predated and outlived the *serial*, since it was born in 1908 in several different countries: France (the Nick Carter series), Norway (the Raffles series), and the US (the Broncho Billy series); England followed suit in 1909 with The Dandy Detective. In the United States, the series was one of the staples of *B-movie* production, particularly *westerns* (such as the Roy Rogers and Gene Autry films for Republic), but also *thrillers* (Charlie Chan, Mr Moto, The Thin Man, Sherlock Holmes), comedies and horror films. Nowadays, it is not always easy to distinguish a feature film series from a run of *sequels*; nor is it particularly enlightening; though, if one were pushed on the point, a useful rule of thumb might be the presence or absence of numerals in the title: thus, *Rocky II*, *Rocky III* and *Rocky IV* could be thought of as pure sequels, where *From Russia With Love*, *Goldfinger* and *Thunderball* are early films in the James Bond series, and so on.

servo mechanism, servomechanism   an electronic system used for the slow, steady adjustment of lenses on occasions when manual operation would be too fast or too irregular.

sestina   the only film made in compliance with sestina form appears to be *Gustave Flaubert. Le Travail de l'écrivain* (1974), a short written by the great Oulipian Georges Perec, and directed by Bernard Queysanne. The film's commentary is a pastiche of a textbook or reference book, read twice over (by Jacques Spiesser), with all the punctuation spelled out as though for a school dictation exercise. Images of Flaubert, of Louise Colet, and of the Flaubert museum at Croisset recur in new and varied combinations in a manner analogous to the repeated end-words of the sestina.

set   the place where a given scene or a whole production is shot, but particularly a location that has been purpose-built for the production; the movies plundered the term from the stage as early as the first decade of this century (OED's first citation is from 1912). *Set decorator*, the person who furnishes the set scene by scene – that is, who installs and arranges the props and other *set dressings*; *set designer*, the person who, after consultation with the production designer or art director, plans the construction of a film's various sets; *setting*, the fictional time and place within which a film's narrative runs its course; *setup*, *set-up*, the positioning (a) of the camera, and (b) of the actors and lighting for a given shot.

70mm film   save for the *Imax* format, 70mm film is the widest gauge used in professional film-making, being twice the size of the standard 35mm gauge, with an *aspect ratio* of 2.2 to 1; it is usually reserved for highly spectacular releases or re-releases, such as that of the reconstructed *Lawrence of Arabia*. See also *65mm*.

sexploitation movie   a portmanteau of *exploitation movie* and 'sex': a medium- or soft-core pornographic feature, such as the lucrative adventures of large-breasted women written and directed by Russ Meyer. The word has been part of US slang since the 1940s, meaning any kind of commercial manipulation of the sex drive, and had become particularly associated with films by the 1960s. For a similar portmanteau label, see *blaxploitation*.

SFX   a common abbreviation for *special effects* (see also *FX*) or, sometimes, *sound effects*.

shallow focus   the opposite of *deep focus*: in an image with shallow focus, only a small depth of field is kept in sharp definition while the rest of the picture is blurred; directors can use the technique to keep the audience's attention fixed on the part of the picture which has the greatest narrative or psychological content.

Shell Film Unit   a documentary production unit set up in 1933, and dedicated to making films on subjects ranging from aircraft manufacture to pest control. It was founded at the suggestion of John Grierson, and continued to make films for more than two decades.

shoot   as a verb: to film all or part of a movie. 'He ... debated whether it should be "shot" with two cameras or three' – B.M. Bower, *Phantom Herd*, 1916; as a noun: either one day's filming, or the whole business of filming a particular movie over the course of several days, weeks, months or (exceptionally) years. Interestingly, 'shoot' – which comes from OE *sceotan*, and has as its earliest denotations various acts of going swiftly or suddenly – has been associated with the activities of light for some three centuries: 'I was as soon sensible as any Man of that Light, when it was but just shooting out, and beginning to travel upwards to the Meridian' – Dryden, *Juvenal*, 1693. The cinema takes on the word from still photography ('Does he shoot when his companion did?' – *Anthony's Photography Bulletin*, 1890), and photography seems to have taken it from archery and gunnery – 'shoot' and its variants has meant 'to let fly from an engine' since the 10th C.

There are many associated cinematic terms, most of them using the form *shooting*, a synonym for *filming*, either in the sense (a) of recording specific actions on camera or (b) of making a whole production. Hence: *shooting call,* see **call**; *shooting company,* another term for the *crew*; *shooting ratio,* the ratio of the amount of film shot to the amount of film in the final release print. Generally speaking, the higher the shooting ratio, the more expensive the film: notorious examples from recent years include Michael Cimino's *Heaven's Gate* and Elaine May's *Ishtar,* though high shooting ratios were far from the only extravagances of these features; *shooting schedule,* the timetable and logistical plan of a production, put together from the breakdown sheets and the production board; *shooting script,* the final version of a screenplay, used on the set or location by director and key members of the crew, and including not just the dialogue and general directions found in the screenplay presented by the writer, but details of the camera set-ups for each scene and other logistical information; *shooting wild,* to film without sound.

short   (in the United States, sometimes called a **short subject**), a film with a running time of around 30 minutes or less, such as the brief dramas or documentaries made by film students for their graduation exercises, or as 'calling cards' for the industry.

short end   the unexposed film left over when the relevant sections of exposed film have been cut away; students, and other poor but resourceful directors, have often shot their films from salvaged short ends.

shot   'Bill and Tommy were both below examining the effect of their "shots" of the evening before' – B.M. Bower, *Parowan Bonanza,* 1923. (a) The smallest individual element of film grammar: a single, continuous image that may last for less than a second (as a subliminal flash) or an entire reel (as in the 10-minute shots of Hitchcock's *Rope,* or the elaborate and self-advertising *tracking shot* which opens Altman's *The Player*), and which may range over any number of different subjects and move through any number of different angles, but only ends with a *cut* to a new shot. The typology of shots is elaborate, though most of these designations simply indicate how the camera moves during the shot (*pan shot, tilt shot* etc.), how many people it contains (*two shot, three shot*), what relationship it has to the subject – how close or far away (*medium shot, long shot* etc.) – and what part it plays in the grammar of the film (*establishing shot* etc.): among the most important are the *crane shot, dolly shot, follow shot, high shot, insert shot, low shot, master shot, pan shot, reaction shot, tracking* or *travelling shot* and *zoom shot.* (b) A shot can also refer to each occasion during filming when the cameras rolled uninterruptedly, and to the celluloid results of that filming; 'We were losing daylight, so we had to try and get the scene in one shot.'

Associated terms include: *shot analysis,* a close study of every shot of a film, either for academic or critical purposes, or as part of a financial review of a production; *shot breakdown,* a list of all the shots to be filmed on a given day or for a whole production, usually printed up with a list of cast, crew, location and logistical details; *shot list,* a list of all the shots that were filmed during a production, arranged in the order in which they were made; *shot/reverse shot*, a standard technique for filming dialogue; see *invisible cutting*.

shotgun mike   a highly directional microphone, often used to record dialogue in circumstances – such as a battle scene – where the background is extremely noisy.

show reel   a film, or more usually videotape, sent out to prospective employers of a performer or director, showing samples of their earlier work.

shutter   the standard device in both still and motion cameras, set between the *aperture* and the film, which exposes film to light when the frame is in position and shields it from light as each frame is advanced; hence the related terms *shutter control*, the mechanism by which the shutter can be opened or closed; *shutter release*, a mechanism, often used in *stop-motion* work, which allows the shutter to be opened and closed from a distance, by means of a cable, so that the camera does not wobble even slightly; *shutter speed*, the length of time for which a shutter opens to expose film.

side car mount   see *camera mount*; *sidekick*, the hero's (or, less often, the heroine's) pal, *confidant(e)* and helper, esepcially in an adventure or comedy-adventure movie: Sancho Panza to the Don, Robin to Batman, Rocky to Bullwinkle; *side light*, another name for a *cross light*, illumination from right or left; *side viewfinder*, a type of camera viewfinder which sits on the side of the casing, parallel to the lens, and is often adjusted for *parallax*.

Sight and Sound   a magazine of criticism, commentary and debate about the cinema, published under the auspices of the British Film Institute. It grew from a journal with rather different intentions, the *Quarterly Review of Modern Aids*, founded in 1932 in response to a series of exhibitions held in London demonstrating the possible educational functions of radio, film and television. The *BFI*, founded in 1934, took the magazine over within a few months, changing its title to *Sight and Sound, a Review of Modern Aids to Learning*; as this suggests, it was still primarily concerned with the educational possibilities of the cinema, but it gradually developed into a forum for discussion of the cinema as an art, and was widely acknowledged – even in North America – as the most distinguished journal of its kind in English. It is now published on a monthly basis, having absorbed and taken over the function of the old *Monthly Film Bulletin*, which gives full production details of every film released in the United Kingdom, as well as a detailed synopsis and short critical assessment.

silent   an actor who has no lines, but whose activity or inactivity plays some significant part in the development of a scene.

silent films   either (a) film shot without sound, whether for technical, economic or aesthetic reasons, or more usually (b) almost all of the films made in the period from the Lumières to *The Jazz Singer*, which is to say

1895 to 1927, before adequate systems of synchronised sound came into general use; the adjective can also be applied to any aspect of that period, as, for example in Budd Schulberg's novel *What Makes Sammy Run?* (1941): 'He was married to one of the big silent stars'. Associated terms include *silent frame*, the aspect ratio of 1.33:1 that was standard for 35mm film in the pre-talkie period, before part of the film had to be given over to the sound tracks; *silent print*, see *picture print*: *silent speed*, the appropriate speed for silent film, which is to say, around 16 to 18 frames per second.

silk (or **butterfly**)   a rectangular cloth used to diffuse light, especially natural light. These were originally made of real silk, but are now manufactured from artificial, fireproof fabrics.

silver halide   the generic name for crystals in film emulsion which respond to light so as to form a latent image which can be brought out by developing chemicals; the halides in question are silver bromide, chloride and iodide.

silver screen   a hackneyed metonymy for the cinema, as in the phrase 'star of the silver screen', which dates from the black and white period when films did have such a silvery glow: 'Somehow there had crept into this new field of endeavour the romance of the silver screen' – R. Brown, *Talking Pictures*, 1931. See also *screen*.

single   a shot of just one person, either speaking or silent – that is, a *one shot*; *single card*, an actor's, producer's, writer's or director's credit that appears on screen alone (this is often a condition stipulated in contracts); where two or more names appear at the same time, the credit is called a *shared card*; *single-frame exposure*, the process of exposing film stock frame by frame rather than at normal speeds; this technique is the basis of both *stop-frame animation* and of *time-lapse photography* (such as that in Godfrey Reggio's *Koyanisqaatsi*); *single-shot technique*, a style of shooting which dispenses with the usual alternation between a *master* shot and various different angles on the same action, and instead relies on a series of individual shots of an action, edited into the illusion of continuous activity; *single system sound*, the technique of recording sound and image onto the same film, generally for news footage; the sound quality that results from this method tends to be poorer than that achieved by the more standard *double system*, in which sound and image are kept separate.

sixteen millimetre, 16mm   a professional film gauge, smaller and less expensive than the 35mm stock which is standard for features, mainly used for *documentaries*, television films and low-budget features. It was first produced by Kodak as a *safety film* for amateur use in 1923; the company had previously considered a gauge of 17.5mm, but opted for 16mm pretty much at random, it is said, because it was feared that crooked dealers would simply slice the highly inflammable 35mm *nitrate* stock in half and pass it off on the innocent.

65mm   is the true gauge on which *70mm* films are shot; the additional 5mm on *release prints* are taken up by sound tracks.

skin flick   common slang for a pornographic film or *blue movie*. OED suggests that the term came into use in the early 1960s or thereabouts.

skip framing   a technique used to speed up action, by passing over every other frame when printing the film; the reverse process is known as *double printing*; *skipping* is another term for the jerky effect otherwise known as *strobing*.

skull shot   uncommon and rather violent slang term for a *close-up*.

slapstick   the violent, knockabout comedy style characteristic of the *Keystone* productions and other comedies of the silent period, and still employed from time to time in less cerebral films today. 'Charlie Chaplin has intimate and painter's qualities in his acting, and he makes himself into a painting or an etching in the midst of furious slapstick' (Vachel Lindsay, *The Art of the Moving Picture*). The term is said to come from a gadget (also known as a flexible lath) which was used by stage performers in Vaudeville to make a tremendous racket when hitting the fall-guy or stooge. For a discussion of the specifically cinematic development of slapstick, see James Agee's essay 'Comedy's Greatest Era' in *Agee on Film*, Volume I.

slasher, slasher film, stalk and slash, slice-and-dice film   a gory sub-category of the *horror* movie, highly popular in the 1980s, which runs minor variations on the theme of young people, especially attractive teenage girls, being mutilated and killed by a knife- or axe-wielding maniac or maniacs. Amomg the best-known of these films are the *Friday the 13th* series, though the vogue for such imbecile productions began with John Carpenter's *Hallowe'en,*, which, despite its unfortunate progeny, was in many repects a tense (rather than merely repellent) and well-crafted thriller. See also *splatter movie*.

slate   (a), another name for the *clapsticks* or *clapperboard*, or more specifically (b) the part of the clapperboard on which production details are written.

sleeper   a film which does poor business on its first release, but which eventually earns a good deal of money (or at least a *succès d'estime* or *cult movie* status).

slide   a transparent print of a *still*, mounted and used, sometimes, in making *rear-projection* shots.

slop mix   jargon for a rough early mix of the sound-track, just as a *slop print* is usually another term for a *scratch print*. A *slop test* is an on-the-spot processing of exposed film, carried out with portable developing equipment, to make a rough check of image quality.

slow   the most important of the cinema's various 'slow' terms is *slow motion*, an effect achieved by filming action at speeds faster than 24 frames per second and then projecting them at normal speed. In most instances, slow motion sequences feel 'lyrical', even when the action shown is violent. Such moments became a trademark of the films of Sam

Peckinpah, who has inspired countless epigones; among the most recent is the Hong Kong director John Woo. Jean-Claude Carrière says that slow-motion is 'almost always an aesthetic disaster', and not without justice, but that qualifying 'almost' is crucial: though the technique is often used crudely or lazily, in the hands of a gifted director it has been and can still be one of the most affecting devices of the medium. The theorist Pudovkin called slow motion 'a close-up in time'. Other significant 'slow' words include *slow film* (or *stock*), which requires longer exposure or more light than ordinary film but produces extremely high-quality images, and *slow in/slow out*, the technique of moving a camera fairly slowly at the beginning and end of a *pan* or *dolly* or other movement so that the visual effect is not too jarring.

slug a length of leader that is cut into a work print to stand in for sequences that have not been edited, processed or shot.

smash cut an extremely abrupt cut from one action to another, often made for comic effect; as I write, I have in front of me a production script for an episode of *The Simpsons* which uses this direction several times.

smellies slang term for the cinema's various gimmicky ventures into the olfactory zone made between the 1950s and the 1970s, from *AromaRama*, which introduced smells into the cinema's usual ventilation system, to *Odorama*, the scratch-and-sniff card system devised by John Waters for his film *Polyester*. The most elaborate of such gimmicks was *Smell-O-Vision*, dreamed up by Mike Todd Jr for *Smell of Mystery* (1960): a series of pipes wafted aromas to each seat in the house. Unkind souls, recalling the producer's earlier gimmick *Todd-AO*, christened it 'Todd-BO'.

Smithee, Alan (or sometimes Allen) a name beloved of all true film buffs: it is the fictitious director's credit (the only one allowed by the Directors Guild of America) put on films when the true director has gone off in a huff after the producers have made unwelcome changes to his final cut. The name is said to have been coined in 1969 for the release of *Death of a Gunfighter*, directed two years earlier by (first) Robert Totten and (second) Don Siegel, both of whom disowned the end product.

sneak preview a one-off screening of a film to the general public before its official release date, either to check the audience's reponse or to stimulate rumours and excitment about it.

snoot a cone fitted on to a lamp to help direct its light.

Socialist Realism a blight on the Soviet cinema, as it was on all the other arts of the USSR. The brief and extraordinary flowering of cinematic brilliance in the early post-revolutionary days ('For us', said Lenin, 'cinema is the most important of the arts') and the freedom enjoyed by the likes of Dovzhenko, Eistenstein, Pudovkin and Vertov under the New Economic Policy, gave way to a era of philistinism, paranoia and slick idiocy which lasted from around 1928 (the beginning of Stalin's first Five-Year Plan) to 1953 (when the mass murderer died). A key year is 1935: the release date of the first full-blooded Socialist Realist movie *Chapayev*, directed by Sergei and Georgy Vasiliev, a highly successful feel-good adventure story about a Red Army hero which tickled Stalin no end; and also the year of the Kino conference before the Moscow Film Festival, at which recent work by Dovzhenko, Eisenstein and Vertov came under fierce critical fire. There have been many accounts of this period; see, for example, Jay Leyda's *Kino; a History of the Russian and Soviet Film* (1960).

soft focus   (a) the accidental fuzziness in an image caused by clumsy focussing of the camera lens, (b) a deliberately hazy effect created with *filters* or *gauze*, usually to create a romantic or dream-like atmosphere, or to flatter the appearance of an actress; *soft light*, either (a) a type of bulb (also called a *softlite*), or (b) a diffused light source which gives a scene a mildly glowing look; *soft wipe* (*soft-edge wipe*), a *wipe* with fuzzy rather than sharp edges.

soubrette   a term taken over from the theatre, meaning the stock type of a flirtatious young woman or the actress who plays such a role. The first soubrettes were lady's maids, who played the part of the *confidante* in French 18th C comedies. The word originated in the Provençale *soubreto*, from *soubret*, 'coy, reserved', itself from the verb *soubra*, 'to set aside'. It has been used in English since the mid-18th C.

sound   broadly speaking, every audible component of films made in the post-silent period – *dialogue, score, voice-over* and so on – recorded either on to magnetic tape or magnetic film. Of the many specific terms associated with the word, the more important include: *sound advance*, the distance – 21 frames in the case of optical sound systems – by which the sound-track must precede the picture frame for image and sound to be correctly in sync (see *advance*); *sound camera*, a modern camera that has been *blimped* so that the noise of its mechanism will not be picked up by microphones; *sound crew*, the team responsible for sound recording; on a standard feature, this will usually be made up of three people: the main *sound man* or *soundman* (otherwise the *recordist* or *production mixer*), the *boom operator* and the *cable puller*. On a more modest production, the recordist may have to perform all three jobs alone; *sound dissolve*, the auditory equivalent of, or accompaniment to, a *dissolve*, created by fading down the outgoing scene as the incoming scene is faded up; *sound effects (SFX)*, the atmospheric and other noises – wind, waves, explosions, bird song, applause – added to the sound track from library (*sound effects library*) recordings or some other source rather than recorded at the moment of shooting (see *Foley*); *sound head*, the component in a projector that reads the optical or magnetic sound track as film passes through its body; *sound mixer*, (a) the technician, also known as the *dubbing mixer*, who is in charge of mixing the various sound tracks, (b) the various pieces of electronic equipment used in mixing; *sound perspective*, the auditory counterpart to pictorial perspective

– sounds in the distance must seem to come from far away and so on; *sound speed*, the rate at which film must pass through the camera when a scene is being shot in sync; *sound stage*, the barn-like studio buildings inside which films are shot; *sound track*, either (a) the individual channel on which a film's dialogue, or its music, or its sound effects is recorded; or (b), more commonly, and abbreviation for the *composite sound track* or *optical sound track* created by mixing these tracks together, and printing them on to the side of the film. It can also mean (c) the CD, tape or album of a film's musical score.

soup   slang name for the chemical bath in which film is developed.

source lighting, source music   respectively, light and music which comes, or appears to come from some obvious, visible source on screen – candles (say, in the interior scenes of *Barry Lyndon*, for which Kubrick used special lenses and stock), a saxophonist jamming (say, in *Bird*). The latter is also known as *direct music*.

Sovcolor   the name of a type of colour film used in the Soviet Union after about 1950; it was based on *Agfacolor*, since the USSR had seized that company's factory at Wolfen at the end of the Second World War.

spaghetti Western   the familiar or jocular term for those low-budget Italian-made *Westerns* which flourished in the 1960s and helped launch the international career of Clint Eastwood, and which might just as logically be known as 'paella Westerns', since many of them were shot on location in Spain. The most famous and accomplished examples of the genre – *A Fistful of Dollars*, *Once Upon a Time in the West* – were made by Sergio Leone; by the time of Alex Cox's curious, partly parodic *Straight to Hell*, and the Comic Strip's wholly parodic *A Fistful of Traveller's Cheques*, the form appeared to be beyond resuscitation. For a scholarly history of the form, see Christopher Frayling's definitive *Spaghetti Westerns*.

sparks   slang term, on British productions, for an electrician.

special effects   also abbreviated to (*SP-FX*), generally (a) any image that is created or contrived by technical means, whether mechanical (that is, created in front of the camera) such as artificial rain storms, fogs, fires and the like, or photographic (created with the camera or in processing), or by some combination of the two. With the flourishing of science-fiction or fantasy movies in the last couple of decades, however, the term has come particularly to mean (b) the fantastic or spectacular images made possible by advances in optical techniques.

spectacle   informal term for any movie which appeals to its audience primarily by flaunting its massive production budgets, manifest in huge sets, elaborate special effects and the like, from the early epics of Cecil B. de Mille to the late 1990s versions of the disaster movie, such as *Dante's Peak* and *Volcano*.

speed   either (a) the rate at which film passes through a camera (or projector, or printer), measured in terms of *FPS* or *Frames Per Second*, or (b) the index of a film's sensitivity to light, usually measured in *ASA* numbers. The cry of *speed!* is the sound man's indication to the director that the sound tapes are running fast enough to synchronise with the film travelling through the camera.

spider   a gadget used to stabilise cameras that are mounted on tripods; not to be confused with a *spyder dolly*. *Spider box*, slang term for a junction box – an electrical box with several outlets.

spill, spill light   accidental illumination, or illumination that is unintentionally bright.

splatter film   an extremely violent *exploitation* film, so called because its major selling point is the gruesome sight of human flesh being splattered across the screen. The term appears to have been made current by the American film writer John McCarty in his book *Splatter Movies: Breaking the Last Taboo of the Screen*; see also his *Official Splatter Movie Guide* (St Martin's Press, New York, 1989). Though their excesses now seem relatively mild, Tobe Hooper's *The Texas Chainsaw Massacre* and Abel Ferrara's *Driller Killer* are the most notorious examples. Hooper and Ferrara both went on to careers in the mainstream cinema, the former directing *Poltergeist* for Steven Spielberg, the latter making the likes of *Bad Lieutenant* and *Dangerous Game*; and Hollywood itself began to borrow certain elements from the splatter movie in the 1980s, indulging in spectacles of violence which would formerly have been thought intolerable. For more detailed discussion of these and related matters, see Kim Newman's *Nightmare Movies*.

splice   the most basic act of editing: to join two pieces of film together, either by overlapping and gluing them (a *hot splice* or *cement splice*) or by joining them end to end and taping them (a *dry splice* or *tape splice*). The tool with which this task is accomplished has the generic name of a *splicer*, and comes in several forms.

split-field lens   a lens so designed that it can hold two distinct planes in focus simultaneously; that is, which can be used to produce *split focus*, a means of keeping actions in the foreground and background in focus at the same time.

split screen   the simple special effect created by combining one or more distinct images within a single frame, usually to suggest simultaneous but physically distinct actions – the two sides of a telephone conversation, for example. Mike Wadleigh's famous documentary of the rock festival *Woodstock* used the device frequently, to give multiple perspectives on the performer's act or to show the responses of the audience.

spool   the cylindrical gadget around which film is wound for filming or projection; in the latter case, then, a synonym for *reel*.

spot, spotlight   a lamp that can be focused so as to cast light quite precisely on the object or person to be filmed.

spotting session   a meeting held in post-production between the director, editor, composer and others to decide where and how the musical score should be placed. *Spotting*, locating dialogue and other sounds by running film through a *Moviola*.

sprockets, sprocket wheels   the tiny notched wheels in a camera (or projector, or printer) which move the film along; they fit into the *sprocket holes* at the side of the film. 'Old, dry films jump because the sprocket holes are shrunken' – F.H. Richardson, *Motion Picture Handbook*, 1910. 'Of obscure origin', says OED, though also of considerable vintage: the account books of St John's Hospital, Canterbury for the year 1536 record a payment 'To Nycoles & Horton for makyng sprokettis . . .'

spyder dolly   a more compact and portable substitute for a *crab dolly*.

spy film   though there had been many films about espionage before the period (including some wonderful movies by Hitchcock, such as *Notorious*) and quite a few since, the Golden Age of the spy movie was obviously the Cold War period, and particularly the 1960s, when the tremendous international success of the James Bond series inspired any number of more or less distinguished epigones, from the relatively serious films based on Len Deighton's unglamorous hero (played by Michael Caine, and given the movie name of 'Harry Palmer' for his outings in *The Ipcress File, Funeral in Berlin* and so on) to sillier or more openly parodic vehicles for the likes of Dean Martin (the Matt Helm series) and James Coburn (*Our Man Flint*, 1966). More recently, James Cameron has attempted to find fun in the old war-horse with the Arnold Schwarzenegger vehicle *True Lies*, and the Bond series looks set to continue into the next millennium.

squeeze lens   an *anamorphic* lens; *squeeze ratio*, the squashing down of an image by means of an anamorphic lens.

squib   a small electrical gadget which, when triggered, gives the effect of a bullet striking its target.

stabiliser   either (a) a camera mount designed to keep the camera steady, for example during *hand-held* shots, or (b) a chemical wash used to fix the image during processing.

stag film   a pornographic film or *blue movie* intended for heterosexual men; like 'Stag Party', the pre-marital debauch at which such films were traditionally shown, the term is now slightly quaint. Susan Sontag once listed 'stag films viewed without lust' as an example of camp sensibility.

stage   see *sound stage*.

stalk-and-slash film   see *slasher*.

stand-in   a person with roughly the same build, features, complexion and hair colour as a leading player, who has the boring job of substituting for their famous counterpart while lighting and camera positions are being worked out.

Stanislavsky method   see *Method*.

star (or **film star, movie star**)   an actor or actress famous enough to attract a sizeable audience by his or her presence in a production, and featured primarily in leading roles or tantalising *cameos*. The word 'star' came to mean a person of brilliant reputation or talents (presumably because they were held to shine like celestial bodies, were looked up to, had heavenly associations . . .) by the late 18th C, and particularly in the theatre. OED's earliest citation of a cinematic sense is from 1914: 'The greatest film stars in the world' – R. Grau, *Theatre of Science*, but the term still seemed to be novel enough by 1923 for *Chambers's Journal* to use inverted commas: 'A number of very beautiful women have earned untold riches as "film-stars".'

star system   the famous method, first hatched by the Hollywood studios in the silent period, for making leading players into well-nigh guaranteed money-spinners by a shrewd combination of well-orchestrated publicity campaigns and stringent contracts. The earliest true star of the star system is said to have been Florence Lawrence (1888–1938), since she was the first player to be given a screen credit in her own name by the producer Carl Laemmele (see *IMP*), having previously enjoyed considerable success with *Biograph* as 'the Biograph girl'. Her career set a precedent which was rapidly followed: studios began to fabricate elaborate myths around the public personae of their contracted players, both female (Theda Bara, Mary Pickford) and male (Douglas Fairbanks, Rudolph Valentino). The studio which carried the star system to its most refined and, in some cases, near-tyrannical degree was *MGM* ('more stars than there are in the heavens'): Judy Garland is often held to be its most conspicuous casualty. The system began to wane as the *studio system* itself went into decline, and was largely defunct by the late 1950s.

starlet   a somewhat dated, and generally rather demeaning term, applied to pretty young actresses whose careers were in the ascendent.

Start   a Polish film society which, during its few years of active life (1930–35), acted both as centre for the discussion and dissemination of film theory, and as a production base for non-commercial film-making; a number of distinguished directors, including Wanda Jakubowska, were among its founder members. The name signifies 'Society of the Devotees of the Artistic Film'.

start marks   small marks made at the beginning of a strip or reel of film, indicating the point at which *printing*, *projection* or the like should begin.

static shot   as the name states, a shot taken by a camera which does not move. Eyes trained by the commercial film-making of Hollywood and its fellow-travellers, which has become ever more fidgety (particularly since the early 1980s, when MTV started to teach younger viewers to be impatient with anything less than a hyperactive style of shooting and editing), may find films composed largely of static shots – those, for example, of the great Japanese director Ozu – rather unnerving; *static marks*, discolourations on film caused either by friction within the camera or by clumsy handling.

Steadicam   the trade name for a widely-used device which balances hand-held cameras gyroscopically so that the resulting images are smooth and fluent. The corresponding device made by Panavision is known as the *Panaglide*.

Steenbeck   the brand name of an editing machine. It has become so commonly used in recent years that, in Britain at least, 'Steenbeck' has become the loose generic term for all editing machines.

step printer (or **step optical printer**)   the optical printer used for *step printing*, a process in which film is developed a frame at a time, so as to ensure the steadiness of *travelling mattes*.

stereophonic sound   an audio system, common in the cinema (as well as professional and domestic audio systems) since the 1950s. Stereophonic recording and reproduction makes for a more realistic and/or dramatic sound quality. *Stereoscopy*, the more formal term for the process of making three-dimensional moving images, more commonly known as *3D*.

still   'A striking "still" from the film "The Fall of a Nation"' – caption to a photograph published in the *Independent* (not the present-day British newspaper of the same name) for 5 June 1916. A still is either (a) any photograph of some aspect of a production, taken while it is in the process of being made – that is to say, a 'production still', or (b) a frame still, blown up from a single frame of the completed film, or (c) the standard 8 x 10 glossy photographs of actors. The on-set photographer employed to produce such images is sometimes called the *still man*.

stock (or **raw stock**)   the raw material of film, stored in *reels*, and used for three main different purposes: shooting, printing and duplicating. (The term is as old as cinema, or very nearly: 'The film is of transparent celluloid, one side of which is coated with a sensitive emulsion, that for the negative being much more rapid than the positive stock' – C.F. Jenkins, *Picture Ribbons*, 1897.) References to 'stock', however, almost always mean 'film stock': as Mr Jenkins's early definition explained, this is made up of a *base*, nowadays usually made of a non-inflammable substance such as cellulose tri-acetate, and several layers of light-sensitive *emulsion*, each one designed to react to a different range of the visible light spectrum. In the early part of the century, film stock was generally based on cellulose *nitrate*, but this was superseded by *safety film* in or around 1951.

stock footage, stock shots   period film, newsreel footage and the like that can be edited together with newly shot dramatic or documentary footage. For example, in Philip Kaufman's *The Unbearable Lightness of Being*, stock monochrome footage of the Soviet invasion of Czechoslovakia is intercut with carefully matched shots of the leading players.

stop, stops (or **lens stop**)   the pre-set positions to which a lens *aperture* (or *diaphragm*) may be opened; hence *stop down*, to reduce the amount of light entering the lens by closing down the aperture; lens aperture is measured in *f-stops*, which go higher as the aperture grows smaller; *stop frame motion* (or *stop motion*, *stop motion animation*), a form of animation which involves the use of models, puppets or other three-dimensional figures, and *single frame exposure*. The technique was once a staple of amateur film-making, and in Agnes Varda's *Jacquot de Nantes*, a touching dramatised documentary about her late husband, Jacques Demy, there are several scenes portraying how the youthful Jacquot made his first steps towards a directing career with cut-out cardboard figures and a second-hand 8mm movie camera. Though dauntingly time-consuming, the stop-frame method can yield delightful effects: recent and notable instances of the stop-frame method include Nick Park's wonderfully funny, Oscar-winning shorts *Creature Comforts* and *The Wrong Trousers*, and the full-length feature by Tim Burton, *The Nightmare Before Christmas*. It is also widely used in television commercials, such as those made by *Aardman* Animation (which is Nick Park's production base).

story analyst another term for a *reader*; *storyboard*, a series of drawings, similar to a comic strip, representing either the sequence of shots in a complictated action scene, or, less frequently, every shot that will eventually make up the completed film. *Story conference*, a meeting between the *screenwriter* or writers and the director, producers or studio representatives; *story department*, the team responsible for judging, summarising and, where appropriate, passing on to executives the many *properties* that are submitted to or solicited by a major studio; *story editor*, a senior member of a story department who supervises the work of a number of readers or analysts.

straight cut a simple cut from one shot to the next, as opposed to a *fade, wipe* or some other transitional effect; *straight man*, as on the stage, the performer who acts as the butt of or foil to the comic hero.

straight-to-video an adjectival phrase designating the kind of production that is either so low-budget, *avant garde*, commercially unappealing, artistically unaccomplished or simply awful that it has no theatrical distribution at all, but is simply dumped on the video market.

street film the critical label for a group of German films made in the years from 1923 to 1930, which told the tales of respectable but bored citizens lured away from their homes by the temptations of the big city. (The reasons for its decline after 1930 will be obvious.) Probably the most famous example of the genre is Pabst's *Die Freudlose Gasse* (*Joyless Street*, 1925), though the most influential was Karl Grune's *Die Strasse*, which began the tendency. The term was coined by the film historian and aesthetician Siegfried Kracauer (1889–1966) in his famous psychological history of the German film *From Caligari to Hitler* (1947).

stretching a technique for converting film shot at silent camera speeds (16 frames per second) to modern speed (24 frames per second), using an *optical printer* to print every other frame twice.

strike (a) as in the expression 'to strike camp': to take down a set when every scene has been completely shot; (b) to make a print from a negative.

strobe, strobing (a) the high speed on-and-off flashing – created by a

strobe light (or *stroboscopic light*) – that gives moving objects the appearance of jerking bizarrely, and became something of a cliché in the disco
scenes of thrillers and psychological dramas of the late 1970s and early
1980s, or (b) an effect which sometimes occurs during projection, when
objects appear to jitter awkwardly across the screen rather than move
smoothly; the most common cause of this visual oddity is a *pan* that is
executed too rapidly, so that the usual *persistence of vision* phenomenon is broken up.

Stroboscope   an early 19th C precursor of the cinema, similar in
principle to the *Zoetrope* and the *phenakistiscope*, and like those
gadgets, inspired by Roget's publication of his discovery of *persistence
of vision* in 1824. The Stroboscope was the invention of Dr Simon
Stampfer (1792–1864), a professor of Vienna; he took out a patent on
his 'stroboscopic discs' on 7 May 1833.

structural film   a term ˙ sometimes applied to a particular kind of
(mostly American) *avant-garde* or *experimental* film, of which the
most famous example is probably Michael Snow's *Wavelength* (1967),
which consists of what appears to be a single zoom shot. As this example
may suggest, structural films are non-representational, non-narrative
exercises, and are more concerned with the fundamental elements of
vision and cinema technology than with the habitual subjects of film-
making. The BFI published a book of writings on the subject, *Structural
Film Anthology* (1976); the term itself is said to have been coined by the
American writer and *avant-garde* apologist P. Adams Sitney in 1969.

student film   a low-budget film, usually a *short*, made by film students
as part of their course. Such films will often be made as graduation
exercises.

studio   today, either (a) the site on which every major aspect of film-
making can be carried out, made up of sound-stages, offices, editing
rooms, commissary and so on, or (b) any large-scale body concerned
with developing, producing and distributing films. The term originally
meant, simply, a room in which films could be shot: 'Covered-in studios
provided with expensive glass roofs for daylight work ... are hardly
among the first flights of commercial Kinematographic enterprise' –
C.N. Bennett, *Handbook of Kinematography*, 1911. It had taken on its
more familiar meaning by the early 1920s: 'Hollywood studios moving
to less costly locations', ran a *Variety* headline on 15 November 1923.

Associated terms include: *studio picture*, a film shot entirely or mainly
on sound stages rather than location; *studio system*. the factory-style
industrial method of production (and distribution) which prevailed in
Hollywood from 1920 to the early 1950s: for a detailed history of this
method, and its consequences for the narrative forms and styles of films,
see Bordwell, Staiger & Thompson, *The Classical Hollywood Cinema:
Film Style and Mode of Production to 1960* (1985); and many other,
largely self-explanatory terms such as *studio lighting*, *studio manager*, and

studio tank, which is a large container for water on which sea and river scenes may be shot.

Studio des Ursulines and **Studio 28**   two of the most celebrated early Parisian *art-houses* (another was the Vieux Colombier) which flourished in the 1920s, which played host to the premières of *Un Chien Andalou* (1928), *L'Age d'Or* (1930) and the like.

stunt   (or, less often, *gag*) any extraordinary or potentially dangerous physical feat, usually carried out by a *stunt man/woman* (or *stunt double*) who stands in for a less expendable star. 'Of obscure origin', says the OED, though it appears to have first been used by participants in American college athletics some time towards the end of the 19th C, to mean something like 'a feat remarkable for skill or strength', and was taken up by pioneer aviators shortly afterwards. John Baxter has written an entertaining study of the unusual trade, entitled simply *Stunt* (1973).

subjective camera   a camera style which suggests that the audience is witnessing the on-screen action through the eyes of a particular character; it is usually achieved with a *hand-held* camera. For some purposes, the term may be synonymous with a *point-of-view* shot, though a subjective shot may also be distorted in some way to suggest the character's disorientation through drink, drugs, nervous breakdown, hallucination, demonic possession and the like.

subliminal shot   a shot that lasts less than a second or so, often used to disconcert or alarm the viewer; for example, in Tobe Hooper's largely undistinguished horror movie *The Mangler* (1995), quick flashes of messy red matter are used to create the impression of a body so hideously mutilated that the sight can scarcely be tolerated by a sane mind.

subtitles   the written translations that appear on the bottom part of the screen when undubbed foreign-language films are exhibited or broadcast.

subtractive process   the principal (nowadays, indeed, near-universal) technique used in colour photography; see *colour*.

sun gun, sungun   a small but powerful portable light.

super-8, super-8mm   the smallest commerically available film gauge, used mainly by home-movie enthusiasts or by avant-garde film-makers; the late Derek Jarman was fond of the gauge, and made a number of charming and arresting films with it, sometimes transferring the results to 16mm and 35mm for theatrical exhibition. The Spanish director Pedro Almodóvar recalls (*Almodóvar on Almodóvar*, ed. Strauss, 1995) that his earliest works, made on Super-8 and shown at festivals in Barcelona, would go down well with the general public because of their strong narrative component, but were derided by other practioners and theorists who held that the Super 8 cinema should deal exclusively in concepts.

superimpose   to print or photograph two or more images over each other, so as to create a *composite* image.

Superscope   a relatively short-lived *wide-screen* process used in the early 1950s.

super-16 a form of 16mm stock which can create much larger images than the ordinary kind (which is masked to create a 1.66: 1 aspect ratio), and which can be used to shoot low-budget theatrical features, blown up to 35mm for projection.

supporting role as in the theatre, a part that is subordinate to the leads but more substantial than a minor role or cameo.

surrealism tempting as it might be to write 'moose' or 'banana', and move on to the next entry, let us begin instead with the words of Phillipe Soupault: 'At the time we were developing surrealism the cinema was an immense revelation to us.' So it was: the first generation of surrealists adored the cinema, loving it for its moments of absurdity and dream-like logic rather than (the quality hailed by other intellectuals) its 'modernity'. Breton, Soupault and Aragon would rush to see such American serials as *The Exploits of Elaine* and *The Perils of Pauline*, or Feuillade's *Judex* and *Les Vampires*, or any of the new comedies with Keaton or Chaplin, watching greedily from the front row (a habit later unconsciously echoed by the young critics of *Cahiers du Cinéma*). Soupault: 'We finally understood that the cinema was not a perfected toy but the terrible and magnificent flag of life.' Hardly surprising, then, that the energies of this group should soon have found issue in surrealist works for the screen. The relationship between surrealism and the cinema is a large and fascinating subject which deserves treatment at book length (and has occasionally received it, for example in Ado Kyrou's *Le Surréalisme au cinéma*, 1953); any brief review of the canonical films would have to acknowledge, *inter alia*, Germaine Dulac's *La Coquille et le Clergyman* (1928), though this was violently rejected by Breton and Co; René Clair's *Entr'acte* (1924), though this is usually described as a product of surrealism's wilder cousin and precursor, Dada; Man Ray's *Le Retour à la Raison* (1924), Fernand Léger and Dudley Murphy's *Ballet méchanique* (1924) and, of course, Buñuel's *Un Chien Andalou* (1928) and *L'Age d'Or* (1930), which the surrealists enthusiastically endorsed. Buñuel was the only major director to remain a staunch surrealist, long after the movement had splintered and dwindled, but surrealism has had a pervasive effect on a great deal of subsequent film-making, albeit in diluted forms which would have disgusted the founding fathers. The word *surréalisme* (or, to be pedantic, *sur-realisme)* was coined by Apollinaire in his advance notice for *L'Excelsior* of the Satie-Picasso-Diaghilev ballet *Parade* on 11 May 1917: 'De cette alliance nouvelle ... il est résulté, dans "Parade", une sorte de sur-réalisme.' André Breton borrowed the term for his *Manifeste du Surréalisme* in 1924, where he defined it as 'pure psychic automatism, by which it is intended to express, verbally, in writing, or by other means, the real process of thought.' For a fascinating anthology of surrealist writings on cinema, see *The Shadow and its Shadow*, edited by Paul Hammond (BFI); for curious observations on Dada and the cinema, see Greil Marcus's *Lipstick Traces*.

surround sound the technique used in well-equipped cinemas, which, by channelling parts of the sound-track through speakers set around and behind the audience, creates the auditory illusion of being right in the middle of the action.

swashbuckler   a type of adventure film, generally with a period setting, a fair dash of humour and a robust, romantic male lead such as Errol Flynn. Recent examples include *The Three Musketeers* and (though these are less humorous in spirit than their precursors) *Rob Roy* (Michael Caton-Jones, 1995) and *Braveheart* (Mel Gibson, 1995). 'Swashbuckler' – literally, 'one who makes a noise by striking his own or his opponent's shield with a sword' – originally meant a bravo, ruffian or braggadocio: 'Too be a dronkarde, . . . a gammer, a swashe-buckeler . . . he hath not allowed thee one mite' – Pilkington, 1560.

sweetening   the process of adding new music or sounds to a sound track.

swing gang   the team which works overnight (or, for a night shoot, throughout the day) on a set to prepare it for filming or to *strike* it.

swish pan   an extremely fast *pan*; see *zip pan*.

switchback   another, less common term for a *flashback*, or for the act of returning to an original action after cutting to some (usually parallel) action.

Symbolism   in his study of the Symbolist and Decadent movements of the late 19th C, *Dreamers of Decadence*, the art historian Philippe Julian suggests that the repertoire of macabre and exotic images evolved by such painters as Gustave Moreau, Franz von Stuck, Felicien Rops and Jean Delville did not perish with the movement and the century, but instead migrated to and took up home in the cinema, and specifically in such films as Murnau's *Nosferatu*. ('The cinema', he writes, 'gave an increasingly mechanised world the images of which Symbolism had dreamt thirty years before.') This interesting observation appears to have been anticipated, at least in part, by Maxim Gorky, in an article of 1896: 'Yesterday I was in the kingdom of shadows . . . I must explain, lest I be suspected of Symbolism or madness, I was at Aumont's café and saw the Lumières' Cinématographe – moving photographs' (cited in Ian Christie, *The Last Machine*, 124).

sync (or, infrequently, **synch**)   a near-universal abbreviation for *syn-chronisation* – the perfect matching of sound to image; the most obvious sign that a film is *out of sync* rather than *in sync* is that the words on the sound-track do not coincide with the movements of the performers' lips. (From the modern L *synchronismus* and the Gk *synchronismus*: 'Syn-chronism' and its related forms are known in English from the late 16th C; OED cites a test from 1588: 'Is there any greater concordance, or Synchronisme, betweene the prophesie of Elias and this text. . . .?') Among the many associated terms are *synchroniser*, the machine that allows an editor to bring sound and image into sync; *synchronous sound*, either simply (a) a movie soundtrack that is in sync with the correspond-ing pictures, or (b) sound that is recorded in sync with the film that is passing through the camera; *sync mark*, a mark made on film or leader by an editor to help align picture and sound; or a mark serving the same for the projectionist; *sync pulse*, an electrical pulse generated by the camera that is sent to the sound tape and recorded on a track running parallel with that which holds the sound. When the tape is transferred to magnetic film, the pulse keeps the sound running at the appropriate speed.

synopsis   in industry terms, a brief plot summary or *outline*, generally submitted to a producer to suggest a possible project.

synthespian   the trade name, copyrighted by the Kleiser-Walczak Construction Co, for an 'actor' made up entirely of digits. At the time of writing (August 1997), there have been only a few synthespian perform-ances – notably in *The Crow* and *Waggons East*, both of which had to fall back on the resources of *CGI* after their lead players, Brandon Lee and John Candy, died in mid-production. But there are rumours to the effect that Marilyn Monroe, Bruce Lee and others are to be brought back from the grave by digital means; and the director James Cameron has declared his intention to make a film called *Avatar* which will have a cast of synthespians. See Jonathan Romney's essay 'Million-Dollar Graffiti: notes from the digital domain' in *Short Orders* (Serpent's Tail, 1997).

synthetic sound   sounds produced by a synthesiser or other electronic means, rather than recorded from an actual source, often used in science-fiction films, horror movies and the like.

T-core the small, round plastic object around which film may be wound.

t-stop an electronically calculated measurement, similar to an *f-stop* but more minute, of the amount of light passed through a specific lens and reaching the focal point of the film stock; the 't' stands for 'transmission'. In practice, the difference between a t-stop measurement and an f-stop measurement is relatively insignificant on modern lenses, but it needs to be taken into account when older equipment is used.

table editing machine, tabletop editing machine any editing machine, such as the *Steenbeck* or the *Kem*, built in the shape of a table, with rotating plates mounted on a horizontal work surface, as opposed to upright editing machines such as the *Moviola*; another term, then, for a *flat-bed editing machine*.

tachometer the gauge which indicates the speed at which a camera is running. From Fr *tacheometre*, drived from Gk *tachos*, 'swiftness'; the technology came into use in the late 19th C.

tail the end of a roll of film; *tailgate*, the name for a projector in an optical printer; *tail-out*, a reel of film with its end, or tail, on the outside, prior to rewinding (the opposite of *head-out*); *tail slate*, a *slate* identifying a take at its end rather than (or as well as) its beginning.

take (a) each of the occasions on which a single, continuous piece of action is recorded on film (though each take of a particular action after the first should, strictly speaking, be called a *retake*); or (b) the result of that filming – a single, continuous *shot*. OED indicates that all such cinematic senses, for which the earliest citation is the *New York Times*, 25 February 1917, are derived from an earlier meaning – 'to obtain by drawing, delineating etc.', known in English since the early 17th C. (Hence: 'I went to the castle . . . and took the ruins thereof' – Wood, 1664.) A take may last as long as ten minutes – the rough time needed for a reel to pass through the camera at normal speed – though in practice takes of this length are rare outside the avant-garde cinema, the most obvious exceptions being Hitchcock's *Rope* (1948), which gives the impression of being filmed without a single cut after its first couple of minutes, or bravura tracking shots such as the one which opens Robert Altman's *The Player*. Each take is distinguished from its successors and precursors by the use of a *slate*; the expression 'That's a take' indicates that the action filmed was satisfactory to the director. Hence the associated terms: *take board*, another name for a *clapboard*; *take number*, the numerals written on to the clapboard so that different takes may be distinguished during editing; and so on.

take up, take-up reel, take-up spool the reel that takes up the film after it has been fed through a camera or projector; the counterpart to a *feed spool*. On an editing machine, the analagous device is a *take-up plate*; in a magazine, the *take-up chamber*.

taking lens a term used to specify which one of the various lenses mounted on a camera *turret* is to be used or has been used for a given take.

talent   a generic term for all the actors, musicians and so on employed on a production; the term can even include dogs, horses and other performing animals; hence *talent agency, talent scout,* etc.

talkies   a colloquial term, now seldom used except in historical writing, for the earliest films to use sound: 'In one of [Jules Verne's novels], *The Castle of the Carpathians,* there was even a forecast of the Talkies' – Lord Berners, *First Childhood,* 1934. Lord Berners might have added that not only did the idea precede the phenomenon – generally dated to 1927, the year of *The Jazz Singer* – the word also came before the deed: 'The silent "Movies", so popular today, will become tame in comparison with the "Talkies"' – *Writers' Bulletin,* 9 March 1913. OED also cites an exhibition of sound cinema from Victoria, B.C. as early as 1921, reported in the local *Daily Colonist*; standard reference books make no mention of this particular precocious display, though most acknowledge that experiments had been going on for a couple of decades. W.H. Auden used the expression 'talkie-houses', meaning cinemas, in *Look Stranger!* (1936).

talking heads   shots composed simply of a person, filmed in close-up or medium close-up, talking directly into the camera or to someone off-screen. A standard technique for television documentaries and news programmes, used in feature films either (i) to create a deliberately documentary or quasi-documentary effect – for example in Michael Winterbottom's *Butterfly Kiss* (1995), which is punctuated by a mono-chrome, video talking-head shot representing the deposition of a young woman who drifts into murdering, (ii) for some other dramatic purpose, or (iii) simply because the director lacked inspiration to shoot in a more creative manner.

tank   a large water container kept in a studio, and used to simulate rivers, lakes, seas, oceans or floods; hence *tank shot.*

tape   (a) the magnetic tape used in sound recording, more technically known as *audio tape*; (b) a common abbreviation for *videotape*; (c) the adhesive tape used to make *splices* (also called *tape splices*); (d) the verb used both for sound recording and shooting on videotape; (e) the measuring tape used to work out the distance between the camera lens and the subject; or the verb for making such measurements.

Associated terms: *tape drive,* the mechanism which moves tape through the recorder and over the *sound heads*; *tape speed,* the standard rates at which magnetic tape moves through a recording or playback mechanism – generally seven and a half and fifteen inches per second; *tape splice,* a means of joining two pieces of film together end-to-end (this is also known as a *butt splice*), using transparent tape and a simple machine known as a *tape splicer.*

target   a type of *flag,* shaped like an archery target, used to block light; *target audience,* the section of the cinema-going or video-renting public which a film's makers hope to attract.

tearjerker a mildly sardonic slang name for any mawkish, grossly sentimental film that owes its commercial appeal largely to its capacity to make susceptible viewers weep uncontrollably, such as *Love Story*, *Terms of Endearment*, *The Color Purple*. By definition, few tearjerkers have achieved much critical respectability – it would seem tasteless to describe, say, *Schindler's List* as a tearjerker – though the novelist and critic Gilbert Adair, for one, has written an eloquent, and not wholly ironic defence of the form. The term, which was originally applied to books, plays, songs, people and, occasionally, events, came into use in the United States some time around the 1920s.

teaser either (a) a short, piquant pre-credit sequence used to snag the audience's attention or (b) a short, piquant and sometimes cryptic early version of a trailer, such as the truly inspired one which helped make *Independence Day* (1996) such an extraordinary hit.

technical adviser a specialist in some field (such as physics, genetics, Roman history, numismatics . . .), or experienced practioner of some profession or trade (rodeo riding, police work, the ER . . .) or the like, employed by film-makers as a consultant – generally, to make sure that the details of a particular milieu or procedure are reasonably authentic-looking or that a plot is sufficiently feasible.

Technicolor though this brand name for a particular colour film process – or, to be pedantic, of no fewer than four distinct different processes all going by the same name – managed to lodge itself in the popular imagination so firmly that it is still pretty much synonymous for any kind of colour film in layman's talk, the process itself has seldom been used since the early 1950s, when it was superseded by the much cheaper *Eastman Color*, itself devised in 1949. Technicolor was originally developed in a prototype form in about 1915; it was the work of a partnership between Daniel F. Comstock and Herbert T. Kalmus, co-founders of the Technicolor Motion Picture Corporation; the company's name was a tribute to the college that had given them their doctorates, the Massachussetts Institute of Technology. An adequate discussion of the culture and technology of Technicolor would demand a monograph, but the four main stages in its history run, briefly, thus: (1) Comstock's first camera used a prism which split incoming light into red and green components, and two negatives; the resulting picture was projected through a camera with two apertures, one with a red filter, the other with green. The company made a film in Jacksonville, Florida (plenty of bright daylight) in 1916, *The Gulf Between*, to show what could be done. (2) Encouraged more by the potential of their first system than its achievements, Comstock and Co. went on to develop a more complex system, still using a beam-splitting prism but recording both the red and green images, in the first instance, onto a single reel of film. Among the best-known of the colour productions made using this method was Douglas Fairbanks's *The Black Pirate* (1926). (3) By the late 1920s, Technicolor had developed the process of *imbibition*, or dye printing, which used two sets of film – sensitive respectively to the red-orange and blue-green bands of the spectrum – which then underwent a series of dye printings. A few years later, in 1932, this basic process was adapted to a more rich and satisfactory 'three-strip' system, using three separate negatives. Among the triumphs of three-strip Technicolor: Rouben Mamoulian's *Becky Sharp* (1935), the first full-length feature to employ the process, and *Gone With the Wind* (1939). (4) Finally, the company developed its Monopack Technicolor, which required only a single stock, suitable for use in any standard 35mm camera. This film was first used in sequences of the Errol Flynn vehicle *Dive Bomber* (Michael Curtiz, 1941) and, by some accounts, reached its apotheosis in 1950 with *King Solomon's Mines*, which won Robert Surtees an Oscar for cinematography.

Technirama   a wide-screen process developed by Technicolor, and employed on productions from the mid-1950s to mid-1960s, which used a double frame on 35mm stock and was similar to Paramount's *Vistavision*; *Techniscope*, a rather longer-lived wide-screen process using 35mm film, developed by Technicolor's Italian division in the early 1960s, and relying on an economical *anamorphic* printing process rather than on the more costly method of shooting with an anamorphic lens.

telecine   (**TC** or, in the BBC's abbreviation, **TK** – the point being to avoid confusion on documents, since within the Corporation, 'TC' generally signifies 'Television Centre'; see *kinescope*) the various systems which can transfer film images onto video tape and/or transmit them as television signals.

telephoto lens   a lens which, because of its extended focal length, allows the camera to film distant scenes as if they were close up; in layman's terms, the cinematographer's equivalent of a telescope. Such lenses are widely used in the cameras which relay sporting events, public ceremonies and the like, but are also fairly widely used for certain types of long shot in feature-film making. One of the disadvantages of the tool is the effect known as *telephoto distortion*, which flattens out distant perspectives, though directors can use this visual oddity for dramatic ends, the classic effect being to show an actor running urgently towards the camera yet appearing to come no closer.

television mask   a *mask* found in a viewfinder which shows which parts of the image will still be in view when the film is broadcast on television – in other words, the *safe-action area*.

tendency drive   an alternative – gentler and less potentially damaging – method of passing film through a machine, which uses a set of rotating rollers rather than a tooth-and-sprocket system, and hence is sometimes called a sprocketless drive.

tenner   a large spotlight with a 10,000-watt lamp.

Thaumatrope   a simple *persistence-of-vision* toy, marketed in England in the 1820s, consisting of little more than a disc and a couple of strings: by spinning the disc around, the pictures drawn on both sides would merge into a composite image.

theater (also **movie theater**)   one of the standard US terms for the building in which films are shown to the public; perfectly neutral in Britain, our usual synonym *cinema* is often, I am told by American friends, felt to be just slightly pretentious in the States. *Theatrical distribution*, the release, or re-release of features to cinemas. In Britain, a brief period of theatrical distribution is often the only factor which determines whether a production is regarded as a true feature film or merely a filmed television drama. *Theatrical documentary*, another, less common term for a *docudrama*. *Theatrical film*, a film made primarily for distribution in cinemas rather than for immediate television broadcast or direct release for the home video market.

Theatrograph   an early form of projector, devised in 1896 by the British inventor and film-maker R.W. Paul, who later changed its name to the Animatographe. Apparently inspired by Edison's *Kinestoscope*, the Theatrograph was itself to inspire an apparatus devised by Méliès, who bought one of Paul's inventions when he was unable to lay his hands on one of the Lumières' *Cinématographes*.

thematic montage   a form of *montage* that sketches out some form of symbolic or thematic association between different objects or actions rather than advancing a narrative: such passages may often be crass (the Monty Python troupe once came up with a hilarious parody of a montage suggesting erection, coitus and detumescence), but they have also provided the cinema with some of its most poetic flights.

theme, theme music   a piece of music, either specially composed or (less often) taken from some other source, that establishes a identity either for the film itself (the *main theme*) or of some mood (such as the *love theme*) or character within the film – the Stravinsky-esque 'shark attack' motif from *Jaws* and the martial, rumbling 'Evil Empire' tune from the *Star Wars* films are a couple of well-known examples. Hence *theme song*, a catchy number played on the soundtrack over the opening titles or with some memorable scene, and calculated both to boost the film's intrinsic appeal and to make money in its own right: the various songs composed by John Barry and others for the James Bond films are good examples.

thesis film   mildly disparaging epithet for a film with a hefty ideological axe to grind, such as the recent movies about American history by Oliver Stone – *JFK* (1991), for instance – or, for those not in sympathy with its aims, any product of the:

Third World Cinema   broadly speaking, a generic term for any of the films produced by developing, non-Western nations, though in practice it tends to refer to particularly the serious, highly politicised, anti-imperialist features and documentaries produced in Latin America and Africa from the late 1950s onwards – such as the works of Brazil's

Cinema Nôvo movement – rather than, say, to the crowd-pleasing products of *Bollywood*.

thirty-five millimetre (35 mm)   the standard gauge of film used for professional feature film-making; the other gauges have various different applications – 16mm for a lot of documentary work, 8mm for amateur and avant-garde efforts and so on. It has been in use for almost the entire history of cinema, since the earliest version of the format was devised by Edison and the Eastman Kodak company in 1899, and rapidly drove all the other competing gauges out of the market. Though it has undergone a number of mutations over the past century – in 1929, for example, the *aspect ratio* of the frame was altered for a time to become somewhat closer to a square, and thus make room for the sound track; viewers found this unappealing, so the frame was shrunk and adjusted back to a rectangular ratio, of 1.33:1 – 35mm film is still much the same today as it originally was: perforated down both sides, with four perforations to the frame.

three-camera technique   the practice of shooting a given scene with three cameras, each placed at a different distance from or angle to the subject, to allow for variety in editing.

three-colour process   any of the *colour* film systems which use all three of the primary colours.

3-D   films shot and projected through a stereoscopic system, so that, when viewed through special glasses (usually with one red and one green lens), they create the illusion of action in three dimensions. The gimmick was introduced and enjoyed a vogue in the 1950s, when it was one of the various emergency measures dreamed up by Hollywood to tempt viewers away from the menace of television; André de Toth's *House of Wax*, *The Creature from the Black Lagoon* and Hitchcock's *Dial M for Murder* are three of the best-known examples. The novelty soon wore thin. *Three shot*, any shot containing three people; see *two shot*; *360 degree pan*, a pan in which the camera rotates on its axis through a complete circle.

thriller   though the term ought to apply to any film which sets out to create excitement, in practice most thrillers are tales of murder, conspiracy, violent action, and/or – in the case of the *psychological thriller* – unusual mental states. The slang term 'thriller' came into use in the 1880s, and was originally applied to sensational plays or stories; today, the cinematic sense is the main one.

through-the-lens   a type of reflex viewfinder which shows exactly the field of vision covered by the lens, and which therefore eliminates the need to compensate for *parallax*.

throw   the distance between the projector and the screen on to which it is projecting; more loosely, therefore, the depth of a screening room or auditorium. In David Mamet's entertaining book of reminiscences about the film business, *A Whore's Profession* (1994), the playwright self-mockingly congratulates himself on having this bit of jargon in his personal vocabulary.

tie-in   usually: the Book of the Film – either a reprint of a classic, with a new cover derived from the publicity campaign and the slogan 'Now a Major Motion Picture'; more generally, any other product, from CD to fast food, marketed by associating it with a new release.

tighten, pull up   to move the camera towards the subject, or to adjust the focus, so that the background disappears and the subject comes to dominate the composition. *Tight shot*, an extreme close-up, in which the subject monopolises the screen; *Tight two*, a close-up version of a *two shot*, showing just the heads of the speakers or characters.

tilt   a common camera move: to swivel a camera up or down on its vertical axis; thus, the vertical counterpart to the horizontal *pan*. (OED's earliest citation is from 1959, though it must have been in use for many years before this.) Hence the self-explanatory *tilt shot*.

tilt plate   see *camera wedge*.

time code   the figures which appear at the top or bottom of an image on a video monitor during the editing process, identifying the reel which is being viewed and the time elapsed within the reel.

time-lapse, time-lapse cinematography   the technique of exposing film slowly, one frame at a time and then projecting it at normal speed so that extremely slow movements, such as the growth of a plant or the passage of the sun, moon or clouds across the sky are greatly accelerated. Godfrey Reggio's *Koyannisqatsi* uses the device relentlesssly; more sparing indulgences can be seen in Coppola's *Rumble Fish*, Oliver Stone's *The Doors*, Chris Menges' *Second Best* and elsewhere.

timing   an American synonym for *grading*, as *timer* is for *grader*.

Tinseltown   a somewhat *passé* slang name for Hollywood – or, as the OED notes, for the Hollywood 'myth' – still to be found from time to time in would-be jaunty prose, such as that written by sub-editors for newspapers, or the front covers of listings magazines. An obvious coinage: tinsel, glitter, glamour . . .

tinting   the counterpart to *toning* – that is, the process of chemically adding a single overall colour, such as sepia, to the light areas of an image: the practice was common in the silent period and was occasionally revived in the sound period.

title, titles   (a) the words printed on screen, usually at the beginning and end of a film, sometimes at intervals throughout its length – to identify establishing shots ('Venice, Italy') or give other information. Hence *Billboard*, 21 October 1905: 'All our films come with red titles, and show our trade mark'; (b) the name of a film.

Tobis   the acronym for the German production company Tonbild Syndikat AG, a major rival for *UFA*, founded in 1928, dissolved – after an extremely complex set of amalgamations, affiliations, take-overs and the like – at the end of the war in 1945. Its first head was the composer Guido Bagier, whose theories and policies were influential in the early development of sound film. One of the company's most celebrated productions was Leni Riefenstahl's *Olympia* (1938).

Todd-AO   a short-lived, 70mm wide-screen process – 65mm of image on the negative, 5 additional mm on the positive, holding six tracks of stereophonic sound – which owes its name to Mike Todd (1907–58), who commissioned it, and the American Optical Company, which developed it. Todd's request was simple: he wanted the AOC to come up with a system with 'everything coming out of one hole', rather than the three-projector system required by the rival process *Cinerama*. It proved a great success in Todd's productions of *Oklahoma!* (1955) and *Around the World in Eighty Days* (1956). Hence the jocular, not to say vulgar name 'Todd-BO', applied by wags to the various attempts made to augment the effects of cinema through the strategic use of smells.

Tohoscope   a wide-screen process developed in Japan for the Toho Company, closely modelled on *Cinemascope*, with an aspect ration of 2.35: 1.

tone, toning   (a) the printing process which gives black and white film an overall colour in the dark areas, and is thus the counterpart to *tinting*, which colours the light areas of the image. Tone can also mean (b) the quality of sound on a sound-track, or (c) an audio signal set at one frequency.

tongue   the order to move a *dolly* to one side ('Tongue right!') or the other ('Tongue left!').

top billing   the most conspicuous, dominant place or order for names in an opening credit sequence, trailer or poster – usually the stars and/or the director; the right to top billing is generally one of the issues negotiated in drawing up a contract.

top lighting   a single light or group of lights mounted directly above the subject.

topsheet   the single sheet of paper at the front of a budget document, summarising the main areas of expenditure.

track, tracks   either (a) the *sound track*, or (b) the rails laid down for the camera to be wheeled along for a *tracking shot*; hence, (c) as a verb, to move the camera laterally along rails, usually so as to follow an action. (Compare *dolly*.) OED gives no citations earlier than 1959; sadly, it also omits a much-repeated English phrase translated from an original maxim by Jean-Luc Godard: 'Tracking shots are a question of morality.' When the dolly shot is taken from a moving vehicle, it is sometimes called a *trucking shot*. In post-production, *tracking* refers to the process of laying down pre-recorded music on a film's sound-track

trades, trade papers   American periodicals (and to a lesser extent, their counterparts in other nations), such as *Variety, Box Office* and the *Hollywood Reporter* which write for and about the film and television industries. The principal British trade is *Screen International*. A *trade show* is a private screening for the benefit of exhibitors and trade press; such shows were made obligatory in Britain by the Cinematograph Films Act of 1909.

trailer   *New York Times*, 11 March 1928: '*A trailer*, a few hundred feet of film announcing a forthcoming picture.' It's hard to improve on this crisp definition, though it can be broadened a little. Generally, a trailer is a brief (one and half to four minutes) advertisment for a feature, made for screening in cinemas or on television, generally put together from tantalisingly quick shots of the most exciting or alluring moments. Trailers which appear long before a film's post-production is complete will sometimes be specially shot and more cryptic or witty than usual, such as that for *The Last Action Hero*, in which the film's star, Arnold Schwarzenegger, suddenly turned away from a scene of mounting tension to admonish the audience that it wasn't time for them to see what was happening just yet. (This wit was not rewarded at the box-office; the film was a flop, though it had its champions among the critics.) Trailers are often made by companies specialising in such work, though perfectionist directors such as Stanley Kubrick prefer to make their own. Within the industry, the term 'trailer' can sometimes be applied to any kind of short film that is not a paid advertisment, including public information shorts and the like. OED records the existence of the verb 'to trailer', though in standard television and radio practice in this country the usual verb (also duly noted by OED) is 'trail'.

trainer   the crew member reponsible for dealing with horses, dogs and other animals; see *wrangler*.

transcendental style   a term coined by the director and screenwriter Paul Schrader in his theoretical study *Transcendental Style in Film: Ozo, Bresson, Dreyer* (1972). This book made the attempt – unusual in American writings on film, though less so in France – to introduce certain theological concepts into a formal analysis of directorial technique. Its argument is hard to summarise; this is an attempt made by the present author in 1989: '*Transcendental Style* argued that directors working quite independently of each other had arrived at an identical way of expressing the Holy in cinematic terms: an austere style of "sparse means" which, by progressively denying the spectator all the familiar gratifications of the cinema – identifying with a protagonist and so on – will ultimately permit an experience of the "disparity" of Spirit's presence in the physical world' (Introduction to *Schrader on Schrader and other writings*).

transfer   the magnetic duplication of either sound or image; as a verb, to copy sounds or images from machine to machine, tape to tape and so on.

transition   any of the effects used to move the action of a film from one scene to the next, including the *cut*, but more particularly the conspicuous transitional techniques such as a *dissolve*, a *wipe*, a *flip* or *flipover*, the old-fashioned *iris-in* or *iris-out* and the like. Today, almost all such effects are produced by *optical printers*.

transparency   an image printed on a transparent surface so that it can be projected.

transport   the mechanisms which pull film through a camera, projector or printer, and magnetic tape across the heads of a recorder; *transporta-*

tion department, the drivers and mechanics responsible for all the vehicles on a production.

travelling matte   a system, often used in science fiction, fantasy or adventure films, for combining two or more separately shot actions into a single image. The adjective 'travelling' indicates that the *matte* changes shape from shot to shot; in simpler forms of the process, the matte remains stationary and simply blocks out part of the image, which is then filled with other images.

travelling shot   see *tracking shot.*

travelogue   an undemanding form of documentary film about travel, usually to exotic places; the term is very mildly pejorative – cruel critics often dismiss exotic but dramatically inconsequential sequences in feature films as 'travelogue' – and would not usually be applied to more serious non-fiction films about the experience of travel and exploration. The term, which originated in the USA, originally meant a lecture about experiences of travel and exploration, and was coined by uniting 'travel' and 'monologue': 'Mr. Burton Holmes, an American entertainer new to London, delivered last evening the first of a series of "Travelogues"' – *Daily Chronicle,* 16 April 1903. It came to be applied to films as early as 1921; the *Glasgow Herald,* in November that year, referred to the film 'With Allenby in Palestine and Lawrence in Arabia' as a 'Travelogue film'.

treatment   an early version of a screenplay, sometimes no more than a few pages long, giving an abbreviated but vivid account of how the action will eventually look. Often used to 'sell' the idea of the film to a producer, director or backer. Aldous Huxley explained the term in a letter to one of his friends in 1938, after working on a treatment for a film on the life of Mme Curie; it had been in use in Hollywood at least since the late 1920s.

treble roll-off   the process of reducing high sound frequencies with a filter, usually during mixing.

tree, Christmas tree   a many-armed stand, abstractly arboreal in appearance, used to support *luminaires.*

trench   as the name suggests: a long hole dug to house the camera (for a low-angle shot) or the performers (to make them seem shorter).

triacetate base, acetate base   a safe, non-inflammable base for film, manufactured from cellulose triacetate and used in place of the more hazardous cellulose nitrate base that was common until 1951.

triangle   the three-armed device which holds the legs of a camera *tripod* in place.

Triangle   an early American film company, in production from 1915 to 1918, so called because – encouraged by the success of D. W. Griffith's *Birth of a Nation* (1915) – it was designed as a home for the work of three directors, Griffith, Thomas Ince and Mack Sennett. Despite a number of successes, including the transformation of Douglas Fairbanks from stage to screen star, the company soon ran into trouble, largely because the public was asked to pay the extravagant sum of two dollars to watch one of the three-film shows (two dramatic five-reelers and a comic short from Sennett's unit).

Tri-Ergon Process   at one time the principal form of cinema sound technology used in Europe, this process was invented by three men (hence the 'Tri'): Josef Engl, Joseph Massole and Hans Vogt, who patented it in 1919. It used an optical track which would produce sound when passed between the projector's lamp and a photo-electric cell; the invention was taken up by the German company Tobis-Klangfilm.

trigger film   an American term for a kind of public-service or information film, usually taking the form of a short, unresolved drama which is meant to provoke its audience – of schoolchildren, servicemen or concerned citizens, say – into lively debate.

trim   as a verb: in editing, to make a shot shorter by cutting part of it; thus, as a noun, the discarded piece (or usually, pieces – *trims*) of film left over after cutting. Hence *trim bin*, an easily movable bin, mounted on small wheels and topped with a rack from which strips of film can be hung.

trip gear   a timer used in *time-lapse photography* that exposes frames at regular intervals, or at pre-set times.

tripack   see *colour*.

triple-head optical printer   an *optical printer* equipped with three projectors, and thus capable of producing *travelling matte* shots and other kinds of optical effect; *triple-head process projector*, a system used for rear-projection in the 1940s, and particularly for films which required a brighter background image than other systems could achieve; it was developed by Farciot Edouart.

triple take   the act of filming the same action as a long, medium and close-up shot, so as to allow for plenty of variety when it comes to editing.

tripod   the three-legged stand, adjustable for height, on which cameras can be mounted. The camera is fixed to a moveable *tripod head*, and so panned or tilted. (From L *tripus*, *tripod-* and earlier Gk forms: 'three-footed': known in English since the early 17th C, it comes to mean any three-legged support by the early 19th C.)

triptych screen   a screen divided into three panels, much like a pictorial triptych: the only notable use of such a screen in cinema history appears to have been made by Abel Gance for early screenings of his epic *Napoléon vu par Abel Gance* (1927); he referred to the gadgetry which made this possible as *Polyvision*.

trombone   a clamp that can be extended (like the slide of a trombone) and is used to hang lights.

trucking shot   see *tracking shot*.

tulip crane   a portable crane commonly used for location work, especially when the director requires only a limited amount of elevation for that day's shooting, since it will go no higher than about 16 feet.

tuner   *Variety*-speak: a film composer – someone who writes tunes.

tungsten bulb   once the standard form of bulb used to light sets, the tungsten bulb was superseded by the tungsten-halogen bulb, which does not blacken or burn out so easily, since the tungsten which evaporates from the filament when electricity passes through it then reacts with the surrounding metal halide gas and is deposited back on the filament.

turnaround   either (a) the stage of development at which a project is dropped by one company or studio and may be submitted to another, or (b) the contractual right of a producer or screenwriter to hawk a project around once the first studio has decided not to proceed with development. *Turnaround time,* the amount of rest a member of crew or cast must be allowed between days or blocks of shooting.

turn over!   the order given to the cameraman, usually by the director, to start the camera running. The shout of 'Camera!', as in the legendary exclamation 'Lights! Camera! Action!' is seldom if ever heard today.

turret   a type of revolving lens mount, holding three or more different lenses that can be brought quickly into play as required. (From the ME *turet, toret, tourette,* etc., OF *torete* etc. and L *turris,* a tower.)

turtle   a low, three-legged stand for *luminaires.*

TV cutoff, television cutoff   another way of referring to the *safe-action area* – the part of the image that will remain in vision when a film is shown; the TV cutoff is either (a) the part of the image that will be lost, or (b) the markings in a camera viewfinder which indicate the safe-action area.

tweeter   a loudspeaker designed to handle higher frequencies only (alternatively, the part of a loudspeaker which can handle high frequencies); jocularly so called because of its capacity to reproduce the tweeting and twittering of birds. (OED notes the onomatopoeic 'tweet' as early as 1845.) The corresponding low-frequency equipment is known, for canine reasons, as a *woofer.*

Twentieth Century-Fox   the major American production and distribution company, founded in 1935 from a merger between the Twentieth Century Picture Corporation (founded in 1933 by Darryl F. Zanuck and Joseph Schenck) and the Fox Film Corporation (founded in 1915). The resulting company's house style, tending towards the lavish, was largely established by Zanuck, who was head of production until 1956, and Spyros Skouras, who was company president from 1942 to 1962, when his career was destroyed by the disastrous flop of *Cleopatra,* which lost Fox forty million dollars. In its early years, Fox tended to concentrate on Westerns – particularly the great films of John Ford, including *Drums Along the Mohawk* (1939) and *My Darling Clementine* (1946); Ford also made *The Grapes of Wrath* (1940) for the company – and musicals, starring the likes of Betty Grable and Shirley Temple. It also pioneered wide-screen cinema with Henry Koster's Biblical epic *The Robe* (1953), shot in the *anamorphic* process *CinemaScope.* Other Fox directors included Henry King, Elia Kazan and Joseph L. Mankiewicz; other stars included Marilyn Monroe, Gregory Peck and, later, Julie Andrews – the success of *The Sound of Music* (1965) helped put the company back in the black, though its fortunes waxed and waned erratically thereafter. Since 1985, the company has been owned by Rupert Murdoch's News Corporation; its television wing, Fox, has rapidly established itself as one of the four major networks in the United States.

Two Cities   a British production company, based at *Denham* Studios, which thrived in the late 1940s and early 1950s, and was responsible for a number of unusually distinguished entertainments, including Lawrence Olivier's *Henry V* (1944) and *Hamlet* (1948). The company was founded by a refugee from Fascist Italy, the former lawyer Filippo Del Guidice (1892–1961), in 1937, and was taken over by the Rank Organisation in 1943: the 'two cities' in question were London and Rome. Among the other notable Two Cities productions: Noel Coward's *In Which We Serve* (1942), Carol Reed's *Odd Man Out* (1947) and *The Way Ahead* (1944), and David Lean's *This Happy Breed* (1944) and *Blithe Spirit* (1945).

two-colour process   any one of the early systems of cinematography, so called because they were sensitive to only two of the primary colours.

two-reel comedy   a format for silent comedies, lasting about twenty minutes or so, such as the ones made by Charlie Chaplin for Mutual.

two-shot   a shot containing two people, usually engaged in conversation or the prelude to an amorous clinch; at one time the basic two-shot was referred to in France and other European countries as an 'American shot', since it was such a staple of Hollywood productions.

Tyler mount, tyler mount   the gyroscopic mount used to attach a camera to a helicopter or plane; named for its inventor, Nelson Tyler.

typage   a term coined by the Soviet director Sergei Eisenstein, and meaning the practice of casting non-professional actors according to their readily identifiable appearances. A term related to, but not wholly identifiable with:

typecasting   hiring an actor for a particular part because their appearance is physically appropriate (fat, emaciated, elderly, short) or because they have previously appeared in a similar role; hence the familiar actors' lament of being *typecast*. OED suggests that the term came into use by the 1940s; it may have been a mild play on words, since 'type-cast' or 'typecast' was a well-established term from the printing industry, meaning 'formed into type for printing'.

U, **U certificate**   the film classification which indicates that a film is suitable for viewing by audiences of all ages; an abbreviation for 'Universal'. It was first introduced by the *BBFC* in 1912 as a category for films that were appropriate viewing for children, and extended to its present use over the next four years. See *certificate*.

UFA (sometimes **Ufa**), or *Universum Film Aktiengesellschaft*   the famous German government-sponsored production company, founded in the last days of the First World War (1917) and wiped out at the end of the Second World War (1945). Despite its origins in the wartime propaganda effort, and its eventual, notorious annexation by the Nazis, UFA is most commonly remembered by cinema historians for launching the careers of three major directors: Fritz Lang (*Die Nibelungen*, 1924; *Metropolis*, 1927), F.W. Murnau (*Nosferatu*, 1922), and G.W. Pabst (*Joyless Street*, 1925; *Pandora's Box*, 1929). Though UFA is credited in some reference books as producing the best-known and most influential of all *expressionist* films, *Das Cabinett des Dr Caligari* (Robert Weine, 1919), this is a retrospective attribution: *Caligari* was in fact made by Erich Pommer's company Decla Bioscop, which was merged with UFA in 1923 when Pommer became its chief of production. (Incidentally, Pommer had originally assigned Fritz Lang to direct *Caligari*, but Lang had been ordered to complete work on his serial *The Spiders*, so the assignment was passed on to Weine.) In brief outline, the history of UFA can be said to fall into five main periods: (1) Its creation, from a merger of several existing companies, as an agency for raising the standards of German production and promoting the nation's image; artists recruited included the director Ernst Lubitsch (1892–1947) and the actor Emil Jannings (1886–1950) (2) Its transition to a more commercial policy after the German defeat in 1918, when the Deutsche Bank bought out the government's shares. To this period belong the likes of Joe May's historical epic, *Veritas Vincit* (1918), which cashed in on the Italian trend for lavish spectacle established by *Quo Vadis* and *Cabiria*, and Lubitsch's *Madame Dubarry* (1919) which had its première at the company's showcase cinema, the Film Palast am Zoo in Berlin. UFA began to acquire a large chain of cinemas and set up its own distribution network. (3) When Pommer became chief of production in 1923, UFA gained access to the studios at *Neubabelsberg*, originally founded in 1911; before long, Neubabelsberg became the best studio in Europe, and the only one in the world to rival Hollywood. Despite this resource, and the acknowledged excellence of UFA's productions (such as Murnau's *Der letzte Mann*, 1924), UFA could not rise above the financial crisis of the decade, and was forced to take out loans from *Paramount* and *MGM*, the terms of which obliged the company to flood its cinemas with American product. By 1927 UFA was in a desperate financial state. (4) At this point, the company was bailed out by a financier, Dr Alfred Hugenberg, who had Nazi sympathies. With Hugenberg on the board of directors, a nationalist bias began to appear in UFA's films once more, though the most famous production of this period, Josef von Sternberg's *Der blaue Engel* (1930) was more notable for its displays of Marlene Dietrich's legs and voice than creeping fascism. (5) After the Nazis came to power, the nationalist bias of UFA productions grew ever more marked, and by 1937, when the government bought out its shares anonymously, it became the Nazi Film Unit in everything but name. The only production of this period to be remembered with anything approaching tolerance is the spectacular *Munchausen* (1943). UFA died with Hitler, and Neubabelsberg was taken over by the DDR's film company Defa (Deutsche Film Aktien Gesellschaft). A new West German company called UFA was set up after the war, but did not thrive. For a more detailed account of these matters and these films, see Siegfried Kracauer's classic 'psychological history' of the German film, *From Caligari to Hitler* (1947).

Uher   the brand name of a portable tape recorder that was once widely used for location shooting; it has largely been supplanted by the *Nagra*.

ulcer   a perforated plastic sheet put in front of a lamp or other light source to create a mottled or otherwise more varied effect; that is, an alternative British term for a *cookie*. Etymology uncertain, but presumably derived from its perforations.

ultrasonic cleaner   a method for removing dirt particles from film, using a cleaning liquid in combination with ultrasonic waves. The word 'ultrasonic' (from L *ultra-*, beyond, and *sonus*, sound) first appears in English in the 1920s. *Ultrasonic splicer*, a *splicer* that uses ultrasonic waves rather than glue or tape to hold strips of film together. *Ultraviolet (UV)*, light with a wavelength that is too short to be registered by the human eye, but which can leave a blue haze on film and so must be excluded by a *haze filter*.

umbrella   a concave reflecting board, resembling an opened umbrella, used to bounce diffuse light on to a subject.

unbalanced   a film emulsion that will produce unwanted tints after exposure and development, because it has not been prepared – that is, it does not have the appropriate *balance* – for a particular light source.

undercrank   to shoot a scene at speeds slower than 24 frames per second, so as to achieve the effect of *accelerated motion*. The term derives from the earliest days of cinema, when film was run through by hand cranking rather than by motors. Not noted in OED. *Underdevelop*, to process a film too quickly, or at the wrong temperature, so producing a washed-out image; *underexpose*, to film with insufficient light, or at inadequate speeds, so that the resulting images are dark and indistinct; hence *underexposure*.

underground films   this now somewhat dated tag for the kind of *avant-garde* or *experimental* films that were being made in America from the early 1950s onwards by the likes of Stan Brakhage, Jonas Mekas, Jack Smith, the Kuchar brothers and so on appears to date from 1959. (The use of the word 'underground' to signify 'hidden, concealed, secret', however, begins in the late 17th C: 'This is their help, that some secret underground hopes which they espy not, do revive, at least sometimes' – Gilpin, 1677.) In the Spring 1959 issue of *Film Culture*, Lewis Jacobs wrote an article entitled 'Morning for the Experimental Film' in which he referred to 'film which for most of its life has led an underground existence'; in the same year, the film-maker Stan Vander-Beek began, so he said, to use the adjective 'underground' to define his own work and that of directors with whom he felt an affinity. Before this period, curiously, 'underground film' had been a term the influential American movie critic Manny Farber had used to describe cheap adventure movies of the 1930s and 1940s. Some of the new generation of 'underground' film-makers were uncomfortable with the connotations of sleaziness in the adjective, but it soon achieved common currency, not least because exhibitors found out that advertisements for 'underground films' would draw larger audiences than those promising 'avant-garde' fare. Sheldon Renan's *An Introduction to the American Underground Film* is an illuminating short history of the genre; Stan Brakhage's *Film at Wit's End* (1989) contains some fascinating, charming and occasionally tragic anecdotes of the movement's leading lights: Jerome Hill, Marie Menken, Sidney Peterson, James Broughton, Maya Deren, Christopher MacLaine, Bruce Conner and Ken Jacobs.

undershoot   (a) to film too little usable material to complete a full-length film, or (b) to shoot too little *coverage* for a given scene or scenes (OED gives the word, but not this sense).

understudy   as in the theatre: (a) a performer who can stand in for a leading player in the event of illness or some other emergency – though understudies are much less commonly employed in the cinema, for the obvious reason that films are made once and for all rather than repeated night after night, and, except in certain surrealist films (Buñuel's *That Obscure Object of Desire*, for example, in which the desired heroine is played by two actresses), it is simply not possible to have more than one actor playing the same part. (b) The act of preparing for such a part, or playing it. OED notes the presence of the word in the *Slang Dictionary* of 1874: 'Some actors of position . . . have always other and inferior . . . artists understudying their parts.'

underwater cinematography   the process of shooting dramatic or documentary footage under water, and which requires special *underwater housing* for the camera.

undeveloped   the condition of film that has been exposed to light but not yet processed; current since the mid-20th C: 'Once they have been exposed, colour films should not be left undeveloped too long' – 1939. *Unexposed*, the condition of *raw stock* – film that has not been exposed to light.

unidirectional microphone   a microphone that picks up sound mostly from one direction; see *cardioid microphone*.

Unipod   a type of camera support, used in news filming or other circumstances requiring rapid set-ups.

unit   an extremely common abbreviation for *film unit* – the crew for a film; or, sometimes, the place where a film is shot, including the *location* itself and all the facilities brought there by the production team. The earliest use cited by OED is in 1959, but it was certainly in use before that date. Hence *unit manager* or *unit production manager*, the person in charge of running all the technical, logistical, financial and diplomatic aspects of a shoot; *unit photographer*, see *stills man*; *Unit publicist*, see *publicist*. See also *second unit*.

United Artists, United Artists Corporation   the well-known and often highly successful American production and distribution company, which was founded in 1919 and continued, with various fluctuations of fortune, until 1981, when it was sold to *MGM*: the resulting company was known as MGM/UA Entertainment from 1983 to 1991, when its new owners, Credit Lyonnais, changed its name to Metro-Goldwyn-Mayer Inc. and so wiped away the final trace of the old firm. The artists who originally made up United Artists were Charlie Chaplin, Douglas Fairbanks, D.W. Griffith and Mary Pickford, all four of them dissatisfied with the lack of power they had so far experienced in their contracts to other studios. Despite owning neither studio buildings nor cinemas, United Artists thrived on releasing this quartet's films throughout the silent era (including Griffith's *Broken Blossoms* and Chaplin's *The Gold Rush*), as well as movies by or featuring the likes of Buster Keaton, Gloria Swanson and Rudolph Valentino. After the coming of sound, Howard Hughes' *Hell's Angels* (1930) and *Scarface* (1932) were also produced with UA, and the company became the American distributor of British productions by Alexander Korda's *London Films*. The company's output tended towards the mediocre throughout the late 1930s and 1940s, but UA was given a tremendous fillip by the *Paramount Decrees*: unburdened by huge overheads, it was well placed to respond to the new, less monopolised state of the industry. Distinguished and/or famous UA productions of the years after the Paramount decrees include *The African Queen* (1951), *High Noon* (1952), *The Night of the Hunter* (1955), *Some Like It Hot* (1959), *The Apartment* (1960), *West Side Story* (1961) and, from 1962 onwards, the James Bond movies. In 1957 UA became a public company, and in 1967 was taken over by TransAmerica Corporation. Though the company continued to make a stir in the 1970s – it won the Academy Award for Best Picture in three successive years with *One Flew Over the Cuckoo's Nest* (1975), *Rocky* (1976) and *Annie Hall* (1977) – UA was seriously weakened by the internal divisions which prompted five of its executives to leave and found *Orion* Pictures. The film which finally slit UA's throat was the notoriously excessive *Heaven's Gate* (1980).

universal camera filter   a type of camera filter, such as a polariser, that does not affect the colour balance of the resulting image.

universal leader   the leader put at the start and end of each reel of a release print, marked with numbers and symbols; it helps the projectionist achive a smooth changeover and reduces the amount of damage done to the film itself. Universal leader has taken over as the standard form from the previously used *Academy leader*.

Universal Pictures   the major production company founded by Carl Laemmle in 1912 by amalgamating his *IMP* company with several others. Though the earliest Universal productions remembered by the general film-going public are probably the outstanding horror films of the early 1930s (James Whale's *Frankenstein*, Tod Browning's *Dracula*), the company was a major force in the silent era: Erich von Stroheim made his most successful films for Universal, Irving Thalberg and Harry Cohn both began their careers there, and the company's stars included Valentino and Lon Chaney Sr. From 1915 onwards, Universal productions were made at Universal City, a 230-acre development in the San Fernando valley – the site, lavishly equipped with rides and other attractions, is now one of California's leading tourist attractions. For most of the late 1930s, 1940s and early 1950s, the company managed to stay in the black thanks to musicals starring Deanna Durbin, comedies starring Abbott and Costello and similarly popular if undistinguished fare. In 1946, Universal merged with International Pictures, and was known as Universal-International until 1952, reverting to its old name just before a takeover by Decca records. In the following years, Universal product became rather more polished: Douglas Sirk's well-known melodramas are products of this new policy. In the 1960s, a decade in which the company became a subsidiary of MCA (Music Corporation of America), Universal became the film wing of Universal City Studios, Inc., a thriving television company specialisng in series. In the 1970s, it produced a series of major box-office hits (*Airport*, *American Graffiti*, *The Sting* and others) of which the most momentous was *Jaws* (1975). The unprecedented box office triumph of that film cemented a relationship between Universal and Steven Spielberg which has continued to the present day: Spielberg's company *Amblin Entertainment* has its headquarters on the Universal lot, and Universal has benefited from the huge profits of, *inter alia*, *ET the Extra-Terrestrial*, *Back to the Future* and *Jurassic Park*. In 1990, MCA was bought out by the Matsushita Electrical Industrial Company.

unsqueeze   to project film through an *anamorphic* lens, so correcting the distortions of anamorphic filming and creating a wide screen image. (See *aspect ratio*.) Hence *unsqueezed print*.

up shot   an alternative term for a *low angle shot*.

UPA   an abbreviation for United Productions of America, a production company formed by a group of former *Walt Disney* animators in 1943 that flourished in the 1950s, and is best remembered for creating the querulous and preposterously short-sighted character Mr Magoo.

upside-down slate   a *slate* used to mark the end of a scene rather than its start – in other words, a *tail slate* – is often presented to the camera upside-down.

uprating   to increase the contrast of film by shooting it at a high speed and then *overdeveloping* it; a synonym for *pushing*.

upstage   as a noun: the part of a set or stage furthest away from the camera, and thus from the viewer. As a verb: for one performer to block an audience's view of another, either literally or (more usually) metaphorically, by stealing a scene.

utility department   the humblest part of a crew or studio, responsible for cleaning, minor repairs and the like.

UV filter   a filter designed to cut down the haze caused by *ultraviolet* light; *UV printing*, the process of printing a sound-track with *ultraviolet* radiation.

V**amp** a *femme fatale* of the early screen; or a slightly arch term for one of her modern counterparts: Sharon Stone, say. The term, derived from *vampire*, is said to have been made current by the shrewdly orchestrated movie career of Theda Bara (*née* Theodosia Goodman, 1890–1955; the stage name is an anagram, possibly unintentional, of 'Death Arab'), who starred in about forty films for Fox between 1915 and 1920, each one a variation on the theme of men being lured to destruction by the sexual magic of a *belle dame sans merci*: *Carmen* (1915), *Cleopatra* (1917), *Salome* (1918) and so on. The prototype for this series of roles was *A Fool There Was* (1915) loosely based on Kipling's poem 'The Vampire'. It should be noted, though, that OED records an occurence of the word in this sense slightly earlier than 1915: 'Thackeray took it for granted that Mary Stuart was a vamp.' – G.K. Chesterton, 1911.

vampire movie an enduringly popular sub-genre of the *horror movie*, featuring the adventures, predations and downfall of the undead: high points include the original (unauthorised) screen adaptation of Bram Stoker's *Dracula*, Murnau's *Nosferatu, eine Symphonie des Grauens* (1922); Tod Browning's Universal *Dracula* (1931), starring Bela Lugosi as the Count; and Dreyer's sublime *Vampyr* (1932). Low points are too numerous to list, though *Mother Riley Meets the Vampire* (also, sadly, starring Bela Lugosi) would have its supporters; at the time of writing, the most recent vampire movie is one of the most lavish, Neil Jordan's *Interview with the Vampire* (1995), adapted from the best-seller by Anne Rice. 'Vampire' comes into English from the French *vampire*, itself an adapatation of the Magyar *vampir* (a word of Slavonic origin), in the early 18th C. David Pirie has written an interesting history of the form.

variable-area a type of *optical sound-track*, which takes the visible form of a single or double white line, running along the side of the film, with variably serrated edge, the peaks and troughs of which correspond to variations in the sound; its appearance is best known to the general public through the amusing 'dancing sound-track' sequence in *Fantasia*. Hence *variable-area sound track*, *variable-area recording*. But the variable-area track has now largely been supplanted by the *variable-density sound track*, another type of optical sound-track; in this case, the visible form of the recorded sound is a sequence of horizontal stripes of varying darkness and brightness at the edge of the film.

variable focus lens see *zoom* and *zoom lens*. *Variable shutter*, a shutter that can create *fades* and *dissolves* in the camera (an alternative to the more usual method of achieving them in printing) by controlling the degree of exposure; it has one fixed and one movable aperture plate. *Variable speed control*, *variable speed motor*, a camera motor used to create slow or accelerated motion sequences, and which usually has a speed range of 4 FPS (or a sixth normal speed) to 50 FPS (just over twice normal speed).

Variety the most famous and influential of all the American *trades*. It

266

was founded in 1905 by Sime Silverman, and originally devoted to vaudeville and other forms of stage entertainment (hence the name: *variety*, from the early 19th C onwards, was the general term for the American counterpart to Britain's Music Halls), but now covers all aspects of the entertainment industries, with a particular emphasis on cinema. Outside the industry, it is best known for its unique sociolect of jaunty abbreviations ('thesp' for actor) and coinages ('oater' for Western), variously amusing or repellent according to one's sense of linguistic propriety; elsewhere in this book, examples of such words are identified as *Variety*-speak and translated into standard English. The most famous example of *Variety*-speak, 'Stix Nix Hix Pix' (which may be translated: the audiences in rural and provincial areas of the United States show little appetite for dramas about their own circumstances) was taken up as the title of a novel, and is also seen as a headline in *Yankee Doodle Dandy*.

vault   the place in which negatives and other valuable films or tapes are stored for safety: a fireproof, temperature-controlled chamber. The word 'vault' was taken over from OF *voute, voulte*, etc. in the late 14th C, and came to mean 'a storeroom for provisons of liquors' by the early 16th C. 'In our dayes we vse to keepe both Wine and Grayne in suche vaultes' – Barnabe Goodge, 1577.

VCR   the standard abbreviation for a *Video Cassette Recorder*.

vehicle   either (a) a film designed as a showcase for the particular talents of a performer, or – though these definitions often overlap in practice – (b) a highly commercial genre film in which the star is the main selling point: a Van Damme action movie, an Eddie Murphy comedy, a romantic thriller starring Madonna. The term was taken over by the film industry from the stage, where it had been current since the mid-19th C: 'Lady Gifford's quasi-comedy of '*Finesse*', which . . . simply served as a vehicle for some of Mr Buckstone's practical drolleries and preposterous costumes' – *Illustrated Times*, 15 August 1863.

velocitator   a mechanical platform, somewhere between a *dolly* and a *boom* in size, that can lift the camera, cameraman and focus puller upwards by about six feet. Not noted in OED, but evidently derived, like 'velocipede' and 'velocimeter', from 'velocity' (from Fr *velocité* or L *velocitas*; it enters English around the mid-16th C).

Venice, Venice Film Festival   this was the world's first international film festival, and established the template for most of the major events of the kind, including *Cannes*. It was launched in 1923 as part of the city's Biennale, was repeated at the 1934 Biennale and thereafter became in principle an annual event, though it has been cancelled on several occasions either because of warfare (1943–5) or less bloody forms of political dispute. The main prize awarded at venice is the Golden Lion or *Leone d'Oro*, the lion of St Mark being Venice's heraldic animal. See *festivals*.

vertical control   a business term, meaning the kind of control that the leading American studios enjoyed until the *Paramount decision* (or

Paramount decrees) of 1948, which said that they were breaking the anti-trust laws. Up to this point, the studios had owned not only production and distribution facilities but also chains of cinemas. After this ruling, they were obliged to sell off their cinemas.

vertical wipe   a *wipe* that crosses the screen vertically; horizontal wipes are more common.

VGIK   or Vsesoyuznyi Gosudarstvenyi Institut Kinematografii, ('All-Union State Institute of Cinematography'), the world's first film school, was founded in 1919 at the behest of Lenin. Despite the crippling poverty of its early years, VGIK proved to be one of the most fertile breeding grounds for talent and technique the cinema has seen, and it employed directors of the first rank as teachers: among others, Eisenstein, Dovzhenko, Pudovkin and Kosintsev. See *Kuleshov effect*.

video   from L *viderere*, and the first person singular of its present tense, *video*: (1) the technology of recording images and sounds on magnetic tape. The principal video system used in the UK is PAL (Phase Alternation Line); the USA has an NTSC system, which, so scornful British technicians will tell you, stands for 'Never Twice the Same Colour' (in reality: National Television System Committee). (2) The common abbreviation for (a) the domestic or industrial *VCR* (*Video Cassette Recorder*), which needs no further description here; (b) the tape cassettes used in VCRs and also (c) the act of recording onto a cassette, either from a television broadcast or from another cassette; or, in video film-making, a synonym for the terms 'to *film*' or 'to *shoot*'. (3) The standard term for the short – usually two to three minute long – musical entertainments made by rock musicians and the like to accompany their songs by way of promotion (hence the synonymous, but much less common *promo*). The term is now, pedantically speaking, anachronistic, since the great majority of music videos have been shot on film for the last decade or so, and their production values can be extremely high; the earliest generation of rock videos, which actually were shot on tape, now tend to look shoddy or quaint. Rock, rap, pop and soul videos provide the staple of cable and satellite television channels such as MTV, VH1 and The Box; the presenters who introduce them are sometimes referred to as VJs, an abbreviation for *Video Jockey*, itself a modification of the familiar DJ or Disc Jockey.

There are many other associated terms for 'video', including *video assist* (a technique used in feature film-making which involves shooting video images at the same time and through the same lens as the film images, so that scenes can be reviewed by the director as soon as they are completed) and many other, usually self-explanatory terms: *video editing*, *video format* (the three main formats being PAL, NTSC and SECAM – *Système Electronique Couleur avec Memoire*), *video leader*, *videotape* and so on. The word 'video' enters the language in the 1930s to designate some technical aspects of the new medium of television. Of the senses listed above, 2a is first recorded in 1958 ('The Video is like a combined tape-recorder and cine-camera'), 2b and 3 in 1968 ('The days of the disc, in the pop world at least, are numbered. For soon will come the video.') and 2c in 1971.

Vietnam movies   in the simplest sense, a sub-genre of the *war movie*, depicting the conflict between the United States and North Vietnam from the American point of view. However, since there are so many examples of the form, and since its defining elements have become so strictly codified – the choppers, the unseen Vietnamese enemy in the foliage, the 'psychedelic' rock soundtrack – it deserves to be considered as a minor genre in its own right, and has been done so, notably by Gilbert Adair in his critical history *Hollywood's Vietnam*. It is also worth stressing the fact that the Vietnam film is almost wholly a retrospective phenomenon: with the sole exception of the ultra-Hawkish John Wayne vehicle *The Green Berets*, released in 1968, all of the films which now define the war for popular memory in the West were made well after the fall of Saigon in 1975: *Apocalypse Now* (1979), *Born on the Fourth of July* (1989), *The Boys in Company C* (1977), *The Deer Hunter* (1978), *Full Metal Jacket* (1987), *Gardens of Stone* (1987), *Good Morning Vietnam* (1987), *Go Tell the Spartans* (1977), *Hamburger Hill* (1987), *Heaven and Earth* (1994), *Platoon* (1986), *Rambo; First Blood, Part II* (1985), *Saigon* (1988), *Uncommon Valor* (1983) and so on. 'The singular achievement of Hollywood's retrospective treatment of Vietnam is not, however, its creation of a terse and potent iconography for the war ... but the thoroughness with which its carefully coded fictions have superseded all other representations. (Not one movie set in Vietnam, incidentally, has so far been based on a Vietnam novel of any literary distinction)' – the author, *The Independent*, 29 April 1995. Though they are not usually treated as examples of the 'Vietnam movie' school, other, rather less well-known films about the Vietnam war (usually bitterly hostile to America's involvement) have been made outside Hollywood: *Loin du Vietnam* (1967) by Chris Marker, Jean-Luc Godard and others, and Peter Brook's *Tell Me Lies* (also 1967), for example; and it can be argued with some plausibility that Vietnam is the true or implicit subject of a good many of the films made by Hollywood during the period of hostilities, no matter their explicit subject-matter. Some cases are fairly obvious – it would take exceptional naïveté to believe that Robert Altman's *M*A*S*H* (1969), nominally set in the Korean War, is actually about the conscript GIs of the 1950s – others (*Bonnie and Clyde? The Wild Bunch? Soldier Blue?*) more debatable.

Vieux Colombier   once a theatre specialising in avant-garde pieces, it was taken over by the writer and director Jean Tedesco (1895–1958) in 1924 and converted into a cinema devoted to similarly experimental films, including works by Vigo and Renoir; this was Paris's first *avant-garde* cinema, and so, since Paris was still the acknowledged capital of such things, probably the world's. The Vieux Colombier also had a small production studio, in which Tedesco and Renoir collaborated on *La Petite Marchande d'allumettes* (1928).

viewer   a noun derived from the Anglo-French *vewe*, *veue*, etc., used from the early 15th C: either (a) a real or hypothetical member of the cinema audience (OED cites a delightfully apt earlier use of this sense from 1579: 'You are such a narrowe vewer of such idle pictures'), or (b) the generic term for any equipment used for viewing film, such as a *Steenbeck* or *Moviola*; OED records the sense 'an optical device for looking at film transparencies or the like' from 1936 onwards.

viewfinder   the part of the camera through which the cameraman (and, sometimes, the director) will look so as to compose the image. Known in English since 1899; OED also cross refers to a slightly earlier photographic sense for the word 'finder': 'The handiest view finder for quick exposure work is to fit a double convex lens . . . to the front of the camera', 1889.

viewing filter, viewing glass   the small circular filter which the director and cinematographer peer through in order to assess light levels.

viewzak   Jean-Claude Carrière has recently suggested (in *The Secret Language of Film*) that we are in need a term for that endless stream of nondescript images on television, video and cinema screens that have the same numbing effect on our visual sensibilities as Muzak is designed to have on our ears. I would therefore like to propose the suitably ugly coinage *viewzak*.

vignette   (from OF *vignete*; it occurs in English as *vinet* and similar variants from the early 15th C, and is readopted as *vignette* in the 18th C), an image that is sharp at the centre but blurred around the edges, in the manner of an early photographic portrait; the photographic sense comes into English in the 1860s.

virgin   an adjective sometimes applied to film that has not been exposed – that is, to *raw stock*. From the Anglo-French and Old French *virgine*, etc., and ultimately from L *virginem*, the accusative of *virgo*, 'maiden'; the metaphorical use of 'purity' or 'freedome from mark' dates from as early as the 14th C.

VistaVision   the trade name for a *wide-screen* system used in the mid- to late 1950s, though a prototype had been tried out as early as 1919. Developed by Paramount, it did not use *anamorphic* lenses but was based on running 35mm film horizontally through the camera; the resulting image had an aspect ratio of about 1.85 to 1. Though the system died young, the word remained in use as a vague metaphor for lavish production values: the *New Musical Express* for 12 February 1976, for example, calls a Diana Ross album 'a vistavision [*sic*] affair'.

visual effects   a term largely synonymous with *special effects*, though it can sometimes be applied to unusual lighting, filters and the like.

Vitagraph   the name (from L *vita*, 'life', plus – *graph*, from Gk *graphos*, 'writing') of an early American production company, founded in 1899, and also of the projector/camera developed by one of its co-founders, Albert E. Smith, from the *Kinetoscope* they had bought from Edison.

The company soon flourished, and, under the guidance of another founder, the British-born James Stuart Blackton (?1868–1941), started to produce longer and more complex films, including a series of one-reel adapations of Shakespeare plays in 1908; they also pioneered *newsreel* and *animation* techniques, though many of their *actuality* films were staged. Vitagraph helped form the short-lived *Motion Pictures Patents Company* in 1909, and in 1915 entered into a consortium with *Essanay*, *Lubin* and *Selig*, which became known as VLSE in 1917. It was taken over by Warner Brothers in 1925.

Vitaphone   the sound system that made the first *talkies* possible, and made the fortune of the company that helped develop it, *Warner Brothers*. Vitaphone was first heard by the public in screenings of *Don Juan* (1926), though the 'soundtrack' for this film consisted of nothing more than some music and a spoken introduction explaining the process; then, most famously, in *The Jazz Singer* (1927), where it provided the songs and a few dialogue scenes; and in the first all-talking talkie, *The Lights of New York* (1928). Unfortunately, the process was immensely cumbersome – it used oversized records – and was soon replaced by *optical sound* systems. 'A method of talking-motion pictures has been developed in America. The invention is called the vitaphone [*sic*]' – *Westminster Gazette*, 20 September 1926.

Vitarama   an early prototype of the *cinerama* system, only shown once in public (in 1939), in which multiple films were projected onto a curved screen. Not cited in OED.

Vitascope   an early form of *projector* using the *Latham loop*; it was bought by Edison from its inventors, and used for the first commercial screenings of films in the United States on 23 April 1986. 'The vitascope [*sic*] throws upon a screen by means of bright lights and powerful lenses the moving life size figures of human beings and animals' – *Columbus Dispatch*, 4 April 1896.

Vitasound   the trade name of a stereophonic sound system used by Warner Brothers in the 1950s. Not cited in OED.

VLSE   see *Vitagraph*.

voice artist   in *animation*, the actor who speaks the lines for a cartoon character. One of the few voice artists to achieve fame in his own right was the late Mel Blanc (1908–89), who rasped, lisped, spluttered, bawled and drawled the voices of Bugs Bunny, Daffy Duck, Sylvester Cat and the rest of the zany menagerie in the course of some 3,000 cartoons for Warner Brothers.

voice-over (VO)   speech that originates from somewhere off-screen, either in the form of *narration* or from a character who has not yet appeared on screen. '. . . it was a matter of judgment whether the voice-over announcer would come on to plug the sexual properties of petrol, hand-lotion or tooth-paste' – *The Listener*, 19 September 1968. First recorded by OED in 1947.

VU meter   the common abbreviation for a *Volume Units meter*, which indicates the peaks and troughs of sound amplitude on a recording or playback machine, usually in decibels. Old recording suite joke: Neophyte: 'What does the VU stand for?' Seasoned pro: 'Virtually Useless.'

W **A** abbreviation for *Wide Angle*.

walkie-talkie a small personal radio transmitter used by assistant directors and others to co-ordinate activities on a set. The device is said to have been originally developed by the US Army Signal Corps, and its name first appears in print in 1939.

walk-on (a) an extremely brief appearance in a film, otherwise known as a *bit part*. 'Or I might get a walk-on in a film' – Rosamund Lehmann, *The Weather in the Streets* (1936). (b) the actor who takes such an unglamorous part. The term was first used in the theatre in the nineteenth century; it sometimes appears in the form *walker-on*.

walk-through a technical rehearsal conducted largely for the benefit of the crew, so that they can work out the relationship of camera, mikes and lights to the subjects.

walla, wallah, walla-walla the general hum and buzz of background activity in a scene, including the 'rhubarb, rhubarb' noise of speech. Origins mysterious, though a *walla-walla* is a small boat used in the waters around Hong Kong, not a city noted for its tranquillity. See *wild track*.

Walt Disney Company formerly **Walt Disney Productions**, often simply known as **Disney** grew from the early partnership of Walt Disney (1901–66) and the gifted cartoonist Ub Iwerks (1901–71). They met in 1919 in a commercial art studio in Kansas, and by 1923 were in Hollywood, working on their first, unsuccessful production *Alice in Cartoonland*, a series which combined live action and animation. By 1928, things were starting to look up: *Oswald the Lucky Rabbit* proved much more popular (though rights to the character were taken by the series' distributor), and the partnership had just dreamed up their most immortal creation, Mickey Mouse, who starred in three productions that year, *Plane Crazy*, *Gallopin' Gaucho* and the landmark film *Steamboat Willie*. Hard on the tail of Mickey came the Three Little Pigs, stars of the *Silly Symphony* series (1929), and the company began to seem unstoppable. By the mid-1930s, Disney employed over 700 production staff, had distribution offices in London and Paris and a vigorous merchandising division which established the precedent for all such operations in the future: in the holiday season of 1933, a quarter of a million Christmas trees had Mickey Mouse railway engines nestling at their feet. Disney productions were marked not only by their founder's notorious perfectionism but by ceaseless technical innovation. *Steamboat Willie* (1928) was the first sound cartoon; *Flowers and Trees* (1933) the first to use three-strip *Technicolor*; the first feature-length sound cartoon in colour was *Snow White and the Seven Dwarfs* (1937) – Ub Iwerks devised the *multiplane camera* in the course of production on this film; and *Fantasia* (1940) achieved an early approximation to full stereophonic sound. But the company also encountered some major setbacks: Disney's authoritarian work practices led to the defection of a number of his animators who set up the rival *UPA* (*United Productions of America*), and the war interrupted work on *Bambi* (1943). The last half-century has also seen various fluctuations in the company's fortunes, notably during the 1970s, after the death of Walt himself. Yet the scope of Disney's franchise on Western childhood remains unequalled, and there can be very few parents who have not contributed to its profits at some time, either through tickets, video rentals, merchandising or visits to the Disney theme parks in California, Florida and the somewhat less popular venue near Paris. Disney also has a production arm which concentrates on slightly more adult fare, Touchstone, and (since 1954), its own distribution company, Buena Vista. In the last few years, the company has managed to revive the full-length animated feature with conspicuous success: *Beauty and the Beast, Aladdin* and *The Lion King* have all attracted large audiences and the approval of quite a few critics.

WAMPAS baby stars   the thirteen young actresses nominated as showing exceptional promise by the Western Association of Motion Picture Advertisers between 1922 and 1934; the group included Joan Crawford (1926), Jean Arthur (1929) and Ginger Rogers (1932).

Wardour Street   'The only street that's shady on both sides' – the traditional London home of the British film industry, it runs through Soho from Oxford Street to Old Compton Street. For about half a century, the name was used as a synecdoche for British cinema: 'A still more ambitious "ten million pound" company died even before it became more than a Wardour Street fairy tale' – *Stage Year Book*, 1920; 'It amazes me how few films we manage to make in a year here: Wardour Street seems to have accepted defeat' – *The Times*, 20 December 1977. (In the 19th century, when the street was best known for its antique and fake-antique shops, 'Wardour Street' was a sardonic term for the pseudo-archaic diction used in historical novels.) Now that the national industry is in such an enfeebled condition, that use is becoming increasingly unusual. However, even though many of the street's former cinematic landmarks have been handed on to other industries, both Warner Brothers and Rank still have their headquarters here, Fox and Columbia Tri-Star are just short walks away, and most of the screening rooms in which the nation's film critics see advance screenings of the latest productions are located either in Wardour Street or in minor streets nearby.

wardrobe   From OF *warderobe*, a variant of *garderobe*, a room in which clothing or valuables are kept; it crossed over to England in the late 14th C: (a) any or all of the clothing worn by actors, or (b) more commonly, an abbreviation for *wardrobe department*, the team which buys, makes, alters and maintains all costumes, under the direction of a *wardrobe master* or *mistress* (or *man, woman*). The cinema takes this use directly from the theatre, and ultimately from the British nobility, for whom 'Warderobe' meant 'the office or department of a royal or noble household charged with the care of the wearing apparel' (OED): 'The which Warantes yf I should paye hem, your Household, Chambre, and

Warderobe, and your Werkes, shuld be unservid and unpaide' (1433). It enters theatrical use around the early 18th C; Addison notes in *The Spectator* that 'It is indeed very odd . . . to observe in the Wardrobe of the Play-house several Daggers, Poniards, Wheels, Bowls for Poison' (1711).

war film   the term originally appears to have been applied principally to *documentary* or *newsreel* coverage of armed conflicts; the *New York Times* for 14 January 1914 reports: 'Real war "movies" shown . . . Moving pictures of real warfare were exhibited in Seventy-first Regiment Armory last night.' But directors had already noted the dramatic possibilities of warfare for the cinema – D.W. Griffith's *The Battle*, which recreated a Civil War skirmish, and *The Massacre*, representing Custer's Last Stand, were made in 1911 and 1912 respectively; Griffith topped both with *Birth of a Nation* in 1915. The success of these and similar productions meant that the term 'war movie' soon became applied almost exclusively to feature films about war; hence the phrasing of a comment in Paul Rotha's *The Film till Now* (1930, the earliest survey of world cinema): 'Like all war films manufactured in Hollywood, *The Big Parade* [King Vidor, 1925] carried little of the real spirit of war.' Among the notable examples of the genre: thoroughly or vaguely pacifist films including *All Quiet on the Western Front* (Lewis Milestone, 1930), *Paths of Glory* (Stanley Kubrick, 1957), *The Charge of the Light Brigade* (Tony Richardson, 1968) and *Gallipoli* (Peter Weir, 1981); prisoner-of-war stories including *La Grande Illusion* (Jean Renoir, 1937) and *Bridge on the River Kwai* (David Lean, 1957); black comedies such as *M*A*S*H* (Robert Altman, 1969), *Catch-22* (Mike Nichols, 1970), *Dr Strangelove* (Stanley Kubrick, 1963) and *Stalag 17* (Billy Wilder, 1953); epics *cum* biopics such as *Napoléon* (Abel Gance, 1927) and *Lawrence of Arabia* (David Lean, 1962); thick-eared adventures such as *The Dirty Dozen* (Robert Aldrich, 1967); semi-autobiographical combat films such as *The Big Red One* (Sam Fuller, 1980); agitational pieces such as Gillo Pontecorvo's *The Battle of Algiers* (1965) or – though its status as a safe 'classic' tends to tame its political energies – Eisenstein's *Battleship Potemkin*; musical laments (Derek Jarman's *War Requiem*, 1988, from the choral work by Britten); fantasies (*A Matter of Life and Death*, Powell and Pressburger, 1946); historical films and literary adaptations (*The Last Valley*, James Clavell, 1970; *War and Peace*, by King Vidor in 1956 and Sergei Bondarchuk in 1967); and so on. For the many films about America's involvement with South-East Asia, see *Vietnam movies*.

Warner Brothers   the major American production company, which grew from a film distribution business organised by Albert, Harry, Jack and Sam Warner in 1917; in 1923, Jack and Sam moved to Hollywood and the quartet founded Warner Bros Pictures Inc. The company's first five years were not particularly distinguished, save for the construction of several major cinemas and the acquisition of *Vitagraph*, and it was their chronic financial instability that led the brothers to gamble on the development of sound pictures. Sam Warner collaborated with Western Electric and Bell Telephone Laboratories on the *Vitaphone*, a disc system, but died just 24 hours before the première of the film which saw its first full exploitation, turned around the company's fortunes and revolutionised the film industry: *The Jazz Singer* (1927). With the profits of this and other pioneering *talkies*, Warner Bros expanded rapidly, taking over the huge Stanley theatre chain in 1932 and various other production companies including First National. Warner Brothers soon became celebrated for their low-budget, high-entertainment value films, and produced many of the most celebrated *gangster movies* of the 1930s, introducing the world to the likes of Humphey Bogart, James Cagney and Edward G. Robinson. They also produced several Busby Berkeley *musicals* (including *42nd Street*, 1933), some social conscience movies (*I Am a Fugitive from a Chain Gang*, 1932) and a few self-consciously 'prestige' features, including *biopics* about Pasteur and Zola. In the 1940s, the company went on to produce *Casablanca* (1942), *The Maltese Falcon* (1941) and *The Treasure of the Sierra Madre* (1948); they also initiated the immortal cartoon series featuring the adventures of Bugs Bunny and his peers. Though the company lost its cinemas after the *Paramount decision* of 1948, it diversified quite profitably into the new growth industry of television, and, much as in the 1930s, managed to produce and/or distribute both glossy musicals (*My Fair Lady*, 1964) and rather more abrasive fare: *Rebel Without a Cause* (1955), *Who's Afraid of Virginia Woolf?* (1966), *Bonnie and Clyde* (1967), *All the President's Men* (1976). The company has been through various changes of identity since the mid-1960s, including a merger with the distributor Seven Arts, an acquisition by the financial concern Kinney National Service and an amalgamation with Columbia. *Warnercolor* was the trade name coined for films shot in *Eastman Color* and processed by Warner.

warning bell   either (a) the automatic bell that rings in a projection room to warn of an imminent reel change, or (b) the bell or other loud signal that alerts everyone on or around a set that a *take* is about to begin. In the latter case, a red *warning light* (or *wigwag*) outside the set usually flashes until the take is complete.

wash   the bath which removes all the developing chemicals from newly processed film.

weave   the accidental sideways wobbling of film through a projector or camera; derived from the common verb meaning 'to move from side to side', current in English since the late 16th C.

wedge   a strip of film sent back from the lab with the rushes to indicate the range of densities that can be produced from the negative.

weenie   a small object – a stolen diamond, say – that offers the excuse for setting a plot in motion; see *MacGuffin*. Presumably derived from other uses connoting smallness – 'a very young child' – and slang adjectival forms such as 'teeny-weeny'.

weepie   jocular term for a maudlin or lachrymose film. 'There are undoubtedly times when a film calculated to raise buckets of tears has its appeal. Someone recently christened this type of picture . . . a "weepie"' – *Sunday Dispatch*, 23 December 1928. See **tearjerker**.

Western, western An action film set in the western states of America, usually some time between the end of the Civil War and the turn of the century, and featuring the exploits of cowboys, Indians, gunslingers, gamblers and the US Cavalry. It can be argued that the Western is the oldest of all cinematic genres, since Edison was shooting *kinetograph* items about Wild West shows in 1894, and in 1898 filmed a quintessential saloon scene, *Cripple Creek Bar-room*. The first true Western, however, was Edwin S. Porter's *The Great Train Robbery* (1903), a reconstruction of the Wild Bunch's raid on the Union Pacific Railroad three years earlier. Among the actors in Porter's film was one Gilbert M. Anderson (1883–1971), who co-founded the *Essanay* company, adopted the identity of 'Broncho Billy' (originally created by the novelist Peter B. Kyne) for *Broncho Billy and the Baby* (1908) and thus created the original Western hero, whose adventures were chronicled in some three hundred short films. The Western was off at a gallop, and scarcely faltered until the 1970s and 1980s, when some pundits assumed that it had finally gone to Boot Hill. OED notes an adjectival use of 'Western' as early as 1909 ('The success of their Western series of last year was abundantly satisfying and added greatly to the reputation of the firm' – *Moving Picture World*, 6 November 1909); by 1912 it had grown up into a noun ('A powerful Western, distinctly unusual among typical "Westerns" containing a beautiful story and a dashing indian battle that will interest and instruct' – ibid, 27 July 1912). Though it was once fashionable for intellectuals to sneer at Westerns as crude, melodramatic and racist (the critic Dwight Macdonald once called the form 'vapid and infantile'), informed consensus has now moved almost to the other extreme (the critic Terrence Rafferty recently speculated that Sam Peckinpah's *The Wild Bunch*, originally released in 1969 and reissued in 1995, was the greatest of all American films) and even those *cinephiles* who could not name a Randolph Scott movie to save themselves from lynching will earnestly inform listeners that John Ford is one of the cinema's great poets. The genre is much too vast to permit the naming of more than a handful of its major practitioners here, though it would be shameful not to list a few credits for the aforementioned Ford (*The Iron Horse, Stagecoach, My Darling Clementine, Fort Apache, She Wore a Yellow Ribbon, The Wagonmaster, The Searchers, The Man Who Shot Liberty Valance*) and Peckinpah (*Ride the High Country, The Ballad of Cable Hogue, Pat Garrett and Billy the Kid*). Other essential director's names include D.W. Griffith (many one-reel Westerns between 1908 and 1914), Thomas H. Ince (*The Bargain*, which gave the screen its first western star in the strong, silent person of William S. Hart), Howard Hawks (*Red River, Rio Bravo*), Howard Hughes (*The Outlaw*), King Vidor (*Billy the Kid, Duel in the Sun*), Raoul Walsh (*The Big Trail*, in which John Wayne had his first starring role), Victor Fleming (*The Virginian*), Budd Boetticher (*Seven Men from Now, The Tall T* – both, potential lynch mob victims might like to know, vehicles for Randolph Scott), Michael Curtiz (*Santa Fe Trail*), Alan Dwan (*Frontier Marshall*), Fritz Lang (*Western Union, Rancho Notorious*), Henry King (*The Gunfighter*) Anthony Mann (*Winchester 73, The Man from Laramie*), Nicholas Ray (*Johnny Guitar*), Sam Fuller (*Run of the Arrow*), George Stevens (*Shane*), Arthur Penn (*The Left-Handed Gun*), Fred Zinnemann (*High Noon*), Marlon Brando (*One-Eyed Jacks*), John Sturges (*Gunfight at the OK Corral, The Magnificent Seven*), Don Siegel (*Flaming Star*) and Clint Eastwood (*High Plains Drifter, Pale Rider*). Though it is the most distinctively American of film genres, even more so than the *musical*, the Western has none the less inspired and been imitated by filmmakers in other nations, notably Kurosawa in Japan and Sergio Leone, grand master of the *Spaghetti Western*, in Italy. Announcements of the death of the Western have since proved premature, though it still looks unlikely that it will ever become the staple of production it once was; there has been a striking, if fitful revival in the last ten years, which has encompassed films as various as *Silverado, Wyatt Earp, Dances With Wolves, Geronimo, Tombstone, Unforgiven* and so on, as well as such relatively novel spins on the genre as the all-black Western (*Posse*; incidentally, it has been estimated that some 30 per cent of real-life cowboys were of African descent) and the female Western (*Bad Girls*). Philip French's monograph *Westerns* (1973) offers an excellent critical introduction by a long-term fan, and one of the best brief characterisations of its extreme adaptability: 'The Western is a great grab-bag, a hungry cuckoo of a genre, a voracious bastard of a form, ready to seize anything that's in the air from juvenile delinquency to ecology. Yet despite this, or in some ways because of it, one of the things the Western is always about is America rewriting and reinterpreting her own past, however honestly or dishonestly it may be done.' Further information and enlightenment can be found in *The BFI Companion to the Western*, edited by Ed Buscombe.

wet gate, wet gate printing   a printing system which greatly reduces the amount of scratching and produces a sharp image; the film is bathed in a solution of tetrachlorethylene just before printing begins, so that minute holes on both sides of the film are filled. The method is also known as a *liquid gate*.

WGA   see *Writers' Guild of America*.

whip pan, whip shot   a sudden panning movement; see *zip pan*.

whodunit, whodunnit   precisely as with fiction and the stage: a slang term for a *mystery film*.

whoofer   a gadget used to blow powder into the air; used in combination with *pyrotechnics*, it helps create the effect of an explosion; from the verb meaning 'to make a sound like that of a sudden expulsion of air.'

wide angle, wide angle shot   a shot which embraces more than 60 degrees, rather than the standard 45 to 50 degrees. Such shots can only be achieved with a *wide-angle lens*, which creates a certain amount of distortion: subjects in the foreground are magnified, those in the backround are reduced; *widen*, to pull back from the subject either by moving the camera or adjusting the zoom; *wide screen*, a film with a broader **aspect ratio** than the standard, achieved by one of several *wide screen processes*.

wigwag   the red light mounted outside a sound stage to warn passers-by that shooting is taking place. A noun unknown to OED, though it notes that the verb wigwag means 'to move lightly to and fro', and especially 'to wave a flag in signalling'. The vovel change from I (wig) to A (wag) appears to be an analogical enactment of to-and-fro motion.

wild   the general adjective appiled to non-synchronous sound recording – *wild sound, wild track* – or, less frequently, to non-synchronous images (or *wild pictures*). *Chambers's Technical Dictionary*, 1940, defines wild track as 'a sound-track which is recorded independently of any photographic track or mute, but is destined to be used in editing a sound-film'. Hence *wild lines*, dialogue that is recorded non-synchronously. A *wild motor* is an alternative name for a **variable speed motor** ; a *wild wall* is an easily removable set wall.

Williams shot   a form of **matte shot** invented by Frank Williams in 1918, and used for several years thereafter.

wind   noun, the direction in which film is rolled on to a core: either with the emulsion side facing outwards (*B wind*) as in shooting, or facing inwards (*A wind*) as in printing. *Winding*, to spool film from one core or reel to another; *wind machine* (or *ritter*), a large fan of engine used to create wind effects. A *wind sleeve* is the fabric covering that fits over a microphone for outdoor filming to reduce the amount of wind noise it will pick up; see **Dougal, zeppelin**.

wipe   a transitional device, achieved with an *optical printer*, in which one scene appears to push another horizontally or vertically off the screen; in the earlier part of the century, often known as a *wipe dissolve* (illogically, since each image remains sharp and there is no *dissolve* effect): 'There is no real equivalent in music even of the "wipe-dissolve" which leads the eye gently but quickly from one scene to another' – Constant Lambert, *Music Ho!*, 1934. Hence *wipe to black*, a wipe in which the outgoing image is replaced by a black image.

wireless microphone   a miniature microphone *cum* transmitter hidden on a performer and used when more orthodox means of sound recording are hard to arrange.

wire-tripping   the traditional method for making a galloping horse fall over.

woman's picture, women's picture   the slightly, or more than slightly dismissive terms for the movies Hollywood once made for a female audience, and concentrating on domestic drama and romance rather than the more violent activities characteristic of genres aimed at men. Classic examples include *Mildred Pierce* (Michael Curtiz, 1945), starring Joan Crawford, and *Now, Voyager* (Irving Rapper, 1942), starring Bette Davis.

woodsman   in pornographic productions, a male actor with the ability to achieve and sustain an erection more or less on command. Hence the expression *waiting for wood*, a delay caused by a male performer's temporary inability to rise to the occasion. 'Wood' (as in 'morning wood') is a common slang term for an erection in the US. See also *fluff*.

woofer   the counterpart to a *tweeter*: a loudspeaker designed to emit low frequency sounds; the term, jocularly inspired by the deep bark of large dogs, has been in common use since the mid-1930s.

work print   the rough version of a film nearing completion, created by editing *rushes* together; *working title*, the title sometimes given to a film in progress, either because the real title is undecided or because the producers have some good reason for wanting to keep its name secret. *Working Title* is a British production company.

wow   the onomatopoeic term for the sound distortion created when a tape runs at an uneven speed. 'Wobble or "wow" – to use the expressive American term . . . is not so troublesome nowadays, most modern sound cameras having anti-wow mechanism' – *Wireless World*, 16 March 1932.

wrangler   an animal handler, often specialising in the care, feeding, grooming, control and safety of a particular species: dogs, horses, tigers. From the 19th C Western American slang term for a herder on a ranch or farm.

wrap   as a noun: the end of a day's shooting, or of the *principal photography* for an entire production; the latter event is usually celebrated with a *wrap party*. As a verb: to finish shooting, or complete a film. OED notes that the verb 'to wrap' has meant 'to bring to completion' since the early 20th C.

Writer's Guild of America (WGA)   the union which represents the interests of screenwriters in the United States. The credit *written by* indicates that both the story and the screenplay are the work of the credited writer or writers.

Wurlitzer   affectionately known as 'the Mighty Wurlitzer', the brand name of the organ, manufactured by the Rudolf Wurlitzer Company, that would rise up in front of the screen in the intervals between films to keep audiences diverted. The glory days of the Wurlitzer were the 1930s and 1940s, but some cinemas maintained such an organ into the early 1960s.

X **(or X-certificate)** In the United Kingdom, the X *certificate* was originally introduced in 1951 by the *BBFC* to bar entry to screenings for those under the age of 16; in 1970 that age limit was raised to 18, and in 1983 the X certificate waṣ superseded here by the '18' certificate. The term appears to have been coined in the original Parliamentary report on 'Children & Cinema' of 1950: 'We recommend that a new category of films be established (which might be called 'X') from which children under 16 should be entirely excluded.' In the United States, the X-rating (American usage prefers 'rating' to 'certificate') still survives, and prohibits entry to a such a film to those under 17 or 18 years – the limit varies from state to state – usually because of its lurid sexual content. As with the other American ratings, it is administered by the *Motion Picture Association of America*. Since an X-rating will usually mean commercial disaster for many mainstream films, which in recent years have needed to draw the youth audience, most companies will happily make enough stragegic cuts to placate the Association. More loosely, the expression 'X-rated' can now be used to refer to any type of real-life or portrayed activity that might be at home in an X-rated film, while an *X film* or *X movie* is the familiar term for any type of pornographic film or *blue movie*. 'Sebastian had gone into Oxford to see an X film ("any X film", he said) and to moon around looking for girls with his spotty mates' – Martin Amis, *The Rachel Papers*, 1973.

XCU see *extreme close-up*.

x-copy the first duplicate of the *transferred sound master*; *x-dissolve*, standard abbreviation for *cross-dissolve*.

xenon lamp the powerful lamp used in most modern projectors; its principal component is a *xenon bulb*, incorporating two tungsten electrodes surrounded by xenon gas. Xenon, from the Greek *xenos*, 'strange' (as in 'xenophobia'), was first isolated in 1898 by Sir William Ramsey. Hence *xenon print*, a print so balanced that it can be satisfactorily run through a *xenon projector* (or *xenon arc projector*).

xerography a process developed by Disney in collaboration with the Xerox corporation, which enables animators to transfer drawings onto cells by xerox-style copying rather than by inking. However, this term is simply a specialised application of the standard meaning of xerography (from Gk *xeros*, 'dry'), the more technical term for 'photocopying'.

xfr or **xfer** abbreviations for *transfer*.

XLS abbreviation for *extreme long shot*.

X-rated see *x-certificate*.

x-rays the name for shadow photographs taken using short-waved electromagnetic radiation (a translation from the German *x-strahlen*, the name given these rays by Prof. W.C. Rontgen when he discovered their existence in 1895; OED states that Rontgen's 'X', indicating their unknown nature, can trage its lineage back to Descartes, who introduced *x*, *y* and *z* as algebraic notations of unknown quantity in his *Geometrie* of 1637, though it has been suggested that this use of 'X' may be derived from a medieval transliteration of an Arabic word meaning 'thing'.) Though film-makers are not usually concerned with x-rays except as a transport hazard (the x-ray scanners used in airports can cause fogging on stock), there are some notable exceptions: in *Thirty-Two Short Films about Glenn Gould*, for example, there is a striking close-up sequence shot in x-rays, showing the skull and limbs of a man (ostensibly Gould himself) playing the piano, and X-ray images have also been used in *science fiction* and some *spy* movies, either for their eerie appearance or to suggest high-tech surveillance equipment and the like.

X-sheet   in animation: a sheet of instructions from the animator to the cameraman, stipulating how each sequence is to be exposed: an abbreviation, then, for exposure sheet.

Y **-cable** or **y-joint**   an electrical junction unit in the form of a Y, with plugs for cables at each of its three extremities.

Yakuza   the Japanese thriller genre devoted to the exploits of Japan's gangsters and racketeers, the *Yakuza*. The young critic (later turned screenwriter and director) Paul Schrader helped to introduce the form to the West in his essay 'Yakuza-Eiga', and went on to write the screenplay for a Hollywood venture into the form, *The Yakuza* (1974), directed by Sydney Pollack and starring Robert Mitchum and Ken Takakura, the latter a leading star of the indigenous product. The word *Yakuza* is built up from three Japanese numerals, *ya*, 'eight', *ku* 'nine' and *za* 'three', 8–9-3 being the worst set of cards you can be dealt in a game and thus figuratively meaning 'the dregs' or 'the worst type'.

yoke   a brace or frame in the form of a Y, used to support a *luminaire*. Yokes will either be mounted on a stand or suspended from overhead rigging.

youth culture movie   films of the late 1960s and early 1970s such as Dennis Hopper's *Easy Rider*, made about, for and sometimes by hippies.

Z **core**   a type of *core* used for winding 16mm stock.

Z-movie   slang: the most extreme version of the *B-movie*: a ramshackle production made on a sub-shoestring budget, with atrocious acting, terrible continuity and incomprehensible plot. *Plan 9 From Outer Space* is generally cited as the classic of this genre, which has become surprisingly popular again in the last decade or so, at least among devotees of kitsch. See *cult movie*.

zeppelin, or **zeppelin windscreen**   a type of *wind sleeve*: a long cylindrical covering for a shotgun microphone, with perforations to reduce wind noise. So called because of its similarity to the famous dirigible, named for the Count Ferdinand von Zeppelin and first constructed in 1900.

zero cut printing, zero printing   a type of *A and B roll* printing, which maintains the shots on the two rolls in their original condition by means of an intermittent shutter.

zero out   to set a counter (usually a footage counter) back to zero.

ZI   an abbreviation for *zoom in.*

zip pan (also **flash pan, swish pan**)   an unusually rapid *pan* (usually though not always lateral) that produces a blurred image and is often used to suggest either (a) a rapid, dramatic or comic transition from one location to the next, or (b) a type of *subjective* or *point-of-view* shot, indicating a character's sudden surprised awareness of the subject that comes into shot. 'Zip', a word mimicking the sound of a bullet as it cuts swiftly through the air, enters the English langauge in 1875.

ZO   an abbreviation for *zoom out.*

Zoetrope   from Gk *zoe*, life and *tropos*, turning. A 19th C device which created the illusion of movement; sometimes called a 'Wheel of Life'. (So W.S. Gilbert, 1869: 'And also, with amusment rife, A Zoetrope, or Wheel of Life'.) Invented in 1834 by an Englishman, William Horner, it consisted of a rotating cylinder with an open top and vertical slits just below its rim; when the viewer peered through the slits, figures drawn on a strip of paper set inside the drum would seem to prance and caper. *Zoetrope*, or American Zoetrope, is also the name of Francis Coppola's production company.

zoom   in the broadest sense, any real or apparent movement of the camera towards or away from its subject. (It appears to be a relatively recent term; OED lists no cinematographic sense of the word before 1948, though it is almost certainly derived from a common early 20th C sense, 'to move at speed, to hurry'. 'Zoom' first appears in English at the end of the 19th C, as an onomatopoeia for a humming noise.) In practice, however, the term almost always refers either (a) to the effect of such movement created by the manipulation of a *zoom lens* – also known as a *varifocal lens, variable-focal length lens*, or most commonly and simply as (b) a *zoom* – rather than to the real forwards or backwards movement of a dolly. A zoom lens can be adjusted from wide angle to long focus, or vice versa, without losing focus or changing the aperture. These lenses were first developed in the 1950s; all earlier approximations to a zoom were really *dolly* or *crane* shots. A *zoom in* (*ZI*), or apparent move towards a subject increases the focal length; a *zoom out* (*ZO*) or *zoom back* (*ZB*), an apparent move away, decreases it. Hence *zoom motor*, *zoom range*, *zoom shot* and so on. It should be noted that a zoom in does not create the same visual effect as a dolly in: the former will enlarge everything at the same rate, whereas physical movement of the camera will enlarge the objects nearest to the camera more rapidly than those in the distance; a zoom shot maintains the same perspective, a dolly shot alters it. Though zooms are usually meant to be noticed, a zoom lens can also be used more unobtrusively, to adjust focal lengths between shots without having to change the whole lens. The main disadvantages of zoom lenses are that they are produce slightly poorer quality images than prime lenses, and their speeds are lower. *Zoom stand*, another term for an *animation stand*, so called because the camera mounted on such a stand can be moved swiftly up and down above the drawings to approximate zooms.

Zoopraxiscope, also **zoopraxeoscope** and, incorrectly, **zoopraxinoscope** as the *Leeds Mercury* noted in 1881 (the year of its development and christening), this was an improved form of the *zoogyroscope*, a form of projector invented by Eadweard Muybridge (*né* Edward James Muggeridge, 1830–1904), the British pioneer of motion photography, in 1879. As is well known, Muybridge had originally become interested in techniques for photographing motion in 1872, when he was asked by the Governor of California to produce an accurate representation of the ways in which a horse walks, trots, canters and gallops. In the course of the next eight years, Muybridge came up with a system involving trip threads and a series of 24 cameras placed at regular intervals. After the results were published in book form in 1878, Muybridge set about devising a means to melt these frozen images back into life-like motion, and eventually came up with a gadget that combined a *magic lantern* and a rotating *Phenakistiscope*. The result was the most advanced photographic projection device so far known; it held that distinction for twelve years, until Edison introduced his *Kinetoscope*.

Zoptic system a type of *front projection* method used to make subjects in the foreground appear to move in or into the deep background; named from a mating between its inventor, Zoran Perisic and the suffix -optic.

Zydeco a device similar to a *Harry*. Zydeco is also and originally, as connoisseurs of folk music will know, the name of the infectious dance tunes played in Louisiana. Conjectured etymology: the Creole pronunciation of a song title, 'Les haricots [sont pas sales].'

Selected Bibliography

A: CINEMA REFERENCE BOOKS

Andrew, Geoff, *The Film Handbook*, Harlow: Longmans, 1989.
Bawden, Liz-Ann (ed.), *The Oxford Companion to Film*, Oxford and New York: OUP, 1976.
Beaver, Frank E., *Dictionary of Film Terms*, New York: McGraw-Hill, 1983.
Browne, Steven E., *Film – Video Terms and Concepts*, Boston and London: Focal Press, 1992.
Katz, Ephraim, *The Macmillan International Film Encyclopedia, New Edition*, London: Pan Macmillan, 1994.
Konigsberg, Ira, *The Complete Film Dictionary*, New York: New American Library, 1987; Meridian, 1989.
Lombardi, F., *The Variety Book of Movie Lists*, London: Hamlyn, 1994.
Milne, Tom (ed.), *The Time Out Film Guide*, London: Penguin, 1989; and subsequent editions.
Monaco, James et al. (eds), *The Encyclopedia of Film*, New York: Perigee Books, 1991.
Penny, Edmund F., *The Facts on File Dictionary of Film and Broadcast Terms*, New York and Oxford: Facts on File Books, 1991.
Singleton, Ralph S., *Filmmaker's Dictionary*, Los Angeles: Lone Eagle Books, 1990.
Thomson, David, *A Biographical Dictionary of Film* (a revised and expanded edition of *A Biographical Dictionary of Cinema*, 1975), London: André Deutsch, 1994
Whitaker, Rod, *The Language of Film*, New Jersey: Prentice-Hall Inc., 1970.

B: OTHER REFERENCE BOOKS

Cuddon, J. A., *A Dictionary of Literary Terms and Literary Theory*, Third Edition, Oxford: Basil Blackwell, 1991.
Harrison, Martin, *Theatre: A Book of Words*, Manchester: Carcanet Press, 1993.

C: OTHER BOOKS ON THE CINEMA

Adair, Gilbert, *Flickers*, London: Faber, 1995.
Adair, Gilbert, *Hollywood's Vietnam* (revised edition), London: Heinemann, 1989.

Adair, Gilbert, *Surfing the Zeitgeist*, London: Faber, 1997.
Agee, James, *Agee on Film: Volume I, Essays and Reviews*, New York: Perigee, 1983.
Armes, Roy, *A Critical History of British Cinema*, London: Secker and Warburg, 1978.
Bach, Steven, *Final Cut: Dreams and Disasters in the Making of Heaven's Gate*, London: Cape, 1985.
Baxter, John, *The Gangster Film*, London: Zwemmer, 1970.
Baxter, John, *Stanley Kubrick*, London: HarperCollins, 1997.
Bazin, André, *What is Cinema? Volumes I & II* (trans. Hugh Gray), Berkeley and Los Angeles, University of California, 1967, 1971.
Bazin, André, *Jean Renoir* (ed. François Truffaut, trans. W. W. Halsey II and William H. Simon), New York: Delta, 1974.
Barnouw, Eric, *Documentary: A History of the Non-Fiction Film* (second revised edition) New York and Oxford: OUP, 1993.
Bogdanovich, Peter, *Fritz Lang in America*, London: Studio Vista, 1967.
Bogdanovich, Peter, *Pieces of Time*, New York; Arbor House, 1973.
Boorman, John, *Money into Light*, London: Faber, 1985.
Bordwell, D., Staiger, J. and Thompson, K., *The Classical Hollywood Cinema: Film Style and Mode of Production to 1960*, London and Melbourne: RKP, 1985.
Brakhage, Stan, *Film at Wit's End: Eight Avant-Garde Filmmakers*, Edinburgh: Polygon, 1989.
Bresson, Robert, *Notes on Cinematography* (trans. Jonathan Griffin), New York: Urizen, 1977.
Buñuel, Luis, *My Last Breath* (trans. Abigail Israel), London: Cape, 1984.
Buzzell, Linda, *How to make It in Hollywood*, New York: HarperCollins, 1992.
Carrière, Jean-Claude, *The Secret Language of Film* (trans. Jeremy Leggatt), London: Faber, 1995.
Cavell, Stanley, *Pursuits of Happiness: The Hollywood Comedy of Remarriage*, Cambridge, Mass: Harvard University Press, 1981.
Christie, Ian, *The Last Machine: Early Cinema and the Birth of the Modern World*, London: BFI, 1994.
Clarens, Carlos, *Horror Movies*, London: Panther, 1972.
Coates, Paul, *The Story of the Lost Reflection*, London: Verso, 1985.
Cocteau, Jean, *Beauty and the Beast: Diary of a Film* (trans. Ronald Duncan), New York: Dover, 1972.
Coppola, Eleanor, *Notes on the Making of Apocalypse Now* (revised edition), New York: Limelight, 1991.
DiCillo, Tom, *Living in Oblivion & Eating Crow*, London and Boston: Faber, 1995.
Dickinson, Thorold, *A Discovery of Cinema*, London and New York: OUP, 1971.
Frayling, Christopher, *Clint Eastwood*, London: Virgin, 1992.

Friedrich, Otto, *City of Nets: A Portrait of Hollywood in the 1940s*, London: Headline, 1987.

French, Philip, *The Movie Moguls*, Harmondsworth: Penguin, 1971.

French, Philip, *Westerns*, London: Secker and Warburg, 1973.

Geduld, Harry M. (ed.), *Film Makers on Film Making*, Harmondsworth: Penguin, 1967.

Gelmis, Joseph, *The Film Director as Superstar*, London: Secker and Warburg, 1971.

Graham, Peter, *The New Wave*, London: Secker and Warburg, 1968.

Giusti, Marco, *Dizionario dei Cartoni Animali*, Milan: Garzanti Editore, 1993.

Hammond, Paul (ed.), *The Shadow and its Shadow: Surrealist Writings on Cinema*, London: BFI, 1978.

Hillier, Jim (ed.), *Cahiers du Cinéma: The 1950s: Neo-Realism, Hollywood, New Wave*, London: BFI/RKP, 1985.

Huston, John, *An Open Book*, London: Columbus Books, 1988.

Infante, G. Cabrera, *A Twentieth Century Job*, London: Faber, 1991.

Jackson, Kevin (ed.), *The Humphrey Jennings Film Reader*, Manchester: Carcanet, 1993.

Jackson, Kevin (ed.), *Schrader on Schrader and other writings*, London and Boston: Faber, 1990.

Jarman, Derek, *Dancing Ledge*, London: Quartet, 1984.

Kael, Pauline, *Reeling*, New York: Warner Books, 1977.

Kael, Pauline, *Hooked*, New York: E. P. Dutton, 1989.

Kael, Pauline, *Taking it all in*, New York: Holt Rinehart Winston, 1984.

Knight, Arthur, *The Liveliest Art*, New York: Macmillan, 1957.

Kracauer, Siegfried, *From Caligari to Hitler: A Psychological History of the German Cinema*, Princeton: Princeton University Press, 1947.

Le Fanu, Mark, *The Cinema of Andrei Tarkovsky*, London: BFI, 1987.

Leff, Leonard J., and Simmons, Jerold L., *The Dame in the Kimono: Hollywood, Censorship, and the Production Code from the 1920s to the 1960s*, New York: Anchor Books, 1991.

Leyda, Jay, *Films Beget Films: A Study of the Compilation Film*, New York: Hill and Wang, 1971.

Lindsay, Vachel, *The Art of the Moving Picture*, New York: Macmillan, 1915; revised edition 1922.

Lumière, Auguste and Louis, *Letters: Inventing the Cinema* (trans. Pierre Hodgson), London and Boston: Faber, 1995.

Macdonald, Kevin and Cousins, Mark, *Imagining Reality*, London: Faber, 1996.

Mamet, David, *A Whore's Profession*, London and Boston: Faber, 1994.

Mayersberg, Paul, *Hollywood the Haunted House*, Harmondsworth: Penguin, 1967.

Milne, Tom (ed.), *Godard on Godard* (trans. Tom Milne), New York: Viking Press, 1972.

Monaco, James, *How to Read a Film* (revised edition), New York and Oxford: OUP, 1981.

Monaco, James, *American Film Now*, New York: OUP, 1979.

Newman, Kim, *Nightmare Movies: A Critical History of the Horror Film, 1968–88*, London: Bloomsbury, 1988.

Peary, Danny, *Cult Movies*, London: Vermilion, 1982.

Pierson, John, *Spike Mike Slackers & Dykes*, London: Faber, 1996.

Pirie, David, *A Heritage of Horror: The English Gothic Cinema, 1946–1972*, London: Gordon Fraser, 1973.

Powell, Michael, *A Life in Movies*, London: Heinemann, 1986.

Pudovkin, V. I, *Pudovkin on Film Technique* (trans. Ivor Montagu), London: Victor Gollancz, 1929.

Ramsaye, Terry, *A Million and One Nights: A History of the Motion Picture*, New York: Simon and Schuster, 1926.

Ray, Satyajit, *My Years with Apu*, London and Boston: Faber, 1997.

Reisz, Karel, and Millar, Gavin, *The Technique of Film Editing* (enlarged from original 1953 edition), New York: Focal Press, 1968.

Renan, Sheldon, *An Introduction to the Underground Film*, New York: E. P. Dutton & Co Ltd, 1967.

Rhode, Eric, *Tower of Babel*, Philadephia and New York: Chilton Books, 1967.

Rhode, Eric, *A History of the Cinema, from its Origins to 1970*, London: Penguin, 1976.

Rivette, Jacques, *Texts and Interviews* (ed. Jonathan Rosenbaum), London: BFI, 1977.

Robinson, W. R. (ed.), *Man and the Movies*, Baltimore: Penguin, 1969.

Romney, Jonathan, *Short Orders*, London: Serpent's Tail, 1997.

Ross, Lillian, *Picture*, London: Gollancz, 1953.

Salamon, Julie, *The Devil's Candy: The Bonfire of the Vanities Goes to Hollywood*, London: Cape, 1992.

Sarris, Andrew, *Interviews with Film Directors*, New York: Avon, 1967.

Sayles, John, *Thinking in Pictures*, Boston: Houghton Mifflin, 1987.

Schrader, Paul, *Transcendental Style in Film: Ozu, Bresson, Dreyer*, Los Angeles and London: University of California Press, 1972.

Spottiswoode, Raymond, *A Grammar of the Film*, Berkeley and Los Angeles: University of California Press, 1967.

Strauss, Frederic (ed.), *Almodóvar on Almodóvar*, London: Faber, 1996.

Tarkovsky, Andrei, *Sculpting in Time* (trans. Kitty Hunter-Blair), London: The Bodley Head, 1986.

Taylor, Richard (ed.), *Eisenstein: Writings 1922–1934*, London: BFI, 1988.

Thomson, David, *Movie Man*, New York: Stein & Day, 1967.

Thomson, David, *America in the Dark*, New York: Morrow, 1977.

Thomson, David, *Overexposures: The Crisis in American Filmmaking*, New York: Morrow, 1981.

Toulet, Emmanuelle, *Birth of the Motion Picture* (trans. Susan Emanuel), New York: Abrams, 1995.

Truffaut, François, *Hitchcock* (updated edition), London: Paladin, 1978.

Tyler, Parker, *Sex Psyche Etcetera in the Film*, Harmondsworth: Penguin, 1971.

Vaughan, Dai, *Portrait of an Invisible Man: The Working Life of Stewart McAllister, Film Editor*, London: BFI, 1983.

Waters, John, *Crackpot*, New York: Vintage, 1987.

Wajda, Andrzej, *Double Vision: My Life in Film* (trans. Rose Medina), London and Boston: Faber, 1989.

Wollen, Peter, *Signs and Meaning in the Cinema*, London: Secker and Warburg; 1969.

Wright, Basil, *The Long View: An International History of Cinema*, London: Secker & Warburg, 1984.

D: FICTION, ESSAYS AND OTHER BOOKS OF RELATED INTEREST

Adair, Gilbert, *The Holy Innocents*, London: Heinemann, 1988.

Antonioni, Michelangelo, *That Bowling Alley on the Tiber* (trans. William Arrowsmith), New York and Oxford: OUP, 1986.

Bryson, Bill, *Made in America*, London: Minerva, 1995.

Emblen, D. L., *Peter Mark Roget: The Word and the Man*, London: Longmans, 1970.

Fitzgerald, F. Scott, *The Last Tycoon*, Harmondsworth: Penguin, 1960.

French, Philip and Wlaschin, Ken, *The Faber Book of Movie Verse*, London and Boston: Faber, 1993.

Fussell, Paul, *Bad, or, the Dumbing of America*, New York: Simon and Schuster, 1991.

Julian, Phillipe, *Dreamers of Decadence* (trans. Robert Baldick), New York: Praeger, 1971.

Marcus, Greil, *Lipstick Traces*, London: Penguin, 1993.

Roszak, Theodore, *Flicker*, London: Bantam 1992.

Sontag, Susan, *Against Interpretation*, New York: Farrar Straus Giroux, 1966.

Sontag, Susan, *Under the Sign of Saturn*, New York: Farrar Straus Giroux, 1980.

Tolkin, Michael, *The Player*, London: Faber, 1988.

Vidal, Gore, *Matters of Fact and Fiction*, New York: Random House 1977.

Wagner, Bruce, *Force Majeure*: New York: St Martin's Press, 1991.